THEY SAY CUT BACK, WE SAY FIGHT BACK!

THEY SAY CUT BACK, WE SAY FIGHT BACK!

WELFARE ACTIVISM IN AN ERA OF RETRENCHMENT

Ellen Reese

A Volume in the American Sociological Association's
Rose Series in Sociology

Russell Sage Foundation • New York

Library of Congress Cataloging-in-Publication Data

Reese, Ellen, 1969–
They say cut back, we say fight back! : welfare activism in an era of retrenchment / Ellen Reese.
p. cm. — (American Sociological Association's Rose series in sociology)
Includes bibliographical references and index.
ISBN 978-0-87154-714-9 (hbk. : alk. paper)—ISBN 978-1-61044-748-5 (ebook : alk. paper) 1. Public welfare—United States. 2. Public welfare—United States—Citizen participation. I. Title.
HV95.R425 2011
361.60973—dc23

2011022409

The paper used in this publication meets the minimum requirements of American National Standard for Information Sciences—Permanence of Paper for Printed Library Materials. ANSI Z39.48-1992.

Text design by Suzanne Nichols.

RUSSELL SAGE FOUNDATION
112 East 64th Street, New York, New York 10065
10 9 8 7 6 5 4 3 2 1

The Russell Sage Foundation

The Russell Sage Foundation, one of the oldest of America's general purpose foundations, was established in 1907 by Mrs. Margaret Olivia Sage for "the improvement of social and living conditions in the United States." The Foundation seeks to fulfill this mandate by fostering the development and dissemination of knowledge about the country's political, social, and economic problems. While the Foundation endeavors to assure the accuracy and objectivity of each book it publishes, the conclusions and interpretations in Russell Sage Foundation publications are those of the authors and not of the Foundation, its Trustees, or its staff. Publication by Russell Sage, therefore, does not imply Foundation endorsement.

Previous Volumes in the Series

American Memories: Atrocities and the Law
Joachim J. Savelsberg and Ryan D. King

America's Newcomers and the Dynamics of Diversity
Frank D. Bean and Gillian Stevens

Beyond the Boycott: Labor Rights, Human Rights, and Transnational Activism
Gay W. Seidman

Beyond College for All: Career Paths for the Forgotten Half
James E. Rosenbaum

Changing Rhythms of the American Family
Suzanne M. Bianchi, John Robinson, and Melissa Milkie

Counted Out: Same-Sex Relations and Americans' Definitions of Family
Brian Powell, Lala Carr Steelman, Catherine Bolzendahl, and Claudia Giest

Divergent Social Worlds: Neighborhood Crime and the Racial-Spatial Divide
Ruth D. Peterson and Lauren J. Krivo

Egalitarian Capitalism: Jobs, Incomes, and Growth in Affluent Countries
Lane Kenworthy

Ethnic Origins: History, Politics, Culture, and the Adaptation of Cambodian and Hmong Refugees in Four American Cities
Jeremy Hein

Good Jobs, Bad Jobs: The Rise of Polarized and Precarious Employment Systems in the United States, 1970s to 2000s
Arne L. Kalleberg

Making Hate a Crime: From Social Movement to Law Enforcement
Valerie Jenness and Ryken Grattet

Market Friendly or Family Friendly? The State and Gender Inequality in Old Age
Madonna Harrington Meyer and Pamela Herd

Passing the Torch: Does Higher Education for the Disadvantaged Pay Off Across the Generations?
Paul Attewell and David Lavin

Pension Puzzles: Social Security and the Great Debate
Melissa Hardy and Lawrence Hazelrigg

Trust in Schools: A Core Resource for Improvement
Anthony S. Bryk and Barbara Schneider

Forthcoming Titles

Embedded Dependency: Minority Set-Asides, Black Entrepreneurs, and the White Construction Monopoly
Deirdre Royster

Exceptional Children, Challenged Families: The Family Consequences of Raising a Child with a Disability
Dennis Hogan

Family Relationships Across the Generations
Judith A. Seltzer and Suzanne M. Bianchi

Global Order and the Historical Structures of Daral-Islam
Mohammed A. Bamyeh

The Logic of Terrorism: A Comparative Study
Jeff Goodwin

The Long Shadow: Family Background, Disadvantaged Urban Youth, and the Transition to Adulthood
Karl Alexander, Doris Entwisle, and Linda Olson

Nurturing Dads: Fatherhood Initiatives Beyond the Wallet
William Marsiglio and Kevin Roy

Repressive Injustice: Political and Social Processes in the Massive Incarceration of African Americans
Pamela E. Oliver and James E. Yocum

Social Movements in the World-System: The Politics of Crisis and Transformation
Dawn Wiest and Jackie Smith

The Rose Series in Sociology

The American Sociological Association's Rose Series in Sociology publishes books that integrate knowledge and address controversies from a sociological perspective. Books in the Rose Series are at the forefront of sociological knowledge. They are lively and often involve timely and fundamental issues on significant social concerns. The series is intended for broad dissemination throughout sociology, across social science and other professional communities, and to policy audiences. The series was established in 1967 by a bequest to ASA from Arnold and Caroline Rose to support innovations in scholarly publishing.

Contents

About the Author

Ellen Reese is associate professor of sociology at the University of California, Riverside.

Acknowledgments

THIS BOOK would not have been possible without the help of many individuals, institutions, and organizations. First and foremost, I would like to thank all of the activists who welcomed me into their world, answered my questions, generously gave me materials, and spoke at protests and other public events. Without their help and inspiration, this book would not have been possible. I am also very grateful for the members of the American Sociological Association Rose Series editorial board and staff, especially Michael Schwartz, for their feedback, patience, and support for this project.

For feedback on research presentations and early drafts of each chapter, I thank my anonymous reviewers and Aldaberto Aguirre, Eileen Boris, Lisa Brush, Amalia Cabezas, Scott Coltrane, Geoffrey DeVerteuil, Volker Eick, Helen Ingram, Rebecca Jean Emigh, Chad Goldberg, Lynne Haney, Valerie Jenness, John Krinsky, Ruth Milkman, David S. Meyer, Joya Misra, Nancy Naples, Karen Pyke, Elvia Ramirez, Dolores Trevizo, and Marguerite Waller. Many conversations with Amy Schur also helped to shape my ideas for this book. For research assistance, I thank Kadambari Anantram, Vincent Giedraitis, Matheu Kaneshiro, Esther Koeshadi, Erin Ladd, Daisy Lomeli, Peter Luu, Acela Ojeda, Elizabeth Sotoj, Sandee Maung, Rosemarie Ostoich, Elvia Ramirez, Eric Vega, and Michael Walker, along with University of California, Riverside (UCR) undergraduate students enrolled in Sociology 197. For child care assistance, I thank Sonia Ninette and Erika Ibanez. I also thank the Ford Foundation, the University of Missouri–Columbia, California State University–San Bernardino, the UCR Division of the Academic Senate, the UCR Center for Ideas and Society, and the University of California Institute for Research on Labor and Employment for financial support for this project. Special thanks to Jennifer Jordan for welcoming me into her Milwaukee home while I conducted research in Wisconsin.

My husband, Ernest Savage, provided loving support during all of the years of research and writing for this project. He has always helped to keep me informed on many of the issues discussed in this book. My family, friends, and many current and former colleagues at UCR, the University of California at Los Angeles, California State University–San Bernardino, and the University of Missouri, also were important sources of support and information at various stages of this project, for which I am very grateful. Finally, I thank my son, Xavier, for providing me with lots of joy during the last stages of writing this book.

Chapter 1

Welfare Reform and Its Challengers[1]

Many books about the politics of welfare reform in the United States provide a top-down perspective. They tend to focus on the role that political, cultural, and economic elites have played in pushing for welfare reforms and in shaping the design of federal welfare reform acts—in particular, the 1996 Personal Responsibility and Work Opportunity Reconciliation Act (PRWORA).[2] Similarly, both feminist and race-centered scholarship on welfare reform highlight the influence of hegemonic ideologies; they emphasize how racist stereotypes of the poor, expectations that poor mothers must work, the stigma of single motherhood, and heterosexism shape the content of, support for, and implementation of federal welfare reform policies.[3] These discussions about contemporary welfare policymaking in the U.S. fail to account for the role that low-income people and their allies have played in reshaping state and local welfare reform policies—policies that were enacted and imposed by those aiming to "end welfare as we know it."

This book seeks to fill some of this gap by examining how welfare recipients and their allies have helped shape the implementation of welfare reform. Elites have certainly dominated the development and implementation of welfare reform policies. They have shaped and constrained national welfare reform legislation, imposing major changes in how the welfare system functions and justifying new regulations by invoking all sorts of negative stereotypes of the poor. Nevertheless, elites' influence over welfare policies has not gone uncontested, and state actors' views towards welfare have been multivocal, varying across state governments and institutions. As Paul Pierson suggests, welfare state retrenchment is politically risky because it threatens to alienate organized interest groups that have developed around particular welfare programs.[4] Along with such interest groups, newly formed membership organizations of welfare recipients and ad hoc welfare rights coalitions and task forces have mobilized to defend the rights of those with little or no income. While these groups were largely unable to block new national welfare reform policies like the PRWORA, they were sometimes successful in reshaping them, altering or moderating the ways in which they were implemented, and challenging the terms of policy debates.

Welfare rights campaigns that emerged over the period of welfare retrenchment surrounding the enactment of the PRWORA provide two important lessons about the challenges of improving our social safety net, and how those challenges can sometimes be overcome through mobilization and coalition-building. First, these campaigns reveal how, even after legislation has been passed, activists can still reshape policies. I argue in this book that in the case of welfare reform, policy implementation at one level was policymaking at another level. The implementation of federal welfare reform measures required states and local governments to redesign their welfare programs, creating opportunities for activists to halt or improve welfare reform policies and practices. Second, these campaigns reveal the importance of building coalitions to make change. When the welfare rights struggle broadened its reach beyond its traditional advocates and the very poor, it gained new allies, which, in turn, helped to make policy gains. While the victories in this period of welfare retrenchment were limited, the alliances that were formed could help to sow the seeds for further gains in the future.

This chapter provides the historical and social context for the rest of my study. I first examine the way in which the 1996 federal welfare reform act (the PRWORA) and its reauthorization changed U.S. welfare policies and how those policies and recent shifts in U.S. labor market conditions have shaped poor people's living and working conditions. Advocates of welfare reform have portrayed these policies as beneficial for both poor people and society at large, but most Americans have little detailed knowledge of these policies or their impacts. Reviewing the research on the impacts of welfare reform helps us to better understand the concerns of poor people and their allies, why the welfare rights movement became reinvigorated in the late 1990s, and why this movement continues to be relevant today.

I then discuss my comparative case study methodology. States and local governments had considerable discretion in how they implemented federal welfare reform policies. In addition, welfare policies varied considerably across space, partly as a result of the uneven influence of welfare rights activists. To capture this diversity, I examine similar welfare rights campaigns in two states—California and Wisconsin—and their two largest cities, Los Angeles and Milwaukee. I review some of the major ways in which California's and Wisconsin's welfare reform policies differed and how political, social, and economic conditions varied between these two states, providing distinct challenges and opportunities for activists to shape the implementation of welfare reform. I then provide an overview for the rest of my book, summarizing the conclusions from each chapter.

U.S. Welfare Reform and Its Failures

The 1996 federal welfare reform act, or the Personal Responsibility and Work Opportunity Reconciliation Act (PRWORA), represented a major overhaul of the U.S. welfare system. Fifteen years after its enactment, politicians both within the United States and around the world continue to hail the virtues of the U.S. welfare reform policies. They claim that time limits, strict work requirements, and other policies adopted in 1996 were effective in reducing welfare dependency among poor families. They also point to the sharp reduction of welfare caseloads that followed the implementation of welfare reform, from a monthly average of 4.8 million families in 1995 to 1.7 million in 2008, as a sign of success.[5]

By other measures, however, this massive reform of the U.S. welfare system was not so successful. The vast majority of former welfare families, even those with employed parents, have remained in poverty since the PRWORA's enactment.[6] And, as the economic situation worsened after 2007 and unemployment increased nationwide, the number of families receiving welfare in the U.S. rose about 11 percent between December 2007 and June 2010.[7]

Compared to welfare systems in other wealthy democracies, the U.S. welfare system is far less effective at reducing poverty. By international measures, the United States has the highest child poverty rate among highly industrialized countries—most of which have a poverty rate that is 50 percent lower than that found in the United States. Other affluent democracies are far more effective at eliminating child poverty than the U.S. They provide better regulation of the labor market and offer families—even middle-class families—far more generous welfare rights and benefits, including universal child allowances, national health insurance, subsidized child care, and paid family leave.[8] Similarly, the U.S. also holds one of the highest poverty rates among women compared to other affluent nations. Cross-national research indicates that the high poverty rate for women in the U.S. is due to America's low wages and lack of public assistance—and not the country's higher incidence of single motherhood.[9]

Using U.S. measures, 43.6 million people (representing more than 14 percent of the population) and more than one out of five children under the age of eighteen lived below the official poverty line in 2009; these figures have undoubtedly risen with the deepening of the economic crisis.[10] Poverty is particularly concentrated among racial minorities and female-headed households. More than one out of every three African American and Latino children in the United States lived in poverty in 2009.[11] Among all female-headed households with children, the poverty rate was 38.5 percent, and for African Americans and Latinos, this rate was even higher (44.3 and 46.0 percent, respectively).[12] The poverty rates among children and female-headed households declined in the late 1990s amid the country's employment boom, but then increased between 2000 and 2009 as economic conditions worsened.[13]

Though shockingly high, official measures of the U.S. poverty rate underestimate the true extent of poverty. These measures presume, based on consumption patterns in the 1950s, that at least one-third of household income should be spent on food.[14] In an attempt to address concerns that the official poverty line was outdated, the National Center for Children in Poverty estimated the actual costs in 2008 of various basic needs, such as rent, utilities, food, child care, medical care, and transportation. Its "basic budget" estimates suggest that the federal poverty guideline should be set more than three times higher than its current level in high-cost urban areas and about twice as high in low-cost rural areas. By those measures, millions more families in the United States would officially be counted among the poor.[15]

Rather than expanding working-class people's access to welfare, efforts to reform the U.S. welfare system in the late 1990s largely restricted poor people's access to income and welfare services by imposing all sorts of new rules and regulations. In the 1980s, the backlash against welfare had risen to new heights. Critics charged that American welfare programs were overly permissive and generous, despite the fact that they provided far less support to low-income families than welfare states in other affluent democracies.[16] In response to such criticisms, in 1996 PRWORA ended federal entitlements for low-income families to receive public assistance through Aid to Families with Dependent Children (AFDC) that had been operational since 1935. It replaced AFDC with a more restrictive and decentralized program called Temporary Assistance for Needy Families (TANF). A central thrust of welfare reform was to put poor mothers to work and prepare them to make the "welfare-to-work" transition. To this end, the 1996 federal welfare reform act introduced two-year consecutive time limits and five-year lifetime limits on welfare receipt. It also required states to expand adult TANF recipients' participation in welfare-to-work programs and authorized states to adopt work requirements for able-bodied recipients of food stamps with no dependent children.[17]

While the public supported welfare reform in general terms, few knew the details of the new policies. As Kent Weaver points out, Republican control of Congress produced harder time limits and stricter work requirements than most people supported.[18] Many states adopted even stricter time limits than those required by federal law for welfare mothers and developed systems of full- and partial-benefit sanctions to enforce work requirements.[19] And, despite strong public support for job training programs, most states implemented "work-first" models of welfare-to-work programs. These models prioritized actual work and initial employment rather than education and training for long-term career development.[20] PRWORA also denied most legal immigrants access to federal public assistance during their first five years in the country, authorized states to contract out welfare administration to private agencies, and authorized state adoption of "family cap" or "child exclusion" policies, which denied greater benefits to women who had an additional child while receiving welfare.

At the same time, General Relief programs, which provide assistance to indigent adults who are ineligible for federal public assistance, also came under attack. Of the thirty-eight states that still had General Relief programs in operation in 1989, twenty-seven enacted new eligibility restrictions by 1998, while twelve states eliminated their requirements that counties provide General Relief altogether.[21]

In 2006, ten years after PRWORA's enactment, congressional politicians not only lauded its success, they adopted even more stringent work requirements for welfare mothers in the legislation reauthorizing PRWORA. Promoters of welfare reform claim that tough rules and regulations are necessary for disciplining the poor and encouraging self-sufficiency, and they highlight stories about recipients who successfully made the transition from welfare to work.[22] They also claim that welfare reform was responsible for the dramatic decline in TANF welfare cases between 1995 and 2007, as well as for the rising labor force participation among single mothers, which rose from 58 percent in 1995 to 71 percent in 2007.[23] Yet these trends were partly the result of the employment boom of the 1990s, not just the change in welfare policies.[24] Indeed, as labor market conditions worsened after 1999, TANF caseloads rose in many states, while recipients' and former recipients' employment rates fell.[25] As labor market conditions continued to decline, TANF caseloads rose in thirty-seven states between December 2007 and September 2009.[26]

Additionally, work was not always the sole reason why all women left welfare. National studies of mothers who left welfare between 1995 and 1999—the height of the employment boom—found that between 40 and 50 percent were not employed.[27] Welfare reform did little to address the structural barriers that keep people in poverty, such as racial discrimination; the shortage of stable, living-wage jobs; and the lack of affordable child care. As a result, it is not surprising that most former welfare-to-work participants who found some employment did not work full-time or year-round and remained in poverty.[28] Indeed, many employed mothers suffered hardships and were worse off financially than before leaving welfare due to the loss of subsidized child care and health care benefits and the increase in work-related expenses, such as transportation. Problems with insecure employment and insufficient paychecks contributed to frequent cycling between welfare and work and the need for welfare to supplement low earnings.[29] Researchers estimate that, at most, only between 10 and 20 percent of former recipients of TANF will permanently leave poverty.[30]

Advocates of the "work first" philosophy argue that "any job is better than no job" and will lead to upward mobility.[31] Unfortunately, these policies have dramatically reduced welfare recipients' access to secondary education and vocational training, even though research has shown that educational attainment improves employment and earnings outcomes significantly for most Americans as well as most welfare recipients;[32] 40 percent of TANF recipients have not completed high school, while only 5 percent have attended any college.[33] In fact, work-first models complement the needs of flexible, low-wage labor markets by ensuring "a continuously job-ready, pre-processed, 'forced' labor supply for the lower end of the labor market."[34]

After the welfare reform of the 1990s, employers across the nation benefited from publicly subsidized drug-testing and skill-testing of job applicants, job training, and job fairs that were organized as part of welfare-to-work programs. Employers also benefited from welfare-to-work (or "workfare") participants' free labor as well as tax breaks for hiring welfare recipients in unsubsidized jobs. Welfare-to-work programs were especially popular among low-wage employers. According to Welfare to Work Partnership, "businesses like Burger King franchises . . . swear by it."[35] In Missouri, the main beneficiaries of these programs were meat-processing plants, temporary agencies, and nursing homes.[36] In Wisconsin, hundreds of welfare recipients were placed in temporary jobs, mainly in light industrial factories or warehouse positions.[37] In areas of high unemployment, local governments lowered municipal labor costs by employing welfare recipients for various public jobs, including picking up trash, scrubbing toilets, doing routine paperwork, and guarding parking garages.[38] This trend was most dramatic in New York City, where almost seven thousand welfare recipients were assigned to work for the Department of Parks and Recreation in 1998.[39]

Most welfare-to-work programs were not as work-oriented as expected, however. Because states received credit for reducing caseloads and because many recipients could be exempted from work requirements (for example, because of a disability or to care for a disabled child), only 31 to 34 percent of adult recipients of TANF in the nation were actually employed between 2001 and 2006.[40] Nevertheless, even when employers did not hire welfare recipients directly, work requirements helped to degrade welfare receipt and reaffirm the work ethic in the wider society, which in turn protected employers' supply of low-wage labor.[41] Restrictive welfare policies also increased competition at the bottom of the labor market, putting downward pressure on wages.[42] For all of these reasons, business lobbyists and corporate-sponsored think tanks actively promoted work-based welfare reforms.[43]

Welfare policies, like criminal justice policies that also target the poor, have become increasingly punitive.[44] New eligibility criteria—time limits on receiving welfare, tougher welfare-to-work requirements, and restrictions on legal immigrants' use of federal public assistance, for example—have disqualified millions of poor people from public assistance.[45] Other obstacles to welfare access had been long-standing barriers, such as the stigma associated with welfare and the low-income ceiling used to determine eligibility. In order to qualify for TANF, the main public assistance program serving low-income families, a family must be extremely poor. As of 2006, only twelve states used the federal poverty guidelines to determine the maximum monthly earnings a family can have while remaining eligible for the program. More importantly, only one state (New Hampshire) uses a standard of need above this poverty guideline, while the thirty-four other states set their income ceilings below the federal poverty guideline.[46] Nationwide, the median annual household income of all families receiving TANF in 2005 was $9,606.[47] There are millions of "working poor" families in the U.S. that have household incomes well below the federal poverty line and that struggle to pay for basic necessities but who still earn too much to qualify for cash assistance through TANF and other public welfare programs.

Yet, even those who still qualified for welfare were using it less frequently after federal welfare reforms were implemented. By 2005, only 40 percent of people eligible for TANF were receiving it, down from 84 percent in 1995 under AFDC. Likewise, 62 percent of poor children received AFDC in 1995 compared to only 21 percent receiving TANF in 2009.[48] According to Kay Brown, director of the U.S. Education, Workforce, and Income Security Department, 87 percent of the decrease in caseloads between 1995 and 2007 was due to the decline in participation of eligible families as welfare rules became more restrictive, the real value of welfare benefits declined, and diversion programs were implemented.[49] The loss of welfare contributed to a rise in extreme poverty among single parent families within the few first years of federal welfare reforms, even though overall poverty rates were then declining.[50]

Low participation in TANF helped to slow the growth in TANF caseloads when economic conditions worsened after 2007, despite a growing need for economic assistance among female-headed households. While the TANF caseload rose 11 percent between December of 2007 and June of 2010, Food Stamp participation increased 55 percent in this same period. Similarly, between 1994 and 2003, TANF participation rates declined while participation in other means-tested public assistance programs—such as Medicaid, Supplemental Security Income (SSI), and the Earned Income Tax Credit (EITC)—rose.[51] And even as participation rates in other welfare programs were increasing, many eligible families were still not using them. One study found that, as of 2002, only 7 percent of "working poor" families received benefits from all four of the core programs established to serve them: the EITC, Food Stamps, Medicaid (subsidized health insurance), and the State Children's Health Insurance Program (SCHIP).[52] Federal housing assistance and subsidized child care are also not fully funded, creating enormous waiting lists for these programs. Poor outreach, the complicated bureaucratic maze of different categorical welfare programs, onerous application procedures, and the stigma associated with receiving welfare all discourage low-income people from getting the help they need.

Qualitative research provides a clearer picture of some of the devastating impacts of welfare reform than is conveyed in survey statistics. One such study was conducted over a three-year period in Cleveland, Ohio, through in-depth interviews. This study found that the implementation of welfare reform led some women into dependency on current or former abusers (often the fathers of their children) for help with child care, transportation, car maintenance, and help in purchasing basic necessities such as diapers or food. These women had serious health problems and no one else to help them. In several cases, recipients who reached the end of their time limits, desperate for money, became dependent on sex work.[53]

Perhaps most alarming are indications that the loss of welfare has contributed to the rise of homelessness. State surveys suggest that between 5 percent and 8 percent of former welfare recipients were forced to rely on a homeless shelter.[54] These surveys likely underestimate the extent of these problems, as they frequently rely on phone communication, thus excluding former recipients with the greatest housing problems. In 2007, families with children made up as much as 23 percent of the urban homeless population nationwide and an even greater percentage in smaller cities. If homeless parents who gave up custody of their children were included, these figures would be even higher. With layoffs and foreclosures rising and more families reaching the end of welfare time limits, homelessness among families rose. By 2009, 76 percent of twenty-seven cities surveyed claimed that homelessness among families had risen over the past year, and more than 50 percent claimed that they could not provide enough shelter to all those in need.[55]

Cutting off access to welfare has also contributed to the breakup of families because it denies parents the means to take care of their children. Follow-up studies found that as many as 4 percent of "timed off" welfare recipients had a child removed from their custody.[56] Other surveys indicate that between 5 and 10 percent of all former welfare mothers lost custody of their children.[57] Quantitative studies also show that, compared to states with more lenient time limit policies, states with shorter time limits experienced greater increases in reported child maltreatment, the number of children in out-of-home care, and the foster care population.[58]

Additionally, even when low-income people do receive federal public assistance, welfare does not provide enough money to lift a family out of poverty or even to pay for all of a family's basic necessities. Because most states did not increase benefits in order to keep up with inflation while twenty states froze or lowered benefit levels, the real value of TANF cash benefits, adjusted for inflation, declined in forty-eight states (including Washington, D.C.) between 1996 and 2010. As of 2010, TANF benefit levels for a family of three were less than half of the federal poverty line in all states and less than one-third of the federal poverty line in more than half of them. And in no state did TANF benefits provide enough to pay fair market rent for a two-bedroom apartment.[59] Even when families received both TANF and Food Stamp benefits, the value of those combined benefits remained below the federal poverty line in all states and less than 75 percent of that line in more than forty states.[60] As a result, welfare families commonly struggle to pay their bills, even when they receive other public benefits. Surveys of welfare recipients and other low-income families found that both groups often relied on friends and family members to survive, which contributed to overcrowded housing. Many of these families had to "make ends meet" by combining earnings from multiple sources, including paid work, welfare, and work in the informal economy.[61] Material hardships are also common among welfare recipients. In 2000, a fifteen-state survey of mothers who received TANF in the past twelve months found that "over 30 percent reported experiencing one or more of the following four hardships: maternal or child hunger; eviction or homelessness; utility shutoff; inability to receive medical care due to cost."[62]

As more poor mothers were denied welfare and pushed into the low-wage labor force through welfare-to-work programs, they faced deteriorating labor market conditions. Even before economic conditions worsened in 2008, a combination of factors undermined the position of most American workers. Union membership continued to decline in the late 1990s and early 2000s, reaching below 13 percent for all U.S. workers in 2008. New rulings and insufficient resources for labor law enforcement undermined labor regulations. In this context, private-sector employer intimidation of unionizing workers ran rampant. Researchers estimate that employers fired workers during about one-third of all union election campaigns held between 1999 and 2003. During half of these campaigns, employers or supervisors threatened workers during mandatory one-on-one meetings about the union.[63] Workers also faced new downward pressures on wages through economic globalization, neoliberal policies, and economic restructuring, all of which contributed to a global "race for the bottom."

The net result was that workers faced what Steven Greenhouse aptly calls the "big squeeze." While worker productivity rose by 60 percent since 1979, the wages for most workers were stagnant or declining: in the same timeframe, "hourly earnings for 80 percent of American workers (those in the private-sector nonsupervisory jobs) have risen by just 1 percent, after inflation"[64] as of 2005. A decline in the real value of the minimum wage contributed to this wage stagnation. Meanwhile, "corporate profits have climbed to their highest share of national income in 64 years, while the share going to wages has sunk to its lowest level since 1929."[65] The percentage of the labor force in contingent jobs (part-time, seasonal, or contract jobs) also rose, increasing job insecurity among workers and leaving fewer workers covered by collective bargaining rights. Along with declining unionization and rising health care costs, the rise in contingent employment contributed to a declining share of workers with employer-provided benefits. By 2009, more than 50 million Americans, representing about 16.7 percent of the population, lacked health insurance.[66] Given the decline in workers' real wages and rise in contingent work, it should not surprise us that, as of 2005, most adults receiving TANF were working, with one-third engaged in full-time employment sometime in the past year. Moreover, among the welfare parents meeting TANF work requirements, the majority participated in unsubsidized employment.[67] While critics of welfare demonize welfare recipients and contrast them to good, hard-working, tax-paying citizens, the vast majority of welfare recipients are tax-paying workers, often with long work histories.[68]

Conditions for U.S. workers and their families deteriorated even further as the economic crisis deepened, leading to a massive wave of foreclosures and layoffs. By March 2009, about 5.4 million mortgages were delinquent as middle- and working-class households faced the brunt of financial deregulation and speculation: rising interest rates on top of overpriced mortgages. Mass layoffs further exacerbated the foreclosure crisis.[69] The following year, the crisis worsened, with 1 in every 389 houses in the nation receiving a foreclosure filing in October 2010.[70] That same month, the official unemployment rate had reached 9.6 percent of the labor force. The long-term unemployed (those without a job for twenty-seven weeks or more), had reached 6.2 million, representing nearly 42 percent of the unemployed.[71] Studies in several states show that the recent economic recession hit single mothers especially hard, as the growth in their unemployment rates between 2007 and 2010 exceeded that for both married men and women.[72]

The current economic crisis has helped to broaden concern around the failures of the U.S. welfare system to reduce poverty, as many workers are confronting the limits of the U.S. welfare state for the first time in their lives. Many unemployed workers have qualified for Unemployment Insurance, but many others have joined (or rejoined) the TANF or General Assistance programs. Others who had received permanent sanctions or reached the end of their TANF time limits found themselves at the mercy of private charities, many of which have been unable to meet the growing demands for their services. And, even as demands for government assistance have increased for low-income people, the nation's safety net, already shredded, has become even more so as state deficits rise and a new wave of welfare cutbacks spread across the nation.[73]

Concerns about the limits of federal welfare reform policies have long been raised by community and labor activists, especially in the wake of the 1996 welfare reform act. The implementation of PRWORA reinvigorated the U.S. welfare rights movement, which had declined considerably since its heyday in the late 1960s and early 1970s. While many of those facing the hardships associated with welfare reform and its shortcomings suffered silently or engaged in individual-level forms of resistance, some low-income people mobilized collectively for their rights.[74] This book examines the lessons of some of those welfare rights campaigns: when and under what conditions poor people's rights can be defended and improved in the context of retrenchment.

Examining Welfare Rights Activism Through Comparative Case Studies

This book provides in-depth case studies of welfare rights campaigns that took place within two states, California and Wisconsin, in the aftermath of PRWORA's passage. The purpose of these comparative case studies is to better understand how and why activists were or were not able to shape the implementation of welfare reform. California and Wisconsin and their two largest cities, Los Angeles and Milwaukee, were chosen for their contrasting contexts as well as their prominence within national debates about welfare reform. Welfare reforms in California and Los Angeles were closely watched by both welfare critics and advocates, mainly because they claimed the largest state and urban welfare populations in the nation. By contrast, Wisconsin's welfare reform program gained its notoriety in the late 1990s because of its plummeting caseloads. While critics of Wisconsin's tough new welfare regulations pointed out how they caused hardships among poor families, proponents portrayed them as a cure for ending "welfare dependency." Many southern states adopted even more draconian welfare policies than Wisconsin and provided less generous benefits to poor families. Nevertheless, Wisconsin's welfare rules, adopted under a Republican-controlled legislature, were a stark contrast to those found in California, where Democrats controlled the state legislature. Indeed, Wisconsin's tough welfare reform program helped to make its largest city, Milwaukee, the "epicenter of the anti-welfare crusade,"[75] or the "world's most famous welfare-eradication zone,"[76] as journalist Jason DeParle put it. I will now briefly review the main differences in the content of welfare reform legislation in these two states and other conditions that shaped the context for welfare rights campaigns explored in this book.

Welfare Reform Legislation in Wisconsin

Wisconsin Works, or W-2, was the culmination of a series of restrictive and work-based welfare reform programs that Wisconsin's Republican governor, Tommy Thompson, actively promoted and passed through the Republican-controlled legislature in 1996.[77] As one observer described,

> Thompson was a relentless campaigner for his welfare reform agenda. This was manifest in each of his statewide election contests, his legislative negotiations, his national policymaking roles, and his extensive interaction with the media. His message was so consistent that a *Chicago Tribune Magazine* cover story dubbed him "Governor Get-a-Job."[78]

Historically, Wisconsin had been a relatively generous welfare state compared to other states in the nation, and conservative politicians sought to reverse this pattern, claiming that it had become a "welfare magnet," despite a lack of clear data supporting that claim.[79] Conservative, corporate-sponsored think tanks also actively promoted the "Wisconsin model" of welfare reform as an example not only for the nation but also for other Western industrialized countries. In the mid-1990s, the Thompson administration hired researchers from the Hudson Institute, a conservative corporate-sponsored think tank, to design W-2 and then evaluate its performance. Not surprisingly, the Hudson Institute's evaluations of the program, widely publicized by the press, emphasized W-2's capacity to reduce welfare dependency.[80] During congressional debates on PRWORA and its reauthorization, various conservative think tanks, including the Heritage Foundation, the Heartland Institute, the Manhattan Institute, and the Wisconsin Policy Research Institute, promoted Wisconsin's welfare initiatives as model programs for the rest of the nation.[81] Largely because of the accolades that Thompson gained from Wisconsin's welfare reform initiatives, in 2001, President George W. Bush appointed him to be the Secretary of the Department of Health and Human Services. In this post, Thompson advocated more stringent work requirements for welfare mothers.

Advocates of W-2 also promoted the program as a model for other Western industrialized nations, many of which were actively seeking ways to reduce their rising welfare caseloads.[82] In 1997, the Hudson Institute promoted the virtues of the Wisconsin model of welfare reform through an international conference that drew experts and policymakers from England, Germany, Holland, and Denmark.[83] Politicians in Germany, Great Britain, and Holland sent delegations to Wisconsin to study the W-2 program, and they later incorporated key aspects of the W-2 program into their own welfare reform initiatives.[84] A Dutch reformer, describing the influence of the Wisconsin model within Europe, also upheld the "Wisconsin model" at a conference in Australia.[85] So did Tommy Thompson when he served as a featured speaker for an event organized by the libertarian Centre for Independent Studies in Australia. Such events helped to build international support for creating work requirements for welfare recipients, a move adopted by the Australian national government in 2000.[86]

Welfare Reform Policies in California Versus Wisconsin

While Wisconsin's welfare rules tended to be tougher than those found in most other states, California's policies were, in general, comparatively lenient. When California designed its new welfare-to-work program, CalWorks, it was ruled by a Republican governor, Pete Wilson. In contrast to Wisconsin, however, Democrats in California controlled the state legislature, constraining Republicans' influence over welfare policies.

Table 1.1 illustrates some of the main differences between the two states' welfare reform programs. The sanction policies in California were more lenient than those found in most other states, and its rate of applying welfare sanctions was among the lowest in the nation. At worst, when TANF recipients in California were sanctioned for not complying with welfare program rules, they were only denied the adult portion of the

Table 1.1 Welfare Policies in California and Wisconsin

Temporary Assistance for Needy Families Policies	California	Wisconsin
Most severe sanction for non-compliance	Adult portion of grant for six months	Entire grant permanently
Application of sanction rate, compared to most other states	Low	High
Permits all work activities allowable under federal law	Yes	No
Exempts adult recipients from work requirements and time limits if they are sick or incapacitated	Yes	No
Exempts adult recipients from work requirements and time limits if they are caring for a sick or incapacitated person	Yes	No
Exempts recipients aged sixty or more years from work requirements and time limits	Yes	No
Exempts victims of domestic violence from work requirements and time limits	Yes	No
Maternity leave from work requirements (months after birth of an infant)	12	3
Exempts recipients from time limits if child is three months or less in age	No	Yes
Exempts from time limits unemployed recipients cooperating with welfare regulations	No	Yes
Other welfare programs		
Number of federal benefits replaced for legal immigrants	4	2
Requires counties to provide General Assistance	Yes	No

Source: Author's compilation of data from Rowe and Murphy (2006), National Immigration Law Center (2002), Geen et al. (1998), and Coughlin et al. (1998).

grant for up to six months and for first and repeated incidences of non-compliance, the state adopted partial sanctions. California families also continued to receive the child portion of welfare benefits even after they exceeded the five-year lifetime limit on welfare. By contrast, Wisconsin's sanction rates were among the highest in the nation, and its sanction policies were some of the toughest in the country.[87] Along with only five other states in the nation, Wisconsin authorized caseworkers to deny recipients their entire benefit permanently as the most severe sanction.[88] California's

TANF welfare-to-work policies and time limit policies were also more lenient than those of Wisconsin and many other states in terms of allowing for more types of exemptions.[89] Like most other states, California permitted all activities allowable under federal law to count towards the TANF work requirement. By contrast, Wisconsin defined "work activities" more restrictively than the federal law and enforced its work requirements more strictly than most states. In fact, Wisconsin was one of only five states that placed more than 50 percent of its welfare-to-work participants in workfare positions.[90] As Jane L. Collins and Victoria Mayer suggest, Wisconsin's welfare reform program "reveals what workfare looks like in its starkest form."[91] However, it should be noted that even before 1996, California policymakers gave counties considerable discretion over welfare policies, and some counties adopted more restrictive rules than others. The welfare program in the Republican-controlled county of Riverside, for example, was actively promoted by conservatives in the 1990s as a model of the "work first" approach to welfare reform that emphasized labor force participation over education and training.[92] California was also more generous toward legal immigrants, replacing their federal benefits for all four major public assistance programs, whereas Wisconsin only replaced benefits for two of these programs. Whereas Wisconsin eliminated its requirement that counties provide General Relief in 1995, California continued to require counties to provide these benefits. Efforts to privatize welfare services were also carried out more extensively in Milwaukee, where TANF administration was completely privatized, as compared to Los Angeles, where only 25 percent of its welfare-to-work case management services were privatized.

Setting the Stage for Welfare Rights Campaigns

The broader context in which welfare reform policies were implemented in these two states and their two largest cities also shaped opportunities for welfare rights activists to mobilize and make gains. Wisconsin's more restrictive welfare policies and lower poverty and unemployment rates, combined with Milwaukee's smaller labor force, produced a smaller welfare population there than in Los Angeles, for example (see table 1.2). Compared to Wisconsin, California also had a much larger population of immigrants and a more racially and ethnically diverse population (see table 1.3). These conditions shaped the size of the populations affected by welfare reform policies, making it more or less easy to mobilize in response to them. In addition to a more liberal legislature, California also had a higher share of legislators that were Latino and spent more on welfare than Wisconsin, as exemplified by its higher average monthly AFDC payments (see table 1.3). Along with broader political differences in the two states and their largest cities, there

Table 1.2 Selected Characteristics of Los Angeles and Milwaukee

	Los Angeles–Long Beach	Milwaukee–Waukesha
Labor Force (PMSA, 1998)[a]	4,645,468	809,079
Unemployment Rate (PMSA, 1998)[a]	6.5%	3.3%
Unemployment Rate (Central City, 1998)[a]	7.4%	5.2%
GR welfare-to-work participants[b]	15,000–26,000	———
TANF welfare-to-work participants[b]	60,537	14,121
All welfare-to-work participants[b]	75,537–86,537	14,121

Source: Author's compilation based on U.S. Bureau of Labor Statistics (1999a, 1999b), Wisconsin Department of Workforce Development (1998), Citizens for Workforce Justice (1998), and Los Angeles Department of Public Social Services (1998). This table appears in part in Krinsky and Reese (2006) and is reprinted with permission of the publisher.
Note: GR = General Relief; TANF = Temporary Assistance for Needy Families; PMSA = primary metropolitan statistical area.
[a]Unemployment rates are annual averages from U.S. Bureau of Labor Statistics (1999a, 1999b)
[b]These welfare-to-work figures are for June 1998 and include participants in educational and training programs, and thus are larger than the actual size of the workfare population (data not available). They give a rough approximation of the relative sizes of the populations that activists sought to organize in each city however. Monthly total from Wisconsin Department of Workforce Development (1998); estimate from Citizens for Workfare Justice (1998); monthly total from Los Angeles Department of Public Social Services (1998).

were also significant differences in movement politics and infrastructure. Milwaukee had been known as an important "center of labor organizing" in the past,[93] while Los Angeles had a long history as an "anti-union city." Yet, by the late 1990s, Milwaukee's local labor movement was relatively more traditional and less vibrant when compared to the innovative labor campaigns underway in Los Angeles.[94]

Table 1.3 Demographic and Political Characteristics

	California	Wisconsin
Percentage of the population that is foreign-born, 1996*	25.6%	2.9%
Percentage of the population that is Latino, 1996**	27.9%	2.1%
Percentage of the population that is Asian, 1996**	11.7%	1.4%
Average AFDC*** payment, 1996	$198	$155
Percentage of legislators who are Latino, 1996****	11.7%	0%

Source: Author's compilation based on *Zimmerman and Tumlin (1999) and U.S. Census Bureau (1997); **U.S. Census Bureau (1997); ***U.S. Department of Health and Human Services (1998); and ****Council of State Governments (1998) and National Association of Latino Elected Officials Educational Fund (1997).
Note: AFDC = Aid to Families with Dependent Children.

To structure my comparisons of welfare rights struggles in California and Wisconsin and their two largest cities, I focus on the rise and outcomes of four different types of welfare rights campaigns: statewide campaigns to restore public assistance benefits to legal immigrants that were denied at the federal level, local campaigns to improve welfare-to-work policies, local campaigns to oppose the privatization of welfare services and to improve the regulation of welfare contractors, and state and local campaigns to improve child care services. I choose these four campaigns because they represent significant lines of conflict around welfare reform and also help reveal how the local politics of race, class, and gender shaped welfare rights activism. Comparing similar campaigns in these two contrasting settings helps to illuminate the complex interplay between popular mobilization and the policymaking process and how these dynamics were shaped by local demographic, economic, and political conditions. Most importantly, these comparative case studies reveal how the actions of welfare rights coalitions altered state and local welfare policies, and under what conditions.

Overview of This Book

My comparative case studies in the chapters that follow show how, and under what conditions, activists built influential coalitions and, in effect, successfully impacted four types of state and local welfare reform policies in California and Wisconsin. As Suzanne Staggenborg suggests, there are three dimensions of measuring success for social movement coalitions: they last long enough to achieve goals or concessions, they consistently carry out collective action, and they manage to influence their targets in desired ways.[95] Although activists seek to achieve their ultimate goals, they seldom do. We would fail to acknowledge most activists' actual influence if we viewed it simply in all-or-nothing terms, particularly when political conditions are not ripe for real, fundamental social change. According to the "collective goods" criterion, social movements are considered to be influential if they "secure . . . collective benefits for the challenger's beneficiary group," even if the benefits won are concessions other than a movement's ultimate goals.[96] This criterion allows us to acknowledge when gains are made, such as when low-income families get greater access to cash assistance or services, as well as the limits of those gains.

Chapter 2 puts my book into the context of prior scholarship on the U.S. welfare state and welfare reform policies as well as the literature on social movement coalitions. I argue that greater research is needed on the collective struggles that sought to influence the implementation of welfare reform policies and challenged the negative construction of welfare recipients in ongoing policy debates. The welfare rights campaigns examined in this book complicate our understanding of how U.S. welfare reform policies are shaped by the politics of race, class, and gender. They also reveal the multivocal character of the U.S. welfare state as state actors' positions on welfare issues and their relationship to welfare rights activists vary across state institutions and levels of government. Drawing insights from social movement scholars, I argue that when new allies joined welfare rights campaigns, activists were better able to make policy gains.

Chapter 3 focuses on state-level campaigns to replace the public assistance benefits for legal immigrants that were lost through PRWORA's passage and how their outcomes were shaped by racial politics. These campaigns forged new coalitions among traditional welfare advocates, immigrants, and the larger ethnic communities to which they belonged. In California—home to the largest immigrant population in the nation—cross-racial and cross-ethnic collaboration between Asian Americans and Latinos produced large demonstrations and grassroots lobbying campaigns in favor of benefit-replacement programs. This, along with the growing size of the foreign-born, Latino, and Asian electorate and the active leadership of Latino legislators, put pressure on politicians to replace benefits for all four major public assistance programs. In Wisconsin, where the immigrant population remained small, there was much less popular mobilization around this issue and far less electoral pressure on politicians to support benefit replacements. Nevertheless, popular mobilization and the visible role played by Hmong refugees in this campaign helped advocates win legislative support for two benefit-replacement programs. This chapter demonstrates the important role that broad-based and multiracial alliances played in preventing the implementation of federal cutbacks to legal immigrants' welfare rights, as well as the importance of demographic and political conditions to welfare policy outcomes.

Chapter 4 focuses on labor and community campaigns that took place in Los Angeles and Milwaukee against the privatization of welfare services. With the passage of the 1996 federal welfare reform act, Congress authorized the privatization of a wider range of welfare services than ever before; state and local governments could now offer for-profit and nonprofit private agencies contracts for eligibility determination as well as case management services for cash aid programs like TANF. After PRWORA's passage, multibillion-dollar companies, such as Maximus Corporation and Lockheed Martin Information Management Systems, aggressively pursued and received multimillion-dollar contracts to administer state and local welfare-to-work programs, claiming that they could provide cheaper and more effective services than the public sector. Because it threatened to displace unionized public-sector workers and erode the quality of welfare services, welfare privatization spurred the formation of community-labor alliances. Public-sector unions and community activists joined forces, seeking to shape the implementation of PRWORA by preventing or minimizing welfare privatization or by reducing the harms caused by private contractors.

While many state and local governments established public-private partnerships to administer welfare services, the extent of "mixed governance" and its terms varied by locale, creating different conditions for influencing the implementation of welfare reform. In Los Angeles, where county officials had discretion over the issue and where support for welfare privatization was already mixed, public-sector unions and their allies mobilized together and succeeded in minimizing the privatization of welfare services. By contrast, TANF administration in Milwaukee County became completely privatized, a move that was imposed from above by conservative state politicians, despite the opposition of community and labor groups. As scandals involving private welfare agencies surfaced, community groups mobilized and demanded greater public oversight of private welfare contractors. Although many of the activists' demands were ignored by distant state officials, a combination of public pressure and bad publicity helped to curb some of the worst practices carried out by private welfare contractors. Chapter 4 demonstrates how public-sector workers and community groups can mobilize together to pressure public officials to minimize welfare privatization and its negative impacts and how policymakers can either help or ignore their demands.

Chapter 5 examines the efforts of community and labor activists in Los Angeles and Milwaukee to organize welfare recipients as workers in response to the expansion of welfare-to-work programs. In Los Angeles, organizers mobilized recipients of both TANF and General Relief to develop multiracial and cross-gender workfare workers' campaigns that were sustained for more than three years. These campaigns called for workers' rights and job creation, challenging the racist stereotype that underemployed public assistance recipients did not want to work, and they resulted in the creation of two transitional jobs programs and a number of small but significant improvements in the implementation of the city's and county's welfare-to-work programs. By contrast, workfare workers' campaigns in Milwaukee never involved more than a few hundred participants and lasted less than one year. I argue that these divergent outcomes were partly related to the political economy of workfare in these two cities. High unemployment levels in Los Angeles helped to create a relatively large workfare population concentrated in the public sector, where they posed a displacement threat to unionized workers. This facilitated the mobilization of workfare workers and encouraged public-sector unions to join forces with community groups around demands for workers' rights and job creation. By contrast, Milwaukee's low unemployment levels, along with the state's highly restrictive welfare policies, produced a small welfare-to-work population that was widely dispersed across worksites that were located mainly in the private sector. The small and largely privatized workfare population in Milwaukee, along with the complete assault on public welfare administration discussed in chapter 4, hindered the development of a union-organizing drive among welfare-to-work participants. Union revitalization processes and employer responses to unionization also shaped the trajectory of workfare workers' campaigns in these cities.

Chapter 6 examines the political threats and opportunities for expanding and improving subsidized child care programs in the context of policymakers' interest in putting more poor mothers to work. Forcing thousands of welfare recipients into the labor market significantly increased the demand for child care services, putting further strains on programs already stretched beyond capacity. Yet, it also increased political support for expanding publicly subsidized child care programs within state and local governments. In both California and Wisconsin, women—including low-income mothers, child care providers, and female policy advocates—played key roles in state and local campaigns to improve child care policies. Taking a stand against work requirements for welfare mothers, local chapters of Wages for Housework and Welfare Warriors defended the right of poor mothers to stay at home and care for their own children, but they found few allies to actively support their demands in either state. More successful was the movement to expand and improve subsidized child care, which challenged the devaluation of paid child care and sought to defend and expand low-income working parents' access to affordable child care. New resources and grassroots energy to state and local campaigns resulted from the efforts of community organizations and unions to organize home-based child care providers and the families relying on their services. They greatly helped to defend, expand, and improve subsidized child care services in California and Wisconsin. Policymakers alternately helped or rejected activists' demands, and the fate of these campaigns ultimately depended upon gubernatorial politics. Whereas Democratic governor Jim Doyle in Wisconsin authorized collective bargaining for home-based child care providers, Republican governor Arnold Schwarzenegger refused to do so.

Chapter 7 draws conclusions about the lessons learned from welfare rights activism in this era. I argue that the implementation of federal welfare reforms became an opportunity for policymaking, but only under certain conditions. The welfare rights movement was generally small and its influence was very limited, especially in rural areas, in conservative states, and at the national level. Policy victories depended upon activists' ability to mobilize welfare recipients and to forge broad alliances both inside and outside of the state. Consistent with welfare-to-work goals, state and local policy gains made by activists often involved expansions of work-based entitlements, such as improvements in subsidized child care or the authorization of new transitional jobs programs. Other policy victories were mostly defensive ones that prevented the implementation of federal or state cutbacks rather than expansions in welfare rights. Although limited, these policy gains represented significant victories for those who benefited from them.

The book ends with a discussion of the challenges and prospects for the welfare rights movement in the United States in the midst of the deep recession that began in 2007. Large corporations and other powerful proponents of welfare reform and privatization remain strongly entrenched within U.S. politics. In the midst of the current economic crisis, the welfare rights movement remains small and weak, and even broader assaults on public social services and public-sector workers' rights are under way. The coalitions formed in response to the implementation of welfare reform—along with new campaigns emerging in response to the economic crisis—could sow the seeds for future policy gains for working families. Broadening support for more universal welfare programs and strengthening the organizational capacity of and alliances between grassroots anti-poverty organizations, unions, and other working-class organizations remain critical tasks for rebuilding the U.S. welfare state.

Chapter 2

Policy Implementation as Policymaking: The Case of U.S. Welfare Reform

THE PASSAGE of the Personal Responsibility and Work Opportunity Reconciliation Act (PRWORA) in 1996, justified through all sorts of negative stereotypes of the poor, represented a massive defeat at the national level for welfare rights advocates. At the same time, the provision of state and local discretion over the design and implementation of welfare reform policies directed energy towards state and local campaigns. Thus, while federal welfare policies have historically provided elites with "multiple veto points" through which they have limited welfare rights,[1] the decentralized and institutionally complex nature of welfare policymaking also provided flexibility and multiple routes for welfare rights activists to reshape federal policies as state and local governments implemented them and to challenge the demonization of welfare recipients. In the post-PRWORA period, welfare rights activists "jumped scale" in light of uneven political conditions and interpretations of welfare policies and rights;[2] in order to maximize their influence, they were able to move welfare rights struggles into federal, state, or local governmental arenas; private welfare agencies; and even into different branches of government. Their campaigns reveal how policy implementation is, in effect, policymaking.

This chapter lays out my theoretical perspective and puts my research into the context of prior research on the U.S. welfare state and social movement coalitions. While previous research reveals how welfare policies in the United States are shaped by the politics of class, race, and gender, more attention needs to be paid to the role that grassroots struggles have played in challenging policies at the implementation stage and shaping how welfare reform policies are put into practice or averted. My research also highlights the multivocal and contested character of the U.S. welfare state, showing how state actors both quashed and supported welfare rights campaigns. In doing so, I seek to add nuance and complexity to our understandings of the interrelationships between the welfare state and the politics of class, race, and gender. I then review scholarship on social movement coalitions, arguing that welfare rights campaigns have tended to be more successful when they involve broad alliances that cut across race and class divisions, thus gaining support from state actors. Combining insights from this literature with Anne Schneider and Helen Ingram's (1993) insights on the construction of policy target populations, I argue that when welfare reform policies cut across policy domains and target multiple social groups, this facilitates the coalition-building process and helps to attract new allies to the welfare rights struggle. Finally, I provide historical background on the immigrant rights and labor movements, exploring the factors that both facilitated and limited their involvement in welfare rights campaigns that emerged in response to the implementation of PRWORA.

Policy Implementation as Policymaking

As Seymour Martin Lipset documented long ago, seldom are laws implemented simply as their original designers envisioned them.[3] Scholars identify at least four kinds of interactive—but analytically distinct—phases of the policymaking process. First, in the agenda-setting stage, problems that require policy solutions are identified. Next, in the policy design and adoption phase, particular policy solutions are chosen from a range of options through the enactment of legislation or through administrative decisions. In the third phase, government officials or judges interpret the policies and determine their specific meaning through administrative rules and regulations governing operational procedures or through legal rulings. In the fourth phase, agents authorized to enforce the policies, such as welfare caseworkers or other kinds of government bureaucrats or private contractors, apply the policies in terms of actual situations or cases.[4] The policymaking process is seldom a unidirectional linear process. Instead, it is ongoing and complex, involving a "series of feedback actions or recursive loops" between phases[5] and "multiple, interacting cycles" occurring at various levels of government.[6]

Much of the scholarship on the U.S. welfare state has focused on the early stages of policymaking, often at the national level. For example, cross-national research has traditionally focused on why the U.S. welfare programs were so minimalistic and restrictive when compared to welfare programs in other wealthy democracies, emphasizing the role of political, institutional, and economic factors to national welfare legislation. This scholarship highlighted the historical influence of business interests, particularly low-wage and conservative employers, in constraining U.S. welfare coverage and the absence of strong cross-class coalitions and working-class parties in favor of welfare spending. It also highlighted the challenges of making welfare gains in a federal system and how policy legacies, particularly the categorical and means-tested nature of welfare programs, hindered efforts to build popular support for welfare spending in the United States.[7] Recent scholarship revives this tradition, showing how work-based welfare reforms and anti-welfare rhetoric were heavily promoted by business groups and various corporate-sponsored think tanks as well as politicians.[8] It also draws attention to how the design and local implementation of welfare-to-work policies or "workfare" programs symbolically uphold the value of paid labor and regulate the low-wage labor market by providing a ready pool of low-wage workers for employers in the service sector and other industries.[9] Scholars have also documented how the privatization of welfare programs reflected the influence of neoliberal ideologies that portrayed the welfare state and public-sector workers as costly and inefficient.[10]

Much of race-centered and feminist scholarship on the welfare state has likewise examined the selection and design of national welfare policies. These studies' historical research has highlighted how racial and gender inequalities and traditional gender roles were reinforced through the development of the "two-tiered" welfare state. As a result, white men were more likely than women and racial minorities to qualify for Social Security, Workers' Compensation, or Unemployment Insurance, which provided relatively high benefits, had comparatively few eligibility requirements and regulations, were viewed as entitlements, and were administered through national agencies. By contrast, women and racial minorities were more likely to receive public assistance, which was more stigmatized, more tightly regulated, and administered through state and local governments. Public assistance for poor mothers was designed to "shore up" the family wage system, reinforcing the patriarchal expectation that mothers' primary responsibility was to care for their children. Historical research shows, however, that state and local "mothers' pensions" and, in its early years, federal Aid to Dependent Children (ADC) benefits were almost exclusively given to "worthy widows" and white mothers.[11]

More recently, scholars have examined the national backlash against welfare that has been on the rise since the 1980s, highlighting its racial and gender dimensions. As they have shown, attacks on welfare have mainly focused on the Aid to Families with Dependent Children (AFDC) program and its adult recipients—by then, mostly single mothers and women of color.[12] Along with corporate-sponsored think tanks and business groups, politicians, keen on capturing or maintaining the support of white voters, stepped up their attacks on welfare.[13] In the 1980s and 1990s, while politicians touted tough new welfare rules, they also championed "tough on crime" policies, leading to a significant rise in the nation's incarceration rates. Whereas restrictive welfare rules mainly targeted single mothers and women of color, tough new criminal justice policies mainly targeted low-income men of color. These twin policies were similarly justified through long-standing racist stereotypes of poor people of color as lacking discipline and in need of greater state regulation. Just as champions of "tough on crime" policies appealed to racist stereotypes of black and brown men as dangerous and prone to crime, critics of AFDC appealed to long-standing racist images of poor black women, portraying them as lazy and promiscuous.[14]

Research has, of course, contradicted many of these denigrating stereotypes of welfare recipients. For example, research findings show that, even before the implementation of the new federal work requirements, most able-bodied welfare mothers were not avoiding work but rather combining work and welfare, actively seeking work, or cycling between welfare and low-wage jobs. Research has also shown that between 80 and 92 percent of adult recipients of welfare were employed prior to receiving welfare. Contrary to the myth that welfare encourages poor women to have children, most welfare mothers also had fewer children, on average, than their non-poor counterparts, and the longer a woman received welfare, the less likely she was to give birth.[15] To justify the denial of public assistance to legal immigrants, politicians and other welfare critics appealed to racist stereotypes of Latino and Asian immigrants; those immigrants were portrayed as overly dependent on welfare and as purposefully immigrating to gain access to public assistance. Again, the research contradicts such myths, showing that immigrants actually have similar or lower rates of welfare use compared to their native-born counterparts and that they contribute more in taxes than they cost the government.[16]

Along with racially charged images, anti-tax sentiment and the notion that welfare programs fostered dependency contributed to public support for several national-level welfare cutbacks in the 1980s as well as the spread of restrictive state welfare reform policies.[17] The rise in maternal labor force participation in the 1980s and 1990s also broadened public support for work requirements for welfare.[18] Blaming welfare recipients for their own poverty was also politically strategic, as it displaced attention away from the role of structural barriers to poor women's mobility, such as racial discrimination by employers, the devaluation of women's work, and the lack of living-wage jobs and affordable child care. Since tackling such problems would be expensive and challenge the elite's interests in minimizing state intervention in the economy, few politicians sought to do so.

In addition to demonstrating the influence of elite interests and hegemonic ideologies on the design of welfare policies, historical research has also uncovered the efforts of various organized groups and advocates to shape U.S. welfare policies. This literature again focuses mainly on the early stages of policymaking, highlighting activists' ability—or inability—to shape the political agenda of public officials and to win support for new kinds of benefits. For example, Theda Skocpol documents the role that organized veterans have played in the creation of veterans' pensions, as well as the roles that social reformers and women's groups played in the establishment of state-level mothers' pensions at the turn of the century, and how the influence of all of these groups was politically mediated.[19] Similarly, several other studies examine how and why poor people's movements emerged during the Great Depression and how these movements helped pass the Social Security Act and establish the Works Progress Administration.[20] In the same vein, a number of books explore the political and cultural constraints on policymaking and why certain proposals failed to win sufficient support. For example, Edwin Amenta examines why, in 1935, Old Age Insurance was adopted instead of the pension plans advocated by the "Share the Wealth" clubs or by the Townsend clubs;[21] Brian Steensland discusses the failure of congressional proposals for a Guaranteed Annual Income in the 1960s and 1970s; and Jill Quadagno explores the forces preventing the enactment of a national health insurance program.[22] When welfare scholars do examine the role of poor people's movements in shaping the implementation of welfare policies, they usually focus on the implementation of benefits rather than welfare restrictions. Thus, a number of studies have highlighted the role of activists in shaping the implementation of War on Poverty programs, encouraging poor people to apply for public assistance and helping welfare mothers to win benefits in the 1960s and 1970s.[23] Likewise, Amenta examines the conditions under which Townsend clubs were able to promote higher old-age pensions effectively.[24]

This book focuses on struggles to shape the implementation of welfare reform policies at the state and local levels. Examining national legislation alone overlooks the tremendous variability in U.S. welfare policies, which complicates our understanding of the welfare state and its race, class, and gender dimensions. This is particularly true in relationship to the Temporary Assistance for Needy Families (TANF) program. State and local government long exercised considerable discretion over AFDC policies, and federal policymakers encouraged states to develop their own welfare reform policies when implementing PRWORA. One study identified as many as seventy-eight different types of TANF policies that varied across different states in the U.S.[25] Of course, much of this variation consisted of just how restrictive welfare policies would be. Many states adopted even stricter eligibility rules for TANF than those required by the federal government. For example, they adopted welfare time limits shorter than those required by the federal government (two consecutive years or five years total). Some states also introduced rules denying additional benefits for children born to mothers already receiving welfare, a policy that was authorized, but not required, by PRWORA. Other states, though less numerous, provided more generous eligibility rules for TANF.[26] For example, some of these states used state funds to replace the federal welfare benefits that PRWORA denied to most legal immigrants during their first five years in the country. PRWORA also authorized state and local governments to contract out the administration of TANF welfare services to private agencies, but the extent and forms of welfare privatization varied considerably across different states and cities. As the balance of political forces and the local politics of race, class, and gender varied across the nation's states and municipalities, so did the implementation of federal welfare reform and the challenges and opportunities that welfare rights activists faced.

States' increasing propensity to contract out welfare and social services to private agencies (or to engage in privatization or voucher programs) further complicates the analysis of policy implementation; implementation increasingly involves a network of state governments and private (nonprofit and for-profit) agencies. Political economy approaches that focus on national legislation tend to neglect "the space between policymaking and policy outcomes."[27] Along with lower levels of government, private agencies that implement national policies establish the everyday contexts through which recipients experience and perceive the welfare state.[28] This trend has been described by scholars variously as "mixed governance" or the "mixed economy of welfare." Indeed, the welfare state is increasingly an "enabler and animator of private action for public service."[29] Empirical scholarship on the "mixed economy" of welfare emphasizes variation in welfare-state restructuring. While many nations and sub-national governments have pursued "public-private partnerships" in an effort to reduce public spending or decentralize services, the extent and forms of privatization vary due to differences in regime type, policy discourses, and institutional legacies.[30] "Mixed economy" scholars emphasize institutional plurality and the differences between nonprofit agencies, for-profit agencies, and public agencies, as well as the considerable variability within these three sectors.[31] While there has been an overall trend toward the commercialization of services, especially as governments fall under pressure to cut costs, the nature and influence of private agencies vary tremendously both within and across nations or states,[32] as private agencies (even nonprofit ones) differ in their organizational missions, size, operating structure, and funding streams.[33] "Mixed economy" scholars provide important insights for understanding the current challenges that welfare rights activists face, as those activists must increasingly confront both public and private institutions in order to improve the treatment of welfare recipients and applicants.

Certainly, other scholars have examined the implementation of welfare reform policies, but these studies tend to overlook the role of grassroots struggles. Much of this research examines the macro-level factors that shape how states and counties implement federal welfare reform policies differently. This research finds that states tended to adopt stingier and stricter welfare regulations where racism towards blacks and Latinos was more prevalent,[34] the demand for low-wage labor was high,[35] fiscal constraints were greater,[36] and conservative politicians and the Christian right were more influential.[37] These findings help explain why the most restrictive welfare reform policies tend to be concentrated in Midwestern and Southern states, where these various forces converge.[38] Similarly, scholars have also shown how county-level variation in the implementation of welfare reform sanctions was linked to the racial and political context of each area.[39]

Other welfare scholars examine the implementation of welfare policies at the "micro-level." Based mainly on field observations and in-depth interviews, these studies focus on the role of welfare staff, or "streel-level bureaucrats,"[40] in interpreting and enforcing policies. The findings reveal that welfare caseworkers and workshop leaders tend to believe in negative stereotypes of the poor and enforce upon welfare recipients normative expectations of "proper behavior" that are rooted in hegemonic ideologies about gender, race, class, and sexuality. The research also suggests that caseworkers' compliance with welfare reform policies is encouraged by governmental monitoring, pressures to meet performance-based goals to maintain welfare contracts, caseworkers' view that they are helping clients, and their agreement with the goals and values associated with welfare reform—"personal responsibilities," "self-sufficiency" through employment, and reducing "welfare dependency."[41] Anna Korteweg's fieldwork at welfare-to-work training sessions found that trainers encouraged participants, who were mostly mothers, to adopt masculine work norms by working long hours and disregarding their family needs in order to get hired or promoted; motherhood was devalued and "generally treated as something to hide."[42] Korteweg further reported that "motherhood was given positive meaning only when it was used to motivate women to find paid work or when the tasks of parenting were described as a set of marketable skills."[43]

In contrast to their strong emphasis on the importance of paid employment, welfare caseworkers paid relatively little attention to the "marriage promotion" aspects of welfare reform in their interactions with welfare recipients.[44] In fact, welfare caseworkers frequently discouraged poor mothers from developing relationships with boyfriends that were "too close" or reporting such relationships during the intake process; they feared that boyfriends' failure to comply with welfare reform requirements might jeopardize families' access to welfare.[45] "Marriage promotion" was nonetheless carried out through special workshops and funded through the PRWORA and the 2005 Healthy Marriage Initiative. Ethnographic research reveals how workshop leaders reinforced white, heterosexist, middle-class ideals of marriage and the nuclear family. They also reinforced patriarchal gender roles and stereotypes, upholding "cultural ideas of men as rational (strong) and women as emotional (weak)."[46]

Ethnographic research on welfare recipients and their interactions with caseworkers and welfare-to-work (WTW) trainers reveals both the salience of racism and the neglect of the racial barriers that impede employment of the poor. For instance, research reveals how caseworkers are more likely to encourage white mothers than nonwhite mothers to finish high school and to obtain education when implementing WTW requirements.[47] Observations of WTW workshops also reveal that trainers discouraged discussions of race and failed to address participants' experiences with racism in the labor market.[48] Likewise, WTW case managers also generally ignored employers' racial discrimination toward their clients.[49]

Qualitative research also shows how participants often questioned or challenged the enforcement of welfare reform policies and the presumptions underlying them. For example, welfare recipients frequently resisted the expectation that they ignore their children's needs in order to comply with work requirements, which led to high rates of procedural diversion from the program.[50] Interviews with black welfare recipients show that many of them viewed WTW programs as "creating a workforce of slave laborers" and that they saw caseworkers' presumptions that they didn't want to work as racist.[51] Meanwhile, the presence of same-sex and other non-traditional couples attending marriage promotion workshops challenged the hegemonic assumptions about family life expressed by workshop trainers.[52]

While otherwise insightful, this scholarship neglects the role of collective struggles over the implementation of welfare reform policies, some of which involved alliances between service providers and welfare recipients. Ethnographers have focused narrowly on everyday interactions at welfare offices or workshops and on capturing the views and experiences of individual welfare recipients—in effect, overlooking the larger-scale efforts of welfare rights activists to shape the implementation of welfare reform policies. As various case studies of national or local welfare rights campaigns have demonstrated, the welfare state remains an important site of collective struggle.[53]

Past research on the design and implementation of welfare policies toward poor, mostly female-headed families tends to highlight the classist, racist, and patriarchal dimensions of implementation. While capturing broad patterns, this research obscures the multivocal character of the U.S. welfare state. Welfare reform policies are developed, carried out, and evaluated through numerous state institutions at multiple levels of government. Moreover, as "mixed economy of welfare" scholars point out, the government increasingly relies on private agencies to administer welfare services, especially welfare-to-work programs and subsidized child care. Welfare policies are thus shaped by many different kinds of policymakers and "street-level bureaucrats,"[54] and both public and private institutions, all of which vary in their views toward, and relationships with, welfare rights activists. As my research reveals, when confronted, state actors can work to support or to oppose the arguments of welfare rights movements. Nor do struggles over welfare policies end when legislation passes. I show how welfare advocates and their opponents—both inside and outside state institutions—work to reshape welfare policies at the implementation stage. They have sometimes succeeded in influencing state and county legislation, as well as the policies of public and private agencies overseeing welfare administration or employing welfare-to-work participants.

I argue that whether or not welfare advocates are able to succeed in making policy gains at the implementation stage partly depends on their capacity to build broad-based coalitions that cross policy sectors as well as social divides rooted in class, race, or gender. This part of my argument borrows insights from the literature on social movements. While the welfare rights movement has been fairly small-scale and only sometimes employs disruptive tactics, it is nonetheless a social movement. By social movement, I refer to "those organized efforts, on the part of excluded groups, to promote or resist changes in the structure of society that involve recourse to noninstitutional forms of political participation."[55] Participants in social movements often work in league with more influential groups, including state actors, and frequently utilize a range of tactics that are more or less disruptive.[56] If we are to fully understand the interrelationships between welfare policies and race, class, and gender relations and ideologies, we must pay attention to how such relations and ideologies shape the demands, rhetoric, and social composition of welfare rights campaigns, as well as actors' responses to those campaigns.

The Power of Coalition-Building

As Frances Piven and Richard Cloward's classic study shows, major gains in welfare rights were won in the United States only in response to massive disruptive protests that emerged in the 1930s and 1960s. Poor people mobilized in response to large-scale socio-economic changes that disrupted their normal routines—namely, the Great Depression and the subsequent mechanization of agriculture, both of which threw millions out of work. Piven and Cloward conclude that elites are most likely to offer concessions to poor people when the poor are highly mobilized and when elites are divided and in competition, as occurs during periods of significant electoral realignment. They use this argument to explain both the passage of the Social Security Act in 1935 as well as significant increases in welfare spending during the 1960s. Consistent with Piven and Cloward's argument, quantitative research on local welfare expenditures and caseload increases in the 1960s shows that these were positively related to popular mobilization, namely levels of welfare rights organizing and the occurrence of urban riots.[57]

While otherwise insightful, Piven and Cloward's analysis overlooks the major role that allied groups played in supporting poor people's struggles and how such support is often critical to making gains, especially during periods of welfare retrenchment. Their study also lacks an analysis of how gender and race interact with class politics to shape both poor people's mobilization and welfare policies. A major argument of this book is that broad cross-class and cross-racial alliances were often critical to the success of welfare rights campaigns. This book seeks to increase our understanding of the conditions under which welfare recipients and their allies were able to forge alliances with groups beyond those who traditionally advocated for welfare rights; how their campaigns challenged classist, racist, and patriarchal underpinnings of welfare policies; and why such alliances mattered to welfare policymaking.

Social movement research suggests that coalitions are often vital to activists' success. Alliances improve access to members, allies, and interorganizational ties as well as the material resources required to mobilize people. Coalitions thus expand the variety and numbers of people who get involved in collective actions (such as letter-writing campaigns, lobbying, demonstrations, or more disruptive forms of protest), which, in turn, helps to gain the attention of power holders.[58] Forming coalitions with other types of groups, such as professional associations, experts, celebrities, or business groups, often adds legitimacy to activists' demands.[59] Alliances can sometimes improve activists' access to policymakers, enabling them to broker agreements with the state.[60] For all of these reasons, coalitions increase the effectiveness of demonstrations, boycotts, and lobbying campaigns.[61] Perhaps most importantly, alliances improve groups' strategic capacity and leverage. As Piven and Cloward argue, poor people's power is constrained by their position within social structures. The main source of leverage for unemployed workers is their power to disrupt daily routines, through sit-in demonstrations or stopping traffic, for example. Creating alliances with workers improves poor people's strategic leverage, since workers are in a structural position to halt production, services, and the flow of capital. Coalitions also enhance activists' strategic capacity when they enable aggrieved groups to carry out "multipronged" strategies or coordinated campaigns involving multiple targets and tactics.[62] Of course, coalitions do have their pitfalls and challenges. Coalition work can interfere with groups' autonomy and their ability to meet their own organizational needs and goals.[63] Political differences, racism, sexism, class inequalities, and other social cleavages also pose challenges for coalition-building.[64] Successful coalition-building requires effort to overcome such challenges if its fruits are to be born.

Scholarship on other movements, such as the civil rights movement, suggests that organizations, institutions, and leaders within deprived communities are key to mobilization.[65] Research on the mobilization of extremely deprived low-income communities in the United States, such as farm workers, homeless people, and welfare recipients, however, suggests that this mobilization often gains ground only after extremely deprived people obtain access to external funding.[66] External funds do not simply facilitate the organization of poor people; they may constrain and channel it, as funding is allocated for specific purposes. When elites control these funds, such as in the case of foundation grants, they often allocate funds for purposes that do not threaten their own interests. Research on various social movements documents how elite patronage can channel insurgency into professionalized forms or encourage organizations' adoption of moderate goals and institutionalized tactics. The extent to which elites exercise control over activists, of course, depends both on the patrons' politics and the social group's internal capacity and willingness to protest.[67] Although there are exceptions, union resources are also frequently allocated in self-interested ways that benefit particular unions and existing members.[68] Most of the welfare rights campaigns examined in this book depended on the resources of other groups, either from foundation grants or union members' dues. These resources made these campaigns possible but also limited their breadth and longevity. Resources were allocated for particular kinds of welfare issues and not others and were often time-limited, which shaped and constrained the kinds of policy gains that could be made.

Other research on poor people's mobilization finds that it tends to be the most successful in winning benefits when reform-oriented politicians, or governmental allies, are present.[69] Evidence presented in this book is consistent with this finding. When reform-oriented or sympathetic policymakers were present, demands were more easily won. When such policymakers were absent, state actors more easily repressed welfare rights groups or ignored them, even when they were highly mobilized and supported by a broad alliance. This was especially the case when activists' demands contradicted the vested interests of powerful groups, such as politicians' and employers' interests in minimizing social expenditures and putting more poor people to work. Demands that did not conflict with such vested interests were more easily won. Nevertheless, within these constraints, and sometimes in spite of them, poor people and their allies managed to shape the development and implementation of welfare reform policies.

Forging Alliances in the "Post-Welfare" Era

As Anne Schneider and Helen Ingram (1993) argue, one of the most important consequences of public policy is the construction of target populations that become subject to particular kinds of treatment. They argue that the political power of target populations and how they are socially constructed or culturally portrayed influences the design of public policies, which, in turn, powerfully shapes groups' social status, access to resources, and their patterns of political participation. They claim that policymakers tend to adopt beneficial policies for "powerful, positively constructed target populations," while enacting punitive policies towards "negatively constructed groups."[70] They suggest that the design of public policies—and the rationale justifying these policies—provide powerful messages that shape how target populations are publicly perceived, as well as how they view themselves in relation to the government. They claim that "groups portrayed as dependents or deviants frequently fail to mobilize or object to the distribution of benefits and burdens because they have been stigmatized and labeled by the policy process itself."[71] By contrast, advantaged groups tend to participate actively in politics, as they frequently view themselves as entitled and worthy of governmental assistance, and they tend to be treated as such by policymakers.

Schneider and Ingram (1993) suggest that it is challenging to mobilize groups that have been stigmatized through the policy process, such as welfare recipients. Perhaps even more challenging is making collective gains on top of mobilization. History has shown that this is not impossible, however. Policies that threaten groups' status and access to resources can spark opposition and contestation even among the most denigrated social groups, especially if they are already organized or if allies invest resources in organizing them. Extending Schneider and Ingram's insights, one would expect the scale of policy targets to shape the incentives and opportunities for coalition-building and mobilization in response to policy changes. If policies have inclusive targets, there are greater opportunities to build broad, influential social movement coalitions against them, especially if political opportunities appear to be relatively favorable. However, if policies have narrow targets, those opportunities tend to be diminished.[72]

When the policy threats or opportunities associated with welfare reform crossed multiple policy domains and symbolically or materially affected groups beyond the welfare population, this helped to draw new groups, often less stigmatized and more advantaged than welfare recipients, into welfare rights struggles. For example, the implementation of "work first" policies that emphasized job placement over education and training affected both welfare recipients and those employed in educational and job training programs. These policies forced tens of thousands of students enrolled in job training and college classes to quit them, frustrating their hopes of obtaining better-paying jobs.[73] In response, students receiving welfare organized at the state and local levels to demand their rights to enroll in community colleges, four-year colleges, and job-training programs.[74] Activists also protested in support of stopping the five-year clock for recipients enrolled in high school, college, or job-training programs.[75] These campaigns, which crossed the educational and welfare policy domains, often involved school administrators, teachers, and other students who were concerned with maintaining access to, and demand for, educational programs.

Other campaigns focused on opposing welfare policies that threatened women's rights, sometimes with the support of feminist organizations. For example, feminist organizations filed legal challenges to the child exclusion policy, which denied additional assistance for a child born to a woman already receiving welfare. These groups claimed that this measure not only discriminated against children based on the conditions of their birth but also restricted women's reproductive choices. Feminist organizations persuaded Congress to adopt a "domestic violence option" that allowed states to exempt battered women from new work requirements and time limits.[76] Various groups also contested the use of federal welfare money to promote marriage, pointing out how it discouraged women's independence and might pressure poor women to stay in abusive relationships. Members of Grassroots Organizing for Welfare Leadership (GROWL, a national coalition of fifty organizations across twenty states), for example, raised awareness about the problems with marriage promotion through protests and a policy briefing in Washington, D.C., which was attended by more than ninety legislative staff members.[77]

Campaigns challenging nativist and racist welfare policies and practices involved immigrant rights organizations, ethnic organizations, and welfare advocacy groups. Such groups joined together in opposition to rules that restricted legal immigrants' right to welfare and organized numerous marches, demonstrations, and legislative visits to prevent their implementation at the state and federal levels.[78] Various advocacy groups around the nation also documented and opposed the lack of translation services and other problems that prevented immigrants, racial minorities, and other poor people from getting access to welfare.[79] Drawing lessons from these local campaigns, activists drafted a national bill, the Racial Equity and Fair Treatment Bill. The introduction of this bill helped to reframe public debates about welfare reform, but it failed to win much congressional support.[80]

Given the limits of existing U.S. welfare policies, it is not surprising that some welfare rights groups, namely the Philadelphia-based Kensington Welfare Rights Union formed in 1991, drew on internationally recognized economic human rights policies to build alliances among various groups of poor people and to challenge the implementation of welfare reform policies. In June of 1997, Kensington members launched a Poor People's Economic Human Rights campaign and organized a ten-day "March for Our Lives" from Philadelphia's Liberty Bell to the United Nations headquarters in New York City. The following year, it organized a "freedom bus tour" attended by poor people and their allies. Visiting thirty-five cities, participants collected testimonies of violations of economic human rights and attended various local protests and marches around the country. The tour ended in a national tribunal at the United Nations Church. Also in 1998, Kensington members and their allies held a Poor People's Summit on Human Rights in Philadelphia, which drew about four hundred people, out of which developed the Poor People's Economic Human Rights Campaign, involving over fifty grassroots organizations. Participants pressured public officials to comply with international human rights standards and used public hearings at state, local, and international levels to raise awareness of poor people's unmet needs, with some efforts more successful than others. As part of this campaign, Kensington members organized a march from Washington, D.C., to the United Nations headquarters in 1999. The group also organized demonstrations at the 2002 Winter Olympics in Salt Lake City, Utah, using the opportunity to gain international media coverage of the plight of poor people in the United States.[81]

Some demands failed to attract much support outside of the traditional welfare advocacy community because they challenged the central thrust of welfare reform policies and the new "gendered consensus"[82] that poor mothers should be employed rather than stay at home to care for their children. In 1999, the People's Network for a New Safety Net campaigned for a national moratorium on time limits for welfare benefits.[83] "Stop the Clock" protests calling for a moratorium on federal time limits were waged in twenty-five states.[84] While these protests involved allied groups such as children's and women's advocates, they mainly involved traditional welfare advocacy organizations and did not find widespread support. Likewise, protests and demands calling for the abolition of welfare-to-work requirements on the grounds that they devalued poor women's caregiving work did not receive much support outside of grassroots welfare rights organizations, limiting their impact.[85]

New Allies for Welfare Rights

The campaigns examined in this book focus our attention on two types of "cross-movement coalitions" that formed in post-PRWORA struggles for welfare justice: coalitions between the welfare rights and labor movements and coalitions between the immigrant rights and welfare rights movements. The boundaries of each of these movements, like all social movements, are blurry and overlapping. Yet, analytically distinguishing these movements helps us to better understand the dynamics and trajectory of the alliances formed in this period of welfare history, as well as some of the interorganizational tensions that occurred. Coalition-building between welfare rights groups and other types of organizations was facilitated by the coincidence of welfare reform with the rise of the immigrant rights movement and efforts to revitalize the labor movement. Labor activists and immigrant rights activists were responding to their own sets of threats, only some of which overlapped with welfare rights issues. In joining welfare rights struggles, they contributed to—and were also shaped by—internal shifts within these two movements. A convergence of political forces thus came together in the late 1990s to broaden the scope and the scale of welfare rights activity.

Coalition-Building with Labor Activists

The labor movement as a whole was not particularly active in the post-PRWORA campaign for welfare justice, but a number of labor organizations did join in the struggle. In 1998, Jobs with Justice rallied thousands in over sixty cities for a national day of action against welfare reform, calling attention to the lack of good job opportunities for welfare recipients.[86] Unions also became involved in joint campaigns to organize workfare workers with community groups in cities where the labor movement was relatively strong: New York City, San Francisco, Los Angeles, several counties in New Jersey, and Baltimore. These campaigns sought to defend welfare-to-work participants' rights as workers, to improve their working conditions, and to increase their opportunities for regular employment.[87] In Chicago, a local chapter of the American Federation of State, County, and Municipal Employees (AFSCME) participated in public hearings and "accountability council" meetings, developed with other labor and community organizations, at which welfare clients and welfare employees brought public attention to the problems associated with the implementation of welfare reform. One such public hearing effectively raised public controversy about the policy of calling clients en masse and on short notice for redetermination of their eligibility, a policy that led to large numbers of wrongful benefit terminations. Soon after the hearing, welfare managers ended this policy.[88] Unions also helped to form Working Massachusetts, an alliance of unions, welfare rights activists, and other advocacy groups. Unions provided staff time, money, and members' support for the organization, which opposed the privatization of social services and time limits on welfare, sought to reduce welfare caseloads, and aimed to improve training opportunities and child care services for welfare recipients. Union members and welfare recipients promoted their welfare agenda through joint lobbying campaigns, protests, and education and outreach efforts. Unions such as AFSCME also promoted welfare rights during congressional hearings on welfare reform reauthorization.[89]

While we should not exaggerate its extent, this level of interest in welfare issues by organized labor was markedly greater than what occurred in earlier decades. Prior to the late 1990s, most campaigns to organize job training participants, unemployed workers, and welfare recipients were initiated by community organizations.[90] Although some unions supported the efforts to organize unemployed workers in the 1930s and supported the National Welfare Rights Organization (NWRO) in the 1960s, most unions ignored these campaigns. Some union leaders even opposed the NWRO's demands, such as demands for a guaranteed income, which they viewed as undermining the work ethic. They also expressed alarm over the expansion of welfare-to-work and job-training programs, claiming that participants would compete with other workers for jobs and reduce unions' bargaining position within the public sector.[91] Many union leaders thus helped to reinforce long-standing divisions between employed and unemployed workers rather than encouraging greater solidarity among them.

Even today, there are many barriers preventing service providers—only some of whom are unionized—from joining welfare recipients in their struggles to improve welfare programs. Fieldwork and interviews in New York, for example, identify multiple obstacles that create social distance between contract welfare caseworkers and their clients, even though both groups are contingent workers. First, welfare caseworkers are high-end contract workers with relatively good wages and benefits, while WTW participants mostly gain employment in low-wage temporary positions with few, if any, benefits. Second, staff frequently view themselves as superior to their clients; they view themselves as positive role models for their clients, and they tend to blame their clients' underemployment on personal defects rather than systemic problems with the low-wage job market. Moreover, caseworkers develop an antagonistic and paternalistic relationship with their clients as they monitor them and enforce welfare regulations through a system of rewards and punishments, providing clients with access to cash aid and services or implementing sanctions and case closures, in an effort to modify clients' behavior. Caseworkers view themselves as enforcers of strict policies that they believe are designed to help their clients become more self-sufficient, glossing over their clients' needs or the structural problems they face, such as the lack of good-paying and stable jobs and racial discrimination by employers. Such views, along with the differential power of caseworkers and their clients, reinforce class divisions between caseworkers and their clients rather than fostering solidarity between them.[92] Similar barriers often create distance between public-sector welfare workers and their clients.

Of course, the challenges of building community-labor alliances are not isolated to welfare issues; such challenges have generally been great within the United States, where workers are divided by race, gender, and ethnicity. Although there were notable exceptions, especially with the Congress of Industrial Organizations (CIO) in the 1930s and the United Farm Workers in the 1960s, U.S. unions were generally reluctant to incorporate social movement tactics and to strengthen community-based movements for social justice.[93] Union leaders feared that community groups lacked sufficient resources to justify a partnership and would divert attention and resources away from workplace issues and union recruitment.[94] Such fears partly stemmed from declining union membership, but they also reflected the influence of "business unionism," which became widespread in the U.S. labor movement after World War II, when the labor movement shifted to the right and leftists were purged from leadership positions. Under the "business unionism" model, unions became top-down "service bureaucracies" that narrowly focused on serving existing members through highly institutionalized collective bargaining and grievance procedures.[95]

There were at least three reasons why labor unions mobilized in response to welfare reform. First, the implementation of welfare reform posed multiple threats to unions and their members. The privatization of welfare services and other rollbacks in social services threatened public-sector unions with job loss. The influx of welfare-to-work participants into the public sector also threatened to displace unionized workers and to erode their bargaining position. The loss of welfare entitlements coupled with the implementation of welfare-to-work programs shredded the safety net for all workers, undermined the wage floor, and increased job competition by pushing millions of welfare recipients into the low-wage labor market.[96] Second, the rising costs of living, stagnant and declining real wages, and the rise in contingent (and insecure) employment increased unions' interest in expanding access to supportive services for low-income workers, such as child care and health care. The implementation of welfare reform created new opportunities for pushing through such expansions as policymakers at all levels sought ways to "make work pay" and to ease the transition from welfare to work.

Finally, the spread of social-movement unionism into the mainstream U.S. labor movement in the 1990s encouraged unions to become involved in welfare rights campaigns. Social-movement unionism refers to a number of internal political orientations and practices, including a broad understanding of the working class, attention toward community and political issues, as well as the use of social movement tactics and bottom-up processes of organizing and decision-making. Of course, actual unions rarely exhibit every dimension of social-movement unionism; many unions, for example, get involved in political issues but fail to use direct action or empower their rank-and-file members.[97] Social-movement unionism encouraged unions to become active in debates about welfare reform policies that affected their members; it also encouraged unions to put more resources into organizing workers, particularly non-traditional and low-wage workers, such as home-based child care providers and workfare workers.

Social-movement unionism spread in the 1990s for a number of reasons. First, the leadership of John Sweeney and the New Voice slate encouraged American Federation of Labor and Congress of Industrial Organizations (AFL-CIO) unions to invest more resources into labor organizing. Greater inclusion of women and people of color within organized labor, as well as organizers with experience in other social movements, also fostered social-movement unionism and a greater interest in community issues.[98] Finally, a sense of crisis rose within the labor movement as membership declined; Republicans gained power; and unions confronted rising threats of layoffs, greater economic insecurity, and other pressures associated with neoliberal restructuring and economic globalization. This perceived crisis encouraged union leaders to embrace tactical innovation.[99] As a result, unions increasingly relied on community support for labor campaigns.[100] Unions and central labor councils also became more active in voter mobilization and efforts to influence public policies.[101] Unions' involvement in welfare rights campaigns thus reflected broader political shifts within unions as well as a recognition of the ways that welfare reform threatened workers' and union members' interests.

Coalition-Building with Immigrant Rights Advocates

Immigrant rights advocates also participated in the struggle for welfare rights in the late 1990s. Efforts to restore or replace legal immigrants' access to welfare benefits that were lost through PRWORA were part of a much broader struggle to defend and expand the rights of immigrants. The immigrant rights movement rose to new heights in the 1990s and early 2000s in response to a backlash against immigrants that had been growing since 1980. That anti-immigrant backlash included the promotion of congressional legislation that aimed to reduce the levels of immigration through tougher border enforcement, country-level restrictions on the numbers of legal immigrants allowed to enter the U.S., and sanctions on employers that hired undocumented immigrants. Nativist organizations also attempted to deny citizenship to U.S.-born children of immigrants and to curtail other rights of undocumented immigrants, including their right to obtain drivers' licenses, public education, and social services. These efforts were particularly strong in California in the early 1990s, contributing support for a series of bills in the state legislature, many of which aimed to restrict undocumented immigrants' access to social services. Electoral support for such efforts was expressed through the passage of California Proposition 187 in 1994, which threatened to deny undocumented immigrants access to public social services, including public education. As welfare reform was being debated by congress in the 1990s, anti-immigrant organizations and politicians promoted the inclusion of federal restrictions on legal immigrants' rights to public assistance and social services.[102]

Immigrant rights advocates sought to counter this backlash and also to shape immigration reform laws. In the 1980s and 1990s, various organizations and institutions, including the Catholic Church, engaged in congressional lobbying. Immigrant rights advocates opposed employer sanctions for hiring undocumented immigrants and guest worker programs, and they pushed for the legalization of undocumented immigrants already residing in the U.S. They also mobilized voters against California Proposition 187. After its passage, advocacy organizations filed a series of lawsuits against the new law. They also organized protests against the measure, including demonstrations by teachers and students, and marches, the largest of which drew together more than 70,000 opponents, mostly Latino, in Los Angeles. Proposition 187 was eventually overturned through a court ruling in 1997.[103] Like many social movements, there were radical and moderate wings of the immigrant rights movement. While radicals called for full amnesty for all immigrants and defended the rights of undocumented immigrants, moderates sought more limited legalization programs and focused on defending the rights of legal immigrants.[104]

Various factors facilitated the mobilization of immigrants and their allies in support of immigrants' rights in this period. These included the growing size of the immigrant population and its various ethnic communities, which were also geographically concentrated. Civic and grassroots organizations providing services or advocating for the rights of immigrants or particular racial-ethnic groups also grew alongside them. Various other organizations and institutions also became more active in the struggle for immigrants' rights, including the Catholic Church, other religious institutions, workers' centers, and labor unions. These civic organizations and institutions helped to provide the leadership and resources that the campaigns needed to mobilize people successfully. Collaboration across race and ethnicity was encouraged by the formation of various formal and informal coalitions in response to anti-immigrant bills and legislation.

While the immigrant rights movement was growing in the 1990s and the early 2000s, it was still maturing and had not yet reached its peak of mobilization. Much of the activity was defensive, responding to the threats to immigrants' rights posed by various state and national laws and policy proposals. In this stage of the immigrant rights movement, much of the activity on behalf of immigrants involved lobbying, citizenship drives, service provision, legal advocacy, and voter mobilization, although various demonstrations and marches also occurred. Protests against California's Proposition 187 in 1994 drew together as many as 70,000 people at a time. Yet, the size of those protests paled in comparison to the immigrant rights marches and rallies that emerged in the spring of 2006. That year, House Resolution 4437, known as the Sensenbrenner King bill, sought to change unauthorized presence in the U.S. from a misdemeanor to a felony. It also made it a crime for anyone to provide aid to undocumented immigrants. As a result, millions of protesters demonstrated against the bill in several major cities across the United States. The historic March 25, 2006, protest march in Los Angeles drew more than half a million people.[105]

In short, the implementation of federal welfare reform presented overlapping threats to the rights of welfare recipients, immigrants, and service providers, which encouraged the formation of cross-movement coalitions in support of welfare rights. The implementation of federal welfare reform also coincided with other threats to workers' rights and to immigrants' rights and rising activism confronting those threats among immigrants, unionized workers, and their allies. This convergence facilitated the formation of new, cross-movement coalitions for welfare rights in the late 1990s and early 2000s. These coalitions—and their success—depended upon the local willingness and capacity of activists to build bridges and to mobilize. Later in this chapter, I explore the conditions under which both unions and service providers were able to join forces with welfare recipients to improve welfare policies, and with what results.

Outcomes of Post-PRWORA Welfare Rights Activism

Even when new groups joined welfare rights campaigns in the late 1990s, most remained fairly small-scale. Local events usually involved only a few hundred people or less, and at most a few thousand. As the former director of the National Campaign for Jobs and Income Support commented, "This has not been a 'movement period' comparable to the welfare rights movement of the 1960s and 1970s. We do not see large numbers of people in the streets or at the welfare office demanding change . . ."[106] While other movements like the anti-war movement, the immigrant rights movement, and the movement for global justice rose to new heights in the late 1990s and early 2000s, welfare rights activism did not gain such wide popularity.

The small scale of post-1996 welfare rights campaigns reflects the enormous challenges that the current welfare system creates for organizing a mass-based welfare rights movement. The U.S. welfare state provides public assistance through means-tested and categorical programs, which minimizes public support for it. Public assistance is provided to only the very poorest citizens.[107] The vast majority of people living in the U.S., including millions of the "working poor," do not identify with welfare recipients or feel directly affected by welfare reform. This is true despite the fact that welfare reform affects all working-class people by keeping the wage floor low and increasing job competition at the bottom of the labor market. These impacts of welfare reform on the working class are indirect and not widely recognized. The provision of public assistance through a variety of categorical programs divides poor people into distinct constituencies with particular claims about their needs and worthiness for assistance.[108]

The implementation of federal and state welfare reform policies also created additional barriers to mobilizing public assistance recipients, even as it brought greater public attention to welfare issues. Tough new welfare-to-work requirements increased the time that welfare mothers spent working and transporting themselves to and from their workplace and their children's daycare, reducing their time to organize or protest. The implementation of welfare reform, coupled with a booming labor market in the late 1990s, also led to rapid declines and high turnover in the welfare population as tens of thousands of welfare recipients left welfare for paid employment and welfare became harder to access.[109]

Even when welfare rights activists mobilize and gain media attention, they face an uphill battle in challenging the marginalization of adult welfare recipients within American society. As Schneider and Ingram (1993) argue, the construction of policy target populations sends powerful messages to both that target group and the broader public. Politicians, corporate-sponsored think tanks, and other groups promoted welfare reform policies in the 1990s by appealing to all sorts of negative, racially charged, and sexist stereotypes of public assistance recipients, portraying them as lazy and irresponsible and therefore in need of strict rules to discipline them. This demonization of welfare recipients discourages non-beneficiaries from empathizing with them.

In the aftermath of PRWORA, welfare rights activists spent considerable energy in trying to reframe the public discourse about welfare reform in order to gain greater support for their goals. Concerned with the biases in elite-sponsored welfare reform evaluations, for example, the National Welfare Monitoring and Advocacy Project involved twenty national and local organizations in documenting and publicizing the negative impacts of welfare reform.[110] In Kentucky, a community-run media group disseminated radio spots and videos that challenged the idea that poverty was due to a lack of the work ethic; it highlighted the shortage of good employment and educational opportunities within Appalachia.[111] Activists affiliated with GROWL attempted to reframe public debates by disrupting a national conference on welfare reform. At the opening ceremony, GROWL members wore gags to represent how they felt silenced by this foundation-sponsored conference, which presented a narrow and conservative perspective on welfare reform and was dominated by white male scholars and policymakers. They organized protests against, or vocally criticized, presentations by various conservative scholars, such as Charles Murray, and presented their own viewpoints during the closing ceremony.[112] Welfare rights organizations faced an uphill battle in these efforts to reframe public debates about welfare, as they seldom had a fraction of the resources or airtime provided to their adversaries in political office and corporate-sponsored think tanks.

Not only are welfare recipients demonized, the groups that organize them are just as often cast in a negative light. The media scandals surrounding the Association of Community Organizations for Reform Now (ACORN) in 2009—which led to the demise of many state and local chapters and the withdrawal of federal funds from the organization—illustrate this point. ACORN, a national federation of multi-issue organizations representing people with low and moderate incomes in more than seventy cities in 2009, was founded in 1970 by former organizers with the NWRO. True to its roots, a number of ACORN chapters responded to the implementation of federal welfare reforms in the 1990s by organizing welfare recipients and providers of subsidized child care. As documented in this book, these campaigns helped to defend low-income people's rights in an era of welfare retrenchment. Other ACORN successes included campaigns to curb predatory lending by banks and in support of local living-wage ordinances. Perhaps because of such success, the organization came under fire by conservative groups and the mainstream media for a series of scandals in 2008 and 2009. First, in 2000, the organization was accused by conservative Republicans of voter fraud. Although a U.S. Attorney General's investigation cleared the organization of these charges, voter fraud allegations quickly resurfaced in the mainstream press in 2008 after Barack Obama was elected as president, even though the organization had reported voter irregularities to authorities. Rumors about the misuse of public funds by the organization's founder, Wade Rathke, and his brother were also circulated by the mainstream news, despite efforts by national staff and leaders to address such problems. Finally, conservative groups and the mainstream media circulated selectively edited videotape of ACORN staff from various offices around the nation giving tax and housing advice to right-wing activists who were disguised as a pimp and a prostitute. Although the organization attempted to improve the management and accountability of its staff, firing many of the workers involved in the scandals, the public image of the organization was ruined. National surveys showed that a majority of those polled had an unfavorable opinion of the organization, and public and private funders alike withdrew money from the organization. Staff and leaders of the organization's largest chapters were forced to close their offices and disaffiliate from the national federation. As John Atlas and Peter Dreier persuasively argue, ACORN's experience reveals both how conservative groups can carry out an "orchestrated campaign" to demonize progressive organizations and activists, and the complicity of the mainstream news media.[113] More commonly, the activities of welfare rights organizations are simply ignored by the mainstream press.

Despite facing enormous challenges, welfare rights activists did manage to make policy gains in the late 1990s and early 2000s. Overall, they were more influential at the state and local levels, where it was both easier to mobilize poor people and their allies and where political conditions were sometimes more favorable than at the national level. Republican control of Congress and the rightward shift in Democrats' positions on welfare issues prevented welfare rights activists from winning very much at the national level. Nevertheless, activists did manage to protect or restore benefits at the national level for certain groups of poor people that were threatened by PRWORA, especially when their demands gained support beyond poor people and welfare advocacy organizations. For example, women's rights groups managed to win congressional support for the "domestic violence option," which allowed states to exempt victims of domestic violence from time limits and work requirements. Immigrant rights activists persuaded Congress to restore some of the benefits that legal immigrants lost in 1996. Child welfare and women's rights groups also persuaded Congress to increase federal funding for publicly subsidized child care.

Even at the state and local levels, the victories of poor people's movements seem puny in comparison to the major policy gains that were made in other historical periods, such as the 1930s and 1960s, when poor people's movements rose to new heights and led to the creation and expansion of welfare programs. Instead, in the decade after the passage of PRWORA, welfare rights actions were fairly small-scale and most often led to the rejection of proposed cutbacks or restrictive regulations at the state or local levels, or improvements in operational procedures. Some welfare rights groups eliminated or eased restrictive policies and practices that prevented poor people from obtaining welfare. Make the Road New York, for example, obtained a favorable federal court ruling and a federal investigation that forced city officials to respond to activists' concerns about the lack of translation services and treatment of immigrants in welfare offices.[114] Members of the Idaho Community Action Network successfully persuaded state welfare officials to adopt many of its policy recommendations, including elimination of the assets test for welfare eligibility, shorter application forms, and ending discriminatory practices in welfare offices towards those not fully proficient in English.[115] In Maine, Kentucky, and other states, welfare rights activists managed to expand the educational opportunities for welfare-to-work participants.[116] In New York City and Los Angeles, they persuaded local politicians to create transitional jobs programs for welfare-to-work participants.[117] Welfare rights groups also prevented or slowed down the privatization of public social services in various cities and expanded state spending on subsidized child care.

These were small but important victories. They made a tangible difference in people's lives, given the political weight and momentum behind efforts to push poor people into the low-wage labor market and to defund, privatize, and restrict access to social services. Even when they were unable to halt cutbacks or make policy gains, welfare rights organizations had a positive impact on low-income people's lives; they helped to give low-income people a collective voice. They helped welfare recipients and other poor people to assert their rights to income and social services while challenging negative stereotypes about the poor and making the claim that the economic system and policymakers perpetuate a cycle of poverty.[118]

Chapter 3

Challenging Welfare Racism: Cross-Racial Coalitions to Restore Legal Immigrants' Benefits[1]

What all these measures and laws do is to create more division, more racism, and that's bad for the city of Los Angeles, for the state, and for the country.

–Lucas Guttentag, Head of the American Civil Liberties Union's National Immigration Law Project

If immigrants don't get the benefits, they are going to be hungry. It is a lot of money, we don't deny that, but we feel the money exists. What could be more important?

–Laurie True, California Food Policy Advocates

Speaking for me and my husband, when you take away [Supplemental Security Income], you take away our lives.

–Supplemental Security Income recipient, Los Angeles[2]

IN 1996, as mounting attacks on welfare recipients coincided with a backlash against immigrants, Congress denied federal public assistance to most legal non-citizen immigrants for their first five years in the country through the Personal Responsibility and Work Opportunity Reconciliation Act (PRWORA).[3] This new rule applied to all four major public assistance programs: Temporary Assistance for Needy Families (TANF), Supplemental Security Income (SSI, which provides cash aid to elderly and disabled immigrants), Medicaid, and Food Stamps. One month later, Congress passed a highly punitive immigration reform act, the Illegal Immigration Reform and Immigrant Responsibility Act, which aimed to restrict illegal immigration and reduce the number of poor legal immigrants entering the country.[4]

One might have expected little resistance to PRWORA's anti-immigrant provisions for several reasons. First, immigrants were geographically concentrated, with about 75 percent living in only seven states in 1996, which meant that they made up a small portion of most politicians' constituencies.[5] Second, the groups most likely to oppose these measures—poor people, Asians, Latinos, and first-generation immigrants—have particularly low levels of political participation in the United States.[6] Third, as Schneider and Ingram argue, social groups that are stigmatized and defined in negative terms by policymakers often fail to mobilize because they view politicians as unsympathetic and punitive towards them.[7] Consistent with this, some legal immigrants contemplated—or, in a few cases, actually committed—suicide when they received news that they were no longer eligible for welfare.[8]

Nevertheless, PRWORA's passage, along with the passage of the 1996 immigration reform act shortly afterward, galvanized immigrants and their allies into action. Partly in response to these two laws, the number of naturalizations rose sharply, more than doubling between 1995 and 1996, as immigrants asserted their rights to become citizens and community organizations increased their efforts to help them do so.[9] The share of naturalized citizens (especially Latinos) registering to vote between 1994 and 1998 also rose, as anti-immigrant legislation at the federal and state levels politicized them.[10] Within this context, a broad coalition of immigrants and community organizations mobilized at both the federal and state levels of government, seeking to block the implementation of PRWORA's anti-immigrant provisions. Through protests, letter-writing campaigns, and public testimonies, they contested the negative construction of immigrants and poor people in policy debates and demanded the reversal of various anti-immigrant provisions in the welfare reform and immigration reform laws. In response, Congress partially restored public assistance to legal immigrants in 1997 and 1998.[11] Meanwhile, slightly more than half of states in the U.S. restored legal immigrants' access to benefits for at least one major public assistance program by 2000 by creating new state-level replacement programs.[12] In doing so, they blocked (at least partially) the contested anti-immigrant provisions of PRWORA before they were ever implemented.

This chapter examines struggles over legal immigrants' welfare rights, which were shaped by the politics of race, class, and, to a lesser extent, gender. I first review prior research on the historical development of and political forces behind restrictive welfare policies toward immigrants. As Cybelle Fox (2009) claims, the anti-immigrant provisions of PRWORA represented the latest chapter in efforts to restrict immigrants' use of federal public assistance—efforts that had been under way since the early 1970s. As welfare scholars have emphasized, these restrictions embodied "welfare racism," as they mainly affected poor immigrants of color, who made up the vast majority of legal immigrants. Negative stereotypes of Latino and Asian immigrants, sometimes directed toward welfare mothers, were commonly used to justify these policies.[13] This literature provides important insights into why efforts to restrict legal immigrants' access to welfare emerged and influenced federal legislation. Yet, as discussed in chapter 1, policy implementation provides opportunities for making—and unmaking—social policy.

By examining the dynamics of campaigns to restore legal immigrants' access to welfare, and the uneven success of these campaigns across U.S. states, I seek to add nuance and contingency to our understanding of how the politics of race, class, and gender shapes welfare policy. I argue that the threats associated with the implementation of PRWORA's anti-immigrant provisions, along with the close timing of PRWORA and immigration reform, fostered cross-racial solidarity among immigrant rights activists, cross-movement collaboration between welfare rights and immigrant rights activists, and collaboration between welfare mothers and other kinds of welfare recipients, such as the elderly or disabled. Local policymakers' concerns about the measure's fiscal impacts on local governments and broad public agreement with providing welfare to poor legal immigrants contributed to the emergence of broad-based support for state-level campaigns to replace legal immigrants' welfare benefits. Finally, I examine how demographic and political conditions shaped the outcomes of these campaigns in California, home of the nation's largest immigrant population, and Wisconsin, home to a much smaller population of immigrants. I also discuss why these campaigns were more successful in some states than others. I argue that it was easier to mobilize grassroots groups to exert more electoral pressure on politicians and to replace legal immigrants' benefits where immigrant populations were large, as the case of California illustrates. Nevertheless, some states with small immigrant populations, such as Wisconsin, replaced welfare benefits that congressional politicians refused to restore to legal immigrants. Broad-based coalitions in support of these demands contributed to the success of these campaigns.

The Welfare Backlash Against Immigrants

Cybelle Fox (2009) claims that the anti-immigrant provisions of PRWORA reflected a restrictionist turn in federal welfare policy that had been under way since the early 1970s. When federal welfare policies were first created through the Social Security Act under the Franklin Roosevelt Administration, they did not include any citizenship requirements or other restrictions on immigrants' access to public assistance.

In fact, the Roosevelt Administration significantly reversed the practice of repatriating indigent immigrants under the "public charge" doctrine. Under that doctrine, thousands of impoverished immigrants, mostly Mexican Americans, were threatened with deportation on the grounds that they cost the public money and because they were indigent and in need of welfare.[14] More than ten thousand immigrants were deported from the U.S. between 1921 and 1930, and hundreds of thousands of indigent Mexican Americans, including women and children, were also persuaded and coerced into leaving the country through various government-funded repatriation programs. Not surprisingly, welfare officials were often involved in these efforts.[15] The Roosevelt Administration significantly restricted these practices after coming to power in 1933. As a result, only 1,886 immigrants were deported under the "public charge" doctrine between 1931 and 1940. This doctrine was rarely applied after 1940, and federal officials did not consider the use of welfare as a reason for applying this doctrine. The Roosevelt Administration also restricted welfare officials from cooperating with immigration officials to identify undocumented immigrants.[16]

According to Fox (2009), there were no federal restrictions on access to public assistance based on citizenship or legal status until 1972. While state-level citizenship restrictions for Old Age Assistance were fairly common in the late 1930s, only one state (Texas) adopted a citizenship restriction on Aid to Dependent Children. Concerns about the cost of implementing these citizenship restrictions contributed to pressure to eliminate them. State poor laws required that local governments provide relief for indigent people not covered by federal public assistance through state and county General Assistance programs. Since the federal government did not contribute to the cost of General Assistance, states had a financial incentive to cover non-citizens through federal public assistance programs. The number of immigrants was relatively small at that time, so providing welfare coverage to them was not as controversial as it later became when immigrants' numbers rose. By 1972, only ten states had any citizenship requirement for public assistance programs. More commonly, new immigrants, along with other new residents, were barred from public assistance through length-of-residency requirements, which were in place in forty states until the Supreme Court ruled them illegal in Shapiro v. Thompson (1968).

Between 1972 and 1976, federal welfare policies shifted, and undocumented immigrants were denied access to most federal public assistance programs through a series of administrative rulings by federal welfare officials and congressional laws. During this period, restrictions limiting welfare officials from cooperating with immigration officials were also lifted. Fox argues that this policy shift represented federal welfare officials' and congressional politicians' rejection of the Supreme Court ruling in Graham v. Richardson (1971) that state citizenship requirements for welfare were unconstitutional. Fox suggests that concerns about the fiscal impact of the Graham v. Richardson ruling, amidst a rising tide of immigrants and welfare caseloads and political pressure to limit non-citizens' access to welfare, led to this restrictive turn in welfare policies towards immigrants. Efforts to restrict non-citizens' access to welfare continued in the 1980s when the U.S. government developed a federal database for checking the citizenship status of all public assistance applicants.[17] The 1986 Immigration Reform and Control Act provided amnesty for nearly three million undocumented immigrants, but it also barred applicants for citizenship from receiving federal public assistance for the first five years after they applied for temporary residency.[18] In the 1980s, new rules for SSI, Food Stamps, and Aid to Families with Dependent Children (AFDC) were also adopted, counting the income and resources of immigrants' sponsors when determining immigrant applicants' need for welfare.[19]

As welfare scholars have documented, attacks on immigrants' rights to welfare continued in the 1990s, appealing to racist stereotypes and resentments. Attacks often focused on the use of social services by Mexican American women and children, reflecting a backlash against the rise in Mexican American women's immigration to the United States and the increasing tendency of Mexican immigrant families to settle permanently.[20] Drawing on long-standing racist stereotypes of Latino immigrants, conservative politicians and anti-immigrant groups claimed that the United States had become a "welfare magnet" that lured poor immigrants into the country through the promise of easy welfare money, creating a fiscal burden on taxpayers. Anti-immigrant organizations, scholars, and newspaper editorials helped to promote these stereotypes. For example, a 1992 mailing by the American Immigration Control Foundation claimed that immigrants were wasting taxpayers' money through their use of social services. Similarly, the Federation for American Immigration Reform's literature highlighted "immigrant-related welfare rip-offs" and described Mexicans crossing the U.S. border "with the sole intention of having a child who is automatically an American citizen" and thereby becoming eligible for social services.[21] Conservative scholars added professional legitimacy to such stereotypes. For example, Dr. Lawrence Mead argued that " 'many of the newer immigrants feel, and display, fatalistic attitudes,' about 'getting ahead' that are 'alien to the dominant culture.' "[22] Politicians frequently associated Latino immigrants with Mexican Americans, who were portrayed as lazy and irresponsible; they were the rhetorical target of the most virulent attacks on immigrants' welfare rights.[23]

By contrast, politicians often viewed Asian Americans as a homogenous "model minority," which rendered invisible the plight of poor Asian immigrants and refugees in the debates about welfare reform.[24] Nevertheless, some pundits targeted Asian Americans in their attacks on immigrants' welfare use. For example, news editorials on the use of SSI by elderly immigrants prior to PRWORA's passage frequently portrayed recipients, disproportionately Asian American, as purposefully immigrating to the United States to obtain benefits while refusing support from their middle-class and affluent relatives.[25] During congressional hearings on welfare reform, one scholar claimed that this practice was especially common among Chinese immigrants.[26] Southeast Asian immigrants, who have high poverty rates, and many of whom are refugees, were also "demonized as culturally unassimilable and overly dependent on welfare."[27]

Research contradicts myths about immigrants' welfare use, however, suggesting that they are driven by race-based nativist prejudice rather than facts. Moreover, immigrants, especially non-refugees, generally have lower rates of welfare use compared to their native-born counterparts.[28] And the National Academy of Sciences found that, rather than being a fiscal burden, the average immigrant worker produces a $278 annual net gain to the U.S. economy.[29] Research on public opinion also indicates that nativism is racialized. Polls show significantly greater opposition to Asian, Latin American, and African immigrants than to European immigrants.[30]

Despite this contradictory research, anti-immigrant propaganda succeeded in shaping public sentiments. Immigrants became increasingly associated with welfare in the public mind. While most Americans viewed recent immigrants as hardworking, national surveys taken between 1985 and 1993 showed that in some years most, or in other years nearly half, of all respondents believed that most immigrants would end up on welfare. Most, or nearly half, depending on the survey year, also believed that immigrants were using up more tax resources through welfare than they were contributing.[31] By 1994, only 27 percent of those polled supported government aid for immigrants who come here with very little, compared to 43 percent in 1986.[32] Undocumented immigrants bore the brunt of such sentiments. Polls showed that less than a third of respondents supported proposals to deny welfare to legal immigrants.[33]

The backlash against immigrants' use of welfare was especially powerful in California, home to the nation's largest immigrant population. There, in 1994, anti-immigrant groups campaigned for Proposition 187 to deny undocumented immigrants' access to public social services, including public education. The media campaign for this measure preyed upon anti-Mexican sentiments and white voters' economic anxieties. One television commercial warned viewers that "those illegal aliens streaming across the border are taking your jobs and abusing your social services."[34] Despite organized opposition to the measure, 60 percent of the state's electorate passed it in 1994. White voters, about 80 percent of actual voters, were the most supportive of it.[35] Proposition 187 was eventually declared illegal since immigration was a federal rather than state matter and its implementation threatened to deny basic rights to U.S.-born children of undocumented immigrants.

Nevertheless, the measure's popularity, together with nativist groups' demands, encouraged national politicians to restrict legal immigrants' access to public assistance. While undocumented immigrants were disqualified from receiving many forms of federal public assistance, legal immigrants and children of undocumented immigrants born in the United States were eligible for it. As immigration increased, so did the share of welfare recipients that were non-citizens. For example, the share of adult AFDC recipients who were non-citizens rose from 5.5 percent in 1983 to 9 percent in 1993.[36]

By the mid-1990s, as the backlash against both welfare mothers and immigrants rose to new heights, anti-welfare forces were pushing for broad restrictions on legal immigrants' rights to public assistance. Anti-immigrant hysteria mounted in the midst of congressional debates over immigration reform. Anti-immigrant groups and conservative think tanks such as the Heritage Foundation urged politicians to restrict legal immigrants' benefits.[37] The Federation for American Immigration Reform lobbied Congress to deny public assistance to non-citizen legal immigrants, arguing that "no federal or state taxpayer should have to pay a dime for immigration . . . Welfare programs are an incentive to attract immigrants without education, skills, or literacy to move to the United States."[38]

Republicans as well as Democrats championed proposals to deny aid to legal immigrants. In 1994, as part of their "Contract with America," House Republicans promised to cut off virtually all welfare benefits for legal immigrants under 75 years of age.[39] Defending the proposal, Republican Representative Clay Shaw of Florida argued, "Our welfare benefits are an attraction to people to come to this country, and they should be cut off. We should take care of our own with the resources we have."[40] President Bill Clinton and moderate Democrats affiliated with the "Mainstream Forum" also supported immigrant cutoffs as a way to finance welfare reform without raising taxes.[41] Through PRWORA, Congress denied federal public assistance to most legal immigrants, viewing it as a politically strategic way to minimize welfare expenditures.[42] As immigrant rights activists pointed out, "'It's welfare elimination for a group of people who are currently out of favor and don't vote.' "[43] Nearly half of the projected savings from PRWORA, $25 billion over five years, was expected to come from restrictions on immigrants' access to welfare.[44]

The passage of the 1996 immigration reform act also concerned immigrant rights advocates. To reduce illegal immigration, this act strengthened border enforcement, raised penalties for forging or misusing immigration papers, and increased resources for deporting undocumented immigrants and those overstaying their visas. Significantly, the act also targeted legal immigrants, expanding the number of crimes for which they could be deported, and increased the income requirements for legal immigrants' sponsors, as well as their obligations. Sponsors now had to prove that they could support immigrants at 125 percent of the poverty line, making it difficult for poor immigrants to enter the United States legally. Congress also increased the required number of years that sponsors' income was deemed available to legal immigrants, making it harder for otherwise qualified immigrants to receive welfare.[45]

These closely timed policies—the 1996 welfare reform and immigration reform acts—posed a considerable threat to legal immigrants' access to income and services. Not only did these policies render most legal immigrants ineligible for welfare, they had a "chilling effect" on immigrants' use of welfare. Even qualified immigrants stopped accessing welfare because of confusion or fear that it would interfere with their naturalization process. After the passage of PRWORA, the number of immigrant welfare applications approved dropped sharply—decreasing 71 percent between January 1996 and January 1998, draining resources away from communities of color.[46] PRWORA and immigration reform also undermined immigrants' social and political standing within the United States. These policies, justified through racist stereotypes, expressed politicians' devaluation of immigrants, most of whom were Latino and Asian. They sent strong policy signals that they were unwelcome and not considered full, or potentially valuable, members of the polity.[47]

Cross-Racial Solidarity for Benefit-Replacement Campaigns

While welfare scholars have brought attention to the ways that racism and nativism shaped efforts to restrict legal immigrants' rights to welfare, there has been relatively little scholarship on how the politics of race have shaped the implementation of these restrictions at the state level or blocked them altogether. These two closely timed policies—the 1996 welfare reform and immigration reform acts—threatened all immigrants and thus strengthened immigrant solidarity across race, ethnicity, and legal status, although the extent of mobilization around these issues varied across ethnic groups.[48] Along with other welfare advocates, immigrant rights activists mobilized at multiple scales of governance, targeting national, state, county, and city officials. Initially, they targeted national-level politicians. Shortly after PRWORA's passage and during congressional debates on immigration reform, immigrant rights activists organized eighty-five thousand people for a march for immigrants' rights in Washington, D.C.[49] Immigrant rights activists also formed new multiracial and multiethnic coalitions, such as the "Fix '96" campaign, which called for the reversal of the anti-immigrant provisions contained in these two laws. New foundation grants for organizing legal immigrants, such as those provided by the Emma Lazarus Foundation, facilitated immigrant mobilization in response to PRWORA.[50]

Campaigns to reverse PRWORA's anti-immigrant provisions brought together the most stigmatized, vulnerable immigrants, such as undocumented Mexican immigrants, with less stigmatized or vulnerable immigrants, such as legal Russian or Korean immigrants. Not only did this increase activists' organizational resources and reach, it helped to legitimize their demands. As noted by Aihwa Ong (1999), immigrants are differentially racialized, or "othered," in the United States. As a result, "some immigrants of color have greater access than others to key institutions in state and civil society."[51] For example, legal distinctions between refugees and other immigrants result in a "discriminatory two-tiered system of access to public assistance and social services."[52] While refugees, disproportionately Asian, are considered "deserving" of aid, "economic migrants," disproportionately Latino, are deemed "undeserving" of government assistance. Such differential treatment results in better services for, and higher welfare utilization rates among, refugees than other immigrants.[53] Since Asian immigrants, especially Southeast Asian refugees and Hmong veterans, were commonly seen as worthy of support, their collaboration in campaigns against the anti-immigrant provisions of PRWORA contributed to their legitimacy. In contrast, the visibility of Latinos, especially Mexican Americans, in benefit-replacement campaigns often provoked ambivalent responses from politicians. Whereas some viewed them as an important constituency and championed their cause, others were hostile to their demands. Working together, Latino, Asian, and other immigrant rights activists challenged politicians' negative construction of immigrants as a fiscal burden. For example, "Fix '96" activists attached mock tax forms from immigrants to letters urging national politicians to restore legal immigrants' rights to welfare.[54]

Because PRWORA's anti-immigrant provisions cut across several policy domains, they also encouraged greater collaboration between

immigrant and civil rights activists on the one hand and welfare advocates on the other. As one activist explained,

> If there is a good thing about welfare reform . . . it is that it has brought all these different types of folks together. So immigrant rights groups who never worked with [anti-] hunger advocates are now working on food stamps. I guess that is the silver lining of welfare reform . . . we have been able to establish a good network, a diverse group of folks who have become invested in these issues of hunger, these issues of fairness to immigrants.[55]

Ethnic and immigrant advocates viewed immigrants' welfare rights as part of their broad agenda of protecting the rights of immigrants and/or racial and ethnic minorities. Welfare advocacy organizations, in contrast, supported immigrants' rights to welfare as part of their broad agenda to improve the social safety net. Because PRWORA threatened immigrants' rights to multiple forms of public assistance that served different constituencies, it mobilized a wide variety of service providers and other kinds of welfare advocates, including senior citizens' groups, anti-hunger activists, welfare mothers' organizations, disability rights groups, and religious organizations. This helped to unite able-bodied welfare recipients, commonly viewed as the "undeserving poor," with non-able-bodied poor people, commonly seen as the "deserving poor." Broad public support for the welfare rights of legal immigrants, who were generally seen as more deserving of aid than undocumented immigrants, facilitated the building of such broad-based alliances.

Together, immigrant rights and welfare rights activists exerted considerable pressure on Congress to overturn the restrictions on legal immigrants' access to welfare. Against the perception that immigrant recipients were not truly in need of help, advocates highlighted the suffering that the impending cutoffs would create. They publicized stories of people who had committed suicide in response to losing their benefits and warned of "mass evictions, increased homelessness, and hunger as aid ceases."[56] They also gathered thousands of letters on paper plates from recipients, providing personal testimonies about how food stamps kept their families from going hungry.[57] Through public demonstrations, lobbying, and high-profile legal challenges, advocates demanded the full restoration of legal immigrants' welfare rights. This mobilization and coalition-building was facilitated by elite donors' and foundations' provision of new funds for immigrant and welfare rights organizing in response to the 1996 welfare reform and immigration reform acts.[58] One of the most notable new funding sources was George Soros's $50 million Emma Lazarus Fund for organizations that helped legal immigrants to naturalize or campaign for their rights.[59]

Politicians' mixed support for welfare reform's anti-immigrant provisions also encouraged mobilization on this issue, as it gave people hope that policymakers would respond to popular pressure. Indeed, even as he signed PRWORA into legislation, President Clinton vowed to restore legal immigrants' rights to welfare.[60] The National Governor's Association, fearing the fiscal impacts of federal cutoffs to immigrants, also urged Congress to reinstate benefits.[61] Even Republican politicians were mixed or lukewarm in their support of restricting immigrants' rights to social services since it might alienate Latino voters, a growing share of the national electorate.[62]

Within a year, most congressional politicians supported partial benefit restorations for the Food Stamps and SSI programs. In an effort to co-opt the resistance movement and save money, Congress subdivided legal immigrants into those who were "deserving" and "undeserving" of aid. In 1997 and 1998, Congress reclassified certain refugees and legal immigrants that were young, disabled, or elderly so that they qualified for federal public assistance.[63] Other immigrants had already been declared "qualified" for benefits in the original welfare reform law. As a result, "qualified immigrants" also included lawful permanent residents, those with Immigration and Naturalization Service parole for at least one year, conditional entrants, and victims of domestic violence and their dependents. "Unqualified immigrants" included those without green cards but who were nevertheless in the United States legally and immigrants who entered the country legally on or after August 22, 1996 (the day the law was passed), unless they were veterans, were refugees, or could prove they had worked in the U.S. for ten or more years.[64] However, new legal immigrants who entered the United States after August 22, 1996, and able-bodied working-age legal immigrants were still deemed the "undeserving poor."[65]

As Lynn Fujiwara (1999) suggests, politicians and the media showed particular sympathy towards poor Asian refugees, especially Hmong, Lao, and Mien veterans who had fought for the U.S. during the Vietnam War. These refugees were reclassified as eligible for benefits and played a central role in gaining congressional support for partial benefit restorations.[66] Although partial benefit restorations narrowed the base of support for subsequent campaigns, many ethnic, welfare, and immigrants' rights groups continued to push for full benefit restorations. In response to such pressure, in 2002 Congress restored access to food stamps for legal immigrants that were disabled or under age eighteen, regardless of their year of entry.

Activists also put pressure on state and local politicians to restore the safety net for legal immigrants, especially when the limits of federal support for their demands became clear. They pressured state politicians to halt the implementation of federal cutbacks in welfare for legal immigrants by creating state-funded benefit-replacement programs. Local policymakers sometimes supported activists' demands, often in response to concerns about the fiscal impacts that immigrant cutoffs would have for local governments, especially those still required to provide General Assistance to the needy. In response to public demands, just over half of all states restored legal immigrants' access to at least one public assistance program by 1999.

Why did some states replace benefits for legal immigrants while others did not? Quantitative studies of states' welfare policies toward legal immigrants highlight various factors shaping states' welfare policies towards legal immigrants. Using data from all U.S. states, Wendy Zimmerman and Karen Tumlin (1999) constructed a scale of welfare generosity towards legal immigrants. Comparing the characteristics of states with more and less generous safety nets for immigrants, they found that states with larger immigrant populations tended to be more generous, although a few states with small immigrant populations were also generous. They also found that more generous states generally had higher per capita income and more well-developed social safety nets. Another study also shows that states were significantly more likely to replace legal immigrants' welfare benefits between 1996 and 1998 if larger immigrant populations resided within them. This is hardly surprising since it would have been easier to mobilize political pressure on state legislators to replace welfare benefits for legal immigrants where immigrant populations were larger, and politicians would have experienced greater electoral pressure to respond favorably to such demands. Consistent with the argument that politicians treated Asian immigrants as more worthy, states were significantly more likely to restore benefits in states with larger Asian populations but not larger Latino populations.[67] Other quantitative research suggests that states were more likely to adopt more inclusive welfare policies toward immigrants when their governments were more liberal in orientation and supportive of civil rights policies, when they were more highly urbanized, when their welfare caseloads were larger, and when state residents were more highly educated and more liberal in orientation.[68] The following case studies of the campaigns to replace legal immigrants' welfare benefits in Wisconsin and California shed greater light on how the dynamics of these campaigns—and their outcomes—were shaped by the local political and demographic conditions in which activists waged their battles.

Benefit-Replacement Campaigns in Two States

Not surprisingly, benefit-replacement campaigns were more successful in California than in Wisconsin. California was one of the two most gener-

Table 3.1 Number of Public Assistance Recipients, 1996–1997

	California (Percentage of Population)	Wisconsin (Percentage of Population)
Food Stamps	3,143,000 (9.8%)	283,000 (5.4%)
Medicare	845,958 (2.6%)	80,945 (1.6%)
SSI	1,044,753 (3.2%)	407,264 (7.8%)
AFDC/TANF	896,000 (2.8%)	291,000 (5.6%)

Source: Author's compilation based on U.S. House of Representatives Committee on Ways and Means (1998, tables 2-40, 3-21, 7-11, 15-9) and U.S. Census Bureau (1999).
Notes: Data for Food Stamps, SSI, and AFDC are for 1996; data on SSI are for 1997; welfare recipients refer to average monthly caseloads; total population estimates are for 1997. SSI = Supplemental Security Income; AFDC = Aid to Families with Dependent Children; TANF = Temporary Assistance for Needy Families.

ous states for legal immigrants to reside in the nation, restoring most legal immigrants' rights to all four major public assistance programs.[69] In contrast , Wisconsin only replaced legal immigrants' access to two programs: TANF and Food Stamps. As I explain further below, the outcomes of these campaigns depended on their grassroots strength as well as the political conditions under which they were waged.

Activists had a far larger group of likely supporters for benefit-replacement campaigns in California than in Wisconsin. As table 1.3 shows, more than one-quarter of California's population was foreign-born and Latino, while more than one-tenth was Asian. By contrast, less than 3 percent of Wisconsin's population was Latino, foreign-born, or Asian. Although the percentage of the population receiving welfare was higher in Wisconsin than California for some programs, California had a much larger welfare population than the less populous state of Wisconsin (see table 3.1). California also had a greater share of welfare recipients who were Latino and Asian (see table 3.2). Given these demographic differences, it is not surprising that demonstrations for benefit replacements were larger and more militant in California than in Wisconsin, and electoral pressure to make concessions to immigrants was greater in the former state than in the latter. Compared to Wisconsin, California also had a far greater share of legislators that were Democrats and Latino, increasing activists' access to powerful allies within the state government.

Both case studies help to demonstrate how common threats helped to forge broad-based and multiracial welfare rights coalitions and how the breadth of mobilization around this issue helped to prevent the implementation of federal-level cutbacks. Indeed, the benefit replacements for the two welfare programs won in Wisconsin represented a significant victory, since most states only replaced benefits for one program. This victory was even more striking given the dominance of Republicans within Wisconsin's state politics and the state's small immigrant population. I

Table 3.2 Percentage of Aid to Families with Dependent Children Recipients by Race–Ethnicity, 1995

	California	Wisconsin
White	25.6	42.8
Black	17.7	40.4
Latino	40.0	8.5
Asian	8.8	4.2
Native American	0.9	2.7

Source: Author's compilation of data from the U.S. House of Representatives Committee on Ways and Means (1998, table 7-24).

argue that, just as in California, the formation of broad-based coalitions helped to prevent cutbacks to legal immigrants' welfare rights in Wisconsin. In both states, Hmong refugees also played a visible role in benefit-replacement campaigns. Based on focus group discussions, Jeremy Hein (2006) found that Hmong immigrants expressed a strong willingness to mobilize against the anti-immigrant provisions in PRWORA, more so than Cambodian immigrants. He concludes that these varied responses were shaped by their different ethnic origins, which led to a more polarized "us-versus-them" group identity among the Hmong and a more individualistic view of adaptation among Cambodians. Public sympathy for these refugees, who were U.S. war veterans, probably helped to increase political support for benefit replacements in these states. Along with Hmong refugees, other influential individuals such as religious leaders and local politicians also lent support and credibility to the demands for replacing legal immigrants' welfare benefits. Activists also benefited from broader public opinion, which generally favored assistance for needy legal immigrants even while it opposed to aid to undocumented immigrants.

California's Campaign

Although California never cut off legal immigrants' access to TANF or Medicaid, activists confronted serious challenges in their efforts to replace Food Stamp and SSI benefits to legal immigrants. First, nativism was strong within the state, and Governor Pete Wilson, a strong supporter of Proposition 187, was a powerful foe of immigrants. Five days after PRWORA's passage, Governor Wilson ordered state agencies to cut off all public services to undocumented immigrants, arguing that they "serve as a magnetic lure drawing illegal aliens across our border."[70] Although Wilson was more supportive of restoring legal immigrants' welfare rights, he strongly opposed benefit replacements for working-age adults and new immigrants.[71] Because of California's large immigrant population, benefit replacements were also very expensive. Food Stamp replacements were expected to cost $175 million a year, while replacing SSI benefits was expected to cost $274 million over two years.[72]

However, California provided a more favorable context for mobilizing on behalf of legal immigrants' welfare rights than elsewhere because of its relatively generous welfare state and large immigrant population. About 26 percent of the state's population was foreign-born by 1996, and on average, more than 200,000 legal immigrants were entering the state each year.[73] Approximately 400,000 legal immigrants received some form of public assistance, out of the state's 2.5 million legal immigrants and 6 million public assistance recipients.[74] The state also had large Asian and Latino populations, which respectively made up 12 and 28 percent of the state's total population in 1996 (see table 1.3). Many of these Asians and Latinos were first- or second-generation immigrants likely to identify with the plight of new immigrants. Electoral participation research also shows that California's immigrants were becoming more politicized in the 1990s in response to the passage of a series of anti-immigrant initiatives.[75] This not only provided a large pool of potential supporters for benefit-replacement campaigns, it also increased electoral pressure on politicians, especially in the Bay Area and southern California, to respond favorably to them.[76] Most of the opposition for providing social services to immigrants was also directed at undocumented rather than legal immigrants.

As table 3.3 shows, 68 percent of California's foreign-born population was concentrated in the Bay Area and three southern counties (Los Angeles, Orange, and San Diego), with 45 percent of foreign-born residents living in Los Angeles. This meant that hundreds of thousands of people affected by the immigrant welfare cutoffs were concentrated in these areas. In Los Angeles County, for example, almost ninety-nine thousand elderly and disabled legal immigrants faced the threat of losing SSI, while 150,000 would lose Food Stamp benefits.[77] Along with poor immigrants, Latino and Asian communities were also concentrated in these areas. This concentration and the well-developed network of ethnic and immigrant organizations within Los Angeles and the Bay Area greatly facilitated mobilization around this issue. Ethnic, immigrant, and anti-poverty organizations provided staff, membership lists, meeting space, coalition partners, and other resources necessary for popular mobilization. For example, an alliance of nearly fifty social service agencies serving Asian Americans in the Los Angeles area organized testimonies for press conferences and public hearings by mobilizing representatives of their member agencies who, in turn, recruited clients.[78]

Table 3.3 Immigrant, Asian and Pacific Islander (API), and Latino Populations in Southern California and the Bay Area

	(Percentage of State's Share)			
County	New Legal Immigrants, 1996*	Foreign-Born, 1990**	API, 1996***	Latino, 1996***
Los Angeles	63,794 (32%)	2,895,066 (45%)	1,129,800 (31%)	3,988,100 (36%)
Orange	17,598 (9%)	575,108 (9%)	314,600 (9%)	720,700 (7%)
San Diego	18,049 (9%)	428,810 (7%)	221,700 (6%)	622,900 (6%)
Bay Area (Alameda & San Francisco)	21,257 (10%)	476,409 (7%)	492,800 (14%)	335,700 (3%)
Four areas	120,698 (66%)	4,375,393 (68%)	2,158,900 (59%)	6,068,400 (55%)
California	199,483 (100%)	6,458,825 (100%)	3,648,860 (100%)	10,966,556 (100%)

Sources: Author's compilation based on *State of California Department of Finance (2000); **U.S. Census Bureau (1991); and ***State of California Department of Finance (1999).
Note: This table appears in Reese and Ramirez (2002a, table 4) and is reprinted with permission of Taylor and Francis, Ltd.

Ethnic and immigrant rights organizations were highly active in California's campaign, as were welfare advocacy groups, civil rights organizations, religious groups, and social service agencies.[79] While legal organizations stalled the implementation of federal cutbacks, these groups organized community support for benefit replacements. While some of these organizations pre-dated 1996, other groups, such as the California Immigrant and Welfare Collaborative, were formed in response to welfare reform through new foundation grants. A variety of Asian and Latino organizations, including those serving Hmong American, Korean American, Central American, and Mexican American populations, frequently worked hand-in-hand in this struggle.

At the same time, Asian American activists portrayed Hmong, Lao, and Mien refugees as "a special case, deserving special treatment."[80] Groups like the California chapter of the Lao-Hmong American Coalition claimed that because these refugees had fought for the U.S. during the Vietnam War, they should qualify for the exemptions from benefit cutoffs that were provided to other U.S. veterans. They portrayed this group as particularly honorable because they had fulfilled military duties for the United States. The Asian Law Caucus filed at least 3,500 appeals on behalf of Hmong immigrants in California who were slated for benefit cutoffs, which led to mass hearings before California's administrative law judges.[81] Even during rallies for benefit-replacement programs that would benefit all legal immigrants, Hmong refugees highlighted their special status, holding signs that read, for example, "U.S. Hmong Veteran fought for the U.S. and denied Food Stamps."[82] In response to impending benefit cuts, two Hmong refugee women in California committed suicide, sparking a storm of media publicity around the issue and drawing attention to the plight of Hmong immigrants.[83]

To put pressure on politicians, activists organized a series of marches and rallies, legislative visits, public statements, and letter-writing campaigns. Within a year of PRWORA's enactment, activists organized at least three mass demonstrations. The first was a two-thousand-person march through downtown Los Angeles in support of benefit restorations. About fifty groups sponsored the march, including immigrant rights groups, social service agencies, and labor unions.[84] Several months later, activists organized two separate "Immigrant Lobby Days," where they visited legislators in small groups and rallied outside the state capitol building. Participants claim that the first event drew about four thousand participants, while the second drew about three thousand.[85] These events brought together immigrants from many countries. As one participant observed, state legislators were confronted by "Hmong women wearing their traditional head dress, and Mien, and Laotian women with other advocates, Latino migrant workers with their jeans and plaid shirts," all of whom demanded benefit replacements.[86]

Despite the strength of nativist forces and fiscal conservatives in California, advocates quickly found governmental allies. The California State Association of Counties urged state legislators to restore benefits to legal immigrants. Although this may have been partly motivated by a genuine concern over the plight of poor immigrants, it also reflected fiscal concerns. County officials estimated that welfare cutbacks would cost counties $850 million, as indigent immigrants would flood state-mandated, county-funded General Relief programs.[87] California counties asked the state for financial help in coping with the impending cutoffs, giving political weight to grassroots efforts. According to former Governor Wilson's spokesperson, their pressure helped to win the governor's support for food stamps for legal immigrants.[88]

Advocates also found powerful allies among Democrats, who dominated the legislature. Politicians felt considerable pressure to replace benefits to legal immigrants because of the state's growing Latino, Asian, and immigrant electorate. In 1998, Latinos composed 12 percent of all voters in California's primary election, more than double their share in 1994.[89] Latino politicians, who made up nearly 12 percent of the state's legislators in 1996,[90] ardently supported benefit-replacement campaigns. Acting as "institutional activists," they mobilized within the state legislature, vigorously lobbying their colleagues and the governor to support benefit replacements. Martha Escutia, Cruz Bustamante, Gil Cedillo, Richard Polanco, Hilda Solis, and Antonio Villaraigosa were especially active on the issue.[91] Villaraigosa (who was elected mayor of Los Angeles in 2005 and reelected in 2009) and Solis (who served as a U.S. Congress representative between 2001 and 2009 before becoming the U.S. Secretary of Labor in 2009) were particularly active in this welfare rights campaign, joining grassroots activists in at least one public demonstration.[92] Restoring aid to legal immigrants was Assembly Speaker Cruz Bustamante's top priority in 1997: "It's because of maybe who I am and where I come from . . . I can't go back home unless I do something important about this issue," he said at a news conference.[93]

By July of 1997, most legislators were willing to support benefit replacements, but Governor Pete Wilson rejected the idea. To pressure Wilson, Latino legislators produced a commercial urging him to assist legal immigrants.[94] Under Bustamante's leadership, the Democratic Caucus spent three weeks refusing to pass Wilson's budget unless benefit replacements were included in it.[95] By the following month, Wilson agreed to compromise. In a face-to-face meeting with Bustamante, he delineated a state Food Stamp replacement plan, although he was willing to provide only $32 million worth of food stamps to children and the elderly, excluding working-age adults and new immigrants.

After this partial victory, immigrant rights activists continued to mobilize grassroots support for expanding benefits for immigrants. Various community groups protested in downtown Fresno and reprimanded Bustamante and Wilson "for not doing enough" for legal immigrants. Members of the Latino Civil Rights Network gave Bustamante a plastic water jug filled with 5,300 beans, representing the number of adult legal immigrants in Fresno County that did not qualify for either federal or state food stamps.[96] Each year, activists participated in "Immigrant Lobby Day" and "Hunger Action Day," where they urged state legislators to reauthorize and expand benefit-replacement programs. Activists also continued to testify at public hearings, wrote letters, made phone calls, and even protested in the governor's office.[97]

With so much mobilization and the support of Latino politicians, especially then-Assembly Speaker Antonio Villaraigosa, advocates scored major victories in 1998 and 1999. In 1998, the California Food Assistance Program was extended to cover working-age adult immigrants, and legislators created exemptions for new immigrants without active sponsors. Legislators also created the Cash Assistance Program for Immigrants (CAPI) to restore SSI to elderly and disabled legal immigrants. Such victories were facilitated by partial benefit restorations at the federal level, which reduced these programs' cost. Nevertheless, California's benefit replacements remained contested. After taking office, Governor Gray Davis, a Democrat, tried to end CAPI to save money. In response, immigrant and welfare rights activists jointly held a sit-in demonstration in his Los Angeles office. Afterward, Davis agreed to extend both programs for another year and later agreed to make them a permanent part of the state's budget in 2000.[98] As fiscal conditions worsened in the state, politicians annually proposed the elimination of these programs and continued to do so in 2010.

While California's benefit-replacement programs served legal immigrants regardless of their country of origin, state and local officials expressed particular concern about the plight of Hmong, Lao, and Mien refugees.[99] For example, then–Lieutenant Governor Gray Davis wrote a letter in support of a Hmong veteran's lawsuit against the California Department of Social Services and its director, Eloise Anderson, for cutting off his food stamp benefits. "As a veteran myself," Davis argued, "I am personally offended that the state of California should fail to acknowledge the sacrifices of fellow veterans and their family members."[100] The judge, who determined that the Hmong veteran was not entitled to the same welfare benefits provided to other U.S. war veterans, also decried "the inequitable treatment of a class of residents that sacrificed much to serve this nation."[101] The Hmong refugee population in California, the largest in the nation, thus received particular sympathy from public officials because of their image as the "deserving poor"—an image that Hmong refugee activists actively promoted.[102] The visible role played by Hmong veterans within benefit-replacement campaigns helped to increase activists' political leverage, as did the multiracial character of this campaign. Because active supporters represented an array of ethnic and racial groups as well as a growing population of immigrants, they wielded greater electoral pressure on politicians; had this campaign been closely identified with only one racial or ethnic group, politicians might have found it easier to dismiss activists' demands. More generally, the breadth of support for benefit-replacement campaigns increased their influence. The active support of local and state policymakers lent political muscle to grassroots activists' demands, while the participation of immigrant rights activists and ethnic organizations widened pressure beyond welfare advocates and the poor.

Wisconsin's Campaign

Broad-based and multiracial mobilization also contributed to the success of benefit-replacement campaigns in Wisconsin. While not nearly as large as the immigrant populations in California (see table 1.3), the foreign-born population in Wisconsin was not puny. An estimated fifty-eight thousand legal foreign-born residents lived in the state, which was home to the nation's second-largest Hmong community in the 1990s.[103] To immigrants' relief, the state restored legal immigrants' access to TANF early on. However, an estimated 7,200 legal immigrants were expected to lose access to Food Stamps, while 4,600 were expected to lose SSI benefits.[104] To push for benefit replacements, concerned advocacy groups formed the Wisconsin Immigrant and Refugee Coalition in 1997.

The coalition was composed of thirty agencies, including organizations serving Asian, Latino, and Eastern European immigrants; social service agencies; welfare advocacy groups; religious groups; and ethnic organizations.[105] It mainly focused on lobbying and increasing publicity about the impending welfare cutbacks by gaining media and local governmental support for its campaign. Toward those ends, the coalition organized several press conferences outside the state capitol in support of legal immigrants' rights to SSI and Food Stamps. Through "action alerts," the coalition also urged its members to contact their state legislators, write editorials in favor of the replacement bills, and contact their local media about the issue.[106] Later, the coalition focused more exclusively on lobbying for Food Stamp replacements, considering legislative support for replacing SSI and Medicaid as more of a "long shot" because of their greater expense and the strength of the opposition to funding benefit replacements within the legislature.[107] The coalition did not organize protests for several reasons. Because legal immigrants in Wisconsin were fewer in number and lived far from the state capital, it would be difficult to organize large demonstrations like in California. The coalition's leaders also feared the emotional consequences of raising immigrants' expectations, especially given the recent spate of suicides by those affected by welfare cutoffs, and worried that protests might provoke greater opposition from Republicans than lobbying would. However, a less-cautious group mobilized several hundred people, including busloads of Hmong immigrants, for a rally at the state capitol building.[108]

In February 1998, the state Senate committee held a hearing on the need for Food Stamp replacements. The coalition and the Wisconsin Child Nutrition Alliance held a joint press conference outside of the capitol to urge legislators to pass the bill. They highlighted the plight of Hmong families, who were expected to lose an average of $300 a month in food money. The coalition's chair remarked, "Do we really want to force parents to choose between feeding their children and heating their homes just because they have not become U.S. citizens yet?"[109] Thirty-one people attended the hearing, including more than a dozen immigrants and members of religious, elderly, and civil rights groups.[110]

While not as large or as militant as California's campaign, Wisconsin's benefit-replacement campaign was broad-based, including a multiracial alliance of immigrants and ethnic organizations. Welfare advocacy groups and religious activists and leaders also supported the cause, concerned with preventing hardship among the needy. For example, four religious organizations of different faiths wrote a well-publicized letter urging politicians to replace Food Stamps for legal immigrants.[111]

As in California, Hmong refugees were highly visible within this campaign. Many of the state's Hmong residents were poor, contributing to the state's high poverty rate among Asians (48 percent), the highest in the nation.[112] There were at least four reported suicides among Hmong residents in response to PRWORA's passage, prompting concerned groups to organize "suicide watches." These suicides helped activists gain sympathetic press coverage of the impacts of impending welfare cutoffs.[113] Immigrant rights groups warned that there could be more suicides if state officials did not replace legal immigrants' Food Stamps and SSI benefits.[114] Focus groups across the state found that the impending loss of welfare benefits was causing tremendous stress and financial hardship among Hmong residents, many of whom expressed suicidal feelings. A university professor produced a videotape of these focus groups and distributed it among Republican lawmakers.[115] Hmong refugees also participated actively in public hearings, press conferences, and rallies. Organizers claim that the visible role of Hmong refugees in this campaign helped to gain legislative support for benefit replacements since the Hmong, as political refugees and U.S. war veterans, were seen as the "deserving poor." In fact, some legislators even argued that they "should just do it [replace benefits] for the Hmong because they fought in Vietnam for us."[116]

Like their counterparts in California, Wisconsin activists also gained support from local policymakers for their demands. For example, in response to immigrants' and advocates' pleas, the Dane County supervisors approved a resolution supporting state benefit replacements, immediate citizenship for Hmong refugees, and the allocation of funds to speed up immigrants' naturalization.[117] Local welfare and health officials also expressed support for restoring legal immigrants' welfare rights, as did many Democratic legislators.[118] Yet, like grassroots support, local officials' support was not as strong in Wisconsin as it was in California. In part, this was because local governments were not required to provide General Assistance to the needy in Wisconsin, like they were in California.

Republican control of Wisconsin state politics also meant that opposition to benefit replacements was also stronger there than in California, where Democrats controlled the state legislature. Republican politicians and top welfare officials—appointed by Republican governor Tommy

Thompson—were strongly opposed to benefit replacements in Wisconsin. Along with Republican legislators, state welfare officials claimed that it was too expensive for the state to replace benefits for legal immigrants.[119] However, since the immigrant population was relatively small, the bill to replace Food Stamps for legal immigrants was fairly modest, expected to cost, at most, $5 million.[120] State welfare officials also claimed that Wisconsin's other welfare programs already provided more generous benefits compared to those of other states, giving needy immigrants and other poor people an advantage that their counterparts lacked in other states.[121] On a party-line vote, the Joint Finance Committee voted twelve to four against restoring Food Stamps to legal immigrants. Representative John Gard, co-chair of the committee, dismissed the possibility of more suicides by Hmong refugees, claiming that, "people who work very closely (with the refugees) say the discussion about violent acts is a natural response to most of their problems."[122] The state assembly rejected the measure in a close vote, with forty-six in favor of the bill and fifty-one opposed to it. Within the Senate, debate over the bill was heated; most of the opposition came from Republicans,[123] while Democrats made impassioned pleas on behalf of Hmong refugees and other legal immigrants.[124] In tears, Democratic Senator Gwendolynne Moore of Milwaukee, a former welfare mother who later became a Congresswoman, urged Republicans to support the measure.[125]

Shortly afterward, Governor Tommy Thompson urged legislators to replace Food Stamps for legal immigrants. In response, a number of assembly politicians reversed their position; benefit replacements for Food Stamps was passed by a wide margin (eighty-six to eleven).[126] Reportedly, Thompson had supported Food Stamp replacements for Hmong refugees for some time, particularly because research suggested that they were in need, but he had waited to intervene until it appeared that the legislature would oppose the measure.[127] His gesture toward immigrants was not simply an act of compassion, however. An election year was a bad time to pass a budget bill that created personal-income tax breaks and property-tax reductions but refused to aid poor immigrants, many of them Hmong veterans of the Vietnam War.[128] As Senate Democrats argued, "If the Legislature can pass tax cuts, surely it can act to restore Food Stamps to Hmong refugees who fought alongside American soldiers in Vietnam."[129] Advocates' lobbying, on top of the publicity they created about hardships among the Hmong, sufficiently pressured Thompson to put his political weight behind Food Stamp replacements, and his support helped to overcome Republican lawmakers' initial opposition. However, Thompson failed to support replacements for SSI and Medicaid, which were costlier than Food Stamps.

Conclusion

The campaigns to restore legal immigrants' access to welfare illustrate how policies could be made—or unmade—at the implementation stage. Although congressional politicians viewed anti-immigrant provisions as a strategic way to cut welfare costs, denying public assistance to legal immigrants proved to be one of the most controversial aspects of the new welfare law. These provisions—which affected most legal immigrants and crossed welfare and immigration policy domains—sparked mobilization and the formation of cross-racial and cross-movement alliances. Campaigns to restore or replace benefits for legal immigrants brought new players and political alliances into welfare politics. Along with a variety of welfare advocacy organizations built around particular public assistance programs, policymakers and middle-class activists affiliated with immigrant rights organizations and ethnic organizations mobilized in defense of legal immigrants' rights to welfare. To maximize their influence, activists mobilized within multiple scales or levels of governance. At the national level, they won partial benefit restorations. At the state level, they waged their battle to replace the benefits that legal immigrants had lost and pressured local policymakers to support their demands. In most states, activists won benefit replacements for at least one of the four major public assistance programs.

Quantitative research indicates that states were significantly more likely to replace benefits for at least one federal public assistance program when the immigrant population made up a larger percentage of the state's population.[130] These conclusions are consistent with the findings from my case studies. California's relatively large immigrant, Latino, and Asian populations facilitated their mobilization and created strong electoral pressure on politicians to make concessions to immigrants. Measured in terms of the size and frequency of mass demonstrations, grassroots support for benefit replacements was strongest in California, which is not surprising given that the state was more populous than Wisconsin and had a larger share of the population that was immigrant (see table 3.4).

Politicians responded not only to the size and militancy of immigrants but also to racially charged perceptions of these groups' "worthiness." The visibility of Asian immigrants and refugees, particularly Hmong refugees, within benefit-replacement campaigns helped to gain political support for them in both Wisconsin and California. Politicians in the two states openly expressed the greatest sympathy for Hmong refugees, whom they portrayed as especially worthy of support because of their

Table 3.4 Mass Demonstrations for Benefit Replacements by State, 1996 to 1997

	Estimated Number of Participants
California	
March in Los Angeles*	2,000
First rally at state capitol**	4,000
Second rally at state capitol**	3,000
Wisconsin	
Rally at state capitol***	200

Source: Author's compilation based on *Albano (1997); **Fujiwara (1999); ***Wisconsin Immigrant and Refugee Coalition leader, personal interview in Milwaukee, 2002; Hmong American Friendship Association staff, personal interview in Milwaukee, 2002.

participation in the Vietnam War. By contrast, politicians expressed more ambivalence towards Latino immigrants, especially Mexican Americans. Whereas Latino politicians and their allies openly defended Latino immigrants' rights to welfare in California, more conservative politicians, such as former Governor Pete Wilson, were reluctant to support benefit replacements, which would largely serve this population. Racial distinctions among immigrants help to explain why advocates succeeded in replacing just as many kinds of benefits in Wisconsin as they did in Texas, where the immigrant population was far larger and more mobilized around this issue, but where the vast majority of affected immigrants were Mexican Americans. Politicians in Texas openly appealed to racist stereotypes of Mexican Americans in order to justify their opposition to benefit replacements. Ambivalence toward Latino immigrants also explains why the success of benefit-replacement campaigns was not significantly linked to the size of the Latino population, as it was to the size of the Asian population.[131]

Activists in both Wisconsin and California also benefited from their states' long tradition of spending relatively more on welfare compared to other states. This was particularly true in California. California's requirement that county governments provide General Relief to indigent people not served by federal programs created strong fiscal incentives for the state to pick up the tab for legal immigrants. Without state-funded benefit replacements, county officials feared that federal cutoffs would drain municipal coffers and therefore lent political weight to activists' demands. Since Wisconsin had eliminated the state requirement that counties provide General Relief in 1995, politicians did not experience the same fiscal pressures to provide aid to legal immigrants as they did in California. Nevertheless, the state tended to be more generous in terms of welfare spending. Plus, its Republican governor, Tommy Thompson, was not as fiscally conservative as Republican governors in other states. These campaigns were also initially waged in the late 1990s, a time when these states had budget surpluses, which undoubtedly eased their success.

In contrast to Wisconsin and California, most states only replaced benefits for one of the four major public assistance programs. Although polls showed strong public support for legal immigrants' welfare rights, fiscal conservatives and nativist groups actively opposed benefit replacements. Legal immigrants were also a relatively small share of the national population and were mainly concentrated in seven states, which limited their capacity to mobilize either political or electoral pressure in many states. For these reasons, they remained vulnerable to cutbacks, especially when economic conditions worsened and state budgets declined. Even when benefit-replacement campaigns were successful, they represented a limited victory; they simply *restored* previously established welfare rights, but they did not create new welfare rights, nor did they extend coverage to undocumented immigrants.

The campaigns to restore welfare benefits to legal immigrants provide important lessons for future gains in immigrants' welfare rights and for welfare scholarship. The success of these campaigns suggests that building broad-based grassroots support for immigrant and welfare rights, forging strong multiracial alliances among communities of color, gaining institutional allies within the state, and countering the negative and racist stereotypes of immigrants are all crucial parts of making future gains in immigrants' welfare rights. For welfare scholars, these campaigns reveal the complexity of the racial and gender politics of welfare reform in the United States. The racial politics of welfare reform went beyond just the politics of black and white. Anti-Latino and anti-Asian stereotypes drove efforts to restrict legal immigrants' rights to welfare, while cross-racial and cross-ethnic coalitions challenged those efforts and the racist stereotypes justifying immigrant cutoffs. These campaigns also reveal how common threats to legal immigrants' rights to welfare, which cut across all four major public assistance programs, inspired alliances between welfare mothers and their advocates and other kinds of public assistance recipients and advocates, as well as immigrant and ethnic organizations. Most importantly, these campaigns demonstrate how building such broad-based alliances helped to defend legal immigrants' rights to welfare at the state level, in opposition to the direction of national welfare policy. They also reveal the multivocal character of the U.S. welfare state; some state and local policymakers, either on principle or in response to fiscal or electoral pressures, actively supported campaigns to prevent the implementation of welfare cutoffs for legal immigrants, while others ignored or actively resisted those campaigns.

Chapter 4

Battling the Welfare Profiteers: Campaigns Against Welfare Privatization[1]

> There has been great concern about welfare privatization and these companies, especially Maximus and Lockheed and the for-profits, just because they have a bad history in other places. They have paid off politicians to win contracts and their concern is to make profits. . . . When your concern is profits and not people, that's going to show in a program to help the poor. There is something wrong with that on a deep level.
>
> –Service Employees International Union (SEIU) Local 660 staff member, Los Angeles

> There was a sense among the agencies that they could do pretty much anything they wanted. Performance standards were so low, expectations were so low, that they never had to work too hard, and what they did was work to the minimum with folks. . . . It's just so darn tempting for these private-sector companies. If they can make money, they will, that's what's going to happen.
>
> –9to5 staff member, Milwaukee

> Maximus was doing insufficient outreach; they were just kind of holed up in their office waiting for people to come to them. . . . We are also concerned about the number of clients that were not getting follow-up service in terms of calls back. As we understood it, they were left to hang, not getting responses back from their Maximus staff. . . . I mean, it's bad enough that they spent the money on frivolous, bizarre activities; they didn't use the money for outreach.
>
> –Hope Offered through Shared Ecumenical Action (HOSEA) staff member, Milwaukee

SCHOLARS ON "mixed governance" point to various forces that have contributed to support for the privatization of welfare and other social services in wealthy democratic countries since the 1980s.

Declining tax bases and increased demands for state services, especially specialized services, put pressure on states to contract out services to private agencies in order to cut costs. Because private agencies tend to employ non-union workers, their services tend to be cheaper than the unionized public sector.[2] Criticisms from both the left and the right also undermined the legitimacy of the welfare state, paving the way for public-private partnerships in the provision of public goods. Conservatives argued that quasi-markets and private agencies were more flexible and efficient than the public sector and that private agencies would be more responsive to consumer demands.[3] Meanwhile, some progressives portrayed nonprofit organizations as sources for "bottom-up, people-centered alternatives to the hierarchical, highly impersonal quality of many state-run welfare agencies."[4] Like critics on the right, critics on the left charged that state-run agencies were "unresponsive, unaccountable and alienating."[5] Private agencies also contributed to criticisms of the public sector. Even as they sought public funds, they differentiated themselves from the state, actively promoting their services and portraying themselves as superior to public-sector alternatives.[6]

Public-private partnerships in the administration of welfare and services were thus portrayed as providing a "third way" between government control and the free market[7] and as enabling a "more fluid process of reform facilitated by the proliferation of new organizational forms and strategies utilized in social welfare provision."[8] Third-sector organizations promised to help the state meet local needs and the needs of special and ethnically diverse populations.[9] Nonprofit organizations in particular promised to provide services with "personalization, flexibility, and 'client'-centeredness."[10] Those who favored the increased use of nonprofits to provide services emphasized these organizations' "ethical and compassionate" qualities.[11] Others claimed nonprofits would be a source for service innovation: ". . . the nonprofit sector can become a field of experimentation, an area for trying out new ideas that may not necessarily have to stand the test of either the market or the ballot box."[12]

Such political claims contributed to support for the privatization of welfare services in the U.S., much as they did in Western Europe. In 1996, the U.S. Congress authorized the privatization of a wider range of welfare services than ever before through the Personal Responsibility and Work Opportunity Reconciliation Act (PRWORA). State and local governments could now offer contracts to for-profit and nonprofit private agencies to handle eligibility determination and welfare-to-work case management services for Temporary Assistance for Needy Families (TANF). The implementation of PRWORA also spurred welfare privatization in other ways. Block-grant funding for TANF constrained welfare spending, increasing the incentives for state and local governments to minimize welfare expenditures. At the same time, state and local governments were required by PRWORA to meet higher federal welfare-to-work participation goals within a short time period; at least 25 percent of household heads receiving benefits had to participate in welfare-to-work programs by 1997, and this rate was then expected to double by 2002. Many policymakers believed that relying on private welfare contractors rather than public welfare offices would not only help to lower their welfare costs but help them to quickly expand their capacity to provide new employment services. They also hoped private contractors would better serve diverse welfare recipients and shift the culture within welfare offices to one that aimed for parental employment and "self-sufficiency." Following neoliberal logic, proponents of welfare privatization also argued that market competition and performance-based contracts would help to ensure that welfare services would be more efficient and cost-effective.[13]

Welfare Privatization: A New Arena of Class Struggle

Proposals to privatize welfare services in the U.S. sparked considerable opposition from labor unions, welfare recipients, and community groups. Together, they challenged the arguments made in favor of privatization, pointing to examples that showed how welfare privatization lowered service quality.[14] In New York, advocates publicized how employees of private contractor Maximus gave incorrect or insufficient information to Medicaid applicants.[15] In San Diego, evaluators revealed that more than 80 percent of welfare clients at another private firm, Lockheed Martin, were not completely appraised within ten days; moreover, 67 percent of participants had a gap of thirty days or more between scheduled work activities.[16] In Chicago, researchers found evidence that staff at other private welfare contractors engaged in "creaming"—encouraging enrollment in welfare-to-work programs among those seen as employable and discouraging enrollment among the "hard to serve."[17] A report by the U.S. General Accounting Office found that five out of eight sites reviewed failed to meet one or more performance standards that had been established for welfare contractors.[18] Concerns were also raised about the capacity of state and local governments to hold private contractors accountable. Government audits revealed deficiencies in states' monitoring of TANF subcontractors in at least one-quarter of states in 2000.[19] In response to the claim that private contractors were cheaper and more efficient than public employees, critics pointed out that much of the cost savings was often gained by replacing higher-paid unionized workers with lower-paid non-unionized workers. They also pointed to examples in which privatization actually increased welfare expenditures or led to the misuse of public funds.[20] In addition, they cited instances in which private contractors failed to deliver the services they promised, such as Lockheed's failed attempt to develop an effective statewide computer system to collect child support payments in California. As one assemblywoman described, "even after six years of development and $82 million in state expenditures," Lockheed's system was "slow, overly complicated, and unable to perform even basic accounting functions."[21]

Such criticisms echo the concerns raised by scholars studying "public-private" partnerships in social service and welfare administration. They question the claim that private agencies really provide "better governance, accountability, and transparency" than the public sector.[22] Some scholars even suggest that nonprofits are often undemocratic and "dangerously unaccountable."[23] Rather than expanding people's rights, participation in planning services, and access to services, public-private partnerships may, instead, impede them. The emphasis on efficiency and cost-cutting in contracts and on their evaluation makes it particularly difficult for private agencies to provide a high quality of services.[24] Managerialist and quasi-market principles embedded in social service contracts undermine private agencies' capacity to provide flexible, individualized services or to involve clients in decision-making,[25] and concerns about efficiency often outweigh those of citizenship involvement or client needs in evaluations of public-private partnerships.[26] Moreover, there is also little hard evidence that public-private partnerships are actually more efficient than the public sector in providing services. Privatization can instead exacerbate service fragmentation, disrupting the flow of information across agencies and leading to poor outcomes.[27] Competition for state contracts can lead to "organized tribalism" among service professionals, hindering private agencies' capacities to cooperate or to focus on overall outcomes.[28] Perhaps most importantly, scholars raise concerns that private agencies, which are driven by competition and market principles, cannot adequately overcome inequalities and market failures compared to the public sector.[29]

Proponents of welfare privatization were powerful and well-resourced within the United States, however, and privatization became increasingly commonplace despite such criticisms. By 2001, more than $1.5 billion worth of federal funds for TANF services was contracted out by state and county governments—about 13 percent of all federal TANF funds.[30] Approximately 87 percent of these funds involved contracts with nonprofit organizations, 13 percent were with for-profit companies, and 8 percent were with faith-based organizations. In eight states, about half of their contracts involved for-profit providers. Most commonly, these contracts involved employment services, education or training, or supportive services designed to address barriers to work or increase job retention, such as substance abuse treatment or transportation assistance. While the contracts involved determination for TANF-related services in eighteen states, only four states had contracts that involved eligibility determinations for TANF cash assistance.[31]

The federal government did set some limits on the extent of welfare privatization. When the state of Texas attempted to privatize the administration of its entire welfare system in 1996, the Bill Clinton administration barred contracting out eligibility determination for entitlement programs, such as Medicaid and Food Stamps.[32] But such federal restrictions did not stop Texas and Florida from contracting out the prescreening of applicants for these public benefits.[33]

After 1996, both for-profit and nonprofit agencies aggressively pursued contracts for welfare services.[34] Among for-profit companies, "Maximus, Lockheed Martin IMS, Curtis & Associates, and America Works have clearly dominated the welfare employment field, with Maximus and Lockheed pursuing mostly large welfare contracts in states and localities with big caseloads and America Works and Curtis & Associates concentrating on somewhat smaller markets."[35] Other companies, such as Electronic Data Systems, were also hired to manage data on welfare recipients.[36] By 2002, Affiliated Computer Services (formerly known as Lockheed Martin Information Management Services [IMS]) had 26 TANF contracts worth an estimated $108 million, while Maximus Inc. had 15 contracts worth up to $56 million, and Curtis & Associates claimed 31 contracts in 13 states valued at $65 million.[37]

In this chapter, I explore the campaigns that emerged in Los Angeles and Milwaukee to prevent welfare privatization, improve welfare contractors' practices, or end contracts altogether. My research combines information from participant observation in meetings, protest events, and public hearings, plus in-depth interviews with activists and information gleaned from newspaper articles and evaluation reports. These case studies provide important lessons about the problems that welfare privatization can create. They illustrate instances in which private welfare contractors amassed profits, non-union staff members were paid less than unionized public-sector workers, and poor people lost access to welfare and services—altogether providing further evidence that privatization tends to increase social inequalities.

These campaigns also reveal how labor and community alliances can be mobilized to defend the public sector against privatization and to protect clients' rights in the context of privatization. Because its TANF program was completely administered by private contractors, a look at the case of Milwaukee is particularly revealing. The breadth of welfare privatization in Milwaukee encouraged broad-based and intense mobilization against private welfare contractors, but political conditions constrained the outcomes of anti-privatization campaigns. Because Wisconsin's politicians favored welfare privatization so strongly, activists were unable to persuade them to give their county's welfare administration back to a public agency. Nevertheless, by generating negative media and publicity about private contractors' bad practices, they managed to curb some of the worst abuses through greater governmental oversight of private agencies and direct pressure on the agencies themselves. In Los Angeles, opponents of privatization both inside and outside the county government succeeded in limiting the extent of welfare privatization. Compared to Milwaukee, county officials in Los Angeles were not wholly favorable to privatization, and they had more discretion over the administration of their welfare program, which provided greater political opportunities to resist privatization locally. Together, these cases show how collaboration between unions and community groups shaped the implementation of welfare reform policies and how this influence was constrained by political circumstances.

Challenging Welfare Contractors in Los Angeles

Even before the implementation of PRWORA, public-sector unions struggled against the privatization of social services. In 1988, Los Angeles County became the first county in the nation to turn over welfare-to-work case management services to a private company. Its Board of Supervisors approved a one-year, $7.8 million contract with Maximus to provide case management work for 80,000 to 100,000 welfare recipients. Initially, the George Deukmejian administration and high-ranking state welfare officials disapproved of the contract. They claimed that it was illegal because case management involved "discretionary" decision-making, which could only be done by public employees. Democrats in the California State Legislature's joint committee overseeing welfare also criticized the contract for its payment of exorbitant wages to Maximus's president, David Mastran (which came out to $238.19 per hour), as well as another corporate official, John Svahn (at $204.16 per hour).[38] County officials, determined to cut welfare costs through privatization, joined hands with Maximus and used high-powered lobbying and personal ties to key Republican leaders to reach a compromise with the Deukmejian administration. The new agreement, approved by the Ronald Reagan administration, required county workers to handle any appeals filed by welfare recipients and required Maximus to use detailed manuals that reduced case managers' discretionary decision-making.[39]

In response to Maximus's contract, SEIU (representing the county and city workers) and Legal Aid challenged the legality of contracting out welfare services, which they believed should be delivered by public civil servants who were better trained and more accountable to the public. They filed two lawsuits, both of which they lost.[40] SEIU Locals 535 and 660 also joined forces with other public-sector unions; black, Chicano, and Asian employees' associations; and the Southern Christian Leadership Conference to form the Coalition to Stop Contracting Out. In 1991, the coalition released a report showing that privatization took away from public employees' jobs, wages, and benefits; cost taxpayers money; and reduced the quality of welfare-to-work services. They also framed their opposition in terms of racial and gender justice, showing that women, blacks, and Latinos were hurt the most by privatization since they made up the majority of the county's public employees.[41] After considerable lobbying, and after a more liberal Board of Supervisors was elected, the coalition at last made headway. In 1993, supervisors voted not to renew Maximus's welfare contract, claiming that it had performed its services poorly.[42]

Yet this victory over welfare privatization proved to be temporary. The implementation of federal welfare reform unleashed a new round of welfare privatization. In 2000, the Board of Supervisors agreed to issue a request for proposals for welfare services contracts. Unlike Milwaukee, where state policymakers completely privatized the county's welfare administration, Los Angeles County supervisors had discretion and only favored a limited welfare contract. The proposed contract was only for administration of welfare-to-work case management services in the San Fernando Valley, where about 25 percent of the county's caseload lived. This contract threatened to displace fifty of SEIU's members. The union warned that privatization would lower the quality of welfare services. Because the proposed contract would reward companies for each welfare recipient they placed in a job, it would encourage them to push people off welfare too quickly. As a SEIU representative told the *Los Angeles Times*, "When you're talking about getting people off the welfare rolls, that's not a profit-driven business."[43] The union quickly mobilized a broad-based coalition in opposition to the proposed contracts. Union organizers hoped that, if they exerted enough political pressure, they could persuade county supervisors to reject the privatization plans, especially since they knew that nearly half of the county's supervisors opposed them.[44] Summarizing their efforts, a SEIU 660 staff member reported: "We tried everything imaginable politically: [building a] community coalition, protests, letters, calls to the board, media attention, different legislators contacting the board with their concerns . . ."[45] Initially, the union gathered signatures on a statement of principles against welfare privatization among service providers, welfare advocates, poor people's organizations, faith-based organizations, progressive legal organizations, and labor groups. It also organized a letter-writing campaign.[46] SEIU's efforts to mobilize community support benefited from its development of ties to welfare rights groups by participating with them in the Welfare Reform Coalition, which was established to coordinate welfare rights activities and anti-workfare campaigns.

In an effort to bring media attention to the issue, opponents of privatization organized sit-in demonstrations in prospective contractors' offices. In the first protest, about eighty Association of Community Organizations for Reform Now (ACORN) members and supporters took over Lockheed Martin's downtown office. In part, the protest expressed ACORN's opposition to the privatization of welfare programs. As one ACORN organizer, Amy Schur, put it, "We think that welfare reform programs should be run by public agencies, so the money saved goes back into creating more resources for the people they are supposed to help, not in the pockets of private industry as profit."[47] Protesters also pressured the company to hire more welfare recipients.[48] Shortly before the board voted on the contracts, members of SEIU, ACORN, and other community activists held a joint protest inside Maximus's office in Pasadena. After occupying the office, protesters brought attention to Maximus's wrong-doings in other cities and states by enacting a court case against Maximus, in which union members and welfare recipients played the part of "witnesses" who testified about Maximus's crimes and misdeeds.[49]

On the day that county supervisors were scheduled to choose the winning bid, anti-poverty activists and union members rallied, filled the meeting hall, and testified against welfare privatization.[50] Supervisors postponed their decision after questioning the county auditor's claim that contracting out the program would cost $32 million more than keeping the program in-house. They hired an outside consulting firm, Orion Consulting, to reevaluate the bids. SEIU criticized this, pointing out that because Orion had its own welfare contract in Ohio, it would be biased in favor of welfare privatization. As expected, Orion found that the county's bid was not the most cost-effective, and the county sought new bids for the contracts. SEIU complained that the process was unfair because their bid had become public and could thus be easily beaten.[51]

Maximus received the highest marks on its bid, which beat the county's bid by $4 million.[52] Staff member Tanya Akel from SEIU Local 660 criticized the decision to the press, claiming, "This money, that is meant to make people self-sufficient, should not be going to stockholders."[53] County supervisor Gloria Molina also criticized the decision, claiming that the quality of the services would decrease because Maximus did not invest in its employees: "It's not the best arrangement for the recipients . . . you're not going to have the [same] caliber of workers working on these issues."[54] At their request, supervisors postponed their final decision to give the union a chance to meet with county welfare officials and to try to narrow the cost difference between their bid and Maximus's proposal.[55]

In the end, supervisors decided to split the disputed contract between two for-profit companies, Maximus and Lockheed Martin IMS. Supervisor Zev Yaroslavsky, who made the alternative motion, argued that, "We are better served by having them out there side by side. Neither can rip us off, shortchange us, or skimp around the edges without being exposed by the performance of the other contractor."[56] He also claimed that privatizing would save the county $4.2 million over two years and would allow the county to trim its workforce if the number of welfare cases dropped.[57] Three out of five county supervisors voted in favor of awarding the contracts to Maximus and Lockheed, and one supervisor abstained. The fifth supervisor, Gloria Molina, opposed the decision, claiming that privatization "is making a profit in the public sector on the backs of the employees . . ."[58] Together, the two-year contracts, which could be extended, were worth a total of $23 million. After the decision, SEIU "turned our efforts to the legal strategy."[59] Union officials hoped that a lawsuit filed by their sister union in San Diego would find a favorable court decision and that private contracts there and in Los Angeles would be overturned.[60]

The union was more successful at preventing the next round of welfare privatization in 2002, when supervisors considered contracting out a portion of the county's job readiness program to Maximus. The proposed two-year contract would award Maximus an $11.2 million contract to run the program in several areas and award the County Office of Education a contract for $7.4 million to serve the rest of the county. The union feared that Maximus would pay lower wages, eliminate up to seventy jobs, and absorb up to 75 percent of the county's welfare-to-work programs.[61] The 2002 privatization plan was also particularly controversial because it would transfer preexisting county jobs into private hands rather than simply prevent the hiring of additional public-sector workers, as the contract in 2000 mainly did.[62] SEIU responded by mobilizing their members and community groups against the proposal. The Los Angeles Coalition to End Hunger and Homelessness circulated a statement, signed by seven community organizations, protesting the proposed contract.[63] Welfare rights groups were responsive to their calls for action. A staff person from SEIU 660 explained:

> The major groups who have been working with people on welfare for years and years [were] concerned about Maximus and Lockheed providing the services to the poor and understand that accountability is threatened and the quality of services is threatened. . . . [They] all joined us in a coalition to let the board [of supervisors] know what we are against.[64]

Former Maximus and Lockheed employees also came forward with stories of poor working conditions, dishonest reporting practices, and staffing problems, all of which were publicized through the press and a research report.[65] Along with union members, welfare advocacy organizations also rallied outside the supervisors' chambers, packed the audience, and testified against the proposal at several key meetings.[66] Union and community supporters celebrated when the county decided, in a unanimous vote, to maintain public administration of its career-training services, and commended public employees for their exemplary services.[67] Maximus's proposal was estimated to save the county as much as $5.1 million, but the savings would be largely derived from reduced staffing and lower employee wages. The vote was considered to be a major victory for SEIU Local 660.[68]

While SEIU and its community allies mobilized considerable opposition to try to prevent the contract proposals in Los Angeles, they failed to do so after the contracts were awarded. SEIU monitored welfare contractors' performance and pursued its legal case against welfare privatization in San Diego. In contrast to the Milwaukee case, neither the union nor community groups launched a public campaign against the disputed contracts. One SEIU staff member attributed the decline in mobilization about the issue to the smaller scope of welfare privatization, which limited its harmful impacts:

> I don't know that there's a frustration level that high. Milwaukee's a bit different because [private agencies] got the whole program . . . whereas in L.A. County it is very limited to [TANF] case management . . . It's not as bad as Milwaukee.[69]

Welfare rights groups in Los Angeles were also busy pursuing other kinds of welfare rights campaigns at the state and federal level.[70] Most of their members were located in areas unaffected by privatization, which may have contributed to their disinterest in the issue.

Poor Quality of Services

Without union and community mobilization around the issue, the local media paid little attention to the quality of private contractors' welfare services in Los Angeles, but this non-coverage was not due to a lack of problems in the welfare services provided by private contractors. Various problems in the quality of welfare services were revealed in interviews with thirteen former employees of Maximus and Lockheed Martin IMS who worked as welfare caseworkers, supervisors, job developers, or employment counselors in Southern California between 1985 and 2001.[71]

These former employees claimed that they engaged in various kinds of questionable practices in order to keep their job placement rates high. Nearly half described fraudulent reporting practices that inflated their companies' job placement rates, such as the manipulation of hours of employment or reporting a temporary job lasting one or two days as a full-time job.[72] Other informants described case managers who would intimidate welfare-to-work participants or give them misleading information so that they could earn larger bonuses. As one interviewee described,

> I know of one case worker . . . she would say "well if you don't do this you know what's going to happen, you know I could push this button on this computer and you could be sanctioned." She would just throw out these threats to them, so people were . . . scared to death about getting the job.

Another way in which employees would make their quota was by funneling welfare-to-work participants into temporary or part-time employment so that they could claim each job as a separate placement. Employees had an incentive to do this because the more temporary or part-time jobs a participant had, the more job placements caseworkers and job developers could claim. Similarly, a former Maximus employee recalled that at one job fair organized by Maximus, the only employer present was a temporary agency.

Former Maximus employees claimed that staff engaged in these kinds of practices in order to receive larger bonuses in their paycheck, while former Lockheed employees claimed they did so to meet their weekly job placement quotas. Job placements "became like gold." While employees were "bonus-driven," managers were "placement-driven." They wanted the company to remain competitive for future welfare-to-work contracts and so pressured employees to do whatever was necessary to keep their job placements high.

Some of these former employees claimed that job applicants seeking work at Maximus or Lockheed were inadequately screened and often had no previous experience with social services, partly because of the pressure to hire many staff members quickly. Employees were inadequately trained—sometimes by staff members unfamiliar with local welfare policies. As one former Lockheed employee put it, "We were all running around like chickens with our heads cut off because nobody knew what to do." Welfare recipients suffered as a result. For example, a former Maximus employee recounted: "There were many times, because of lack of training, that participants did not even receive their supportive services." Lacking the transportation or child care assistance required to fulfill their welfare-to-work assignments, welfare recipients were sometimes sanctioned for non-compliance. Compounding such problems, supervisors sometimes lacked sufficient knowledge to assist employees, especially when contracts were new. Insufficient staffing also led to high caseloads (200 clients or more per staff person), leading some harried case managers to hide cases or fail to complete all of the paperwork on time.[73] When Lockheed first began its contract, the company lacked sufficient numbers of bilingual staff to adequately serve its Spanish-speaking clients, which led to a complaint with the California Department of Social Services.[74]

Case reviews conducted between 2000 and 2001 by the County's Contract Management and Monitoring Division suggest that problems similar to those described above persisted after the new wave of welfare privatization. Both Maximus and Lockheed Martin were faulted repeatedly for "multiple entries of employment record on the same job."[75] Reviews revealed repeated problems with the provision of incorrect or insufficient employment information.[76] Monitors also found a lack of verification that child care, transportation, or other supportive services were offered or provided on time.[77]

In sum, union and community mobilization managed to limit the extent of welfare privatization in Los Angeles. Additionally, the small scope of welfare contracts in the county reduced community concerns about them. Meanwhile, perceived opportunities to oppose welfare privatization through the court system channeled union opposition into legal channels. With little mobilization around the issue, problems with private welfare contractors' services, though existent, were not widely publicized.

Challenging Welfare Contractors in Milwaukee

In Wisconsin, pro-privatization forces—including the Hudson Institute, which designed the state's welfare reform program—were more influential than in California.[78] In 1997, Wisconsin's state officials contracted out to private agencies the administration of cash aid eligibility and welfare-to-work case management for Milwaukee County's TANF program (known as Wisconsin Works, or W-2) in twelve counties that either chose not to run W-2 or failed to meet the state's performance standards.[79] As of 2002, Wisconsin was one of only four states to privatize the administration of TANF eligibility determination (along with Arizona, Florida, and Texas). It was also one of only four states (along with Idaho, Mississippi, and New Jersey) to privatize more than 40 percent of its TANF funds in 2001.[80] In Milwaukee, the county's Private Industry Council was given oversight of these agencies.[81] State officials claimed that privatization was justified in Milwaukee because public employees were performing below the state's required standards. Union leaders, however, claim that the county's relatively high error rate was partly due to its higher-than-average caseloads and the implementation of a new computer system; they contend that the county was targeted for welfare privatization because it was home to the vast majority of the state's welfare recipients and was a Democratic stronghold in a conservative state.[82]

In the first round of welfare contracts, multimillion-dollar contracts for W-2 services were awarded to two for-profit agencies, Maximus and YW Works (an affiliate of YWCA), and three nonprofit private agencies, Opportunities Industrialization Center of Greater Milwaukee, United Migrant Opportunity Services, and Goodwill Industries' Employment Solutions.[83] According to Jason DeParle,

> Maximus wasn't just the new face in town but the ultimate symbol of privatization: a welfare agency that traded on the New York Stock Exchange! The state saw a paragon of market-based virtues—efficiency, discipline, accountability—and considered letting Maximus run the whole Milwaukee program before bowing to the political imperative to include local groups.[84]

Despite Maximus's appeal, the largest contract was actually given to Employment Solutions, run by Will Martin, a former aide to Wisconsin's then-governor, Tommy Thompson.[85]

Wisconsin's state and welfare agencies benefited from the arrangement. The Wisconsin Policy Institute boasted that privatization saved the state at least $10.3 million over the first two years of operation.[86] Most of these savings were due to the dramatic decline in welfare caseloads as W-2 agencies implemented Wisconsin's tough new welfare rules and labor market conditions improved. While welfare recipients lost access to income, private agencies enjoyed large profits—a combined total of $12.4 million in the first year alone.[87]

Meanwhile, advocacy groups grew increasingly alarmed by private welfare agencies' policies and practices and were quickly drawn into the battle against welfare privatization. At least twelve different groups, including welfare advocacy organizations, grassroots welfare rights groups, and faith-based groups, mobilized their members to lobby against or protest the administration of W-2 by private welfare contractors (see table 4.1). Popular mobilization around this issue was facilitated by the dense network of welfare rights groups in Milwaukee. Along with more traditional welfare advocacy organizations, this network included faith-based organizations concerned about the impact of W-2 and private welfare contractors' practices on their members' families. It also included at least three organizations that employed staff to organize

Table 4.1 Groups Lobbying or Protesting Against Welfare Contractors in Milwaukee

Anti-Poverty & Welfare Advocacy Organizations
Association of Community Organizations for Reform Now, Milwaukee branch
Coalition to Save our Children
Emergency Alliance on Poverty
Hunger Action Task Force
W-2 Monitoring Task Force
Welfare Warriors
Faith-Based Organizations
Hope Offered through Shared Ecumenical Action (HOSEA)'s Welfare Reform Task Force
Milwaukee Inner-City Congregations Allied for Hope (MICAH)
Interfaith Conference of Greater Milwaukee
Labor Organizations
American Federation of State, County, and Municipal Employees
Milwaukee Central Labor Council
9to5, Milwaukee branch

Source: Reese, Giedraitis, and Vega (2006), reprinted with permission of the publisher.

welfare recipients: ACORN, Welfare Warriors, and 9to5. These three groups organized press conferences, protests, and rallies, each involving twenty to forty people.[88]

In contrast to Los Angeles, anti-privatization activists in Milwaukee confronted highly unfavorable political conditions for resisting welfare privatization; local politicians had no discretion over the issue, while state officials and politicians strongly believed that the privatization of social services, especially in Milwaukee, would be more cost-effective and efficient because private agencies were more responsive to market pressures.[89] As one official at the American Federation of State, County, and Municipal Employees (AFSCME) described it, state policymakers' will to privatize W-2 in Milwaukee was "overwhelming."[90] Along with privatizing Milwaukee's W-2 services, state officials also privatized other county services, including child welfare services. Governor Thompson, the state welfare officials that he appointed, and Republican politicians (who controlled the state legislature in the late 1990s) were also strongly in favor of both the current W-2 policies and welfare privatization.[91] As one welfare advocate put it, "We knew, frankly, that as long as Jean Rogers was there [as head of the state welfare department], nothing was going to change."[92] Although Milwaukee County officials were sympathetic to advocates' concerns, they had no authority over the administration of TANF, limiting their capacity to respond.

Given the strength of opposition at the state level and local officials' lack of authority over this issue, opponents of privatization had to find other targets in order to gain influence. At first, they targeted federal officials to try to prevent welfare privatization. After the welfare contracts were awarded, activists went "straight to those [welfare] agencies with concerns" to try to put direct pressure on them. They viewed welfare contractors as vulnerable to popular pressure because of their desire to maintain a good public image.[93] They pressured contractors to improve their services or terminate their contracts through large public forums, joint press conferences, eligibility hearings, and protests.[94] Activists also obtained state and federal investigations of W-2 agencies, hoping that their findings and the publicity surrounding them would undermine support for the contracts among legislators. Labor and community campaigns against welfare contractors highlighted three kinds of concerns about welfare privatization: its negative impacts on public-sector workers, the poor quality of private agencies' welfare services, and private agencies' appropriation of and misuse of public funds. Gaining media coverage of the problems associated with welfare privatization helped to improve activists' leverage with state officials and private contractors to improve the quality of welfare services, even if state legislators were steadfast in their support of privatization.

Negative Impacts on Workers

The proposed privatization of welfare services threatened to displace members of AFSCME 594, the union that represented Milwaukee's social workers and eligibility caseworkers, which belonged to District Council 48. While District Council 48 claimed more than fourteen thousand members, it had no organizing director or staff when welfare was privatized. Union leadership, later replaced, was also weak. According to a high-level union official, "There was a lot of hand wringing as opposed to a concerted coordinated attack on the efforts to privatize. [There was] a lack of effective leadership within the union."[95] Nevertheless, union officials mobilized their members against privatization and managed to avert layoffs.

Originally, state officials considered contracting out Medicaid, Food Stamps, child welfare services, and TANF in Milwaukee County. Union leaders believed that privatization of all these welfare services would have gutted union membership and led to at least 300 layoffs. The union sent hundreds of postcards, letters, and phone calls to federal welfare officials and congressmen to oppose the state's waiver request to privatize Food Stamps and Medicaid and urged state legislators to halt the privatization of W-2. Occasionally, the union also participated in public demonstrations with other welfare advocates concerned about the governor's proposed welfare plan.[96] In 1996, for example, AFSCME participated in a 500-person rally against the W-2 plan. At the rally, the vice president of AFSCME 594 proclaimed publicly that, "it has been proven that privatization costs more."[97]

Although the union failed to halt the privatization of W-2, public-sector unions celebrated when federal welfare officials refused to authorize the contracting out of the administration of the state's Food Stamps and Medicaid programs.[98] AFSCME officials estimate that it lost about one hundred positions through the privatization of W-2. It did not lead to involuntary layoffs, however. In anticipation of privatization, many caseworkers had already left their jobs, "looking for . . . something more secure."[99] Nearly 300 caseworkers also continued to administer Food Stamps, Medicaid, child care, and transportation services. Other county workers were transferred into other positions through a union-negotiated settlement.

After the decision to contract out the county's W-2 services, the union tried to organize private contractors' social workers and child welfare workers, who worked in the same offices as public welfare employees. But their efforts to unionize these employees failed, partly because of union-busting activities, some of which were illegally paid for with public money.[100] For example, just before child welfare workers were about to vote on whether to have a union election, a private contractor held a mandatory meeting for employees on "a boat in Lake Michigan." As an AFSCME Local 645 official explained, they "wined and dined them and promised them all these things that they would do for them if they didn't sign union cards."[101] Moreover, agencies' turnover rates were high, making it difficult to organize: "Whenever we'd get enough members to sign cards for a vote, by the time we could set up the vote, those people had already left, the turnover is so great."[102]

From the beginning, the union allied itself with community groups in opposition to welfare privatization.[103] As the president of Local 594, who was an African American woman, explained,

> To me and anybody that represents AFSCME . . . it's about what's happening in my community. And if we can't ensure that our community base remains strong, we don't exist either. . . . I have to live in this community and so whatever affects my community is going to affect me, so I have to ensure that . . . the services are provided the way they should be.[104]

AFSCME lobbied for public employees' right to bid for welfare contracts and to maintain control over W-2 eligibility. Its leaders also raised public and legislative awareness of private contractors' shortcomings. At a public hearing on W-2, for example, the president of AFSCME 594 proclaimed that

> one of the reasons W-2 is not working in Milwaukee is because those private companies are not so much concerned with the unfortunate and poor, but with how much of the money intended for the poor can be used to increase their own profits.[105]

Union officials also participated in the W-2 Monitoring Task Force, which opposed the privatization of welfare services.[106]

To further their cause, labor organizations also highlighted W-2 agencies' unfair employment practices by generating negative publicity about it and getting plenty of media coverage. AFSCME encouraged former employees of Maximus to file complaints of gender or racial discrimination to the Equal Opportunity Employment Commission (EEOC). At least eighteen complaints were filed and got coverage in the mainstream press and other newspapers.[107] Meanwhile, 9to5, an organization representing working women, and Welfare Warriors, an organization of welfare mothers led by Pat Gowens, a former welfare recipient, also issued reports and statements to the press about Maximus's practice of hiring W-2 participants through its own temporary agency. Through press conferences, they also brought attention to Tracy Jones's wage discrimination complaint against Maximus. Jones, an employee through Maximus's temporary help firm, was paid less than men for similar work while on a job with American TV and Appliance. The EEOC determined that discrimination had taken place and settled the dispute out of court.[108] Journalist Jason DeParle's description of the welfare staff hired by Maximus—which he claimed included former criminals; workers suffering from gambling and drug addictions; and the corporate vice president's family members, mistress, and mistress's mother—also raised controversy about private welfare agencies' hiring practices.[109] Even before the publication of DeParle's book, negative media coverage of welfare contractors' bad labor and employment practices increased the pressure on welfare agencies to respond to advocates' other concerns and helped to build the case for greater governmental oversight of private welfare agencies.

Poor-Quality Services

Together with unions, community groups drew public attention to the poor quality of services provided by Milwaukee's welfare contractors and called on state officials to regulate them more carefully.[110] Advocates criticized welfare privatization in the press, claiming that welfare contractors failed to inform applicants and clients about services that were available to them, in effect turning people away instead of trying to assist them.[111]

While the county's rapid declines in caseloads were partly due to the strong economy as well as the increased hassle of obtaining welfare under the strict new regulations, W-2 agencies had financial incentives for diverting recipients and minimizing client services. Agencies tried to maintain their contracts by catering to politicians' desires to reduce "welfare dependency" and obtaining federal "caseload reduction credits."[112] Moreover, the agencies were allowed to keep up to 15 percent of the value of their welfare contract as profit or extra program revenue, and the less they spent on clients, the more money they could keep.[113] Agency employees even received bonuses for caseload reductions or meeting other performance standards.[114] A 9to5 staff person pointed out: "Agencies were rewarded . . . by moving people off of W-2. . . . The lower the number of people [that received] benefits, the more the agency could gain in terms of bonuses and incentives."[115]

To make matters worse, state auditors determined that the Private Industry Council was not providing sufficient oversight of Milwaukee's welfare contractors to ensure that they were using funds properly or providing adequate services to welfare applicants and recipients.[116] W-2 agencies denied cash assistance to many recipients on the grounds that they were "job-ready," even when they had no source of employment. As Collins and Mayer explain,

> At the top of [the W-2 job] ladder were unsubsidized positions. If the agencies implementing W-2 deemed individuals to be "job-ready," even if they had been looking for work and been unable to find it, they could place them in this tier and require them to continue searching for a job. From 1997 until 2007, individuals in this tier (sometimes called 'case management only') received no cash assistance but might receive child care subsidies, foods stamps, medical assistance, or other kinds of state aid.[117]

The state's "light touch" policy, intended to reduce welfare dependency, discouraged welfare staff from informing applicants and clients of their rights to supportive services, such as child care and Food Stamps, unless they directly asked for them.[118] High caseload numbers also made it difficult for welfare staff to communicate with each client adequately.[119] Community groups publicized these problems and other diversionary tactics through various reports, statements to the press, and public forums. They urged the state to reward agencies for increasing former recipients' self-sufficiency, rather than reducing caseloads, and to require agencies to better publicize their services.[120]

The Hunger Action Task Force obtained a federal investigation of private agencies' diversionary practices, which they believed violated poor people's right to obtain food stamps. The number of people seeking food stamps dropped by 32 percent over a three-year period, while the demand for emergency food pantry services increased by 15 percent. Although PRWORA ended poor families' federal entitlements to cash assistance through TANF, their federal entitlements to food stamps, administered by the U.S. Department of Agriculture (USDA), remained intact. Compared to other federal welfare officials, USDA officials were less invested in the goal of reducing welfare dependency, and they maintained a strong commitment to ensuring that all those eligible for assistance were served. In 1999, USDA officials determined that welfare agencies had created various illegal obstacles that kept poor people from applying for Food Stamps.[121] In 2000, under pressure from the USDA and negative media coverage, state welfare officials shifted away from the "light touch" policy, and welfare agencies agreed to better publicize the right to food stamps through signs in their offices.[122] After state audits revealed that private W-2 agencies failed to inform applicants and clients of services and to adequately assess their needs, the state awarded county welfare workers a $5 million contract in 2001 to provide initial assessments of clients' needs for services and to inform them of services for which they were eligible.[123] However, this shift away from the "light touch" policy was unevenly enforced, and contradictory language remained in place for years in W-2 policy manuals. In response to advocates' concerns, state welfare officials issued additional state directives to clarify that caseworkers were expected to be proactive about informing clients about Food Stamps and other services for which they were eligible.[124]

Meanwhile, as fiscal conditions worsened, welfare officials encouraged agencies to deny welfare to participants considered to be "job-ready." Collins and Mayer explain:

> In July 2004, the Department of Workforce Development (DWD) circulated an administrative memo advising the remaining agencies on how to reduce payment caseloads. These directives instructed staff to emphasize upfront workforce attachment, that is, to require those who applied for assistance to search for jobs in the local economy for some period of time prior to becoming eligible for benefits.[125]

State officials also "distributed new guidelines, instructing agencies to reduce their caseloads by closing the cases of women deemed most likely to be able to find work, even if they had not done so at the time, and had not exhausted their time limits."[126] In 2007, Legal Action of Wisconsin successfully challenged these practices, winning a lawsuit that allowed eligible families to receive W-2 cash benefits even when they were deemed "job-ready."[127] However, enforcement of this ruling was problematic, especially when budget constraints put pressure on agencies to reduce their welfare rolls; people continued to complain that they were instructed to keep searching for work for several weeks before applying for W-2 on the grounds that they were "job-ready."[128]

Welfare and immigrant rights advocates also raised concerns about W-2 agencies' treatment of immigrants and racial minorities. They complained to the regional civil rights office about agencies' lack of interpreters and failure to translate forms to be more accessible to non-English-speaking clientele. After federal investigators determined that these problems violated immigrants' civil rights, agencies increased their use of interpreters and translated forms into multiple languages.[129] In 2002, the National Association for the Advancement of Colored People (NAACP) and the American Civil Liberties Union (ACLU) requested a federal investigation of racial inequalities in the use of welfare sanctions for non-compliance with program regulations.[130] To reduce legislative support for welfare privatization, activists generated even more media publicity about these problems and more through press conferences and interviews with journalists.[131] State audit reports and federal civil rights investigations provided legitimacy to activists' concerns, revealing disturbing inequities across agencies in the services provided to W-2 participants in Milwaukee and evidence of discrimination on the basis of disability and racial disparities in the use of welfare sanctions (although those disparities were even greater outside of Milwaukee).[132]

Another strategy that community groups pursued was to put direct pressure on welfare contractors to improve their practices. For example, faith-based activists tried to improve Maximus's outreach by holding a large public forum, which was attended by several hundred people as well as Maximus executives. There, Maximus executives promised to improve their outreach and provide information about their services to a long list of food pantries. It proved difficult to hold Milwaukee executives accountable for their promises, however; it later turned out that only two food pantries received any information from the agency.[133] Legal Aid lawyers also pressed agencies to reconsider eligibility and sanction decisions that they considered to be illegal. This advocacy, on top of greater oversight by the DWD's regional office, led to some local improvements in agencies' implementation of W-2 policies.[134]

Other groups used more disruptive tactics to pressure welfare agencies to shut down or improve their services. For example, in 1998, ACORN organized about fifty people, including W-2 recipients, in a protest at Goodwill's Employment Solutions. The group demanded that the agency provide more emergency assistance, child care, and job training to W-2 clients; several participants were pepper-sprayed by police.[135] Welfare Warriors, a welfare mothers' organization based in Milwaukee, protested W-2 agencies' implementation of time limits and high sanction rates, organizing actions in front of four different agencies.[136] 9to5, which organized W-2 clients, held a forty-person rally outside of Maximus's office. The group tried to deliver an "award" to Maximus for providing the worst welfare services but were stopped by security guards armed with pepper spray, who "yell[ed] and scream[ed]."[137] These sorts of actions did not yield immediate results. However, they may have contributed to Employment Solutions's decision to end its welfare contract after it came under fire for misusing public funds.[138]

Misuse of Public Funds

Welfare and labor advocates raised controversy over private agencies' use of public funds. Initially, they focused on demanding greater public accountability over the agencies' use of state-mandated community reinvestment funds. Advocates pressed W-2 agencies to hold public forums where community members could advise them about how to best spend this money.[139] As Jack Murtaugh, executive director of the Interfaith Conference, explained to the press, they urged greater public input into the use of these funds because "these funds are entirely public dollars and were earmarked for services to low-income families."[140] When their demands were not met, the Coalition to Save Our Children organized a "public speak-out" before W-2 agency heads and elected officials to voice public opinions about how the agencies should spend their $14 million worth of community reinvestment money. The event drew more than ninety people. Various welfare advocates and faith-based organizations also lobbied for the passage of a state bill to require W-2 agencies to seek community input on the use of community reinvestment funds.[141] In 2002, the agencies drew fire from community and labor advocates for failing to use the funds at all.[142]

In 2000, accusations by former and current employees and advocates' lobbying led the state to audit Maximus for questionable expenses.[143] Wisconsin's DWD and a newly created joint legislative audit committee each conducted audits of Milwaukee's W-2 agencies.[144] While the legislative committee identified $415,000 worth of questionable expenses, state officials found $1 million worth, including $50,000 worth of work for welfare contracts or contract proposals in other states and cities, $23,000 for motivational speeches and songs by actress and singer Melba Moore, $6,700 for a holiday party, and more than $22,000 for restaurant meals. The state responded to the findings by temporarily withholding $7.6 million from Maximus and negotiating a $1 million settlement with the company.[145] Audits by state officials also found that Employment Solutions had misspent $370,000, some of which was used to bid for other welfare contracts out of the state, which it agreed to repay. State officials also questioned $67,000 spent by Opportunities Industrialization Center, $5,000 spent by United Migrant Opportunity Services, and $4,168 spent by YW Works.[146]

DeParle suggests that welfare contractors' misuse of public funds ran even deeper than the state's official estimates. As he points out, "The true extent of the waste will never be known because the records were in such disarray. In nearly three-quarters of the transactions later examined by legislative auditors, Maximus either couldn't show what it had purchased or explain its relevance to W-2."[147] Whereas state auditors estimated that Maximus spent about $1.1 million on its marketing campaign, former staff members DeParle interviewed claimed that the figure was closer to $2.3 million; this included hundreds of thousands of dollars spent on promotional items such as backpacks, fanny packs, visors, and even golf balls and creating commercial jingles for radio advertisements. In response, the company aggressively sought the favor of politicians and tried to soften its image among community groups; it donated generously to local organizations, hiring a public relations chief and half a dozen "community outreach specialists" to promote the company's work in Milwaukee as a model for other cities and states.[148] Moreover, DeParle claims, "Among the expenses the state subsequently deemed proper was a share of the costs of hiring two of Tommy Thompson's cronies, for advice on how to target political donations and win new contracts."[149]

Even if they underestimated private contractors' misuse of public welfare funds, the state audit reports were significant because they helped to add legitimacy to activists' concerns about welfare privatization. After state auditors announced their findings, anti-privatization activists stepped up their activity, organizing public meetings, letter-writing campaigns, press conferences, and protests at welfare contractors' offices. Union and community activists criticized the state for being too lenient with the agencies and simply fining them without much more admonishment. While some called for greater state regulation of W-2 agencies, others demanded the end of welfare privatization or the termination of particular agencies' welfare contracts. Faith-based organizations were highly active in this effort.[150] Religious activists jointly held a press conference, demanding the governor to require greater public accountability from its private W-2 agencies, which have "enriched themselves instead of spending the money to assist W-2 clients [to] gain full employment."[151] Several months later, faith-based activists hosted a public meeting that drew two hundred people, where six legislators supported their call for the termination of Maximus's contract. Through meetings, letters, and postcards, faith-based organizations continued to lobby state officials to terminate Maximus's contract. They also called for the end of welfare contractors' "right to first selection," which gave existing contractors the right to bid first on the next round of welfare contracts.[152] Meanwhile, Welfare Warriors carried out a letter-writing campaign, urging Milwaukee District Attorney E. Michael McCann to prosecute Maximus and Employment Solutions for welfare fraud.[153] Welfare Warriors further brought attention to agencies' misuse of public money with a "photo bus tour" of "Wisconsin's bloated welfare empire," a press conference, and a protest urging the end of Goodwill's Employment Solutions's contract.[154]

Despite such activities, legislators were steadfast in their support of welfare privatization. Rather than terminating the contracts held by Maximus and Employment Solutions, they upheld them and negotiated financial settlements instead. Shortly afterward, the Wisconsin Audit Bureau determined that Employment Solutions was guilty of misspending even more money (a total of $560,000). The agency then agreed to give up its W-2 contract, citing "community dissatisfaction" as one of the reasons.[155] Welfare Warriors, and residents from Casa Maria, a local Catholic Workers' house, celebrated the "end of Goodwill's reign in Milwaukee" by holding an "eviction party" outside of Maximus's headquarters, where it warned them that they could be the next W-2 agency to lose their contract.[156] Rather than returning administration to the public sector, however, state officials simply reassigned Employment Solutions's welfare cases to other private agencies (as they did again when YW Works lost its contract in 2003 and when Opportunities Industrialization Center lost its contract in 2005); they also created a regional W-2 office to provide better oversight over the administration of W-2. Advocates' efforts to publicize the problems with private welfare contractors' misuse of welfare funds also had unintended consequences: "Emboldened by the reports of agency misspending, and anxious to close the budget deficit, the legislature cut welfare program funding; 2003 service and benefit allocations were reduced."[157]

However, the negative publicity of agencies' misuse of public funds did help to make welfare contractors more accessible to advocates. As one advocate for Hmong immigrants explained,

> Right now, [Maximus officials] tend to take community agencies' influence very seriously and if they hear something, they respond quickly. Before they were like a big giant . . . It's getting better . . . because they were under threats and are trying to become more popular in the community.[158]

With greater access to agencies, advocates gained modest—but nonetheless significant—improvements in the implementation of welfare reform policies, such as improving agencies' outreach about services and improving immigrants' access to translators.

But even greater public oversight and community pressure failed to prevent additional scandals from occurring or to derail policymakers' penchant for privatization. In 2005, another W-2 agency, Opportunities Industrialization Center, shut down its operations in response to criticisms by state auditors and a criminal investigation. State officials determined that the agency misused at least $2.4 million, including $500,000 for an illegal kickback scheme involving a state senator. To activists' dismay, state officials simply reassigned the agency's welfare cases to other private contractors, kept the same local W-2 oversight staff in place, and promised to include tougher regulations in the next wave of welfare contracts.[159]

State policymakers had a similar response to charges that private agencies were turning away prospective W-2 clients and other criticisms of the uneven quality of their welfare services; they simply reassigned the intake and assessment tasks to another private agency in 2009 and allowed W-2 participants in Milwaukee to choose their welfare agencies from available vendors. The new system allowed private contractors to earn up to $1 million in "incentive bonuses" if they scored high in placing participants in jobs and keeping them employed.[160] Thus, state officials responded to the problems associated with welfare privatization by reforming the terms of welfare contracts rather than returning welfare administration to the state or the county.

In short, state politicians completely privatized the administration of TANF in Milwaukee, which posed threats to both welfare clients and to service providers. This helped to mobilize both groups against welfare contractors and to broaden public concern about the implementation of welfare reform policies. By gaining media and federal officials' attention, community and labor activists managed to gain better public oversight over welfare contractors and pressured them to make welfare more accessible to welfare clients. However, these campaigns also show that broad-based alliances are insufficient to make major policy gains when political conditions are not ripe and neoliberalism is firmly entrenched; despite the scandals surrounding welfare contractors' misuse of public funds and other practices, state legislators remained steadfast in their support of welfare privatization, and local officials lacked authority over the matter.

Conclusion

Campaigns against welfare privatization in Milwaukee and Los Angeles illustrate the important role that public-sector workers can play in welfare rights struggles. In both cities, mobilization to prevent welfare privatization was facilitated by public-sector unions' willingness to invest resources to help organize against it, which is not surprising, given how welfare privatization threatened to displace public-sector workers and erode their bargaining power. Because welfare privatization also posed threats to welfare clients and applicants, it was not difficult for unionized public-sector workers to mobilize community groups to join in their struggle. The prior formation of welfare rights organizations and pre-existing ties between those organizations and unions facilitated the development of community-labor alliances around this issue.

Public-sector unions and their community allies in Los Angeles mobilized under more favorable political conditions than their counterparts in Milwaukee. In Los Angeles, the decision to contract out welfare services was left up to county supervisors, giving activists opportunities to exert pressure on local decision-makers, who were already divided in their support for privatization and who only favored limited welfare privatization. Joint protests and lobbying by SEIU and welfare rights groups, mainly initiated by SEIU and ACORN, were partly successful; while supervisors contracted out about 25 percent of the county's welfare-to-work case management services, they rejected a proposal to privatize part of the county's job-readiness program.

By contrast, in Milwaukee, the state government favored the complete privatization of welfare services in the county, and local officials had no say over the matter. This forced opponents to put pressure on federal and state policymakers to prevent welfare privatization. While federal officials rejected the state's waiver to contract out the administration of Food Stamps and Medicaid, the privatization of the administration of the W-2 program was authorized by PRWORA. State politicians were strongly in favor of privatization, imposing privatization of the county's entire TANF program and dismissing activists' concerns. Given these differences in political conditions, it is not surprising that campaigns to prevent welfare privatization were more successful in Los Angeles, where only one-quarter of welfare-to-work case management services were privatized, than in Milwaukee, where TANF administration was fully privatized.

These case studies also provide evidence that welfare privatization erodes public accountability and exacerbates social and economic inequalities. After welfare privatization was implemented, welfare contractors engaged in highly questionable and illegal practices in both cities. In Milwaukee, these included civil rights violations of welfare clients and employees, misuse of public funds, failure to spend community reinvestment money, funneling welfare recipients into temporary jobs, diverting welfare applicants from obtaining cash assistance, and obstructing low-income families' use of supportive services. In Los Angeles, former employees of welfare contractors reported similar problems, such as funneling welfare recipients into temporary jobs and failing to adequately process their requests for social services.

In Milwaukee, labor and community activists continued to mobilize against welfare privatization after welfare contracts were issued. They fanned the flames of controversy, drawing media and political attention to scandals involving private welfare contractors. They used these scandals to mobilize popular opposition to, and to reduce the legitimacy of, welfare privatization. Activists also used disruptive protests, large public forums, and lobbying to pressure welfare contractors to improve their services and end their contracts. Remarkably, despite the scandals that unfolded, Wisconsin's public officials remained steadfast in their support for welfare privatization. Nevertheless, negative publicity and activists' pressure on welfare contractors and public officials led to increased government regulation of welfare contractors and the termination of several welfare contracts. The negative media coverage that activists helped generate increased their own leverage with policymakers as well as welfare contractors. Under fire from journalists, as well as federal officials and state auditors, welfare contractors curbed some of their worst abuses and made welfare somewhat more accessible to the poor. These campaigns targeting private welfare contractors in Milwaukee demonstrate the importance of gaining broad community support, as well as the importance of targeting multiple kinds of power-holders for making gains under unfavorable political conditions. By contrast, in Los Angeles, there was virtually no public opposition to welfare privatization after the welfare contracts were issued. The smaller scale of welfare privatization in Los Angeles reduced popular interest in the issue, as did union leaders' belief that welfare contracts could be overturned through lawsuits. Together, these campaigns thus show how broad-based mobilization shaped the implementation of welfare reform in Wisconsin and California but also how political conditions in each state constrained activists' mobilization and influence.

Chapter 5

Confronting the Workfare State: Community and Labor Campaigns for Workfare Workers' Rights[1]

We're working for slave labor. Do you think that $212 is enough money to survive?

–Deborah Harris, member of the Association of Community Organizations for Reform Now (ACORN) Workfare Workers' Organizing Committee, Los Angeles

The time limits start this month . . . so you know we're in a desperate mood [to] have jobs created in this system for people to work.

–Abdullah Muhammed, Chair of ACORN's Workfare Workers' Organizing Committee, Los Angeles

I came to the United States from Puerto Rico, where I was a registered nurse. I wanted to be a nurse here, but I needed to learn English. I asked to take English classes full-time, but I was denied. Instead, they told me that in order to get some assistance, I had to take a community service job doing unskilled labor at a thrift store.

–Marisol Rivera, welfare recipient, Milwaukee

We call again for the union movement in the state of Wisconsin to take up a serious organizing campaign among W-2 workers. It's six months into the program. What's the delay?

–A Job Is a Right Campaign, Milwaukee[2]

THE EXPANSION of welfare-to-work programs alarmed both union and welfare rights activists. They feared that welfare-to-work participants would become extremely exploited workers and that governments and other employers would use them to displace and erode the bargaining strength of higher-paid unionized workers. To address the problems associated with the spread of "workfare," unions and community groups in at least five areas—Los Angeles, New York, Milwaukee, San Francisco, and several counties in New Jersey—organized welfare-to-work participants as workers rather than as welfare recipients. While the expansion of workfare programs did create a new population of workers for unions to organize, it was a declining population and one with very low income levels. Unions' interests in organizing this population was thus not driven so much by their interest in capturing more dues-paying members; instead, they sought to protect public-sector workers' bargaining power and to achieve justice for a highly oppressed group.

Although these organized groups of "workfare workers" never gained collective bargaining rights, they acted like and sometimes called themselves "unions." Like unions, they built solidarity among workers and fought to protect and improve their working conditions. As part of this goal, they sought to ensure that welfare-to-work participants were treated like regular workers and protected by existing labor laws, such as minimum-wage laws and federal health and safety standards. They also organized workfare participants around demands for job creation as well as for education and job training.[3]

Since challenging the expectation that welfare recipients should work seemed politically impossible, many activists instead sought to exploit the opportunities that the expansion of welfare-to-work programs presented for improving poor people's labor and employment rights.[4] As two of ACORN's lead organizers explained:

> The basic paradigm for welfare recipients had shifted under the Temporary Assistance for Needy Families Act (TANF) by redefining "work" not "need" as the precondition for assistance. Welfare recipients would now be workers under the Act—albeit forced work in oppressive conditions. But, philosophically and as a matter of public policy and the political process, workers had substantially different rights and entitlements than prevailed for welfare recipients. . . . ACORN sought to create organizations of these "new" workers in order to call the question through direct organization and action, and fold the whole house of cards constructed around the myth of available work, non-existent job training, and employment opportunities.[5]

By framing their struggle as a "workers' struggle," anti-workfare activists strategically linked their demands for better employment and training opportunities to the purported goal of welfare reform: moving welfare recipients from welfare to work. At the same time, they countered the racist stereotype of welfare recipients as lazy people who avoided work—a stereotype often used to justify welfare cutbacks. In these ways, activists made it difficult for opponents and the media to dismiss them as welfare recipients wanting another handout. ACORN's "workfare workers' " campaigns drew on the organization's previous experiences in organizing poor people around demands for job training and employment.[6] By framing welfare recipients' demands in terms of labor rights, ACORN and other community groups sought to build bridges between the welfare rights movement and organized labor, both of which were under attack and threatened by the expansion of welfare-to-work programs.

Building such alliances was no easy task, given organized labor's long history of failing to support—or even opposing—the demands of welfare rights organizations.[7] Indeed, only a handful of unions in the nation participated in these workfare workers' campaigns, and in most of these cases, their participation was a response to community organizations' initiatives. ACORN chapters formed close working relationships with Communications Workers of America (CWA) in Milwaukee and New Jersey.[8] Public-sector unions American Federation of State, County, and Municipal Employees (AFSCME) and Service Employees International Union (SEIU) also joined workfare workers' campaigns involving other community groups, namely Workfairness in New York City and Action for Grassroots Empowerment and Neighborhood Development Alternatives (AGENDA) in Los Angeles. Public-sector unions' interest in these campaigns primarily stemmed from their short-term concern with protecting their members from displacement and, against potential competition from ACORN, defending their rights to bargain collectively for municipal workers. The involved unions, which were both private- and public-sector, also saw these campaigns as part of their long-term commitment to obtain social justice for low-wage workers and to revitalize the labor movement by building alliances with community groups and organizing new workers.

Why did only a handful of unions invest in organizing workfare workers? While there are certainly exceptions, pragmatism pervades much of the American labor movement; many unions have a weak commitment to mobilizing unorganized workers and fighting for social justice on behalf of poor workers and people of color who are themselves not union members.[9] Arguably, the expansion of welfare-to-work programs and the degradation of workfare workers threatened all workers by normalizing forced labor, weakening labor laws, and putting downward pressure on wages—yet, these impacts were mostly indirect.[10] Moreover, racist stereotypes of welfare mothers and other public assistance recipients portrayed them as lazy, irresponsible "dependents" who drained the resources of so-called hard-working, "self-sufficient," and tax-paying citizens; such images, on top of broad public support for putting welfare recipients to work, discouraged union leaders and members (most of whom were white) from developing concerns about the plight of welfare-to-work participants (who were mostly people of color).[11] Finally, many unions were confronting a crisis in declining memberships, but it was not readily obvious that workfare workers' campaigns would result in payoffs like union growth and the collection of more dues-paying members. This was especially true since workfare workers' legal status and their rights as workers were still uncertain. The Department of Labor issued regulations in 1997 that declared that minimum-wage laws should apply to TANF welfare-to-work participants, and in 1999, federal welfare regulations clarified that these and other federal labor laws applied to TANF welfare-to-work participants; yet these regulations were not self-executing. Violations of federal labor laws, especially minimum-wage regulations, remained common in many workplaces.[12] Organizing workfare workers was also difficult. While many welfare-to-work participants were eager for the chance to improve the policies affecting them, most had little time to organize, as working parents. Fulfilling new work requirements—along with the other requirements necessary to gain or maintain access to welfare, subsidized child care, and other supportive services—was time-consuming, especially for welfare recipients who relied on public transportation. Organizing was especially difficult in places where workfare workers were widely scattered across many different worksites or were highly mobile either because of high rates of welfare sanctions or obtaining regular employment. All of these factors discouraged unions from investing in workfare workers' campaigns.

In this chapter, I explore the factors shaping the rise and outcomes of workfare workers' campaigns in Los Angeles and Milwaukee. In Los Angeles, union and community groups organized workfare workers receiving General Relief and TANF. These campaigns were sustained for about three years and led to various improvements in the implementation of welfare-to-work programs. In Milwaukee, the General Relief program had been abolished in 1995, and efforts to organize workfare workers focused only on TANF recipients. There, unions failed to invest in workfare workers' campaigns or invested very little in them; within eight months these campaigns were aborted without achieving any significant policy gains in Milwaukee.

I argue that these divergent outcomes between Los Angeles and Milwaukee reflected differences in unions' internal politics as well as differences in the local political economy of workfare and welfare. The local political economy of workfare in Los Angeles created more incentives and opportunities to organize workfare workers than in Milwaukee because it worked with a large concentration of workfare workers in the unionized public sector, whereas workfare workers were widely dispersed across non-unionized private-sector settings in Milwaukee. Milwaukee's public-sector unions were also confronted with a greater threat of privatization than were public-sector unions in Los Angeles, leaving them less resources and energy to organize workfare workers. Political conditions in Los Angeles were also more favorable than in Milwaukee, making it easier to win concessions.

One might suspect that Milwaukee's unions were not interested in organizing workfare workers because of racism and because such a large share of them were African American (compared to the more racially diverse welfare population in Los Angeles, as shown in table 3.2). However, this explanation does not seem very plausible for several reasons. First, Milwaukee's public-sector unions were active in other welfare rights campaigns and participated in local welfare task forces alongside community organizations. One of the main public-sector unions was also led by an African American woman who expressed great concern about the impacts of welfare reform on the community. Second, at the time that workfare workers' campaigns emerged, local unions affiliated with the Central Labor Council participated in the Milwaukee Jobs Initiative and Wisconsin Regional Training Partnership, programs that sought to link underemployed, mostly black inner-city workers to good jobs through job training and transportation assistance.[13] Before examining and comparing the workfare workers' campaigns in Los Angeles versus Milwaukee, I first discuss the problems associated with the welfare-to-work programs in these two cities.

Workfare Workers' Grievances

In the late 1990s, employment outcomes for former welfare mothers in Milwaukee and Los Angeles mirrored those in the nation, although they were somewhat better in Milwaukee, where the official unemployment rate was lower (see table 1.2). Of course, these official unemployment rates, which exclude information on discouraged workers, who have given up searching for work, and many undocumented workers, who avoid interactions with the government, including census takers, underestimate the true extent of joblessness. Yet, given the relatively large undocumented population in Los Angeles, many of whom are actively searching for work, the true difference in these two cities' unemployment rates may have been even greater.[14] While higher shares of Milwaukee's TANF participants found jobs compared to Los Angeles's TANF participants, employment rates declined in both counties over time as labor market conditions worsened after 1998 and remaining welfare-to-work participants encountered greater barriers to employment.[15] The placement rate for Los Angeles's "Job Skills" program for General Relief recipients was the most dismal, with only about 11 percent of participants—merely 450 out of 4,000—obtaining jobs in 1998.[16] In both counties, most former welfare mothers that managed to find work earned below-poverty wages in service and retail jobs, although their poverty rate was higher in Los Angeles. Temporary agencies were leading employers of former welfare mothers in both counties, contributing to high rates of return to welfare use.[17] Within Los Angeles, welfare-to-work participants with limited English proficiency, especially recent Asian immigrants, fared the worst in terms of their earnings and unemployment rates.[18] By 2001, almost one in five recent Asian immigrants that left welfare for work in 1998 obtained jobs in the garment industry, notorious for its sweatshop conditions.[19]

Although approximately 44 percent of adult TANF recipients lack a high school diploma or General Equivalency Diploma (GED), new welfare regulations, time limits, and the "work first" philosophy created many obstacles for welfare mothers who wanted to improve their long-term employment prospects by getting more education and training.[20] Wisconsin was one of only five states that placed more than 50 percent of its TANF recipients in work activities; more than 75 percent were given workfare assignments.[21] In 1998, a survey of 670 TANF participants in Milwaukee found that most were doing nothing but their job assignments and had received no additional training or education.[22] On-the-job training was often quite minimal. As one participant explained, "At regular jobs, I have done factory work, packing, and cashiering. Through welfare, I have done the same type of work. Even though they call it training, I am already experienced in this work."[23] This experience was common among W-2 participants, many of whom had long work histories prior to receiving welfare; some participants even experienced a downgrade in their work assignments compared to prior jobs they had held.[24] Describing other common job assignments given to welfare recipients, an advocate said, "One of the things they used to have them do was count hangers in order to get a grant . . . They're not giving them any skills."[25] According to Collins and Mayer's research, W-2 participants in Wisconsin were sometimes employed by public agencies but more commonly were employed by private employers. They performed a variety of jobs: They "plant[ed] flowers and water[ed] shrubs on the islands of highways, and cut brush along the shoulders of roads. They clean[ed] public housing and the offices of private agencies administering welfare programs. They sort[ed] clothing for Goodwill and work[ed] alongside the disabled in sheltered workshops."[26]

In 1999, only 16 percent of Milwaukee's TANF participants were enrolled in Jobs Skills training programs.[27] Those training opportunities dried up even further when, "by 2003, budget cuts had forced an end to most training programs."[28] Survey research found that even though more than 90 percent of Hmong welfare mothers in Milwaukee in the late 1990s read little or no English, only 10 percent received any skills training or English-language instruction.[29] Thousands of Milwaukee's welfare mothers were pressured to quit higher education and extended training programs in order to get a job.[30] In 1994, there were about 7,000 welfare recipients enrolled at the Milwaukee Area Technical College, but only 274 were enrolled in 1997.[31] When Wisconsin's TANF program (known as Wisconsin Works or W-2) was first implemented, even teen parents complained of pressure to find work and comply with program requirements rather than stay in high school, where they had difficulty obtaining child care.[32]

The most frequently assigned work activity in Los Angeles was Job Club, which provided participants with three weeks of motivational classes and "soft-skills" training such as how to "dress for success," apply for jobs, and prepare resumes.[33] The share of welfare-to-work participants who were enrolled in education and training programs fell from 25 percent in 1994 to 6 percent in 2001.[34] As in Milwaukee, many students in higher education and long-term job training were pressured by their caseworkers to quit their programs in order to work.[35] Opportunities for education and training were even more limited for Los Angeles's General Relief recipients. The only kind of job training they received focused on improving their job-seeking skills or on-the-job training for various menial jobs, such as janitorial work, routine clerical work, or factory work.[36] The lack of education and training opportunities within welfare-to-work programs is consistent with critics' claims that their main purpose was to fulfill employers' need for low-wage labor.

Testimonies of welfare recipients reveal that work requirements were rigidly enforced through sanctions; they also illuminate the reasons why many recipients who left welfare remained unemployed. As one former welfare mother in Milwaukee testified, "A child gets sick and you cannot go to your W-2 work. . . . You will be sanctioned because it wasn't 'good cause.' " Likewise, a welfare-to-work participant in Los Angeles was sanctioned after one of the two buses that she took to get to her required class was ten minutes late; she subsequently became homeless.[37] The sanction rate in Milwaukee varied considerably across the county's private welfare agencies, ranging in 2001 from 18 percent in some places to 48 percent in others; African American and Latino recipients were sanctioned at nearly twice the rate as white recipients.[38] Los Angeles County also enforced its welfare-to-work requirements aggressively, approving absences for "good cause" in only 2 percent of cases; in 2002, 23 percent of TANF participants were sanctioned.[39]

Complaints about abusive working conditions within workfare programs quickly surfaced in both cities. For example, in Milwaukee, workfare workers hired to do asbestos removal at a private hospital were not given the proper safety equipment.[40] In Los Angeles, workfare workers assigned to janitorial work were given thin gloves that failed to protect them from the toxic cleaning agents they used. Other workfare workers were asked to do heavy lifting but were not given back braces. Supervisors frequently refused to give letters of recommendations to General Relief recipients and consistently denied them opportunities to fill regular job openings.[41] Complaints also surfaced regarding minimum-wage violations in welfare-to-work programs in both California and Wisconsin. It was grievances like these, plus the general lack of legal clarity regarding workfare workers' labor rights, that encouraged community organizations and unions to organize welfare-to-work participants.

Unequal Opportunities to Organize

While welfare-to-work participants had similar grievances across cities, anti-workfare activists in Los Angeles faced more favorable opportunities for organizing than their counterparts in Milwaukee because of differences in the political economy of workfare and union politics in the two cities. There were far more participants to organize in Los Angeles than in Milwaukee (see table 1.2). Los Angeles's relatively high unemployment and poverty rates, coupled with the county's large labor force and its comparatively lenient welfare policies, produced the largest TANF welfare-to-work population in the nation.[42] Moreover, in contrast to Milwaukee, which eliminated General Assistance in the late 1990s, Los Angeles provided General Relief. In 1998, between 15,000 and 26,000 able-bodied General Relief recipients—approximately 25 to 43 percent of the caseload—were placed in county-mandated work assignments.[43] Milwaukee County's relatively low unemployment rate, along with enforcement of Wisconsin's tough new welfare reform policies, led to a dramatic 48-percent decline in the number of welfare-to-work participants between 1997 and 2000.[44]

Of course, a larger population of welfare recipients is not necessarily easier to organize if recipients are widely dispersed across space or across employers, or otherwise difficult to find. Workfare workers were not only more numerous but also more concentrated in the public sector in Los Angeles than in Milwaukee, creating more incentives and better opportunities for unions to organize them in Los Angeles. The relatively low demand for unskilled labor in Los Angeles (dampened further by the ample supply of undocumented workers), plus fiscal pressures to lower labor costs, encouraged local officials to place workfare participants in the public sector. SEIU's research found that nearly 99 percent of General Relief work assignments in 1994 were in the public sector, with 65 percent at county worksites.[45] Reliance on workfare labor—particularly in clerical, parks maintenance, and cleaning work—minimized labor costs and compensated for hiring freezes imposed during the county's worst fiscal crisis since the Great Depression. For example, between sixty and one hundred workfare workers per day were employed at a county-run hospital in 1998 where there had been a hiring freeze for the past three years.[46] This trend continued with the implementation of CalWORKs, California's TANF program. The county allowed most recipients to fulfill their welfare-to-work requirements by participating in programs that helped recipients find jobs and prepare for job interviews, though about one-third were exempt because they were already working.[47] Nevertheless, SEIU and community groups *feared* that "work experience" placements would quickly swell up to 200,000; the expansion of welfare-to-work programs thus presented a large potential displacement threat for unionized public-sector employees in Los Angeles.[48]

By contrast, in Milwaukee, participants in W-2, Wisconsin's TANF program, were widely scattered across many different worksites, the vast majority of which were located in the private sector.[49] Some W-2 participants were assigned to public-sector jobs, such as cleaning roads and highways, but they mostly worked for local businesses and nonprofit agencies in inventory, food service, child care, cleaning, and clerical jobs.[50] Collins and Mayer report, "In 2003, Milwaukee caseworkers placed 68 percent of CSJ [Community Service Jobs] participants with private nonprofits, 21 percent with private, for-profit firms, 6 percent with public agencies and 4 percent with combined nonprofit/for-profit enterprises."[51] Groups of six to twenty women were assigned to various private agencies, including affiliates of the agencies administering W-2. They sorted clothes for Goodwill's thrift stores, produced sweatshirts and counted bottles for YWCA's subsidiaries, and sorted food for emergency food distributors. Alone or in small groups, they also washed dishes for restaurants or did janitorial or routine clerical work for nonprofit agencies.[52]

As I discuss more fully below, contrasts in workforce size and distribution shaped the opportunities to organize workfare workers as well as unions' willingness to invest in these organizing campaigns. In Milwaukee, the scattering of workfare workers across many different private-sector worksites created considerable barriers to organizing them, as they were difficult to locate. It also created few incentives for unions to invest many resources in these campaigns since few unionized workers faced the threat of displacement by welfare-to-work participants. By contrast, in Los Angeles, the large concentration of workfare workers in the public sector facilitated their organization and encouraged public-sector unions to join these organizing campaigns. Public-sector unions were also more fully revitalized in Los Angeles than in Milwaukee, providing greater resources for organizing welfare-to-work participants. The greater longevity and success of workfare workers' campaigns in Los Angeles as compared to in Milwaukee was partly due to greater union investments.

Anti-workfare activists also faced better political opportunities to win concessions in Los Angeles than in Milwaukee. As discussed in chapter 4, Milwaukee's W-2 program was administered by five private agencies that held contracts with the state welfare department. Activists had to gain concessions from private W-2 agencies or from state policymakers, who were dominated by political conservatives ideologically committed to upholding a strict, work-oriented welfare reform program. By contrast, the Los Angeles local government had considerable discretion over the implementation of TANF and General Relief. Both the Los Angeles local government and the California state legislature were dominated by Democrats, who were more sympathetic to activists' demands.

Workfare Workers' Campaigns in Los Angeles

As in Milwaukee, there were two separate campaigns to organize workfare workers in Los Angeles. The first, carried out by ACORN, initially focused on General Relief. The second campaign, which focused exclusively on TANF participants, was carried out by an organizing partnership between AGENDA, a community organization, SEIU 660, and SEIU 347, which respectively represented the county's and city's public-sector workers.

Unlike the short-lived campaigns in Milwaukee, Los Angeles's campaigns lasted for more than three years and led to a number of small but significant victories. In Los Angeles, community and labor organizations had sufficient resources to hire organizing staff and faced relatively favorable conditions in several respects. First, unlike Milwaukee, Los Angeles had a large workfare population that was concentrated in an already unionized public sector, which made it easy to find and recruit large numbers of potential members. The sectoral placement of workfare workers and the decision to organize workfare workers without a traditional union election helped to protect these campaigns from the kind of union-busting campaign that occurred in Milwaukee. Second, local officials in Los Angeles had considerable discretion over welfare programs, and their administration remained largely in the public sector. Activists thus did not face the same constraints as their counterparts in Milwaukee, where local officials had little say over welfare policies.

ACORN's Workfare Workers Organizing Committee

At the end of 1996, ACORN formed the Workfare Workers Organizing Committee, a committee run by General Relief recipients. Members were multiracial and multilingual, though largely African American and Latino, as General Relief workers were. Using bilingual organizers, flyers, and literature, ACORN enlisted many Spanish-speaking members who actively participated in the organization. ACORN's staff organizers trained grassroots leaders through weekend "leadership development" workshops so that they could participate actively in the organization. ACORN also hired a full-time staff person to advocate for thousands of individual recipients whose welfare checks, food stamps, or bus tokens were unfairly denied or delayed. Reportedly, this service helped to recruit new members and increase their loyalty to the organization. By 1998, ACORN claimed to have collected union authorization cards from more than half of the number of active General Relief workfare participants. It did not pursue an official union election, but instead pressured county officials for union recognition through public rallies. However, it lacked sufficient disruptive power to gain official recognition of its "union" by county supervisors.[53] But even without union recognition, ACORN managed to gain concessions from employers and local policymakers through a series of militant actions.

ACORN strategically framed its campaign as a workers' rights campaign. It referred to its members as "GR workers," and its agenda mainly focused on improving their labor and employment rights. ACORN demanded that welfare-to-work participants be covered by existing labor legislation, called for pay equity between workfare workers and regular county workers, sought improvements in job training, and urged policymakers to create more jobs—especially jobs designed to improve low-income communities.[54] As Abdullah Muhammed, chair of the Workfare Workers Organizing Committee, explained, "We want to force the county to change its policy—to hire us full-time at livable wages with benefits."[55] To highlight their desire for regular employment, members completed job applications and brought them to protests at county agencies.[56] ACORN's members, who are mostly African American, also expressed resistance to the racist overtones of welfare reform by drawing on a symbolically powerful analogy between slavery and workfare for their slogan: "Workfare Is Slave Labor." The slogan frequently appeared on T-shirts and protest signs and was often invoked in public protests. Because ACORN required continued flexibility to organize around goals that were identified by its members, it sometimes focused on more traditional kinds of welfare rights. For example, its welfare mothers' organization protested against welfare agency employees' rude treatment towards recipients, while its General Relief group organized against the implementation of five-month time limits for their program.

Through militant protest, ACORN managed to win a number of improvements in the implementation of welfare-to-work policies. ACORN organized a series of protests at worksites, ranging from fifty to one hundred participants, which led to improvements in workfare workers' working conditions. One of these protests targeted a public medical center that employed more than eight hundred workfare workers.[57] In response, administrators agreed to provide workfare workers with new uniforms and an employee discount at the hospital cafeteria.[58] Another group of ACORN members won themselves back braces to protect their backs from the impacts of heavy lifting on the job.[59]

Protesters nabbed an even greater victory when top welfare officials agreed to establish a grievance procedure for workfare participants, responding to a series of protests that drew large crowds and sympathetic media coverage. The first agreement of its kind in the country, the procedure enabled workfare workers to resolve grievances about unfair or unsafe work conditions in a timely, protected manner.[60] Welfare officials also agreed to adopt new rules in their contracts with agencies to improve work assignments for workfare employees. These included requirements that sponsors file specific job descriptions and that caseworkers assess workers' skills and interests when making job assignments. The new rules also allow workfare workers to ask for letters of recommendation from their supervisors.[61]

In response to numerous protests organized by ACORN, county officials also agreed to change the hiring practices that agencies used when assigning jobs to workfare workers. First, they agreed to create a special hiring list of workfare employees who had passed the civil service exam. According to the new policy, county agencies were required to use this list to prioritize the hiring of workfare workers when new job positions opened up.[62] Second, an administrator from the Department of Human Resources agreed to count work experience acquired by workfare participants in relevant, entry-level job assignments when they applied for regular county jobs.[63] Although the hundreds of new jobs obtained via "priority hiring lists" were a mere fraction of the total unemployed workfare laborers seeking work, it represented an incredible victory for those who obtained regular jobs through these lists.[64] In addition, ACORN persuaded the county to create several hundred new child care training slots at community colleges to meet its members' demands for these opportunities.

ACORN also pressured government contractors to hire workfare workers. While private-sector employers were generally more resistant to workers' demands than public-sector employers, there were exceptions.

For example, Lockheed Martin executives agreed to post entry-level job openings through ACORN's "Community Hiring Hall" five days in advance of any other postings. Although only a handful of members obtained jobs through this agreement, it set an important precedent for other government contractors.[65] Lockheed was particularly vulnerable to public pressure because it was seeking a welfare-to-work contract at the time, so it sought to avoid negative publicity that might portray the firm as reluctant to hire welfare recipients.

The majority of ACORN's victories did not cost very much and were improvements that were made under employers' or local officials' discretion. County officials failed to support ACORN's more costly demands for a job creation program, although they did eventually create a very small transitional jobs program in response to AGENDA and SEIU's campaign, which I will describe in the next section. Local officials sought to minimize social expenditures. Their resistance to job creation also reflected the view of that workfare workers were unemployed because they were undisciplined. Despite the county's well-documented job shortages, Pat Knauss, Chief of the General Relief Division, claimed that there were plenty of employment opportunities for welfare recipients:

> Right now we have more jobs than we have people to fill them. Anywhere you drive around here, look for the help wanted signs. They're everywhere in this county, particularly for the entry-level [sic].[66]

Without the county's workfare program to teach them how to structure their time and other work habits, Knauss claimed that General Relief recipients would "sit around on [street] corners."[67] In a statement to the press, she said that if these recipients failed to find employment, it was because they "choose not to take responsibility for themselves."[68]

More costly policy demands, such as extending General Relief time limits, required the help of allies. In July of 1998, about eight thousand General Relief recipients were scheduled to lose aid and about forty-eight thousand recipients would be denied assistance within six months. Weeks before these losses were scheduled to happen, ACORN and other welfare advocates and service providers held a large protest of about four hundred welfare recipients and their supporters, calling for a moratorium on the time limits. Participants disrupted the supervisors' meeting, loudly chanting, "We're fired up; we can't take it no more!" When the crowd surged forward, ten or twelve sheriff's deputies, clad in riot gear and wielding batons, formed a line to protect the supervisors, who quickly retreated behind closed doors. Eventually, supervisors agreed to listen to the group. More than a dozen General Relief recipients, service providers, and advocates testified about the hardships that the cutoffs would create. Abdullah Muhammed expressed the concerns of many of these recipients when he said, "Now once these time limits kick in . . . what are the people going to do? . . . We're in a desperate mood to have jobs created in this system."[69] ACORN thus strategically linked their opposition to time limits to their demands for job creation.[70]

This protest was one of a series of actions opposing the General Relief time limits. Already, a coalition of religious leaders held a press conference where they criticized supervisors' decision to fund the Twin Towers Jail in downtown Los Angeles rather than extend welfare time limits.[71] Later, six members of the "Women of Conscience," calling for a moratorium on time limits, were arrested for blocking traffic and refusing to disperse. At its height, this protest against time limits included about one hundred people, including members of ACORN, a delegation from the Kensington Welfare Rights Union of Philadelphia, and other welfare advocates.[72] On the day that General Relief time limits were implemented, the Welfare Reform Coalition held a large public hearing on welfare reform and urged county supervisors to rescind the five-month time limit.[73]

However, supervisors, seeking to minimize welfare expenditures, stubbornly defended the General Relief time limits. Activists had to jump scales of governance, from the county level to the state level, in order to make headway. With help from then-assemblyman Antonio Villaraigosa, welfare advocates negotiated with county welfare officials over policy proposals. While the county wanted to avoid a state-mandated grant-level increase, welfare advocates wanted to extend the General Relief time limit and improve job training. As a result of these negotiations, county supervisors were allowed to retain the $221 monthly grant level, and they agreed to allow recipients to have up to nine months of aid and to improve their job-training program.[74] Afterward, county supervisors changed General Relief policies accordingly, a significant concession.

ACORN formed partnerships with unions in other cities but had a difficult time forging alliances with SEIU, which represented municipal workers in Los Angeles. In the late 1990s, ACORN was new to the city and its staff was not well known among SEIU staff and leaders. Local union leaders viewed ACORN's organizing drive as an encroachment on their bargaining units; ACORN's demand for union recognition for its Workfare Workers Organizing Committee threatened SEIU's jurisdiction over city and county employees. Though ACORN's demand for union recognition was mainly meant to demonstrate that workfare workers should be accorded the same rights as regular workers, it alienated SEIU from working together with it. Relations between ACORN and SEIU were further strained as both groups began to organize welfare-to-work participants in the TANF program.

Nevertheless, after ACORN turned to issues beyond union recognition (which it never obtained), SEIU began to cooperate more.[75] Together, SEIU and ACORN collaborated in several coalitions that aimed to improve the county's welfare-to-work policies for TANF recipients. Through lobbying and public demonstrations, one coalition demanded minimum-wage protections for TANF participants, some of whom were paid sub-minimum "training wages," in violation of federal policy.[76] Despite protests against this practice, the county did not change its policy. A second coalition demanded that the community service program, established for TANF participants who were unable to find a job after two years, provide participants with a wage rather than a welfare check. At one protest, ACORN members wore large cardboard chains around their bodies to symbolize their enslavement by the current grant-based program. Only after state legislation authorized the creation of a wage-based program did the county agree to implement it, although it did so begrudgingly with little outreach to welfare recipients. As of April 2003, it had benefited only one recipient.[77]

Through these coalitions, ACORN and SEIU formed close ties, supporting each other's campaigns beyond workfare. As an ACORN organizer explained, "The relationship we have now . . . is in terms of 'every worker is a worker'. . . . [They] lend their voice with our voice."[78] When the city's health clinics faced closure, the two groups quickly mobilized community groups and health care workers to save them. They also collaborated in the campaigns against welfare privatization and the campaigns to improve subsidized child care, as described in chapters 4 and 6.

A combination of factors contributed to the longevity and success of ACORN's workfare workers' campaign in Los Angeles. First, the organization had sufficient resources to hire full-time organizers. Second, a large number of workfare workers were concentrated in the public sector, making it easy to locate them and to negotiate for improvements in the welfare-to-work program. To make gains, ACORN organized a series of disruptive protests through which they won improvements in welfare-to-work participants' working conditions, a grievance procedure, and the creation of priority hiring lists. More costly demands, such as extending General Relief time limits and creating a wage-based community service program, required the help of other allies, including sympathetic state legislators. Democratic control of California's county and state governments may have created favorable political conditions for winning policy concessions, but those gains required militant action and sometimes the formation of broad-based alliances.

AGENDA and SEIU's Campaign

While ACORN was in the midst of its General Relief campaign, another community group, AGENDA, began working with SEIU to start a second campaign to organize workfare workers. The organizing partnership included AGENDA, SEIU Local 660 (which represented county workers), and SEIU Local 347 (which represented city workers).[79] Unlike AFSCME District Council 48 in Milwaukee, SEIU 660 and 347 were eager to organize workfare workers. In part, this was because they believed that workfare placements, mostly in the public sector, could expand up to 200,000 after the implementation of TANF. This threatened to displace their members and reduce their bargaining power.[80] As a Local 660 staff member explained:

> We immediately [fore]saw thousands of people on welfare being exploited and not being paid to work in county jobs, and alongside our workers, and displacing our workers, and undercutting wages, and being denied workers' safety [provisions], being denied health [benefits], and being denied everything we've fought so hard for all of these years.[81]

SEIU sought to avoid the kind of displacement that affected public-sector workers in New York.[82] In addition, SEIU was "concerned about the potential for conflict developing between unemployed workers and [employed] workers in a time when everyone was being squeezed." The union sought to build a model welfare-to-work program that would "bring community and labor together" and better serve both.[83] To achieve this, SEIU sought non-displacement agreements and assurances that workfare participants were "entitled to all the rights that other workers enjoy." They also sought to expand welfare-to-work participants' employment opportunities to become regular county workers through a transitional jobs program.[84] SEIU staff viewed the implementation of TANF as providing "historic opportunities for building a powerful labor/community alliance around an economic justice agenda" and believed that their new organizing campaign could possibly lead to "thousands of potential new members."[85]

Compared to AFSCME District Council 48 in Milwaukee, SEIU's local chapters were more fully revitalized and had greater resources for organizing. After the union's international leaders put the union into trusteeship in 1992, SEIU 660 relied on innovative tactics to avert privatization, wage cuts, and layoffs. For example, in 1995, SEIU 660 prevented layoffs by allying with community groups, lobbying for state and federal funds, and holding protests.[86] SEIU also led several successful labor-community campaigns for living-wage ordinances.[87] Thus, it is not surprising that SEIU responded to welfare reform by building alliances with community groups.

SEIU viewed AGENDA as a good coalition partner because of its experience in community organizing and past cooperation with unions.[88] Prior friendships between SEIU 347 and AGENDA staff provided effective bridge-builders between the two organizations. The joint campaign was also initiated after a year of joint planning and input from other unions and community groups, giving the two groups time to build an effective working relationship.[89] Through this planning process, SEIU and AGENDA formulated a five-point action plan that included the following goals: (1) developing a model job creation program, (2) protecting the rights of workfare workers, (3) protecting the rights of public employees against displacement, (4) improving the quality of jobs eligible for welfare-to-work funds, and (5) providing essential support services.[90] To carry out this plan, AGENDA and SEIU pooled their resources and hired four full-time organizers to recruit workfare participants into SEIU's existing bargaining units and into a welfare organizing committee of AGENDA.[91]

AGENDA and SEIU mobilized hundreds of workfare workers and their allies for press conferences and public hearings. They solidified support from local politicians for their goals through office visits, public forums drawing hundreds, and lobbying; the coalition avoided the militant protest tactics used by ACORN, viewing them as unnecessary. As one SEIU organizer put it: "When you bring a couple hundred people to a city council meeting, they consider that disruptive."[92] While organizing hundreds of people to attend a city council meeting and offering testimonies surely helped to display the group's organizational capacity, it was hardly disruptive.

AGENDA and SEIU persuaded the Los Angeles City Council, which was sympathetic to the group's demands, to create a "vocational workers program" with federal welfare-to-work money. The program paid nine dollars an hour and compensated union employees for mentoring participants. Participants were trained for the civil service exam and received vocational training. By 2002, the program trained 237 participants and had a 71 percent retention rate.[93] The coalition hoped to persuade the county to create a similar program. County supervisors, who were more ideologically conservative than the city council, agreed to create a program—but not the kind that organizers desired. As a SEIU staff person explained, county supervisors

> wanted part-time, temporary, minimum-wage jobs. What we had with "city jobs" in L.A. was permanent, civil-service, living-wage jobs with benefits from day one, moving into a career with a pension at the end, et cetera. The county was totally unwilling to consider that.[94]

The county's transitional job program funded only fifty participants, paid the minimum wage, and did not include the paid peer mentorship by unionized workers. SEIU and AGENDA faced even greater resistance from officials in other municipalities who refused to create any type of transitional job program.[95] With neither a militant campaign nor a broad-based coalition behind them, the organizing partnership failed to win more than a few hundred jobs.

The coalition was more successful in securing anti-displacement agreements with the city and county. The Los Angeles City Council prohibited city managers from contracting workfare workers; SEIU negotiated an agreement with the county to protect their members from displacement. Afterward, most TANF welfare-to-work participants were placed in private, nonprofit worksites; only a few hundred worked for the county government. These anti-displacement policies greatly reduced the potential threat posed by workfare to union members and led to SEIU's withdrawal from its partnership with AGENDA. Afterward, AGENDA continued to push for additional public funds for job training and employment programs mostly on its own, although it continued to consult with the union.[96]

In sum, the SEIU and AGENDA campaign benefited from many of the same conditions that helped ACORN's campaign in Los Angeles. The large concentration of workfare participants in the public sector made workers easy to organize; it also increased the incentives for public-sector unions to hire multiple staff organizers for the campaign. Democratic majorities in the county and city governments, with their discretion over the implementation of welfare-to-work programs, also provided opportunities for activists to win policy concessions. While SEIU and AGENDA collaborated with ACORN and other welfare advocacy groups to push for minimum-wage protections and the creation of a wage-based program, they carried out the transitional jobs campaign mostly on their own. Lacking both militancy and broad-based support, and facing policymakers eager to keep costs low, the campaign only managed to win support for the creation of nearly three hundred transitional jobs for welfare-to-work participants. Nevertheless, for most of those who participated in the program, these programs were life-changing.

Workfare Workers' Campaigns in Milwaukee

As in Los Angeles, there were two campaigns to organize W-2 workfare workers in Milwaukee. However, compared to their counterparts in Los Angeles, community activists in Wisconsin had more difficulty gaining and maintaining union support and were unable to sustain these campaigns for long periods of time. A Job Is a Right, an all-volunteer organization of labor and community activists formed in 1994, initiated the first campaign, forming W-2 Workers United. Many members of A Job Is a Right were affiliated with the Marxist-Leninist group Workers World Party (WWP), which organized a similar campaign by Workfairness in

New York City. A Job Is a Right failed to gain union support and, lacking sufficient resources of its own, disbanded W-2 Workers United within a year. ACORN and a local chapter of the CWA carried out the second campaign, which carried out a unionization campaign among W-2 workers at one workplace. The campaign met with strong employer opposition, and the union quickly withdrew its funding from it after it failed to win the election campaign.

W-2 Workers United

A Job Is a Right viewed W-2 as an attack on workers' rights that created "a large, captive low-wage workforce" and put downward pressure on wages for all workers.[97] To fight against the bill that created W-2, members mobilized grassroots opposition, visiting about eight hundred homes in Milwaukee's North Side, where many of the county's welfare recipients lived, and organizing demonstrations against the proposed legislation.[98] After the bill's passage, the group carried out a three-pronged attack on W-2. First, it documented and publicized the corporate and right-wing forces that designed and pushed forward the W-2 system. Second, it organized a "Pledge of Resistance and Non-Cooperation with W-2" campaign to discourage local businesses, nonprofit organizations, and religious groups from hiring W-2 workers.[99] It urged employers to refuse to provide job slots for W-2 participants because the program violated basic rights, such as the right to voluntary employment. Along with other local employers, the pledge was signed by local labor leaders. Third, the organization formed W-2 Workers United to organize welfare-to-work participants and other unemployed workers.

Aware of their limitations as an all-volunteer group, W-2 Workers United had as its primary goal to gain sufficient members to convince unions that W-2 workers could and should be organized by them, an idea A Job Is a Right discussed with state and local labor leaders.[100] Janice Thurman, who was a former welfare mother, felt compelled to organize W-2 workers because "even though they say jobs are plentiful, livable jobs aren't plentiful."[101] As a black woman herself, she appealed to other black mothers in particular to join the organization in order to protect against the added discrimination they would face as W-2 participants.[102]

The formation of W-2 Workers United was announced at a press conference in August of 1997, where various speakers, including then-senator Gwen Moore, criticized W-2.[103] As Janice Thurman explained to the press, "We deserve the right as working people to work side-by-side with other workers and be treated equally." Thurman called for "real training programs for real jobs." She warned unions to "take us on. Otherwise, who's going to get all the jobs?"[104] Flyers for the event criticized W-2 for paying workers below the minimum wage and for giving lucrative tax breaks to their employers. W-2 Workers United demanded "better wages, good benefits, and decent working conditions," as well as union representation.[105] Ironically, the W-2 program officially began on Labor Day in 1997. AFSCME Local 82, which represented university clerical and maintenance workers, most of whom were women and people of color, invited W-2 Workers United to join in the city's annual Labor Day parade.[106] W-2 Workers United were able to use the occasion to raise awareness about W-2 and its participants' need to unionize by marching alongside thousands of union members in the parade.[107]

Although W-2 Workers United managed to organize several hundred workfare workers, they never gained sufficient union support to sustain their campaign. This was not because labor leaders lacked concern about W-2 and underemployed workers. Milwaukee's unions, including AFSCME District Council 48, participated in other welfare rights activities, such as the county's W-2 Monitoring Task Force and campaigns to improve state welfare policies.[108] Public-sector unions vocally supported job creation and participated in a multimillion-dollar project to connect inner-city residents with family-supporting jobs.[109] Labor leaders also endorsed events and demands by W-2 Workers United, but they failed to commit any resources to the organizing drive because they believed union members faced little displacement by workfare workers.[110] W-2 Workers United organizers warned AFSCME that their members would face displacement by thousands of workfare participants, hoping to gain their interest in the campaign.[111] This strategy proved to be effective in New York City. There, actual displacement, along with pressure from the union's international leaders, led AFSCME District Council 37 to join and finance Workfairness's campaign to organize workfare workers.[112]

In Milwaukee, the displacement of large numbers of public-sector workers by workfare workers never really materialized, since only a small fraction of W-2 participants were placed in public-sector jobs. Whereas large numbers of workfare workers in Los Angeles were placed in the public sector, most W-2 participants were instead widely scattered across private-sector worksites. This gave public- and private-sector unions in Milwaukee little direct incentive to organize them. Unions' fears about displacement were probably also allayed by the inclusion of "non-displacement" provisions in Wisconsin's W-2 program that prohibited employers from using workfare participants to replace regular workers, even if those provisions were later violated in some instances. As Collins and Mayer point out, the *Milwaukee Journal Sentinel* underwent restructuring in the context of a merger, which enabled it to "lay off some regularly salaried workers and hire workfare participants without repercussions."[113]

Labor and other community activists considered organizing workfare workers in Milwaukee, but they quickly concluded that they had no "captive population to organize" and that the costs of organizing W-2 participants were too high.[114] The president of the American Federation of Labor and Congress of Industrial Organizations South Central Labor Federation did not believe that a traditional union campaign for W-2 workers was viable because workers were so widely dispersed across job sites.[115] A Central Labor Council official also cited the compounding effects of high turnover that resulted from the relatively favorable labor market conditions in the county:

> [Local labor unions] would have been very involved in trying to organize, had there been a concentration of W-2 participants . . . but there wasn't any. It really is different than, let's say, New York, where there [were] huge concentrations of [the] labor force . . . [Here], they are very scattered . . . the people did not stay in placements for more than a couple of weeks at a time. . . . There was no organizing opportunity because people were never around long enough.[116]

A top official in AFSCME District Council 48, representing the county's public-sector workers, provided a similar analysis of his union's decision not to organize workfare workers despite being pressed to do so by community groups:

> [Workfare workers] were mostly placed in private-sector settings . . . [I]n New York . . . you can get your hands around twenty thousand workers who are now displacing the ten thousand parks employees who used to work there. . . . Here, in Milwaukee, we didn't have that kind of concentration. They were just all over the place.[117]

With workfare workers highly dispersed, mobile, and mainly concentrated in the private sector, Milwaukee's public-sector unions did not have strong incentives or good opportunities to organize them like in Los Angeles. Moreover, the places where the largest numbers of workfare participants were employed were in non-unionized agencies, such as Goodwill Industries or YWCA. Without the help of an already unionized workforce in place, it was difficult to gain access to these participants.[118]

Joint work between Milwaukee's public-sector unions and anti-workfare groups was also impeded by incomplete union revitalization projects. AFSCME District Council 48's leaders, though personally committed to social-movement unionism, had only recently gained control over the union and lacked the infrastructure to put their principles into practice. As one union leader explained:

> I was brought in . . . to reform the union [in 1997] . . . to activate it. . . . I wanted to put resources into organizing because we had none. . . . I had to fight to get the resources. . . . The [International] was very helpful, but we've had to build an organizing program from the ground up.[119]

The union was also preoccupied with mobilizing its members and the community to prevent the privatization of the county's welfare and child-welfare programs, a grave threat to its members; it lacked sufficient organizing staff to carry out both campaigns simultaneously (see chapter 3).

Frustrated by the labor movement's failure to commit resources to its W-2 Workers United campaign, A Job Is a Right halted its organizing drive but continued to mobilize around welfare issues. For example, in 1998 it assembled a march calling for "an emergency moratorium on W-2 suffering" to draw attention to the material hardships caused by the implementation of welfare reform, which led to a rise in the number of people who were denied welfare benefits or who lost income through welfare sanctions. The march drew between one hundred and two hundred people, including labor leaders.[120] Led by former and current welfare recipients, participants called for legislation "for an immediate halt . . . to all W-2-related sanctions, evictions, heat or light cut offs, or the taking of children due to loss of income as a result of the W-2 program,"[121] more funds for child care, and legislation to allow W-2 participants to count more hours in education and training toward their welfare-to-work requirements. A Job Is a Right highlighted the racial dimensions of W-2 suffering, calling W-2 "modern-day slavery," and proclaimed, "Poor people in every neighborhood—but particularly in communities of color—are facing an emergency situation and we are demanding emergency relief!"[122]

The hardships caused by W-2 were becoming increasingly evident, especially for those in the inner city. Utility cutoffs rose, sometimes leading to tragic consequences. For example, in 1997 three young boys tragically died in a house fire caused by a faulty space heater while their mother was at her W-2 assignment. Two families (a total of twelve people) shared the home and used the space heater after the gas was shut off because they couldn't pay the bill.[123] Deputy-assisted evictions rose from 1,337 in 1988 to 3,251 in 1998. There was also a rise in overcrowded apartments, which quickly became nicknamed "W-2 stacks." A sheriff's deputy who supervised many of the county's evictions described the poor living conditions he had encountered on the job: "We had a small place the other day with eight people living there. They couldn't even open the door, there were so many people sleeping on the floor."[124]

A Job Is a Right later formed the Coalition to Ban Winter Evictions with homeless and welfare advocacy organizations.[125] Twenty members of the coalition urged the Milwaukee County Board of Supervisors to declare a state of emergency and ban all evictions during the winter months. One study showed that about 39 percent of former W-2 participants surveyed had been evicted or threatened with an eviction. Local homeless shelters also reported a rising demand for their services from women and children. Three months later, county supervisors voted unanimously in favor of a resolution calling for the creation of a fund, developed by the county's W-2 agencies, that would provide emergency relief for people facing an eviction as a result of W-2.[126] Although supervisors were supportive, they lacked authority over W-2 and could do little to improve the program directly.

Lacking resources to hire staff and unable to gain union support, W-2 Workers United became inactive within the first eight months of W-2's implementation.[127] The conjuncture of three factors discouraged unions from supporting this campaign. Workfare workers were highly mobile, in sharp decline, and widely scattered across private-sector worksites, making it difficult to organize them on site. Although workers could have been organized through neighborhood canvassing, unions had little incentive beyond a commitment to social justice to invest resources in organizing workfare workers. The expansion of welfare-to-work did not threaten to displace workers who were already unionized. Since few W-2 workers were placed in the public sector, public-sector unions faced a more imminent displacement threat from the privatization of W-2 and other social services, and thus they invested most of their scarce organizational resources into their antiprivatization campaign. Finally, county officials lacked authority over welfare policies, making it difficult to win meaningful concessions.

ACORN and CWA

The second campaign to organize workfare workers in Milwaukee was initiated in 1998 by the Milwaukee chapter of ACORN, which assigned staff to organize W-2 participants. After collecting membership cards from W-2 participants, ACORN held its first demonstration outside of Goodwill's Employment Solutions, one of Milwaukee's five private welfare contractors. About fifty protesters gathered, demanding that the agency provide W-2 participants with better services, including better child care, job training, and job placement services. They also opposed welfare agencies' denial of benefits to poor mothers who had been deemed "job-ready" even when they lacked employment and were not informed of job openings. The protest ended when agency officials called the police, who arrested two of the protesters and pepper-sprayed the crowd.[128]

Like A Job Is a Right, ACORN sought to expand their organizing campaign with support from a union that would negotiate on their members' behalf. AFSCME's District Council 48 agreed to "sponsor" ACORN's initiative but would not fund it.[129] A local chapter of the CWA, however, agreed to assign one of their organizers to work full-time on the campaign.[130] According to the agreement, organizers would sign up W-2 participants as both ACORN members and "associate members" of CWA. The two organizations would jointly organize workfare workers and seek improvements in W-2 participants' rights as welfare recipients and workers.[131] Union officials viewed the campaign as an opportunity to fulfill their mission to organize low-income workers. A union staffer who supervised the campaign recalled:

> When [ACORN] visited with me . . . we had just had a series of discussions within CWA regarding our role in terms of low-income workers. . . . And we were really feeling that we were not fulfilling our mission . . . that we needed to get involved, even if jurisdiction was not ours, in assisting low-income organizing.[132]

She claimed that "old guard" leaders within the local union were not completely enthusiastic about the campaign, however, because its benefits for union membership growth were unclear. They provided only a small, temporary investment in it and, in contrast to SEIU in Los Angeles, they insisted on using a traditional union election campaign model.

The union staff person assigned to the campaign was an effective "bridge builder."[133] An African American woman experienced in organizing low-income nursing home workers, she worked well with ACORN staff and members, many of whom were low-income blacks.[134] The site that was selected for the campaign was the Product Development Corporation (an Ameritech contractor), where an ACORN member was employed. The company, which produced telephone directories and sold ads in them, employed about fifty-five workers. Nearly all the employees were women, and about forty of them received W-2. The campaign sought to organize both workfare workers and regular workers into a single bargaining unit.[135]

Initially, the campaign went well. An ACORN member quickly collected membership cards from most of her W-2 coworkers. Workers filed their membership cards and their petition for a union election at the National Labor Relations Board (NLRB) during ACORN's national convention in Milwaukee. At the convention, about 1,500 ACORN members and supporters demonstrated outside of a fundraising dinner for Governor Tommy Thompson. Later, they collected about five thousand signatures on petitions that called for better education and training opportunities for W-2 participants. The following day, members of ACORN, the union, and their supporters marched to deliver their petitions to the governor's office. Marchers also stopped by the Ameritech headquarters to demonstrate their support for the union campaign and then arrived at the National Labor Relations Board office to file the workers' union cards.[136]

After these initial activities, the Ameritech company began an aggressive anti-union campaign. They used many traditional union-busting tactics observed in other union election campaigns, especially in the private sector.[137] For example, they offered incentives to workers who agreed to vote against the union. One worker was told that she could have health insurance if she voted "no" in the union election. The employers also had "one-on-one" meetings and small group meetings with workers to persuade them to reject the union. The company strategically divided the workers for these meetings. As the CWA organizer who was assigned to the campaign explained, "They put the strong ones . . . in with some mouthy people that were against the union and then the weaker ones, they would really lay in on them."[138] Together, the company and anti-union workers warned employees that the company would move and eliminate their jobs if they voted for the union and distributed anti-union flyers, buttons, and T-shirts.

The union-busting campaign that Ameritech ran was typical in many respects, but the company also used gender-focused tactics to manipulate employees. The employers took advantage of the workers' needs as single working mothers to punish and intimidate union supporters. Before the union campaign, the company had allowed workers to leave early to pick up their children from school. During the unionization campaign, however, the company suddenly became inflexible. According to the union organizer,

> they intimidated them terribly. Like before, the women who had kids, they said "I have to go early today, fifteen to twenty minutes early to go pick up my child." "Oh go right ahead. No problem." . . . But then they started to make examples. . . . If you left fifteen to twenty minutes early, they would mark you absent for the whole day.[139]

The use of attendance records to intimidate pro-union workers became a central problem for their campaign in the fall: "That was a key issue. We were winning all the way up until the time that school started." Managers told workers that they would overlook their attendance problems if they voted against the union. They also fired several union supporters because of their attendance. In response to these firings, ACORN and CWA organized a lunchtime rally, which drew about fifty protestors, including union leaders.[140]

Despite organizers' efforts to maintain support among the workers, the company's bribery and intimidation were effective. As the union organizer put it, the workers' "voices became smaller because they were scared."[141] Eventually, the union lost the election campaign. Whereas at least forty out of fifty-five employees signed union membership cards, only fourteen voted in favor of the union.[142] As the union organizer explained, "It was unbelievable the support we had, and then they really came in. . . . That did take a lot of wind out of the sails."

Shortly after the union's defeat, CWA ended its partnership with ACORN. The union supervisor overseeing the campaign believed that the partnership with ACORN still presented opportunities for organizing low-income workers and building community support for labor issues. Yet, she claimed that CWA's "old guard" leaders became frustrated with ACORN staff and the union organizer assigned to the campaign when they failed to keep them updated about their activities. Union officials preferred more traditional styles of union organizing and did not think that the joint campaign would accomplish much, especially given the recent election defeat.[143] After the union pulled out of the campaign, ACORN turned to other issues.

This campaign illustrates the challenges of organizing workfare workers within the private sector, where union-busting campaigns are rampant, as well as the problems with trying to organize a non-traditional labor force through traditional union-organizing methods. Welfare activists might have found more success canvassing neighborhoods and putting pressure on policymakers and employers through collective action instead of organizing workfare workers at a single worksite and pursuing a NLRB-style union election. But moreover, existing political conditions were not as favorable in Milwaukee as they were in Los Angeles. Because the county held little sway over welfare policies, activists had to seek policy improvements at the state level, which proved to be a formidable task. For example, ACORN, A Job Is a Right, union organizers, and other welfare rights groups sought to expand W-2 participants' educational opportunities through lobbying, collective action, and sympathetic press coverage of this issue. In 1998, activists managed to gain bipartisan support for legislation that would allow W-2 participants to count any additional hours spent in educational and training programs as part of their required welfare-to-work hours, but the legislation was vetoed by Governor Tommy Thompson.[144] It wasn't until 2009, when the Democratic governor Jim Doyle came to office and Democrats took control of both legislative houses in Wisconsin, that welfare-to-work participants were given more access to education and training.[145]

Conclusion

The expansion of welfare-to-work programs blurred the boundaries between welfare recipients and workers that have traditionally divided employed and underemployed workers. It also increased the pool of super-exploited labor and, in some places, threatened to displace unionized workers and reduce their bargaining power. In these ways, the expansion of welfare-to-work programs increased the opportunities and incentives to organize welfare recipients. Even so, only in a handful of cities did unions invest in campaigns to organize welfare-to-work participants.[146] Welfare-to-work participants, like welfare recipients more generally, have "few allies and little voice," as they are a stigmatized group in our society.[147] The racialization and demonization of welfare recipients ran deep, preventing many unionized workers, mostly white men, from identifying with the plight of workfare workers, most of whom were African American or Latino single mothers. Moreover, the short-term payoffs for organizing welfare-to-work participants were not readily apparent for unions; increasing membership seemed difficult in the context of organizing a highly vulnerable and mobile population of workers, whose legal status as employees was ambiguous. As Collins and Mayer point out,

> As federal guidelines, state laws, and court cases have accumulated, they have moved in the direction of establishing that workfare participants are employees entitled to a broad range of rights and protections. Nevertheless, ten years after the promulgation of welfare reform, the ground for this interpretation is still shaky.[148]

Short-term pragmatic interests—in defending existing members' rights or increasing dues-paying membership among workers with clear legal rights to organize—unfortunately overshadowed unions' commitment to help some of the most disenfranchised workers fight for social justice. Not only has this unwillingness to help left welfare-to-work participants vulnerable to abuse, it threatens to erode the rights and the wage floor for all workers, unionized or not.[149]

The Los Angeles case illustrates the promises of labor and community collaboration for improving welfare-to-work policies. Compared to Milwaukee, conditions in Los Angeles were far more favorable for organizing workfare workers and gaining union interest in collaboration. Large numbers of workfare workers were initially concentrated in the public sector where managers and public officials were willing to negotiate. This made it fairly easy for community and union staff to organize workfare workers, to negotiate concessions at worksites, and to win anti-displacement agreements. The high concentration of workfare workers in the public sector—and the impending entry of hundreds of thousands more—also gave public-sector unions incentives to invest resources in the campaign. Indeed, when SEIU won anti-displacement agreements from municipal officials, it lost interest in the campaign; protecting existing union members' interest was its primary goal. Finally, though SEIU also confronted the threat of privatization, this threat was not nearly as extensive as it was in Milwaukee, as discussed in chapter 4.

Political conditions were also relatively favorable in Los Angeles, facilitating the success of workfare workers' campaigns. Welfare administration remained largely in the public sector, and local policymakers had considerable authority over welfare policies and the use of federal welfare funds. This made it easier to win policy concessions there than in Milwaukee. Although county supervisors resisted various demands, liberal state legislators helped to push them forward. Activists in Los Angeles won a number of small but significant policy victories. Through militant protest, ACORN pushed for and won a grievance procedure for workfare workers, improvements in welfare-to-work placements and employers' hiring practices, expanded child care training slots, and improved working conditions at worksites. It also helped thousands of welfare recipients obtain or maintain eligibility for cash grants, bus tokens, social services, and emergency services by providing them with information or advocating on their behalf to welfare caseworkers. Together with other allies and support from state legislators, ACORN pushed for and won a wage-based community-service program and extensions in General Relief time limits. The SEIU-AGENDA partnership also persuaded local officials to create two transitional jobs programs that led to nearly three hundred jobs for welfare-to-work participants.

In contrast to Los Angeles, the case of Milwaukee illustrates the challenges workfare advocates faced in gaining union involvement when the expansion of welfare-to-work policies did not pose immediate threats to union members' interests. In Milwaukee, the scattering of highly mobile welfare-to-work participants across private-sector, mostly non-unionized worksites meant that unions did not face significant displacement by workfare workers. It also meant that workfare workers would be difficult to locate and organize at worksites. These factors discouraged unions in Milwaukee—especially those in the public sector—from investing resources in these campaigns. Lacking resources to hire staff and without financial support from unions, A Job Is a Right could only sustain their campaign for workfare workers for less than a year. Incomplete union revitalization within Milwaukee created other obstacles to union involvement. Public-sector unions lacked a well-developed organizing infrastructure, making it difficult for them to invest in these campaigns, especially as they confronted a major wave of privatization. A local chapter of CWA joined ACORN's campaign to organize workfare workers; it viewed it as a way to fulfill its mission to low-income workers and to build a relationship with a vibrant community organization. Yet, the partnership was limited in both resources and strategic vision. CWA only hired one full-time staff person to organize a single worksite, and it pursued a traditional NLRB election. When the campaign failed in the face of a powerful union-busting campaign, the union was quick to withdraw its resources from the campaign. Activists seeking to improve welfare-to-work policies in Milwaukee were also constrained because of the political atmosphere. Because private agencies ran Milwaukee's W-2 program and had contracts with state officials, anti-workfare activists were unable to pressure local policymakers to make meaningful concessions on their behalf. At the same time, conservatives dominated state politics in Wisconsin, making it difficult to win support for state-level improvements in welfare-to-work programs. Even in Los Angeles, workfare workers' campaigns confronted many of the same challenges that more traditional welfare rights campaigns faced. They were mostly defensive campaigns that sought to organize a targeted—and highly stigmatized—social group for minor improvements in existing policies. These limits made it difficult to gain wider political support for demands for job creation.

Perhaps what was most significant about workfare workers' campaigns was that they helped to forge closer ties between community organizations and unions. They challenged racist stereotypes of African American and Latino welfare recipients as being lazy or shirking work, and they blurred the boundaries between welfare recipients and workers that have long kept those groups divided. As the next chapter shows, community-labor alliances that initially developed through workfare workers' campaigns later reappeared in Los Angeles—and grew stronger—through campaigns to organize child care workers.

Chapter 6

But Who Will Watch the Children? State and Local Campaigns to Improve Child Care Policies[1]

Sometimes the wages that my clients make don't allow for child care. And it's only because of [government support] that it is possible for them to even have child care. If they had to pay for it on their own, they would be right back where they started in welfare-to-work because of the [lack of] child care. . . . If they raised the [child care] fees, more than likely, I would be out of business in the area that I live in.

–Child care provider, Los Angeles

I haven't been reimbursed for ninety days for one child and it doesn't look like it's going to happen any time soon because [of] all the red tape and paperwork and everything. Eventually child care providers are not going to want to bear the burden of subsidized care. . . . We can't operate ninety days behind on payments, especially when those payments aren't even going to be at the market rate. What's the benefit in it for us to not get paid what we deserve and then not get paid in a timely manner?

–Child care provider, Los Angeles

Refusing to . . . honor and respect and validate unwaged workers means you refuse to recognize the majority of our women on earth. . . . This is mothers who care for their children, the mothers who care for the elders, the mothers who care for the disabled, the mothers who care for the churches, and the mothers who care for the community, the mothers who care for the schools, the mothers who care for the neighborhoods. . . . Our goal is government-guaranteed child support until children are eighteen.

–Pat Gowens, founder of Welfare Warriors, Milwaukee[2]

IN ADDITION to sparking campaigns over workfare workers' rights, the implementation of new welfare-to-work requirements also gave new life to long-standing struggles over policies that regulated the care of children. This chapter examines three types of struggles over child care policies that ensued in Wisconsin and California in the wake of welfare reform. First, some welfare rights activists defended poor mothers' right to take care of their children, pushing for various exemptions from welfare-to-work requirements. Second, child care providers and children's advocates pushed for improvements in child care providers' rights as workers, such as higher wages and better working conditions as well as their right to influence the development of child care programs through collective bargaining. Finally, providers, low-income families, and other children's and welfare advocates demanded improvements in the availability of child care services. These three struggles over child care were certainly not the only ones. Other struggles, often involving professional associations and child care officials, focused on improving the quality and regulation of subsidized child care. In this chapter, I focus on these three demands—low-income parents' rights to provide care for their own children, working parents' access to affordable child care, and child care providers' labor rights—because they were the primary demands of base-building organizations that represented low-income parents and child care providers, a group composed mostly of racially and ethnically diverse women.

State policies had contradictory impacts on unions' and community organizations' efforts to shape child care policies. The emphasis of putting poor mothers to work within welfare reform created major setbacks in terms of poor mothers' rights to care for their own children at home. As Nancy Naples argues, the "new gendered consensus" on the U.S. welfare state was that poor, able-bodied mothers were unworthy of aid and expected to work.[3] Although federal-level work requirements for welfare mothers had been in place since 1967, states were now required to expand participation dramatically in welfare-to-work programs. The "new gendered consensus" discouraged all but a few welfare rights organizations from defending every mother's right to care for her own children. Instead, most welfare advocacy groups focused on expanding the exemptions from work requirements for particular groups of welfare mothers, such as the mothers of very young or disabled children, building alliances with children's and disability rights advocates around those demands. These more limited demands met with uneven success as policymakers across states and institutions varied in their views regarding the conditions under which welfare mothers should be exempt from work requirements and whether poor mothers' obligation to care for their own children sometimes outweighed their obligation to fulfill welfare-to-work requirements. The fate of these campaigns thus illustrates the multivocal character of the state and the difficulty of making policy gains in the absence of a broad-based coalition.

In contrast, the implementation of new welfare-to-work policies stimulated an expansion of subsidized child care programs, facilitating a new wave of union organizing among child care providers and increasing the opportunities to improve state-subsidized child care programs. To ease the transition from welfare to work, politicians at all levels invested to expand and improve the subsidized child care system. Although insufficient to meet the full demand for it, Congress authorized additional funds for subsidized child care through Temporary Assistance for Needy Families (TANF) and other federally funded programs.[4] State legislatures and local governments also increased their investments in subsidized child care. By 2002, thirty-three states were spending more in state and federal funds on child care than on cash assistance for poor families.[5] The expansion of subsidized child care, along with tough new work requirements, increased both the numbers of low-income working mothers reliant on these services and the numbers of home-based child care providers, many of whom were women of color. Both groups confronted problems in the administration of welfare reform and subsidized child care and became more organized. When community organizations and unions initiated new, multiracial campaigns to organize home-based child care providers, they also organized the families relying on their services, who also would benefit from improvements in the subsidized child care system. Thus, the implementation of welfare-to-work policies led to a coalescence between the labor movement and the welfare rights movement, and unions brought new resources and grassroots energy into state and local campaigns to improve subsidized child care programs.[6] While welfare recipients generally had antagonistic and impersonal relationships with the welfare contract staff who enforced welfare reform regulations,[7] they tended to have positive and personal relationships with contract child care providers—relationships that facilitated building community-labor alliances around child care issues. Unions mobilized child care providers statewide, bridging geographic as well as professional and ethnoracial divisions among them. Existing labor laws created challenges for unionizing home-based child care providers, however. As independent contractors or businesswomen, they lacked the right to collective bargaining and could only establish this right through the adoption of new state policies.[8]

As the case studies in California and Wisconsin illustrate, the fate of these various struggles over child care policies was often shaped by whoever held office at various levels of government. Support for extended maternity leave for welfare mothers was relatively stronger in California than Wisconsin, but it was still uneven. California county officials were allowed to exempt mothers from work requirements for up to twelve months after the birth of a child. County discretion over the implementation of welfare-to-work policies also gave advocates, particularly those in more liberal counties, the opportunity to push for other kinds of work exemptions for poor mothers. In the early years of welfare reform, efforts to defend the rights of poor mothers in Wisconsin to care for their own children faced staunch opposition from conservative legislators and the Republican governor, Tommy Thompson. State politicians in Wisconsin generally favored strict welfare-to-work requirements, which were enforced as soon as three months after childbirth. Nevertheless, persistent lobbying of state welfare officials by a small group of advocates led to modifications in the implementation of the state's welfare reform policies so that parents of disabled children could seek exemption from the state's welfare-to-work requirements and time limits.

Winning the governor's support was critical to the fates of both states' campaigns to unionize home-based child care providers. California's Republican governor, Arnold Schwarzenegger, a former professional body-builder and Hollywood actor, repeatedly vetoed legislation authorizing the right to bargain collectively for child care providers. Schwarzenegger was a fiscal conservative who was often at odds with unions; he first came into office in 2003 through a well-financed special recall election against then-governor Gray Davis and was re-elected in 2006. In both campaigns, Schwarzenegger promised to reduce taxes and to balance the state's budget through expenditure reductions. In contrast, Wisconsin's Democratic governor, Jim Doyle, was strongly supported by organized labor; through an executive order, he established home-based child care providers' right to unionize and negotiate with the state. These unionization campaigns thus illustrate how state actors could be the friend or foe of labor and welfare rights activists. They also show how broad-based alliances help to make policy gains. In both states, organized child care providers, their clients, and other child and welfare advocates managed to improve low-income parents' access to subsidized child care when welfare reforms were first implemented. After 2001, when fiscal conditions worsened, they succeeded in preventing or reducing various proposed cutbacks in child care spending.

Swimming Upstream: Struggles to Defend Maternal Caregiving in California and Wisconsin

Research on the implementation of welfare-to-work requirements documents how caseworkers and employment trainers encouraged welfare mothers to prioritize paid work over their obligations to take care of their children. It also reveals how welfare mothers resisted such expectations in their interactions with welfare staff and when they did not show up for appointments or welfare-to-work classes in order to take care of children or address family emergencies.[9] Such resistance is understandable, considering welfare-to-work participants often had to balance their families' needs with their work obligations while complying with other time-consuming welfare regulations, such as meeting with caseworkers and providing the necessary documentation to maintain eligibility.[10]

Evaluations of welfare reform suggest that increased work activity by welfare recipients has had mixed impacts on child well-being. On one hand, when poor mothers' transition from welfare to work leads to increased income, research suggests that it has positive effects on elementary-school children's educational achievement. On the other hand, some research indicates that this transition also has negative effects on adolescents' behavior and school performance, as more work also increases parental absence and stress.[11] The New Hope Project, a three-year experimental program in Wisconsin, gave low-income parents access to work supports, including an earnings supplement that raised their household incomes above the poverty line and subsidized child care and health insurance. Evaluations of the project found a largely positive impact of parental employment on children's outcomes in terms of behavioral problems and school performance, particularly for boys. A random assignment experiment showed that children's behavioral and educational outcomes were better among New Hope participants when compared to their counterparts in the Wisconsin Works program (W-2, Wisconsin's TANF program).[12] Interviews with W-2 participants suggest that many were critical of the rigid work requirements in the program, which interfered with their capacity to care for their children properly or to ensure that they received proper care from child care providers.[13] Based on their experiences, Collins and Mayer conclude that welfare reform "confront[s] single mothers with frequently untenable choices between degraded jobs and family well-being."[14]

California and the Every Mother Campaign

Many of the struggles waged in Wisconsin around welfare mothers' rights to care for their own children had already been won in California, when the state designed its welfare reform program, CalWorks. Unlike Wisconsin, California, along with thirty other states, exempted adult recipients from welfare-to-work requirements and welfare time limits if they were ill or incapacitated, or if they were caring for an ill or incapacitated person.[15] California also showed more initial support for providing an extended maternity leave from welfare-to-work activities, but support for it was still uneven. Prior to the implementation of welfare reform in

California, welfare mothers were only required to work after their child's third birthday. As state legislators designed their new welfare program, Governor Pete Wilson proposed that adult recipients of TANF be required to work as early as twelve weeks after childbirth, the same policy that was adopted in Wisconsin. Democrats proposed a more generous policy of providing recipients with twelve months of paid maternity leave. The executive director of the Coalition of California Welfare Rights Organizations condemned all of the proposals, claiming that they represented "the start of the coming slaughter that poor babies and children with families will be facing in 1998."[16] Finally, California adopted a policy that allowed counties to exempt mothers of young children up to one year of age but not less than twelve weeks old—representing a compromise between Republicans and Democrats.[17]

After California's new work requirements for welfare recipients were established, few groups challenged them. One such group was the Los Angeles chapter of the Every Mother Is a Working Mother Network (EMWM). Formed in 1997 by members of the International Wages for Housework Campaign, Every Mother had a fairly large mailing list but was mainly run by a small, racially diverse group of about ten to twenty volunteers, virtually all women.[18,19] Like Welfare Warriors in Wisconsin, Every Mother was committed to work on a long-term process of raising consciousness about the goal of compensating caregiving work, even if gains on this issue were unlikely in the short run. Appealing to socialist feminist ideas, Every Mother argued that poor mothers should be entitled to welfare as compensation for their unpaid—but socially significant—caregiving work:

> 'Women's work' of producing and daily reproducing the entire workforce is the basic ingredient of every economy and of all profit. Counting the value of that work, we establish our entitlement to welfare. . . . These are rights, not charities, wages we are owed for the unwaged work we do and have done for centuries.[20]

The group opposed the forced employment of welfare mothers on principle because it presumed that welfare mothers were not already working: "[Every Mother] seeks to establish that the time spent by mothers raising children and the economic value of their work must be reflected in welfare reform."[21] Their claims that mothers' caregiving work deserved compensation from the state revived the original arguments that reformers at the turn of the twentieth century made for the creation of state and local mothers' pensions and later for the creation of the federal Aid to Dependent Children program.[22] They also reflected radical and socialist feminists' demands in the 1960s and 1970s for "wages for housework" while echoing the critiques made by the National Welfare Rights Organization (NWRO) about federal welfare-to-work requirements.[23]

To protect low-income mothers' rights to welfare, Every Mother participated in numerous demonstrations, including the national "Stop the Clock Campaign," which urged the president to support a moratorium on time limits for welfare receipt.[24] They also urged that welfare benefit levels be raised to better compensate welfare mothers for their caregiving work, claiming, "Good care deserves good cash."[25] The organization also organized community dialogues, forums, and teach-ins, where its members publicly criticized the lack of a family allowance in the United States, the lack of paid maternity leave, and welfare cutbacks.[26] Members defended welfare rights both as "carers' right to payment" as well as "children's right to care."[27] They denounced welfare reform as "a racist attack," pointing out that "the majority of those on welfare are women and children of color."[28]

Like Welfare Warriors in Wisconsin, Every Mother found few allies among welfare rights groups or policymakers who would actively support welfare mothers' right to stay at home with their children, and thus they were unable to influence the design of state welfare reform policies.[29] In Los Angeles, most local welfare rights groups and unions mainly worked within the basic framework of welfare reform. From their perspective, challenging the devaluation of poor mothers' caregiving work within welfare reform policies was not an attainable goal in the short term. Every Mother found greater political support for modest expansions of poor mothers' rights to provide care for their children. Through meetings with Los Angeles County welfare officials, they obtained an agreement to require caseworkers to inform TANF recipients that they could not be sanctioned for refusing child care that they found unsuitable. They also had to inform recipients that they might be eligible for payment as "home-care workers" if they were caring for a family member.[30]

Wisconsin and Campaigns for Work Exemptions and Caregivers' Rights

In Wisconsin, advocates defending poor mothers' rights to take care of their own children faced greater challenges than their counterparts in California. As Collins and Mayer suggest in their extensive study of the program, W-2 was "the most work-focused [TANF program] in the nation."[31] The expectation that adult welfare recipients must work in exchange for their grants was so strongly enforced that parents who were unable to work due to a severe disability were removed from W-2 and given Supplemental Security Income (SSI) supplements instead.[32] As of 1999, Wisconsin was one of only ten states that required mothers receiving welfare to return to work three months after the birth of their child. Twenty-three other states allowed for a one-year work exemption, and five states allowed for an even longer period of time.[33] Various advocacy groups in Wisconsin urged politicians to allow welfare mothers more time to care for their children.

Like Every Mother in Los Angeles, Welfare Warriors, which represented former and current welfare mothers, ultimately sought to exempt all mothers of children under eighteen from work requirements, arguing that their work as caregivers should entitle them to receive welfare benefits. Like their counterparts in California, Welfare Warriors had difficulty finding allies in Wisconsin to support the goal of completely abolishing welfare-to-work requirements. Leaders of other welfare and children's advocacy groups believed that such demands would get little support from state policymakers. Disagreements over this issue were heated and ended Welfare Warriors' affiliation with the Coalition to Save Our Children, a broad coalition of children's advocacy organizations.[34] Welfare Warriors continued to fight for poor mothers' right to receive welfare as caregivers, often through public protests.

Most other welfare advocacy groups in Wisconsin sought limited exemptions from work requirements (for example, for mothers of infants or disabled children) through concerted lobbying. As a co-chair for the coalition explained, its agenda was mainly driven by "what's feasible and what some legislators are willing to work on."[35] Advocates pushed for welfare-to-work exemptions for women with high-risk pregnancies, pointing out how the rigid enforcement of work requirements among such women caused hardship. As a former welfare mother testified,

> I will have to move to a [homeless] shelter because my benefits were cut off mainly because I [have a] very high risk pregnancy (losing my baby possibly) and they still want me to work! I couldn't do it.[36]

Along with other groups, the coalition, the Interfaith Conference of Greater Milwaukee, and Wisconsin Council for Children and Families sought to exempt mothers with children under the age of one from work requirements.[37] The latter group pointed out how this policy would improve early childhood brain development by allowing for infants to receive intensive care from their mothers in their first months of life.[38] Its "Women of Change" group, composed of about sixteen W-2 participants, also testified at hearings, wrote letters, and visited legislators about the need for more time to care for their children.[39] Participants of the Wisconsin Works=Prosperity conference, which drew close to eight hundred people, also supported a one-year maternity benefit for W-2 participants.[40]

Democratic state policymakers also called for extending the work exemptions for mothers of infants, but not for a full year. In 2003, Democratic governor Jim Doyle and his administration actively promoted a six-month work exemption for welfare mothers, claiming that it would save about $4.2 million in child care subsidies.[41] Supporters pointed out how the policy would reduce state expenditures and allow more bonding time between parents and children.[42] In 2004, even as the governor urged W-2 agencies to reduce caseloads and to "re-emphasize that W-2 has a work focus," he continued to support a sixth-month maternity leave for W-2 participants. That year, state welfare officials estimated that the policy would save about $2.9 million in child care costs.[43] When the economy continued to decline as the decade wore on, Governor Doyle continued to promote a six-month maternity leave for W-2 participants as a cost-saving measure.[44]

The proposed six-month work exemption was vehemently opposed by state legislators, especially Republicans, however. They claimed that it undermined the emphasis placed on work within the W-2 system. Assemblyman John Gard vocally attacked this proposal, claiming that it represented a return to the old Aid to Families with Dependent Children (AFDC) model. In 2003, the state legislature's joint finance committee rejected the governor's plan to extend maternity benefits for the first six months after childbirth. Opponents claimed that this was a more generous maternity leave plan than other working women received. Democratic senator Gwen Moore urged her colleagues to reconsider the plan in light of recent findings by the U.S. Census that only 34 percent of mothers with infants less than twelve months old worked full-time.[45] She described the Joint Finance Committee's decision as reflecting a "mean-spirited grudge against women for reproducing when they are poor."[46] The governor's spokesman, Dan Leistikow, also criticized the decision: "They are going to spend an extra $4 million so that they can force new mothers to go to work instead of spending time with an infant."[47] In 2005, 2007, and 2008, state legislators repeatedly rejected both the six-month maternity leave plan and work exemptions for high-risk pregnancies.[48] Rejection of the proposed maternity leave extension reflected the balance of power within the state legislature and the strength of the "work first" philosophy in the legislature. The state senate was closely divided between the two parties in these years, but Republicans maintained firm control of the state assembly. This gave Republicans the upper hand in legislative debates, especially when Democrats sided with them, as they often did on welfare policies. When Democrats took control of the state assembly in 2009, the legislature finally approved W-2 benefits for women who experienced problem pregnancies during their last trimester. Yet, the proposed six-month maternity leave was defeated once again in 2009 when Democrats failed to unite behind it.[49]

Building Alliances with Disability Rights Advocates Given the strength of support for strict work requirements in the state legislature, welfare advocates sought help from state welfare officials to gain greater leniency for W-2 recipients who were parents of disabled children. Crossing policy domains, this demand also helped to gain the support of children's and disability rights advocates.[50] Even before W-2, mothers of disabled children, who found it difficult to find child care for their children, were being sanctioned for non-compliance with work requirements when they stayed home to care for their children. The Wisconsin Council on Developmental Disabilities was further alarmed when they learned that under W-2, "there was no ability for parents who took care of kids with disabilities to stay home."[51] The council documented the struggles that these women faced in an effort to persuade state officials to reconsider this policy:

> We did some surveys with families. We went into their homes and did interviews and [made] a videotape called "My Work Is at Home." It tells a story of three women who were taking care of kids with extreme disabilities and how they were caught. . . . We tried to show the range of disabilities in the video and the extent of what the women had to do at home. We produced some [reports] about how much work it took to take care of a child with disabilities.[52]

After meeting with welfare and disability rights advocates, state welfare officials agreed that, for parents of disabled children, their "work at home" could count toward their welfare-to-work requirements. Disability rights advocates also sought to better inform caseworkers on the rights of parents of disabled children and the need to be more flexible in terms of determining when they had a "good cause" to be noncompliant:

> We produced a W-2 record book so that a parent could take notes on all their activities and how many doctors they go to and come in and show it to the W-2 worker. There's a hell of a lot of ignorance in the W-2 caseworkers. When they went into the caseworker's office, they had something to show them. Otherwise, it was very hard for the family to keep track [of their doctor visits]. They could have seen fifteen doctors. This helped them to prove their cases of why they couldn't be in the workforce. . . . To help them with self-advocacy . . . we funded the W-2 disability hotline, and the Wisconsin Council on Children and Families implemented it. . . . We felt we made real progress.[53]

The highly publicized death of DeAndre Reeves, a thirteen-year-old boy with cerebral palsy in 1998, helped to give disability advocates leverage in their negotiations with welfare officials. Reeves accidentally scalded himself to death in a bathtub after his mother, a W-2 participant without access to subsidized child care, left him in the care of her teenage son. The teenager was downstairs making lunch when DeAndre, unable to call for help, turned on the hot water faucet. Yvette Reeves, a single mother, had previously been exempt from work in order to take care of her disabled son during the summer months. But implementing the new rules under W-2, her caseworker required her to take a job at Pizza Hut.[54] The dramatic story of DeAndre Reeves's death underscored the need to give parents of disabled children greater leeway in terms of fulfilling their work requirements. State welfare officials sought to distance themselves from accusations that W-2's tough new welfare rules were endangering the lives of vulnerable children.

Publicity surrounding DeAndre Reeve's untimely death also gave disability and children's rights advocates the leverage needed to push through a legislative expansion of subsidized child care services for these children in 1999.[55] As a disability rights advocate explained,

> [Originally] the child care was only available to kids up to age twelve. If you had a child who was thirteen and had severe disabilities, you received no child care assistance, a significant problem. One of the women [we interviewed] had a child who was turning thirteen, a boy with MD [musclar dystrophy]. She kept saying, "What am I going to do?" She's only making minimum wage and if she had to pay child care that would eat up her whole salary. Unfortunately, one child died and that is often how laws get changed. . . . And [Senator] Gwen [Moore] successfully advocated for that language to be changed. It's one of the first changes we got in W-2. . . . They changed the law so that if you have a child with a severe disability you can get child care assistance up to age eighteen.[56]

A broad coalition of disability, welfare, and children's rights advocates in Wisconsin also pushed for a legislative increase in the benefits given to severely disabled parents for the care of their children. Because they were unable to work, parents with severe disabilities were denied access to the work-based W-2 program and instead given a supplement to their regular grant from the SSI program a federal subsidy provided to disabled adults). Initially, this SSI supplement was set at $77 per month per child, far less than the amount these parents received under the old AFDC system (a basic grant of $363 per month for a parent with one child, plus $77 for each additional child). To advocate for higher benefits for these parents, advocates built a broad coalition—which eventually included as many as seventy different organizations—representing groups with an array of different types of disabilities and diseases, children's rights organizations, welfare rights groups, and women's groups.

To document the hardships that the dramatic reduction in these families' benefits would create, the Wisconsin Council on Developmental Disabilities collected about two thousand surveys and letters from affected families. The group then delivered these to their ally in the legislature, Senator Gwen Moore, who read them on the senate floor. "[She] would point to a different person and say, 'This one is from your district,' and so on. She worked nonstop to make change."[57] Disability rights advocates also teamed up with university researchers and women's groups, including the League of Women Voters, to interview about one hundred of the affected mothers about how the benefit cuts impacted their families. As one advocate explained, "We had people all over the state who volunteered to interview them, assuming that each time somebody interviewed you'd be so emotionally caught up that you'd become the good advocate for them, which people did."[58] In response to this public pressure, the state legislature raised the benefit to one hundred dollars per month per child in 1998.[59]

While the grant increase was helpful, it was still insufficient, so advocates pushed for a bigger increase. They produced more reports, including a booklet titled "Fragile Families" that documented the stories of the affected families. Advocates delivered the booklets to each legislator, using strategic timing:

> The day before we handed these out, this woman died. . . . She was in a house fire, a woman in a wheelchair, and she couldn't get out of the house. Her children were not with her. She was in a house with a lot of other people. She didn't have a lot of money and there were mattresses all over the floor. So [she] died and we released these the next day . . . [with] a letter about [the woman].[60]

The coalition also coached mothers receiving the Caretaker Supplement to speak and advocate for themselves. They organized a press conference and produced a video called "Parents on SSI Speak Out" that featured these mothers. Unable to obtain an official legislative hearing, advocates also organized their own public hearings.

> This woman traveled four hours each time we had a hearing to speak; she has a double lung transplant and it was failing. So she was severely disabled and came with all her equipment each time we asked. Quite a few parents came each time we asked and they wrote letters. They became their own self-advocates.[61]

Meanwhile, Senator Moore continued to build more support for the grant increase in the state legislature. Eventually, they prevailed. In 1999, the Wisconsin state legislature increased the Caretaker Supplement so that for the first child, parents would receive $250 and $150 more for each additional child. As one disability rights advocate put it, "The victory was tremendous . . . and now I don't think it will ever change for them again. . . . I don't think anyone will dare try to touch them again."[62]

Summary

In summary, Welfare Warriors in Wisconsin and Every Mother in Los Angeles found few allies, even among other welfare advocacy organizations, to support their goal of abolishing work requirements for adult TANF recipients, and the protests that they organized around those demands tended to be rather small. Even so, these groups' demands were significant because they openly challenged the "new gendered consensus" that requiring welfare mothers to work was good.[63] In addition, they drew attention to the classist, racist, and patriarchal assumptions underpinning this consensus and its devaluation of welfare mothers' caregiving work.

Most other welfare advocacy organizations turned their focus to gaining more limited work exemptions for certain kinds of welfare recipients through concerted lobbying. Their efforts brought new allies—such as disability rights advocates—into the struggle over the implementation of welfare reform. In California, welfare advocates and liberal politicians had greater influence over welfare reform legislation, which granted exemptions from welfare work requirements and time limits for disabled parents and those caring for disabled family members. Like their counterparts in Wisconsin, welfare advocates in California expanded the exemptions from work requirements by intervening in the implementation stage. For example, in Los Angeles, Every Mother persuaded county welfare officials to require their staff to inform TANF recipients that they could not be sanctioned for refusing child care that they found unsuitable. They also had to inform recipients that they might be eligible for payment as a "homecare worker" if they were caring for a family member.[64] When sympathetic officials were in office and advocates were mobilized, as they were in Los Angeles, such agreements were possible. In other California counties, however, less sympathetic welfare officials adopted strict work requirements and faced less pressure from welfare advocates to loosen them.

In Wisconsin, the state legislature included few exemptions from its tough new work requirements in its welfare reform policies. Nevertheless, policy implementation provided the opportunity for further policymaking. Advocates collected personal stories of hardship from welfare mothers with disabled children and used them for leverage with state policymakers who sought to distance themselves from these incidences. Disability and children's rights advocates expanded the opportunities for parents of disabled children to stay at home with their children through quiet and concerted lobbying of state welfare officials and caseworkers, taking advantage of the multivocal character of the state. Advocates also won legislative support for a larger grant for severely disabled parents, access to W-2 for women with problem pregnancies in their last trimester, as well as new rules allowing parents to enroll their disabled children in subsidized child care until they reach age eighteen. Yet not all battles were won. Efforts to change state welfare legislation to expand other low-income mothers' rights to stay at home with their children were stymied, even for mothers of young infants over three months of age and those with partial disabilities. Such demands conflicted with the "work first" ideology embraced by Wisconsin's legislators, especially Republicans who dominated the state assembly.

Subsidized Child Care: A Mountain of Grievances

Despite policymakers' efforts to expand and improve subsidized child care services to ease the transition "from welfare to work," there were new and persistent problems in the administration and delivery of these services. Even with increased funding in the late 1990s, subsidized child care programs were insufficient to meet the growing demand for them. The demand for affordable child care rose considerably in the 1990s as maternal employment increased, rates of single motherhood rose, and real wages stagnated and declined for most Americans.[65] When states were beginning to implement welfare reform in 1997, national surveys of working families with children under thirteen showed that the need for child care subsidies was great and especially acute among low-income, single-mother households. On average, child care used up to 9 percent of monthly earnings for all working families and 19 percent of earnings for low-income single parents. Nearly one-third (27 percent) of low-income families surveyed were spending more than 20 percent of their monthly earnings on child care.[66] Despite the high demand for affordable child care, national studies found that only about one-third of parents who left welfare for work received child care subsidies, while, at most, 15 percent of eligible families received them. These low figures were the result of multiple factors, including poor outreach, cumbersome application procedures, high co-payments, and shortages in child care spaces (particularly for infant care and night care).[67]

To make matters worse, when fiscal conditions declined after 2001, many states—at least half of them by 2008—began to roll back funds for subsidized child care.[68] These cutbacks, somewhat slowed by the infusion of federal stimulus funds, were carried out in various ways, including lowering real income limits for eligibility, creating waiting lists, increasing co-payments, or reducing reimbursement rates for providers or funds to improve the quality of child care. By 2010, two-fifths of states reported waiting lists for child care assistance or intake freezes.[69]

The staffing crisis was another major problem in the U.S. child care system, one that was exacerbated by child care workers' low wages. Average turnover among child care workers in centers is about 41 percent per year. A study of ninety-two centers found that between 1996 and 2000, 76 percent of all child care workers had left their jobs.[70] Expansions in child care funding did little to raise child care workers' salaries or improve their training or career prospects. Instead, as child care services for welfare recipients and low-income families increased, "voucher payments limited by market rate reimbursement policies increased as a proportion of public funding, and the lion's share of the public resources flowed increasingly to the least-trained and worst-paid sectors of the industry."[71] Most welfare recipients, like most parents, relied on informal, license-exempt child care workers or licensed family-based providers who were paid the least.[72]

The U.S. Bureau of Labor Statistics reports that child care workers nationally earned a median hourly wage of $9.25 and a median annual income of $19,240.[73] State policies contributed to these low wages and salaries. As fiscal conditions worsened, states lowered or froze their payment rates. By 2010, only about one-eighth of states set their reimbursement rates at the federally recommended level (75 percent of market rate), compared to over two-fifths of states in 2001.[74] Salaries for in-home providers were the worst in the industry. National labor statistics from the late 1990s showed that the median hourly wage for home-care providers ($3.37), who often worked long hours, was below that for fast food cooks ($5.42) and parking lot attendants ($6.38) and even below the national minimum wage.[75] Providers' financial difficulties were further exacerbated by bureaucratic delays and problems in the approval and payment of child care subsidies.[76]

In short, insufficient funding and poor administration of subsidized child care created numerous barriers in access to these services for welfare recipients and other low-income parents. Child care providers meanwhile received low wages, lacked benefits, and were often paid late for their services. Providers' and parents' many grievances with the child care system made both groups ripe for organizing. When community organizations and unions began to invest in organizing home-based child care providers and their clients, vibrant multiracial campaigns emerged and succeeded in protecting and improving the system of subsidized child care.

The Worthy Wage Campaign and Unionization of Child Care Providers

The post-1996 expansion of subsidized child care and the growing crisis of affordable child care helped foster an increasing level of activism among child care providers. This activism helped to bridge the divides between the welfare rights movement and the union movement. Efforts to organize these home-based child care providers grew out of two interrelated movements: the "Worthy Wage" movement and the union movement. As early as 1970, child care teachers in various cities began to raise consciousness about their need for higher wages, a cause that was later championed by the Worthy Wage Campaign. In these early years, child care activists were mostly young, college-educated white women who formed small support groups. They framed their demands in terms of economic justice and women's liberation and as part of a broader movement for a better child care system. Initially, they raised consciousness within their professional associations about the need for higher wages, producing research that demonstrated links between wage levels and quality of services. After gaining support from their professional associations, they began raising public consciousness about the issue through community and labor organizing. The movement was largely coordinated by the Child Care Employment Project, which later became a Washington, D.C.–based research and lobbying organization called the Center for the Child Care Workforce. The Worthy Wage Campaign, a multi-year public awareness campaign, was launched in 1991 and quickly spread across the country. This campaign involved a variety of actions, including provider walk-outs, marches, demonstrations, and public forums.

After 1995, the Worthy Wage movement grew increasingly visible. As home-based child care and the child care industry expanded in the wake of welfare reform, more and more child care workers joined in the movement, finding allies in unions, researchers, program administrators, and policymakers. Widespread support for various child care initiatives expanded as the child care staffing crisis unfolded, activism among child care providers and their clients increased, and new research on brain development showed the importance of quality of care during children's early years. As a result, state and local governments in the 1980s and 1990s funded various pre-kindergarten programs; they also developed initiatives to compensate child care workers' training. Most of these wage improvement initiatives were small, temporary programs that linked compensation to workers' levels of education, training, and experience in an effort to improve the quality of services by increasing workers' retention and professional development.[77] Activists within the Worthy Wage movement came into greater contact with both unions and the welfare rights movement; together, all three groups responded to the challenges and opportunities associated with the expansion of subsidized child care services.

Although the Worthy Wage Campaign was largely a public awareness and lobbying campaign, some activists in the movement and other child care workers formed unions in their effort to improve their wages and working conditions. In the 1960s, child care workers in New York City joined the American Federation of State, County, and Municipal Employees (AFSCME), while in the 1970s, workers in Massachusetts, Michigan, and Wisconsin joined the United Auto Workers (UAW). In the 1980s and 1990s, other unions got involved in organizing providers in child care centers and Head Start programs, including Service Employees International Union (SEIU), the American Federation of Teachers (AFT), the International Brotherhood of Teamsters, and the International Union of Painters and Allied Trades. These early unionization campaigns were small-scale and mainly waged "in response to requests by center employees to join a union, not as part of a strategic effort to organize the entire profession."[78]

As of 2004, only about 3 percent of the total child care workforce belonged to a union or was covered by a union contract.[79] Home-based providers organized in the 1980s and 1990s but did so through independent associations such as Direct Action for Rights and Equality in Rhode Island rather than through unions.[80] Until the late 1990s, unions had little interest in organizing family-based child care workers partly because the child care workers counted as small-business owners and thus were not covered by existing labor laws and lacked the legal right to bargain collectively. There were three other major challenges as well that discouraged unions from investing resources into organizing child care workers. Job turnover was extremely high, and the work was highly decentralized, scattering workers widely across job sites that usually employed only a few workers. Moreover, many child care providers saw themselves as professionals and did not identify readily with unions. Nevertheless, their low wages, payment problems, long work hours, and lack of health insurance made child care providers a group ripe for organizing. Formal and informal social networks created through their professional associations and training experiences also facilitated their organization.[81]

Renewed interest among unions in organizing child care workers, including home-based providers, emerged from the coalescence of unions' interest in gaining new members and advocates' interest in improving child care policies. From unions' perspective, home-based child care workers represented a growing sector of the low-wage labor force. By 2007, there were approximately 1.8 million home-based providers, 99 percent of whom were women. They provided care for about 42 percent of all children receiving child care services in the United States. About 804,000 of these providers were related to the children, while 650,000 were unrelated to them. About 298,000 were non-relatives that worked in the child's home. Some of these providers were regulated home-based centers, while others were friends, family, or neighbors who were license-exempt.[82]

Various new campaigns to organize child care workers emerged in the late 1990s. SEIU and AFSCME collaborated with child care advocates in two successful campaigns to organize providers in Seattle, Washington, and Philadelphia, Pennsylvania. These positive experiences encouraged both unions to organize more child care workers. SEIU also found there was considerable interest in unionization among home-based child care providers when it began organizing the sector in 1996 in Illinois. Keystone Research Center and other child-advocacy organizations organized two national conferences (in 1996 and 1998) to discuss how to unionize child care workers, generating new strategic ideas. At about this time, the Center for the Child Care Workforce also discussed the formation of a national child care union with several unions. The Association of Community Organizations for Reform Now (ACORN) also began to organize home-based providers in the late 1990s. By 2002, it was engaged in these campaigns in six states. These early campaigns to organize home-based child care providers by SEIU, AFSCME, ACORN, and Direct Action for Rights and Equality attracted the attention of organized labor and showed them that this sector could be organized.[83]

Eventually, both SEIU and AFSCME pursued large-scale efforts to organize child care workers, focusing initially on workers in Head Start centers and then on home-based providers. The unions developed a model for organizing home-based providers based on home health care campaigns, which gained national attention in 1999 when SEIU organized 74,000 of these workers in Los Angeles. Home-based child care providers were very similar to providers of home-based health care in many ways. In both cases, the labor performed by these providers—mostly women of color—was highly devalued. The home-based nature of this intimate labor rendered the social contributions of these workers even more invisible to the public. Additionally, the skills involved in caring for others have long been presumed to come naturally to women, rather than through training and experience. Like home-based health care workers, home-based providers sought greater public recognition of their skills and training. In public testimonies, they emphasized how they were not "babysitters" or "playmates" for children but serious workers with knowledge about child development. Moreover, like home health care providers, home-based child care providers were paid through subsidies from the state, providing a rationale for treating the state as the employer of record and as a political target for campaigns to improve these services. Like home health care workers, home-based child care providers had to first gain the legal right to collective bargaining through new state legislation or gubernatorial executive orders before unionization was possible. They otherwise lacked these rights as independent contractors or small-business owners. Finally, both industries involved personal services whose clients could be mobilized in support of organizing campaigns.[84]

By the start of 2007, campaigns to unionize home-based providers had occurred or were underway in at least fourteen states.[85] Most of these campaigns were conducted by SEIU and AFSCME, but the AFT, UAW, Communications Workers of America (CWA), and ACORN were also involved. Initially, there was a bitter turf war between SEIU and AFSCME over which union should represent child care workers. In 2006, the two unions signed an agreement through which they split up seventeen states, including split regions in Minnesota, and formed a joint union, the United Child Care Union, in California and Pennsylvania.[86] AFSCME also formed partnerships to organize child care providers with UAW in Michigan and CWA in New Jersey.[87] The AFT, whose educational foundation merged with the Center for the Child Care Workforce in 2002, also formed a national Child Care Workforce Alliance, an "associate membership program" for child care providers to join together to improve their working conditions and unite "Worthy Wage" activists both inside and outside of labor unions.[88] While unions' organizing models varied slightly across states and counties, they generally sought to gain legal recognition of their right to bargain collectively with the state through passage of special legislation or executive orders by governors.[89]

Between 2005 and February of 2007, seven states—Illinois, Iowa, Michigan, New Jersey, Oregon, Washington, and Wisconsin—had authorized unions the right to organize and represent home-based child care providers and to negotiate with state officials on their behalf. Between March of 2007 and June of 2010, an additional seven states joined them: Kansas, Maine, Maryland, New Mexico, New York, Ohio, and Pennsylvania. By June of 2010, union contracts had been negotiated in twelve of these fourteen states. Child care providers' unions also obtained local authorization to represent providers in three Minnesota counties. In three states—Rhode Island, California, and Massachusetts—authorizing legislation was passed but was vetoed by the governor, and providers lacked rights to unionize as of June 2010.[90]

Unions' efforts to organize child care providers brought new vitality to state and local campaigns to improve child care services. Not only did unions invest resources into organizing child care providers, they also organized families receiving state child care subsidies around shared concerns, such as maintaining funding for these services. Home-based child care workers provided a service that was intimate in nature, creating close bonds between clients and workers that could be used to forge community-labor coalitions. These workers often provided clients with flexible scheduling not offered at larger child care centers. Since they worked at home, many home-based providers would allow parents to drop off their children at early hours in the morning or to pick them up late at night; they renegotiated child care schedules in order to accommodate parents' shifting work schedules. Providers also gained parents' trust and friendship through the intimate care that they provided to their children as well as regular personal interactions with them. Providers and their clients, often both women of color, frequently lived in the same neighborhood and were linked through personal referrals and relationships, including those between their children; these commonalities and shared ties helped to strengthen clients' loyalty to providers. The children under providers' care also frequently developed feelings of adoration and respect for these workers, as well as personally benefiting from state subsidies. All of these factors, in addition to parents' own grievances with the child care system, helped providers to solicit the support of their clients in their campaign to improve the subsidized child care system and to gain collective bargaining rights. Moreover, because these services were grossly underfunded, both clients and workers had joint interests in improving state funding for child care work. Since improving compensation has been shown to reduce worker turnover in these industries, many clients were supportive of providers' demands for higher wages.

Unionization was presented as a way to strengthen providers' capacity to improve their wages and working conditions as well as the quality and accessibility of child care services.[91] Child care providers' struggles were motivated not simply by interests in improving their labor rights but also by the "ethic of care."[92] As other scholars have found, child care providers and their advocates strategically deployed a "vocabulary of skill" as well as a "vocabulary of virtue."[93] They emphasized their training and skills in order to justify better wages and benefits and highlighted research linking higher wages with lower turnover rates among providers. They also expressed their concern for their clients' welfare and fought for policies to improve the quality and accessibility of subsidized child care for low-income families.[94] As they did in home-based health care campaigns, unions organizing providers drew on social movement and community-organizing tactics, on top of strategies developed by earlier efforts to organize these workers outside of unions. Such strategies included the formation of client-worker alliances, which would pressure states to recognize workers' rights to collective bargaining as well as maintain and improve funding for their services.[95] From the perspective of the unions, expanding funds for subsidized child care promised to expand the size of their membership and increase their members' wages. There was thus a coalescence between the traditional goals of unions (increasing wages and expanding union membership) and those of the welfare rights movement in expanding low-income parents' access to subsidized child care and improving its quality. This is why unions invested in organizing state-level lobby days around this particular welfare rights issue but not other ones.

As the campaigns in California and Wisconsin illustrate, child care organizing campaigns confronted different political conditions across U.S. states, leading to different outcomes for child care providers' unionization. The failure of the unionization campaign in California versus the success of the one in Wisconsin was largely due to differences in gubernatorial politics. Whereas child care unions found a friend in the statehouse in Wisconsin, they found a foe in California. Yet, in both states, organized providers helped to maintain and improve low-income parents' access to subsidized child care.

Struggles to Improve Subsidized Child Care in California

As in Wisconsin, California witnessed an expansion and restructuring of subsidized child care with welfare reform that generated new opportunities for child care advocacy and unionization. And like their counterparts in Wisconsin, California's home-based child care providers organized—first outside of unions and then within them—to expand and improve low-income families' access to subsidized child care as well as providers' rights to collective bargaining. Yet, whereas Wisconsin's Governor Doyle authorized providers' collective bargaining rights, those rights were blocked through gubernatorial veto in California. The California campaign helps to illustrate the challenges that existing labor laws created for providers' unionization, but also how providers could improve child care policies through mobilization even without union recognition.

In California, eligibility rules for child care subsidies were more liberal than they were in Wisconsin, but funding was inadequate.[96] In the wake of welfare reform, total state and federal child care funding more than tripled in the state between 1996 and 2005, from $926 million to $3.3 billion.[97] Nevertheless, insufficient funding left many qualified children without subsidized child care. By 2003, the California Department of Education estimated that as many as 260,000 families were on waiting lists for subsidized child care in the state. The study, based on data from nine

California counties, found that nearly 71 percent of families waiting for subsidized child care had been waiting for over one year; about half had been waiting for at least four years.[98] Families were technically eligible to receive child care subsidies if they earned up to 75 percent of the state's median income. However, funding limits, plus rules giving priority to current and former welfare recipients and the lowest-income families, meant that only families earning 35 percent of the state's median income typically received the subsidies.[99] Child care shortages were particularly deep in the state's largest county, Los Angeles, where more than forty-two thousand low-income families in the county—mostly families of color—remained on waiting lists for subsidies, while fewer than one in ten children served by TANF received them in 1999.[100]

For all families, licensed child care centers were also scarce, partly because low worker wages made it difficult to maintain staffing. Statewide, there was only one licensed day-care space for every five children in need in 1999. In at least seven counties, this ratio was more than one-to-six.[101] In Banning, which had one of the lowest number of licensed day-care spaces per child in the state, about sixty children regularly used the public library in the afternoon because they had nowhere else to go.[102] The Fresno County Child Care Planning Council found that "many rural areas have no licensed child care facilities."[103] Especially lacking were providers who spoke languages other than English, making it difficult for immigrants with limited English proficiency to utilize subsidized child care. For example, a 2001 study found that just over one-third of child care centers serving Spanish-speaking children had providers that spoke the same language.[104]

The implementation of welfare reform in California presented new opportunities to push for improvements in subsidized child care and increased the interest in this issue, stimulating the formation of new kinds of child care advocacy groups and action by local officials. In Los Angeles, the county formed a Child Care Task Force that included broad community representation. Partly through their participation on this task force, about 250 community organizations pressed for expansions in after-school child care. In response, county supervisors agreed to allocate $74 million to create a free after-school program in 225 public schools for low-income families. Once created, Every Mother and its allies pushed for more improvements through meetings with local school officials and "community dialogues" involving about fifty community members.[105] Pressed by Every Mother and other advocates, local welfare officials also agreed to provide child care for eleven- and twelve-year-olds.[106] Similarly, the Asian Pacific Policy Planning Council, representing over fifty Asian American service organizations, formed a child care committee. Through its participation in the county's Child Care Task Force and other meetings with county supervisors, the group persuaded county officials to allocate funds to increase the supply of Asian American child care providers and to provide more outreach to low-income Asian Americans to inform them about child care subsidies.[107]

As welfare reform unfolded, actions to increase the availability of child care occurred in various municipalities. In San Francisco, about two hundred people marched to City Hall during "Speak Up for Kids Day" and urged local politicians to provide more funds for child care services and to support universal child care.[108] In Fresno County, where six thousand children remained on the waiting list for subsidized child care, the Children's Services Network held a two-hour vigil to highlight the need for more child care money. Participants held hundreds of green balloons to symbolize all of the families waiting for child care, some of whom had been waiting since 1985, and urged state legislators to add $300 million to the child care budget.[109]

The expansion of subsidized child care created new opportunities to organize the workers and independent contractors providing these services. By 2000, there were about forty-seven thousand child care providers in California, with eleven thousand located in Los Angeles County. In 1999, two groups, the Welfare Reform Coalition and ACORN, began to organize these providers in Los Angeles.[110] The Welfare Reform Coalition, a coalition of welfare rights activists and social service providers, organized licensed providers and working parents around child care issues.[111] In 1999, the group drew 270 low-income parents for their "Parents' Convention on Child Care." Out of their discussions with parents, the Welfare Reform Coalition formulated a "families first" child care agenda. They called for maintaining quality and choice in child care services. In particular, they urged for all to support a simpler application process; greater flexibility in hours and care for infants and sick or disabled children; more prompt responses by county agencies to applications, referrals, payments, and complaints; and greater stability in the services provided.[112] To increase the public's attention on child care issues, staff members wrote several reports and articles documenting problems in the county's bureaucratically complex and underfunded child care system.[113] The Welfare Reform Coalition also educated low-income parents about their rights to child care subsidies through the distribution of small, easy-to-read palm cards.[114] But despite these seeming victories, the Welfare Reform Coalition's child care campaign proved to be short lived. In 2001, the coalition lost both its director and most of its staff. Under its new director, the organization shifted its focus to other issues.

Meanwhile, ACORN expanded its child care campaign (which initially focused on license-exempt providers) to include licensed providers. ACORN's campaign grew out of its efforts to organize welfare mothers, many of whom had difficulty finding child care. County officials frequently paid their child care providers late or failed to pay them for all the hours they worked. In response, many child care providers refused to take care of welfare mothers' children, creating an obstacle to welfare recipients' employment.[115] As welfare mothers began to organize around these issues, they brought their child care providers to meetings and actions.

In 2000, welfare mothers and child care providers organized by ACORN—mostly African American and Latina women—jointly protested the county's pay structure for child care services. For state-subsidized child care, license-exempt (in-home) providers were paid $2.93 per hour, while licensed providers were paid under $4/hour per child. Some of these providers, especially the unlicensed child care providers caring for relatives' or friends' children, only took care of one child. As a result, they were paid less than the state-mandated minimum wage. In protest, a group of about twenty welfare mothers, child care providers, and lawyers held a press conference in the State Labor Commissioner's office, calling on him to investigate these minimum-wage law violations. Wielding giant stuffed dogs, they expressed outrage that the county's child care providers were paid far less than the county's dog catchers. One welfare mother explained how these low wages harmed not simply the child care providers but also the parents and children who relied on them:

> When we have to leave our children in the hands of under-paid and resentful providers, we as parents have a much harder time staying focused on our work. How can the state place such a low priority on the well-being of our children?[116]

Welfare mothers also pointed out that the county was encouraging many of them to become paid child care providers, which would leave them in poverty given the current wage structure. At the time of the protest, the state had a surplus of $12 billion, which ACORN members argued should be used to increase the wages for child care providers.[117] While the Labor Commissioner agreed to look into the matter, there was never any official change in the county's pay scales. Nevertheless, the protest illustrates how activists attempted to use one branch of the state to pressure another.

After a few such joint actions between welfare mothers and their child care providers, ACORN formed Child Care Providers for Action. Within a year, the group grew into a three-hundred member organization of mostly Latina and African American women who paid dues to ACORN and participated in meetings, events, and actions that aimed to improve state and local child care policies and providers' working conditions. Many Latina members were Spanish-speaking, so ACORN staff took measures to maximize their participation within the organization. They hired a bilingual organizer, used simultaneous translation equipment at meetings, and translated all flyers into both Spanish and English. Members were also careful to elect a balanced number of African Americans and Latinas to leadership positions in the organization.[118] Although an African American male organizer was initially assigned to the campaign, the campaign was reassigned to two female staff organizers, one Latina and the other an African American, in order to more closely match the demographic makeup of home-based child care providers in Los Angeles.[119] Membership meetings drew about seventy-five to eighty-five people, while a child care providers' Health and Safety Fair attracted several hundred people.[120]

At first, ACORN focused on holding the county's resource and referral agencies accountable for their irregular payments to providers.[121] About a dozen of these agencies, working on contract, administered Los Angeles County's subsidized child care program.[122] In earlier meetings with other child care advocates, local welfare officials promised to hold these agencies accountable for late payments, but problems with late payments persisted.[123] Like the private welfare contractors in Milwaukee described in chapter 4, these agencies sought to maintain their contracts and so were vulnerable to public pressure, especially if it was combined with negative publicity. ACORN negotiated agreements with the agencies to create a grievance system and to process providers' complaints in a timely fashion.[124] The most resistance to their demands came from an agency called Equipoise. Only after Providers for Action stormed Equipoise's offices did the agency agree to adopt the new grievance procedures. Through this new grievance system, many child care providers obtained their backpay.[125] Resource and referral agencies were both targets and potential allies for child care providers as both groups sought to increase funding for publicly subsidized child care. Recognizing such shared interests, the Los Angeles Alternative Payment Alliance, representing the county's resource and referral agencies, allowed ACORN to use their facilities to hold a candidates' forum. At the forum, Providers for Action members urged legislative candidates to increase reimbursement rates for subsidized child care, a demand shared by resource and referral staff.[126]

Organized providers also provided new energy behind statewide child care advocacy. Beginning in 2001, as fiscal conditions worsened, various new eligibility restrictions for child care subsidies were proposed, child care funding began to decline in real dollars, and the income ceiling for eligibility was administratively frozen.[127] In 2001, Governor Davis also vetoed $24 million from the state's TANF budget, telling policymakers that he would only restore the funds after they agreed to restructure the child care system so that current and former welfare recipients were not prioritized over working poor families for access to child care subsidies.[128]

Former welfare recipients who had received subsidized child care for more than two years were notified that they would be cut off from subsidies. In response, organized providers, low-income parents, and other children's advocates mobilized against these cutbacks. For example, Providers for Action initiated a postcard campaign, collecting signatures from parents using subsidized child care, including welfare recipients and other low-income families. The postcards opposed the governor's proposed cutbacks and urged him to increase funds for subsidized child care.[129] The group also pushed for increased state funding to expand child care services and to provide for living wages and health insurance for child care workers, sending hundreds of people to the state capital to demonstrate and lobby.[130] In response to this and other widespread pressure, the governor restored $18.7 million to the child care budget to prevent cutoffs that were expected to affect about three thousand families per month.[131]

In 2002, California experienced what one reporter described as the "steepest revenue drop since World War II."[132] New struggles to protect subsidized child care services emerged, and Democrats and advocates of the poor lobbied for increasing state revenues through new taxes and fees. Governor Davis opposed these proposals and instead pushed for various cutbacks in social services, including subsidized child care.[133] The governor proposed to "increase parent fees, reduce provider rates, and cut about 20,000 children out of the system"[134] through new eligibility rules in order to create nearly 125,000 new child care placements.[135] Advocates of children and the poor criticized the plan, claiming that it would cause hardship and create those new child care slots by taking child care away from other low-income families.[136] In response, participants at the Working Families Policy Summit called for a comprehensive child care plan and urged the state to subsidize $1.2 billion more for child care services in order to cover the 232,000 children who were not receiving the care they needed.[137] Proposed child care cutbacks were also criticized at a forum for nonprofit organizations.[138] Organized providers signed petitions against the plan and expressed concerns in a meeting with the state welfare director, claiming that proposed fee increases were too high.[139] Along with parents and other child care advocates, child care providers testified before state policy advisors against the proposed cutbacks, emphasizing how they would force parents back onto welfare and put child care centers out of business.[140] They also organized a public forum on child care, attended by state and local politicians, to draw attention to the proposed cutbacks and promote improvements in the state's child care policies.[141] In response to advocates' pressure, the governor backed down from the proposed cutbacks. As one reporter put it: "After months of intensive lobbying, 'stakeholders meetings' and parent protests, the state's $3.2 billion child care industry was left untouched."[142]

In 2003, the governor proposed another round of budget cuts, including a proposal to end guaranteed child care subsidies for former welfare mothers.[143] The governor also proposed giving control over child care funds to counties, which could lead to cutbacks if counties reallocated the money to other services.[144] The proposal sparked protests even in smaller cities around the state. Almost one hundred concerned parents and child care providers gathered in downtown Redlands to protest the plan, for instance.[145] Parent Voices (an organization of parents receiving subsidized child care) organized a rally at the state capitol in opposition to the proposed cutbacks in subsidized child care.[146] In 2004, about one thousand people in Los Angeles marched in opposition to another round of proposed cutbacks in social services for children. The march, organized by the Say Yes to Children Network, included a broad alliance of preschoolers, Providers for Action, children's advocacy organizations, service providers, and various unions.[147]

By 2004, Providers for Action claimed 1,200 members in Los Angeles, attracting the interest of SEIU. Interest in unionization was strong among child care providers, who were eager to improve their working conditions and to oppose proposed cutbacks in subsidized child care. Although ACORN mainly organized providers within the city, its office received calls from providers throughout the county, and even from neighboring counties, who were interested in joining the organization. ACORN's success also attracted the interest of SEIU. Interested in initiating a statewide campaign to organize home-based child care providers, the union offered a large sum to ACORN to hand over its campaign to SEIU. Believing that this move would be best for providers since the union had more resources for organizing, ACORN staff recommended the organizational transfer to the members and leaders of Providers for Action, whose members ratified the transfer agreement. Shortly afterward, Providers for Action's move to SEIU was announced at ACORN's 2004 national convention in Los Angeles.[148]

After taking control of Providers for Action in 2004, SEIU engaged in a statewide "organizing blitz" that involved as many as forty organizers to collect union cards from child care providers. Organizers from other cities were sent to Los Angeles, where about one thousand union authorization cards were collected. About seven hundred cards were collected in other cities in California.[149] Afterward, SEIU assigned a team of local organizing staff to organize regional meetings, distribute local newsletters, and develop members' leadership skills. Child care providers in California had also been organized by AFSCME, causing a bitter turf war between AFSCME and SEIU. Eventually, the two unions brokered an agreement that SEIU would represent child care providers in thirteen California counties, including Los Angeles County, while AFSCME represented providers in the rest of the state's counties. The two unions agreed to pool resources for common campaigns.[150] Yet tensions between SEIU and AFSCME persisted for some time despite this agreement. Some AFSCME staff and leaders resented SEIU, believing that they were pressured into this agreement and forced to cede ground to SEIU, which had raided their unions.[151] SEIU, meanwhile, was disappointed when AFSCME organized its own statewide lobby day in 2006 and did not participate in the one that SEIU planned.[152] Despite these difficulties faced by the two unions, they both continued to work toward the same goals, and by 2007 relations had improved, and SEIU and AFSCME engaged in a joint child care lobby day.

A major goal of both unions was to obtain legislation that gave home-based child care providers the legal right to form a union—a right they lacked as small business owners. Toward this goal, union activists organized lobby days at the state capitol that drew hundreds of child care providers, plus hundreds of their clients and other supporters from around the state. Parents and children also gave letters of support to their providers to hand to legislators. AFSCME and SEIU repeatedly won legislative support for a bill that would give child care providers the legal right to form a union and engage in collective bargaining, but Governor Arnold Schwarzenegger—a Republican and no friend of organized labor—vetoed it each time.

While the lack of collective bargaining rights limited the power and capacity of organized providers considerably, it still managed to improve the lives of child care providers. In 2008, Child Care Providers United offered a basic health and dental insurance plan to its "associate members." A survey carried out by ACORN revealed that most of its organized child care providers were licensed, worked full-time, and had children who were minors. About 60 percent of them earned less than $39,000, while nearly half (46 percent) lacked health insurance.[153] Although this plan represented a major step forward, the union was unable to obtain a comprehensive health insurance plan because it lacked formal collective bargaining rights.[154]

Through lobbying, SEIU and AFSCME members and other child care advocates also helped to avert or reduce a series of proposed cutbacks in subsidized child care and to obtain support for an increase in the reimbursement rates for providers. Facing a deficit of $14 billion, Governor Schwarzenegger's budget plan for 2004 included $165 million worth of cuts in child care services through more restrictive eligibility rules and increased fees.[155] In 2005, the governor proposed even harsher restrictions, limiting guaranteed subsidies to former welfare recipients to one year.[156] Child care providers, working parents, and children joined together with other advocacy organizations to protest these proposals.[157] Even county supervisors expressed concerned about the local impacts of the proposed cutbacks.[158] The Central Valley Children's Services Network pointed out how the proposed cutbacks would hurt workers' jobs, especially impacting low-wage agricultural and service workers, who, in Tulare County, spent about 32 to 42 percent of their income on child care for one child.[159] Parent Voices organized a letter-writing campaign against the proposed cuts to subsidized child care.[160] Democrats urged tax increases and ends to prior tax breaks, calling the proposed service cuts "a tax on the poor" and "immoral." At a forum of child care providers and advocates, five legislators in the Bay Area vocally opposed proposed cuts to subsidized child care.[161] Mobilizing hundreds of providers from around the state, unionized child care providers held statewide lobby days in Sacramento, urging politicians to reject the proposed cutbacks.

In response to all this public pressure, and because tax revenues were higher than expected in 2004, the governor softened his proposed time limits for subsidized child care.[162] Parent Voices, child care providers, and other advocates also celebrated the prevention of $67 million worth of proposed cuts in child care in 2006.[163] Speaking at a rally of working parents in Sacramento, Patty Siegel, director of the California Child Care Resource and Referral Network, remarked, "We've had such huge fights these last five years just to keep what we have. This has been the first year that we've had a little reprieve." The group further urged policymakers to raise the income ceiling for eligibility for subsidized child care, which had been frozen at 1998 levels at $35,000 a year for a family of three.[164]

Ballot initiatives, promoted by organized providers and other children's advocates, also helped to generate new child care funds, even as legislators were rolling them back. Proposition 10, a state tax on tobacco for childhood health and development projects for children during their first five years, provided an important new source of revenue for child care programs. In 2002, Los Angeles officials voted to spend $100 million on a pilot program for universal preschool for every three- to four-year-old in the county, initially targeting low-income children; at the time, at least one hundred thousand toddlers were on the county's waitlist for subsidized child care.[165] Other California counties used Proposition 10 money to improve child care workers' salaries or for capital improvement projects for child care centers.[166] In 2006, voters passed Proposition 49, authorizing funds to expand after-school programs.[167]

Also in 2006, children's advocates and child care providers' unions promoted a state ballot initiative, Proposition 82, to create a statewide universal preschool program for all four-year-old children. But wealthy donors and business groups funded and organized a campaign to defeat the proposition. Opponents vehemently attacked Rob Reiner, head of the state's Proposition 10 commission, for using state funds to advocate for the initiative. They managed to defeat the proposition despite early polls showing broad support for it. In response to the strong support for expanding the state's preschool programs, the legislature and the governor passed a bill to authorize $50 million to expand preschool programs for children living in the areas of the lowest-performing schools and another $50 million to improve preschool facilities.[168] The bill was expected to serve about 8,500 four-year-olds in California, representing a significant gain for the families served by it. However, there were 500,000 four-year-olds in California, and the new program paled in comparison to preschool initiatives authorized in other states. For example, Georgia, with only about one-quarter of California's population, spent $245 million for preschool for four-year-olds.[169]

Union investment in California's home-based child care campaign was uneven, making it difficult to maintain support from members and leaders. For example, while SEIU assigned half a dozen organizers to the Los Angeles campaign in 2005, by 2008, SEIU had only two organizers for the entire state.[170] Unions were hesitant to fully invest in the campaign when Governor Schwarzenegger repeatedly vetoed bills authorizing their right to represent home-based child care providers. Yet even without steady union investment or collective bargaining rights, organized providers and their clients, together with a broad array of children's and welfare advocacy organizations and organized parents, had helped to safeguard the state's subsidized child care system from various proposed cutbacks and to gain support for additional public funds for child care services. Despite these victories, shortages in the availability of affordable child care remained. Hundreds of thousands of low-income families remained on waiting lists for subsidized child care in California due to insufficient funds, and voters rejected a ballot initiative to create a statewide universal preschool program.

Improving Subsidized Child Care in Wisconsin

Just as in California, the implementation of welfare reform in Wisconsin increased the state's investments in subsidized child care. As Jean Rogers, state welfare administrator, explained to the press, "From the beginning, Governor [Tommy] Thompson has emphasized the need to invest heavily in child care as a supportive service for working parents."[171] With the adoption of W-2, the state tripled its investment in subsidized child care, investing $20 million, on top of another $5 million in capacity building, and succeeded in eliminating the state's waiting list for child care subsidies.[172] As in California, expansions in the subsidized child care system encouraged mobilization by providers and clients in two ways. First, it expanded their numbers. Second, the implementation of new child care policies and funds created new problems, or exacerbated long-standing issues, around which they could organize.

Poor outreach, high co-payments, burdensome regulations, inflexible care schedules, and poor administration of the program prevented thousands of qualified parents from using these subsidies, causing problems for parents and providers alike. Although the state allocated enough child care money to provide coverage for seventy-seven thousand parents, only twenty thousand were using child care subsidies in 1998.[173] A survey by state welfare officials found that more than half of former W-2 participants who did not use subsidized child care relied instead on informal care arrangements with family members.[174] Such arrangements were often preferred because family members charged less than centers and were more likely to offer evening and weekend care.[175] Low-income mothers also had difficulty getting approved for child care subsidies or found the co-payments too expensive.[176]

Many low-income parents were not aware that they were eligible for child care subsidies because of insufficient outreach, especially in the early years of W-2. Consistent with W-2's "light touch" philosophy, in the early years of W-2, caseworkers frequently did not provide information about welfare services, including subsidized child care, unless they were directly asked about them.[177] As discussed in chapter 4, in response to pressure from advocates, federal U.S. Department of Agriculture officials, and negative media coverage, state W-2 officials agreed to end the "light touch" approach and directed agencies to provide more information about benefits and services to welfare applicants and recipients through policy memos and training sessions. Although problems with outreach remained, these policy shifts improved recipients' access to subsidized child care and other supportive services.[178]

There were numerous complaints, from both parents and child care providers, about the inefficiency of Wisconsin's child care system, especially during the initial implementation of W-2. By November 1997, about nine hundred requests for child care subsidies were backlogged, and a similar backlog was reported in April 1998. School officials complained that delays in approvals for child care subsidies caused teenage parents to miss school.[179] A university-based survey found that child care problems were common among current W-2 participants in Dane County; about one-third claimed they had missed work because of lack of child care, while nearly one-quarter claimed they had to quit a job for this reason.[180] On average, W-2 participants in Milwaukee had to wait five to six weeks after a job placement to receive approval for subsidized child care.[181] Once approved, participants had to renew their eligibility every three months, a difficult task for many working mothers.[182]

Bureaucratic problems in verifying eligibility for child care subsidies caused hardships. These problems were particularly acute during the first year of the program, when these subsidies had to get approved by both W-2 agencies and county workers, located in two different offices. Although Milwaukee County set up a hotline to resolve problems with the new child care system, the answering machine was often full and responses were often delayed.[183] A staff member of 9to5 explained:

> We have a number of people who have experienced job loss because they couldn't get their child care. . . . This is partly due to the bureaucracy. . . . They'll be assured that their W-2 placement will be there and their child care will be set up and then come the first day of work there is no child care. Then they can't get to work obviously, and it begins a cycle. They get sanctioned and the [caseworker] starts thinking, okay this person isn't serious. And often it's just a situation where things didn't come together as they were supposed to and people don't have anyone with whom to leave their children.[184]

Problems in accessing subsidized child care undercut W-2's purported aim of putting poor mothers to work; it contributed to a job turnover rate of 34 percent among W-2 participants in Milwaukee and an unemployment rate of 40 percent among former W-2 participants.[185] Insufficient child care also endangered children, leading to eight reported child deaths among W-2 recipients. In one case, a W-2 participant brought her two-year-old to the hotel where she worked. While she was speaking to her supervisor, he wandered away and drowned in the hotel's pool.[186] Such incidents helped advocates to generate press coverage of their concerns.

Delays and breakdowns in child care approvals and payments also negatively affected child care providers. The problems became so severe in Milwaukee that several groups began to mobilize. Day Care Advocates of Milwaukee, representing about forty child care centers, criticized the new system. Providers Taking Action, representing about seventy-five home-based child care providers, also began to mobilize; they soon gained support from sympathetic county supervisors, who helped to prod county employees to fix individual payment problems and pay providers more quickly.[187] This pressure led to temporary improvements in providers' payments, but problems quickly returned, resulting from the reductions in county staff and employee turnover.[188]

Home-based providers in Wisconsin, like their counterparts in California, did not simply mobilize around their own financial concerns; they used a "language of virtue" and displayed an "ethic of care."[189] As providers organized and sought to maintain or increase state investments in subsidized child care, they highlighted the virtuous contributions they made to working parents, welfare-to-work participants, and their children. For example, at a Worthy Wage event held in Wisconsin, Peggy Haack from the Center for Child Care Workforce proclaimed, "We must recognize that child care is as much part of the infrastructure of a community as its roads, its schools, its public services like police and fire protection, and everything else that helps a community to thrive."[190]

Organized providers lobbied for more than just timely payments and better reimbursement rates. Along with a broad coalition of advocates, they promoted various policy changes to expand low-income families' access to subsidized child care. For example, they lobbied state welfare officials to eliminate the co-payment for teen mothers. While the state welfare director supported their elimination, Governor Tommy Thompson initially rejected it.[191] Thompson claimed that teen mothers, like other working parents, should pay for child care services. However, as advocates began to spread controversy about how W-2 policies were causing teenagers to drop out of high school through the media and other outlets, Governor Thompson eventually relented. The governor agreed to reduce significantly the co-payments required of teen parents to a maximum of $5 per week, which represented a significant victory for advocates.[192]

Along with many other advocates, providers also urged state officials to reduce the co-payment for adult recipients. The Ad-Hoc Committee on W-2, a coalition of welfare advocates, school officials, and policymakers in Milwaukee, called on state officials to suspend co-payments until W-2 participants earned a "sustainable wage" of at least $7.70 per hour for at least two years.[193] Other activists urged state officials to reduce the maximum co-payment from 16 to 10 percent of parents' income. Child care providers rallied at the capitol with "day-care dolls," demanding that the state use the expected $65 million in unspent child care funds to reduce parents' co-payments.[194] Even the mayor of Madison, Sue Bauman, urged the governor to reduce parents' co-payments, claiming that it was causing too many child care centers to close.[195] As a member of 9to5 reported:

> There are a lot of women that had child care, got a little raise and lost it, and now they are about to lose their job or [lost] their job because they can't afford the child care. . . . The ceilings are too low. . . . We have been lobbying for raising the ceilings so that more folks are included.[196]

A report by the Children's Defense Fund validated advocates' concerns, highlighting the lack of outreach to low-income parents, the low income ceilings for eligibility, and the high co-payments required of parents.[197] In response to such concerns and public pressure, and because they were consistent with the goal of increasing poor mothers' employment, Governor Thompson approved legislation to reduce the maximum co-payments from 16 to 12 percent of families' gross income and lowered the income ceilings for eligibility.[198]

Child care providers and various advocacy groups also sought to prevent state-level cutbacks to subsidized child care. As fiscal conditions worsened after 2001, and as more families began to use child care subsidies, budgets were stretched thin. State politicians proposed various ways to reduce child care spending, including increasing parents' co-payments, creating a waiting list for subsidized child care, and lowering the income ceiling for eligibility. The state American Federation of Labor and Congress of Industrial Organizations opposed such proposals, along with child and welfare advocacy groups and faith-based advocates. According to a staff person from 9to5:

> Our child care was threatened in terms of its funding and we were in a deficit. There was concern that they would not be able to find funding for the next fiscal year. And they were able to do that in part because there was very real pressure on them from a number of groups who were advocating for families to be able to access the child care. . . . [Funding] is going to be maintained and that was a huge victory.[199]

Child care providers also organized against administrative cuts in subsidized providers' rates, bringing together more than five hundred people to draw attention to the issue.[200] In 2005, providers, parents, and advocates celebrated when Democratic governor James Doyle, elected with union support, prevented deeper cutbacks to subsidized child care when he vetoed a proposed increase in co-payments that would have cost families as much as $500 more per year and when he restored $8 million for child care improvement projects.[201]

The expansion of subsidized child care and prior organizing by providers facilitated providers' unionization by AFSCME. The existence of professional associations and groups such as Providers Taking Action enabled union organizers to engage in bloc recruitment. Union organizers persuaded many such organizational leaders to encourage other members to join the union.[202] AFSCME's campaign began in Madison and then moved to Milwaukee and other parts of the state. Providers located in both urban and rural areas joined AFSCME's Child Care Providers Together. The statewide branch of the AFSCME union was racially and ethnically diverse and included both Spanish- and Hmong-speaking providers.

In contrast to their counterparts in California whose unionization campaign was stymied by a gubernatorial veto, child care providers declared victory in October 2006 when Governor James Doyle issued an executive order permitting all subsidized and unsubsidized family child care providers and subsidized "family, friend, and neighbor" providers to form a union and to negotiate with the state. The governor's executive order lists various bargainable issues, including "quality standards, training and certification requirements, reimbursement and payment procedures, health & safety conditions, and 'any other matters and regulations that would improve recruitment and retention . . . , encourage certified providers to become licensed and improve the quality of the programs they offer.'"[203] AFSCME's Child Care Providers Together was certified to represent the providers after registering union authorization cards from a majority of the seven thousand certified and licensed providers covered in the governor's order.[204] After Democrats gained control of the legislature, home-based child care providers' legal right was further strengthened through the authorizing legislation passed in 2009.[205]

In June of 2008, Child Care Providers Together ratified a three-year agreement with the state that was "contingent on necessary regulatory or statutory revisions, including appropriations." The agreement established a "bill of rights" for providers and included provisions regarding providers' reimbursement rates and payments, access to health care, and training.[206] As part of implementing the union's agreement with the state, the union worked with other advocates to expand the subsidized health insurance program to cover low-income childless adults through enabling legislation, which has helped to meet some of child care providers' demands for health insurance since 2009. As of 2010, the union was working with state officials to develop a special federal Medicaid waiver to provide health insurance specifically for family child care providers. The union has also worked to expand the state training provided to child care providers in order to make it more accessible to providers, including Spanish- and Hmong-speakers, and has pushed to include a union perspective on training issues. The union also negotiated improvements in the state's process for recouping overpayments to providers.

Unionization of child care providers spurred further mobilization against proposed cutbacks to the state's subsidized child care system. In 2007, state welfare officials froze providers' reimbursement rates to 2006 levels, stopped filling vacant positions, and began to reimburse providers based on attendance rather than enrollment. They also considered other policies to reduce child care spending, including creating a waitlist, reducing income ceilings for eligibility, and lowering reimbursement rates. Oma Vic McMurray, a child care provider from Madison, criticized these proposals: "Once again they're trying to stretch [the budget] on the backs of child care workers. It's just not the answer."[207] Proposed cutbacks were also opposed by Milwaukee-area legislators and welfare advocacy organizations.[208] Hundreds of child care providers attended a series of legislative budget hearings, where they urged full funding for the program.

Despite other cutbacks made in the governor's child care budget proposal, legislators did not reduce the reimbursement rates for providers of subsidized child care in 2007; this was considered an important, albeit partial, victory for child care providers and advocates.[209] The union's agreement with the state required it to set basic reimbursement rates for subsidized child care at 75 percent of the current market rate, consistent with federal guidelines, but the agreement was undercut by legislators' failure to authorize sufficient funding. As of 2010, the basic reimbursement rates have remained frozen since 2006 at 75 percent of 2005 market rates, with 10-percent-higher rates given to providers meeting higher quality standards; legislation prohibited the state from raising those rates in 2011, but at least further cutbacks in these reimbursement rates were averted through mobilization by the union and other child care advocates. The union also successfully lobbied to end the state's policy of only reimbursing providers based on children's attendance rather than enrollment, since providers could not usually fill slots for absent or sick children.[210]

The union also worked to advocate on behalf of providers of subsidized child care when providers came under fire in 2009, first when a series of investigative reports about the subsidized child care program by the *Milwaukee Journal Sentinel* "uncovered a trail of phony companies, fake reports, and shoddy oversight."[211] Soon after, a state audit of the program revealed that it "handed out nearly $19 million in improper payments last year because caseworkers didn't verify participants' eligibility." The audit also identified other documentation problems in about 11 percent of the four hundred participant case files that it reviewed from 2008.[212] As of May 2010, an estimated $45 million was saved through the state's effort to tighten regulation of the subsidized child care system, reduce fraudulent payment claims by providers, revoke licenses from providers who failed to meet state standards, and recoup overpayments from providers.[213] AFSCME's Child Care Providers Together advocated on behalf of child care providers during this period; in their negotiations with state officials, they obtained more reasonable repayment schedules for overpayments when overpayments were unintended or due to errors made by caseworkers rather than providers and an agreement to increase communication between county licensors, the union, and providers through "meet-your-licensors" events. The union also worked to improve training and make it more accessible to providers, as well as to develop peer advocates among members to improve providers' understanding of state laws and rules.[214]

In short, organized child care providers and a broad coalition of advocates, including policymakers, school officials, parents, and more traditional child and welfare advocacy organizations, made a number of important advances in Wisconsin. In the early years of welfare reform, they managed to expand eligibility for subsidized child care through lower fees and higher income ceilings for eligibility. When fiscal conditions later declined, they protected subsidized child care from various proposed cutbacks and protected providers' reimbursement rates. Under Governor James Doyle, home-based child care providers also formed a new union that successfully negotiated various improvements in providers' working conditions and access to training.

Conclusion

The emphasis of putting poor mothers to work within welfare reform policies, and broad public support for welfare-to-work programs, created setbacks in terms of welfare mothers' rights to provide care to their own children. Only a few groups, such as Welfare Warriors in Milwaukee and Every Mother Is a Working Mother in Los Angeles, were willing to denounce the new work requirements for adult TANF recipients and call for a moratorium on enforcing them. Those groups upheld radical feminist demands for "wages for housework," and they also drew attention to the race, class, and gender dimensions of the devaluation of the caregiving work of welfare mothers within federal welfare reform policies. Yet the lack of broad support for abolishing all work requirements for adult TANF recipients made it difficult for these groups to gain much traction.

More commonly, welfare rights organizations pushed for targeted exemptions from welfare-to-work requirements. The implementation of federal work requirements within states and counties provided activists with opportunities for policymaking around this issue. To maximize their influence in Wisconsin and California, activists pressured multiple kinds of state actors and institutions. In Wisconsin, legislators authorized work exemptions only for parents with infants three months or less in age. A broad coalition of welfare and children's rights groups pushed for a one-year exemption for parents of infants and those with difficult pregnancies, but they failed to get sufficient support in the state legislature, which was dominated by political conservatives until 2008. A coalition of disability and children's rights advocates made greater headway for the parents of sick and disabled children by lobbying state welfare officials, who agreed to recognize these parents' caregiving work or to grant them "good cause" exemptions from work requirements. The highly publicized death of DeAndre Reeves, the disabled child who died while his mother was at her W-2 work assignment, gave them greater leverage in their negotiations with welfare officials who sought to avoid allegations that welfare reform endangered children. Reeves's death also helped to push through legislation that raised the age limit to eighteen for subsidized child care for the parents of disabled children. Similarly, publicity surrounding a disabled mother's death helped to increase legislative support for disability rights, children's rights, and welfare advocates' demand that benefit levels be raised for severely disabled parents of young children. In California, thanks to the greater influence of liberal politicians, the parents of disabled and sick children were exempted from work requirements in the state's initial welfare reform legislation. The struggle over mothers' rights to care for their children was pushed to the county level since counties were authorized to exempt mothers whose first child was between three months and one year old, and between three and six months for subsequent children. In Los Angeles, where parents could be exempt from work requirements for the first full year of their child's life, welfare rights activists persuaded county welfare officials to agree that they would not force parents that lacked suitable child care for their children to go to work.

The implementation of welfare-to-work also presented opportunities to expand and improve subsidized child care programs. To maximize their influence around these demands, activists targeted both state and county officials, all the while building broad-based and multiracial community-labor alliances. The growth of welfare-to-work programs was accompanied by an expansion of subsidized child care, increasing the numbers of both home-based child care providers and their clients. In the wake of welfare reform, both these groups became more organized.[215] Campaigns to organize home-based child care providers—first outside of unions and then within them—provided new resources and political muscle behind efforts to expand and improve publicly subsidized child care. Providers highlighted their training and skills, as well as their contributions to society, in order to justify better wages and benefits. Additionally, they mobilized on the basis of an "ethic of care" for low-income families, fighting to expand and improve the quality of publicly funded child care services. This helped to gain clients' active support for their unionization campaign, as did the strong personal bonds that providers had with the families they served.[216] Other parents groups were organized by child care resource and referral agencies, which helped working parents to find child care. A coalescence thus emerged between the labor movement, early education–child care movements, and the welfare rights movement.

The payoffs of unionization for home-based child care providers appear to be substantial. By 2010, child care unions negotiated statewide contracts in twelve states: Illinois, Iowa, Kansas, New Jersey, New York, Maine, Maryland, Michigan, Ohio, Oregon, Washington, and Wisconsin. Summarizing the achievements of these unions, and the movement to unionize child care providers more generally, Helen Blank and her colleagues write, "Since February 2007, unions in a number of states have negotiated increases in reimbursement rates, additional opportunities and incentives for training, access to health insurance, improved payment procedures, and a voice for providers in shaping policies that affect them. In some states, union bargaining and advocacy have helped win increased investments and improved policies for child care centers and parents as well."[217]

Two important challenges facing these unionization campaigns are home-based providers' lack of legal rights to bargain collectively and declining fiscal conditions, which, since 2007, have increased pressure on state policymakers to cut back spending on subsidized child care and other welfare programs. Even when providers and their clients were both highly mobilized, those who held office in the statehouse mattered to the outcomes of providers' unionization campaigns, as the Wisconsin and California cases illustrated. Whereas the Democratic governor James Doyle authorized home-based providers' legal right to collectively bargain, Republican Arnold Schwarzenegger refused to do so. Even when they lacked recognition, however, organized providers and their clients put pressure on public officials to make child care more accessible to working families by raising the income-eligibility ceilings for subsidized child care, keeping parents' fees low, and maintaining funding for these services.[218] Thus, both child care providers and working families have much to gain from these unionization campaigns.

Perhaps most importantly, the success of these campaigns illustrates the power of building broad, multiracial community-labor coalitions for protecting and improving public social services. Public employees and public contractors (in this case, publicly subsidized child care providers, resource and referral agencies, and public child care administrators) helped to provide both legitimacy and leverage to welfare recipients' demands for improving publicly subsidized child care programs and defending them against proposed cutbacks. In the next chapter, we will examine how community-labor coalitions seeking to protect subsidized child care and welfare rights have fared in the face of rising state deficits and the deepest economic crisis since the Great Depression.

Chapter 7

Challenges and Prospects for the Welfare Rights Movement

As other scholars have shown, the design of U.S. welfare policies, including those governing welfare-to-work programs, reflects the influence of dominant-class interests and ideologies: minimizing the redistribution of income, keeping the wage floor low, reinforcing the work ethic, normalizing forced work, and creating legal challenges for the enforcement of federal labor laws.[1] Scholars have also documented how corporate interests promote the privatization of welfare programs, while neoliberal rhetoric fuels policies that portray unionized public-sector workers as costly and inefficient.[2]

Feminist and critical race scholars extend these insights, drawing attention to how gender and racial politics have interacted with class politics in the historical development of a stratified welfare state in the U.S., as well as in the design and public support for federal welfare reform policies.[3] As they point out, dominant discourses justifying tough new eligibility rules and regulations have historically drawn upon and reinforced classist, racist, and sexist stereotypes of welfare recipients that portray them as unworthy of funding and in need of greater regulation.[4] Quantitative research also reveals that states where racial minorities were prevalent, and where conservative politicians and ideologies were influential, tended to adopt the most restrictive welfare reform policies.[5] Ethnographic studies, meanwhile, have shown how negative stereotypes of welfare mothers and the value of "self-sufficiency" through paid work or heterosexual marriage tend to be upheld by the "street level bureaucrats"[6] who implement and enforce welfare reform policies.[7]

Together, this scholarship shows how dominant interests and ideologies powerfully shape the design and implementation of U.S. welfare reform policies. It also helps to reinforce the arguments made by Schneider and Ingram, who claim that when target populations are weak and constructed in negative terms, politicians tend to adopt punitive policies towards them, which sends powerful messages to the public about those groups' low social status and unworthiness.[8] Even so, welfare recipients have exercised considerable individual-level resistance in the form of high rates of absenteeism from required appointments and classes and verbal confrontations with job trainers or caseworkers, as documented by ethnographic research and agency records.[9]

Largely overlooked in much of the scholarship on U.S. welfare reform are the extraordinary and dynamic processes through which grassroots activists and other advocates collectively mobilized to shape the state and local implementation of welfare reform policies and the outcomes of their efforts. Seeking to fill some of that gap, this book has examined various welfare rights campaigns that, beginning in the late 1990s, emerged in response to the implementation of federal welfare reform.

This wave of welfare rights activism provides important lessons for both scholars and activists. For scholars, these campaigns provide nuance to our understanding of how U.S. welfare policies are shaped by the politics of gender, race, and class, highlighting how those politics are dynamic, contested, and uneven across institutions. For activists, these campaigns provide important lessons for future efforts to strengthen and rebuild the U.S. welfare state, given the many challenges facing such efforts. In this chapter, I compare—across issues and contexts—the various welfare rights campaigns examined in earlier chapters in order to identify these larger lessons for both scholars and activists. I then turn to the current challenges and prospects for expanding the U.S. welfare state in the context of the deepening economic crisis.

Lessons from the Post-1996 Welfare Rights Movement

The welfare rights campaigns examined in this book challenged the broader gender, race, and class politics of welfare reform through coalition-building and by asserting the rights and worthiness of both welfare recipients and service providers through grassroots mobilization. Refuting the racist stereotype of welfare recipients as work-avoidant, welfare rights activists and their allies highlighted the shortage of living-wage jobs. Disproving the racist stereotype of immigrants as tax burdens, activists emphasized their tax contributions. Fighting against the devaluation of carework, they emphasized the social importance of this work and the skill associated with it. Union activists, meanwhile, challenged the negative constructions of public-sector workers as inefficient and expensive that were used to justify the privatization of welfare services. They also pointed to problems with the quality of welfare contractors' services. Each of these struggles highlight individual victories in different policy sectors. More generally, they shed light on how popular mobilization can influence public policies.

Perhaps the most important lesson to be gleaned from this book is that policymaking does not end when legislation is passed—*policy implementation is policymaking*. As this book has demonstrated, grassroots activists and other welfare advocates were unable to prevent the passage of the 1996 federal welfare reform act (the Personal Responsibility and Work Opportunity Reconciliation Act [PRWORA]) and lacked much influence over the details of this legislation or its reauthorization. Nonetheless, they and their allies mobilized and sometimes managed to shape the state and local implementation of federal welfare reforms in small but significant ways that improved the lives of low-income Americans. Mobilization was largely defensive, emerging in response to threats to poor people's access to income, education and job training, and social services, as well as threats to public-sector workers' jobs and bargaining power. This type of mobilization paralleled what occurred in the 1980s, when federal cutbacks in social programs serving the poor stimulated a wave of defensive activism among poor people's activist and advocacy groups. As in the 1980s, popular mobilization helped to minimize rollbacks in public welfare programs and poor people's rights to welfare.[10] It also helped to protect welfare recipients' access to education and training. Other campaigns capitalized on the new resources and rights associated with the welfare-to-work aspects of PRWORA, leading to expansions in subsidized child care and the creation of transitional employment programs.

The second important lesson to be gleaned from this book is *the importance of coalition-building, both inside and outside of the state, for making policy gains*. In this period of retrenchment, welfare rights campaigns were generally more successful in making policy gains or halting or reducing cutbacks when broad-based mobilization was coupled with political support within the state. The welfare rights campaigns examined in this book reveal the complex and multivocal response of state actors to activists' demands; state policymakers were both friend and foe to welfare rights activists. Finding governmental allies or sympathetic policymakers often required activists to "jump scale"—that is, to move upward or downward in the level of governance[11]—and maneuver through various political and legal institutions (federal administrative agencies, state audit bureaus, the judicial system, county supervisors, city councils, and state legislators, for example).

The active involvement of allied organizations—such as unions, faith-based organizations, and immigrant rights groups—in state and local welfare rights campaigns in the post-PRWORA period contrasts with earlier periods of welfare rights activism when such allies were noticeably absent.[12] Extending Schneider and Ingram's insights on the importance of social policies in constructing target populations and subjecting them to certain kinds of treatment, I have argued that welfare rights coalitions were shaped by the contours of PRWORA's cross-cutting target populations. The passage of PRWORA created a whole host of symbolic and material threats and opportunities that affected particular types of welfare recipients—teenage mothers, legal immigrants, working parents, students, disabled parents, and the like—as well as groups that extended far beyond the welfare population (Latinos, Asian Americans, public-sector unions, educators, child care providers, and the physically handicapped, for example). Those joint policy threats and opportunities increased the incentives for coalition-building and expanded support for welfare rights campaigns beyond the usual suspects—grassroots organizations of the poor and other welfare advocacy groups. Because the implementation of PRWORA involved extensive rollbacks in poor people's rights to education, services, and cash aid, publicity about the actual or impending hardships associated with those cutbacks also encouraged the active support of allied groups, including religious leaders, children's advocates, and service providers motivated by the "ethic of care."[13]

Whether or not allies actually joined welfare rights struggles, and to what extent, partly depended upon local movement politics. Local economic and demographic conditions, as well as the content of welfare reform policies, also shaped the size of the groups affected by welfare reform, making it more or less easy to mobilize around particular issues. As discussed in chapter 3, the capacity to mobilize in support of restoring legal immigrants' welfare rights varied considerably across states because of the uneven size of the immigrant population and the uneven development of immigrant and ethnic advocacy organizations. Yet, even in states such as Wisconsin, where the immigrant population and advocacy community was quite small, campaigns around this issue forged new multiracial alliances and brought together activists from the welfare and immigrant rights movements. Such broad participation helped to win state-level benefit replacements for legal immigrants during their first five years in the country in Wisconsin, California, and many other states.

While most unions in the U.S. failed to respond to the implementation of welfare reform, some unions, mostly in the public sector, formed community-labor alliances to improve it. As chapters 4 through 6 revealed, unions' commitment to welfare rights campaigns tended to be greater when union leaders recognized common interests with welfare recipients and when efforts to revitalize unions through coalition-building and grassroots mobilization were better developed. Most commonly, public-sector unions mobilized to prevent or limit welfare privatization, which threatened to displace existing union members. Only a handful of unions invested in campaigns to organize welfare-to-work participants, as chapter 5 revealed.[14] Welfare-to-work participants, like welfare recipients more generally, have "few allies and little voice," as they are a marginalized group in our society.[15] Organizing welfare-to-work participants also had uncertain short-term payoffs for unions in terms of increasing membership, given the ambiguous legal status of these workers and the perceived or real difficulties of organizing a declining, highly vulnerable, and mobile population.[16] Chapter 5 helped to illustrate the uneven results of these campaigns. The Milwaukee effort to gain collective bargaining rights for workfare workers at one private-sector worksite through a traditional union election failed amid a concerted union-busting campaign by the employer. In contrast, anti-workfare activists in Los Angeles successfully pushed local policymakers to create a transitional jobs programs, a grievance procedure for welfare-to-work participants, and improved working conditions at a variety of public-sector worksites. More commonly, public-sector unions invested in campaigns to organize home-based child care providers, viewing them as an expanding sector of low-wage workers. As chapter 6 showed, unions maintained these investments in states, such as Wisconsin, where their rights to unionize were achieved through legislation or gubernatorial fiat. However, they pulled back investments from those campaigns in states where those rights were denied, such as California.

Political conditions varied across states and municipalities, making it more or less easy for activists to identify friends in office and to influence the implementation of welfare reform. Political conditions tended to be less favorable for welfare rights activists in Milwaukee, where local politicians had little authority over the implementation of welfare reform, than in Los Angeles, where local politicians had greater decision-making power. This helps to explain why the anti-privatization campaign and the workfare workers' campaign was more successful in Los Angeles than in Milwaukee. In California, where liberals dominated the state legislature, activists generally had greater success in shaping welfare reform policies than they did in Wisconsin, where Republicans controlled the legislature until 2009. This helps to explain why Temporary Assistance for Needy Families (TANF) eligibility policies were generally more lenient and welfare-to-work policies less restrictive in California compared to Wisconsin. It also helps to account for California's greater success in restoring public assistance benefits to legal immigrants compared to Wisconsin. Whereas California legislators created four separate benefit-replacement programs, Wisconsin legislators created only two of them for legal immigrants. One exception to this trend was the initial outcomes of campaigns to unionize providers of subsidized child care, which succeeded by gubernatorial fiat under Wisconsin's Democratic governor, Jim Doyle, but failed by gubernatorial veto under California's Republican governor, Arnold Schwarzenegger.

Overall, promoting welfare rights has been an uphill battle in the United States. The failure of welfare programs to serve most working-class families, on top of the demonization of welfare mothers and other public assistance recipients, has made it difficult to build broad-based support for welfare rights in the United States. Welfare rights campaigns also face concerted opposition from powerful corporate and political interests who benefit from minimizing welfare expenditures and keeping the wage floor as low as possible. In this context, allied groups have frequently abandoned welfare rights, turning to other issues that they believed are more easily won. For example, frustrated with its inability to influence congressional debates about welfare reform reauthorization, the Center for Community Change withdrew its resources from the National Campaign for Jobs and Income Support, an effort to build a national alliance among welfare rights organizations. Instead, they put more of their energy into other issues that were getting more national attention and promised to gain broader support: immigrants' rights, health care reform, and justice for workers.[17]

The current economic crisis political moment presents many new challenges, as well as some opportunities, for the struggle for welfare rights. I first discuss the national situation, where the challenges to expand welfare rights are particularly daunting. I then turn to the state level, where the situation is more contradictory and where resistance to mounting public-sector cutbacks has helped to revitalize both the labor movement and student activists.

Hope and Frustration Under the Obama Administration

The current political situation in the nation presents many challenges for welfare state expansion, despite the mandate for change that was expressed in the historic 2008 election. That year, growing economic discontent and voter mobilization by unions and other groups helped to broaden support for the Democratic Party.[18] Barack Obama, the first African American to be elected as president, entered the White House in 2008 with a Democratic majority in both houses of Congress. Once in office, the newly elected Obama administration pushed through Congress various large-scale measures to address the economic crisis over the first few years of his presidency. These measures, however, have mainly just injected large sums of capital and cash in an effort to stabilize an already broken economic and welfare system. With hopes for deeper change frustrated, many of those who voted for Obama stayed at home during the 2010 midterm election while a resurgent right wing mobilized, leading to an end to Democrats' control of the House of Representatives.

Even in 2008, corporate domination of U.S. politics ensured that those at the top of the economic pyramid received most of the federal assistance given to address the economic crisis. Congress authorized trillions of dollars to bail out the largest and most powerful financial and insurance companies, with very little government control or oversight over the use of the funds.[19] Scandals soon emerged. American International Group (AIG), a company that received tens of billions of dollars in federal stimulus money, paid out a total of $165 million in bonuses to current and former employees, including those who were responsible for the toxic derivatives that bankrupted the company and sent ripple effects into the global economy.

The Obama administration also pushed through Congress various measures to assist ordinary Americans, but the scale of these measures paled in comparison to the growing demand for economic assistance. In an effort to prevent close to four million foreclosures, it authorized up to $75 billion in incentives to lenders to lower home loan payments for troubled borrowers.[20] But by April of 2011, only 630,000 borrowers received permanent loan modifications through the Home Affordable Modification Program, and the program came under fire for its lack of binding regulations, confusing rules, and inadequate oversight.[21] Even more troubling, after five months in existence, only thirty-eight homeowners had refinanced their mortgages through the Federal Housing Administration's Short Refinance program, a program designed to help up to 1.5 million borrowers.[22] As in the case of U.S. welfare reform, ineffective implementation of federal programs to assist homeowners has spurred popular mobilization. Already, various community organizations around the nation have organized protests at banks, home auctions, and eviction sites. Meanwhile, scandals surrounding improper foreclosure proceedings continued to mount. Federal banking regulators, after reviewing 2,800 foreclosure cases in 2010, determined that at least fourteen mortgage services had violated various rules, regulations, and laws.[23]

As part of the economic recovery package, the Obama administration authorized $167 billion for health and human services over the next ten years to help state governments, which were facing massive deficits and declining revenues as well as rising demands for welfare and other social services. Much of these funds were targeted for Medicaid, but an additional $5 billion was allocated for TANF, $2 billion for subsidized child care, and $2.1 billion for Head Start programs. The government also increased federal funding for food assistance programs. As economic conditions worsened and populations grew, the economic recovery act adjusted the rules so that states would no longer be punished for rising TANF caseloads.[24] TANF recipients still faced state and federal time limits on welfare receipt, however. Even so, before it expired on September 30, 2010, the TANF Emergency Fund helped states meet the growing demand for welfare and put more than 260,000 low-income adults and youth into paid jobs.[25]

Following the precedence set by the George W. Bush administration, the Obama administration also authorized new extensions of unemployment benefits. It additionally provided federal incentives for states to expand eligibility for Unemployment Insurance to allow part-time workers and workers who left the job for compelling family reasons to qualify. As of April 2009, less than half of all unemployed workers received benefits. Many unemployed workers, disproportionately low-income and female, were ineligible because they were employed part-time, had not been on their job long enough, or failed to meet other state rules for eligibility.[26] By 2010, thirty-nine states had responded to federal incentives and popular mobilization by expanding eligibility for Unemployment Insurance. All of these states allowed workers to use more recent pay periods to qualify, and thirty-three other states adopted two other rule reforms. These reforms have significantly improved unemployed workers' access to benefits, although many barriers to qualification remain.[27] By 2011, various states have considered, or actually adopted, cutbacks in their unemployment benefits as fiscal conditions have worsened.

Along with many other groups, Health Care for America Now, a campaign involving more than one thousand membership organizations in forty-six states (including labor federations, religious groups, health care professionals, and senior citizens' organizations), pushed for comprehensive health care reform. Along with lobbying, health care activists organized a nationally coordinated day of action that involved about 150 demonstrations across the United States at large health insurance company headquarters and the homes of their executives, highlighting the problems associated with for-profit health insurance. This campaign faced stiff challenges, however, in shaping congressional health care debates, including neglect by the mainstream press and well-resourced opponents. In the first half of 2009, "the insurance companies and HMO industry increased its lobbying expenditures and campaign contributions to some $700,000 a day."[28] Not surprisingly, a robust national public insurance option failed to gain sufficient support within Congress, and the Obama administration quickly ruled out a single-payer plan as politically impossible.

The national health care reform legislation that passed in 2010 promised to expand low-income people's access to subsidized health insurance significantly; it also gave private insurance companies and pharmaceutical companies a captured market. One year after its passage, many of the law's promises of expanded and improved health care coverage were not fulfilled or faced severe challenges. First, the legality of the "individual mandate," which requires that most Americans purchase health care insurance by 2014 or face a tax penalty, has been hotly contested in the court system, with twenty-seven states challenging the law and more than twenty lawsuits filed against it. Second, expansions in health care coverage were much slower than expected and could be significantly challenged by proposed state-level and federal cutbacks in Medicaid benefits and coverage. Newly created health care plans for those with existing medical conditions, expected by the Medicare actuary to serve 375,000 by the end of 2010, were only serving 12,000. Many of those who could have benefited from these plans could not afford them. Similar problems may also constrain the number of parents taking advantage of the new health care regulations allowing them to keep their young-adult children (aged eighteen through twenty-nine) covered through their health insurance plans. Meanwhile, for many workers with health insurance, health care premiums continued to rise while health coverage was reduced. Making matters worse, federal officials failed to enforce the newly enacted health insurance standards; by March 2011, they granted more than one thousand waivers from the law's coverage standards—97 percent of those requested—to states, employers, and unions.[29] Just as was the case for federal welfare reform, the implementation of state and federal health care laws is likely to incite fierce political struggle in the years to come.

Labor law reform was similarly watered down in Congress. Labor unions promoted the passage of the Employee Free Choice Act through concerted lobbying, letter-writing, and demonstrations. The American Federation of Labor and Congress of Industrial Organizations (AFL-CIO) president, John Sweeney, claimed that it was "the largest grassroots campaign in labor history."[30] While this statement was hyperbole, it expressed the seriousness of the issue for union activists and just how rare this national-level mobilization was for the U.S. labor movement. Polls showed strong public support for the measure, which would make it easier for workers to form a union and stiffen penalties on employers that intimidated or harassed pro-union workers. Activists faced concerted business opposition, however; business associations organized letter-writing campaigns and air-lifted members to lobby Congress. In response to such pressure, Congress eliminated a key provision of the proposed law that would allow workers to unionize by collecting union authorization cards from a majority of workers, and the bill failed to gain sufficient support to pass under a Democrat-controlled Congress. With Republicans in control of the House in 2011, the measure has little chance of succeeding in the near future.

As can be seen from the discussion above, labor and community activists were not idle as economic conditions worsened after 2007. There was a flurry of activity as community organizations, unions, and other groups vigorously pushed for moratoriums on home foreclosures, expansions in subsidized health insurance, and the Employee Free Choice Act.

They also vigorously opposed cutbacks in state and local public social services. Unions and other groups also organized unemployed workers; they called for recall rights and severance pay from employers; they protested for job creation programs and against bank bailouts; and they actively lobbied for extensions on Unemployment Insurance benefits. Immigrant rights activists, meanwhile, protested and lobbied for amnesty and other pathways to citizenship for undocumented immigrants while vigorously opposing the rising tide of immigrant deportations under the Obama administration.

Yet, these activities have been highly fragmented, cautious, and generally small in scale. They pale in comparison to the national wave of union-organizing and sit-down strikes that spread like wildfire during the Great Depression, the Bonus March of 1932 (in which unemployed World War I veterans demanded access to the government bonuses promised to them), and other mass mobilizations for pensions, government relief, and jobs that emerged in that era. They also pale in comparison to more recent mass marches and street protests against layoffs and austerity measures in Latin America and Western Europe, where the labor movement and leftist parties are much stronger.[31]

Why has a vibrant national movement of poor and working people in the U.S. failed to emerge in response to what some have called the largest economic collapse since the Great Depression? Working-class movements and other leftist forces in the United States have long been weak compared to their counterparts in other wealthy democratic nations, especially in Western Europe. As many scholars have pointed out, the relative absence of class consciousness, a highly individualistic culture, and deep racial-ethnic divisions—as well as other rifts—among U.S. workers have historically discouraged broad mobilization by poor and working-class people. Moreover, weak labor laws and virulent employer resistance—along with the post–World War II purge of leftist activists from unions—discouraged the growth of a broad, vibrant, and militant labor movement in the U.S., which could have counteracted those forces. In this context, poor people have, in general, been less likely than non-poor people to participate in politics in the United States, while high unemployment has been more likely to stir fears of economic insecurity and to dampen labor solidarity than to increase it.[32]

Unions were generally cautious in their tactics during Obama's presidency. There were, of course, exceptions. About 240 laid-off workers gained national media attention in December of 2008 when they occupied the factory of Republic Windows and Doors in Chicago for six days until their demands for severance pay and earned vacation time were met. A demonstration for jobs and peace, organized by the AFL-CIO and its allies in October of 2010, drew tens of thousands to the streets, while a general strike protesting the proposed layoffs of 17,000 public-sector workers in

Puerto Rico drew 150,000 in October 2009. Otherwise, unions generally mobilized dissent by lobbying; they organized letter-writing campaigns, call-in days, and visits to congressional offices. If they protested, it was mainly in the form of relatively small public rallies or marches. Union leaders feared that they would alienate politicians if they took more militant kinds of actions, such as sit-in protests or disrupting traffic.[33] Chris Tilly suggests that unions' failure to mobilize mass protests in these years was greatly constrained by their close ties to the Democratic Party. After investing nearly $450 million and countless organizers to mobilize millions of voters in the 2008 presidential election, and in response to growing right-wing attacks on the president, unions were hesitant to criticize the Obama administration. Internal divisions and competition (between and within the AFL-CIO and Change to Win) and declining union membership dues in the context of the recession further constrained unions' capacity to mobilize.[34]

Outside of the labor movement, there is a general lack of vibrant national networks of citizenship groups, and even electoral politics tend to be run in a top-down fashion. As Theda Skocpol puts it,

> Even as top-down, professionally-led, and Washington-centered advocacy groups have become more prevalent and active in U.S. politics at the relative expense of locally rooted membership groups, parallel changes have occurred in the political party and electoral systems. Since the advent of television advertising, computerized mailing lists, and continuous polling, U.S. electoral politics has been an increasingly top-down affair.[35]

Many organizations that advocate for the poor at the national level are mainly staff-driven, non-membership organizations that are heavily reliant on foundation and government support, constraining their activities.[36] Many of these organizations also never fully recovered from the loss of federal revenues that sharply decreased under the Ronald Reagan administration. Private donations, more commonly targeted for direct services for the poor, were unable to make up for those losses.[37]

In the absence of a broad, militant national movement for economic justice, national policymakers showed little leadership in challenging corporate interests and adopting far-reaching government support for ordinary Americans. As the economic crisis deepened and federal deficits continued to rise, political support for social spending quickly diminished. By early 2011, the Obama administration and Democratic leaders in Congress agreed to carry out $38 billion worth of domestic spending cuts. As the case of U.S. welfare reform suggests, however, the passage of federal cutbacks in social services is not the end of the story, as their implementation is likely to spur popular mobilization.

State-Level Attacks on Welfare and Other Public Services

The situation across U.S. states is more contradictory. On the one hand, the denigration of welfare recipients left them vulnerable to state-level cutbacks as fiscal conditions worsened after 2007. Welfare cutbacks generally reduced poor people's access to cash aid or the real value of benefit levels. However, some states began to loosen work requirements, as providing subsidized child care for parents of young children was costly, and rising unemployment increased the scarcity of jobs. While this reduced assistance for welfare mothers who were seeking immediate employment, it did provide some welfare recipients with greater opportunities to care for their own children at home or to gain more education and training. As was the case for federal welfare reform, the threat of actual or proposed cutbacks has helped to spur popular resistance and coalition-building. Because cutbacks to welfare programs were often coupled with other social service cuts—sometimes with threats to public-sector workers' collective bargaining rights—this has helped to expand and revive community and labor alliances in many states and regions around the country.

Cutbacks to state services quickly became a national trend as state revenues from income, sales, and other taxes declined in the context of the economic crisis. Federal economic recovery funds only covered about 30 to 40 percent of states' deficits. Increases in tax revenues, enacted in over thirty states since 2007, were insufficient to make up the difference, increasing the pressure to roll back social services. At least forty states cut back spending on state services in their 2009 to 2010 budgets, and forty-six states did so in their 2010 to 2011 budgets. Altogether, in the 2010 to 2011 state budgets, thirty-one states reduced spending in health care, twenty-nine states cut back services to the elderly and disabled, thirty-three states spent less on K–12 public education, and forty-three states cut back spending in higher education.[38] By 2011, Congress indicated that it would not extend as much recession-related aid to states as it had in the past few years, and governors' initial budgets in forty-eight states included proposals for cutbacks in public social services.[39]

Services for low-income families were common targets for cutbacks. In their 2010 to 2011 state budgets, at least thirty-one states authorized cutbacks that restricted low-income children's or families' eligibility for health insurance or reduced their access to health services. Besides California, at least three other states—Texas, Massachusetts, and Ohio—authorized spending cuts for their child care assistance programs, while Michigan and Minnesota reduced spending on welfare-to-work initiatives. In Arizona, politicians shortened the time limit on TANF from sixty months to thirty-six months, cutting off assistance to an estimated 10,000 families. Other states made it more difficult for low-income people to get access to assistance by authorizing staff layoffs and office closures, even as TANF caseloads were rising.[40] As of 2010, state welfare administrators reported that cutbacks in TANF staff occurred in at least twenty-two states, reductions in staff work hours occurred in at least eleven states, and office closures occurred in at least seven states.[41] As in the late 1990s, efforts to cut back welfare spending also targeted immigrants and their children, leading to a slate of new state propositions and bills to further restrict immigrants' access to social services, most of which were defeated in 2005 and 2006.[42] As the economic recession deepened after 2007, support for such state measures continued to grow, along with support for a federal constitutional amendment to deny citizenship to the children of illegal immigrants born in the U.S.[43]

The forces behind retrenchment were particularly powerful in California, which had been hit hard by the economic recession and the collapse of the housing market. By 2009, the state faced a record decline in revenue and a deficit of $26 billion. Welfare advocates and a Democrat-controlled legislature prevented Governor Schwarzenegger from the drastic cuts he proposed in 2009 and 2010: eliminating the entire CalWorks program, all funds for subsidized child care, and benefit replacements for legal immigrants.[44] However, the 2009 and 2010 state budgets included massive cuts in social programs for low-income people, including a $510 million reduction in the CalWorks budget in 2009. In part, these savings were obtained through lower grants and by expanding exemptions from welfare-to-work requirements for mothers of young children, and thereby reducing child care expenditures.[45] The state also adopted a shorter time limit (forty-eight months) for adult recipients of CalWorks, beginning in July 2011 and increased the sanctions for non-compliance with welfare-to-work requirements.[46] The 2009 state budget also included a $178.6 million cut in the Healthy Families program that provided subsidized health insurance for low-income children.[47] The state legislature also froze the income eligibility for subsidized child care to the 2007 to 2008 level for the third year in a row and reduced the reimbursement rate for license-exempt child care providers.[48] In 2010, various cuts to the CalWorks budget were enacted, and the governor cut, through a line-item veto, an additional $366 million from the CalWorks program and another $256 million worth of state child care funds for stage 3 child care, a program that served low-wage families that had successfully transitioned from welfare to work.[49]

While federal assistance promised to help restore some of the funding cut from the CalWorks budget,[50] implementation of the cuts to the state's stage 3 child care program was hotly contested. As earlier welfare rights campaigns illustrated, simply signing legislation did not guarantee its implementation. Similar to the earlier campaign to restore welfare benefits for legal immigrants in California, a combination of broad-based mobilization and help from allies in the state helped to prevent the implementation of the cutback in stage 3 child care. The program served about 55,000 children, and many of their families, along with organized child care providers and welfare and child advocates, successfully mobilized to keep the program running. They also found support for their cause from Assemblyman John A. Perez and other legislators. With bridge funding from the state legislature and state and county child development commissions, plus a judge's approval of a settlement to keep the program running, the program remained intact until state funding for it was restored in 2011 under Governor Jerry Brown's leadership.[51]

Yet, even while activists were hard at work protecting access to subsidized child care, attacks on welfare continued to mount in 2010 and 2011. In her unsuccessful bid for governor, billionaire Republican Meg Whitman ran a series of ads attacking the state's welfare system as overly generous and called for reducing the lifetime limits to two years for adult CalWorks recipients. Although Whitman lost the election to Democratic candidate Jerry Brown, the race was a close contest and her anti-welfare, "anti–big government" messages resonated with many voters.[52] In March of 2011, Democratic governor Jerry Brown and a Democrat-controlled legislature passed an initial budget with at least $12.5 billion worth of expenditure cuts, closing about half of the state's projected deficit. While a broad array of social services was cut back, including public higher education, programs serving low-income families were greatly affected. The legislature adopted roughly $1.2 billion worth of cuts to the CalWorks program and cut the state General Fund support for CalWorks by 50 percent.[53] Specific cuts included a forty-eight-month lifetime limit for CalWorks adult participants (effective June 1 of that year), reductions in benefits, reduced services for teen parents, cutbacks in mental health and substance abuse services, and a $426 million reduction in funds to counties to administer the program. Although in 2011 the governor restored funding for stage 3 child care, he made major cutbacks in subsidized child care to help pay for it, including the elimination of care for eleven- and twelve-year-old children, a lower income ceiling for eligibility, lower reimbursement rates for providers, and an increase in parents' fees. Some welfare advocates supported the decision to extend the welfare-to-work exemptions adopted in 2009 for mothers of young children until July 1, 2014, allowing them to provide care for their own children, although others criticized the policy for reducing training, employment services, and supportive services for these mothers.[54]

Some aspects of the 2011 California state budget are being legally contested through the court system, while other aspects of it may be reshaped in response to protests, lobbying, and voter mobilization. The breadth of state cutbacks has helped to mobilize and unite students, public-sector workers, and a wide variety of service clients across California in a fight to raise revenue in order to prevent the implementation of existing cutbacks and to avert even more severe cutbacks in welfare, public education, and other social services. Such broad-based alliances could help to revive support for public social services, public-sector workers' rights, and demands for a more equitable system of taxation. A range of groups have promoted various increases in corporate taxes and fees as well as tax hikes for the wealthiest state residents in order to protect state services. Governor Brown and other Democratic leaders have also emphasized the importance of raising revenues to avert further cutbacks, although the governor has promised not to raise taxes without permission from voters. He has also promoted an extension on temporary increases in taxes and vehicle license fees to raise revenues and close the remaining budget gap for 2011 (about $14 billion) and has proposed a special election in 2011 to give voters the opportunity to support such measures. Both elite and grassroots proponents of increased taxes confront fierce opposition from Republicans, corporate lobbyists, Tea Party activists, and other anti-tax forces.

Even so, public opinion polls show that, as of April 2011, most voters support Governor Brown's proposed special election and efforts to raise revenues in order to protect public services, especially K–12 education. Polls also indicate that 60 percent of California voters favor raising the income tax for the wealthiest citizens in order to help protect the public education system from cutbacks, although about the same percentage oppose general increases in income and sales taxes.[55] Polls also reveal that 60 percent of California's voters generally approve of Governor Brown's plan to close the deficit through a combination of taxes and cutbacks, but opposition increases when specific cuts already approved by the legislature are described. For example, 67 percent of voters expressed opposition to limiting health care for low-income children, eliminating adult day care for the elderly, and reducing welfare benefits.[56] Given such public sentiments, the broad and loose alliances that are emerging across California to raise revenue and protect public education and other social services could help to protect welfare programs from future cutbacks if these groups can mobilize sufficient numbers of voters, often a challenge during a special election. Of course, the unity of these alliances is likely to be tested if the legislature appeases certain constituents more than others in future budget negotiations. Even so, increased mobilization by public-sector workers, students, and service clients is likely to help shift the public discourse about public services, government spending, and taxes.

The Wisconsin case helps to further illustrate the importance of broad-based mobilization and allies within the state for welfare rights struggles. In contrast to the series of draconian cuts to welfare and other programs serving low-income families adopted in California, under Democratic governor Jim Doyle's leadership and a Democrat-controlled legislature, Wisconsin largely spared such programs from cuts in its biennial 2009 to 2011 state budget, instead authorizing a number of improvements to those programs. While state legislators enacted cuts to most state agencies, the Medicaid program, local governments, and public schools, the state actually increased funding for various programs serving low-income families. With help from federal stimulus funds and new taxes, Wisconsin legislators increased funds for the state's subsidized child care and health insurance programs to meet growing demands for these programs and adjusted state tax credits for low-income families to keep up with inflation.[57]

Wisconsin politicians even adopted various improvements in the Wisconsin Works (W-2) program. Responding to the growing demand for W-2 as economic conditions worsened, the legislature increased the W-2 budget by $12 million, resulting in a 12.2 percent increase in spending in the first year and a 3.3 percent increase the following year. For the first time since the program began, the legislature also approved W-2 benefits for women with at-risk pregnancies. They also authorized a one-time increase of $50,000 for W-2 emergency assistance and expanded a transitional jobs program to serve 2,500 underemployed people. Legislators also removed the twenty-four-month time limit for participation in one of the four welfare-to-work categories created by W-2 in light of employment barriers, such as medical problems and the shortage of unsubsidized placements, both of which made it difficult for many participants to move up the W-2 ladder. The new policy promised to reduce the administrative costs associated with extending those time limits for participants.[58] Wisconsin policymakers also loosened welfare-to-work requirements in an effort to save money and in response to deepening job shortages as well as advocates' concerns about the lack of educational opportunities for W-2 participants. In 2009, they authorized W-2 participants to spend all forty work hours required per week in technical college classes.[59]

Why did Wisconsin protect and even improve some welfare programs while many other states, like California, imposed drastic cuts to them? Such decisions reflect divergent political as well as fiscal conditions in the two states. Alliances were built between unions, welfare advocacy, and other community organizations to improve policies for low-income and working families, a population that had been growing for some time in Wisconsin. These groups found Jim Doyle and other Democrats in the legislature sympathetic to many of their demands and, together, helped to elect them to office. Thanks to Doyle, home-based child care providers were unionized in Wisconsin, and their three-year union contract with the state, negotiated in 2008, gave them greater access to state policymakers than their counterparts in California, who in 2010 still lacked the right to collective bargaining.[60] And, whereas the Pew Center on the States ranked California as the state in the gravest fiscal peril in 2009, Wisconsin was only ranked tenth.[61]

Of course, some of the improvements adopted in Wisconsin, such as welfare benefits for pregnant women and educational opportunities for welfare-to-work participants, had long ago been won in California. The W-2 program also remained highly restrictive so that improvements adopted under the Doyle administration were not very expensive. Indeed, while Wisconsin politicians increased funding for W-2 in its 2009 to 2011 state budget, that increase "barely touche[d] Wisconsin's share of the $5 billion TANF Contingency Fund in the federal stimulus bill, which will finance 80 percent of increased state spending for caseloads, training, or emergency assistance."[62] As the economic crisis deepened, welfare advocates continued to raise concerns about the failure of the program to serve more needy people. W-2 caseloads grew between 2008 and 2010; the May 2010 caseloads were 86 percent higher than those in May of 2008. Yet, "the May 2010 cash caseload is only about one fourth of what it was when W-2 started in 1997, and only about one seventh of the AFDC enrollment two decades ago."[63] Growth in W-2 caseloads also did not keep pace with the growth in the use of other welfare programs, such as Unemployment Insurance, Food Stamps, and Medicaid.[64] A report by state welfare officials released in 2010 provided legitimacy to advocates' concerns. The report focused on explaining why 14,114 parents of dependent children received food stamps but not W-2. Researchers found that two-thirds of such families surveyed or interviewed said they didn't know about the W-2 program, while others claimed they were discouraged from applying or treated rudely by caseworkers.[65]

Hopes for further improving the W-2 program in Wisconsin were quickly dashed, however, by the 2010 election, which brought a Republican governor, Scott Walker, into office under a Republican-controlled state legislature in 2011. Under Governor Walker's leadership, Republican politicians gained the national spotlight for their efforts to reduce the state deficit through cutbacks in public services and public-sector workers' rights. Similar to the case of federal welfare reform, cross-cutting threats helped to mobilize opposition and build new alliances. Only this time, the severity of direct threats to the rights of unionized workers unleashed a historic wave of national protest by labor and community activists.

Governor Walker's proposed biennial budget bill in 2011 included $1 billion worth of cutbacks to welfare and a broad array of other vital social services in an effort to fill a deficit of $3.6 billion. These included the elimination of the state program that restored Food Stamps for legal immigrants; a $41 million reduction in tax relief for low-wage earners; a $500 million reduction in Medicaid; a $227 million reduction in subsidized child care; plus the elimination of the state's new transitional jobs demonstration program, which was designed to serve up to 2,500 unemployed non-custodial parents. Proposed cutbacks to W-2 included a $20-per-month benefit reduction for participants. Other proposed changes to the W-2 program included restoration of the old twenty-four-month time limit for certain W-2 participants; restoration of the previous limits to education and training for welfare-to-work participants; elimination of the rule requiring W-2 agencies to notify participants before they will be sanctioned and provide them the opportunity to improve their behavior; and elimination of the requirement that, before imposing sanctions, agencies must determine that a W-2 participant did not have "good cause" for not participating in W-2 activities or offering a "conciliation period" in which a participant can "make up" for the lost hours. Also proposed was a 75 percent reduction in the grants provided for legal services for the poor.[66] Many of these W-2 policies would reverse the policy gains previously made by welfare rights advocates.

Even more contested than these proposed cutbacks was the passage of a non-fiscal budget bill championed by Governor Walker and Republican policymakers. This new law limited collective bargaining rights for most of Wisconsin's public-sector workers, allowing bargaining only on wage issues, and eliminated them for others, including home-based child care providers. For state, county, and municipal employees, the law imposed a host of new regulations that would make it very difficult for unions to survive and operate: it ended requirements for union members to pay dues, prohibited payroll deductions for dues, required unions to win votes from a majority of members each year in order to remain certified, banned decertified unions from attempting recertification for twelve months, limited contracts to one year, prohibited contract extensions until new agreements were reached, and eliminated binding arbitration to settle disputes.[67]

In passing this law, Wisconsin's Republicans followed the lead of Indiana's governor, who in 2005 had already eliminated public employees' bargaining rights by executive order, allowing that state to outsource government operations, enact pay freezes, and demand higher health insurance payments.[68] Similar bills limiting public employees' collective bargaining rights quickly spread to other states. In 2011, Ohio's governor signed into legislation a bill that severely weakened public employees' collective bargaining rights by barring them from striking, replacing seniority with merit promotions, and putting an end to binding independent arbitration. Advocates of these laws portray unionized public-sector workers as earning too much or having pensions that are too expensive. Such arguments strategically draw attention away from the exorbitant salaries and benefits of CEOs, which have risen far more than those of public-sector workers in recent decades. They also overlook research showing that, when age and education are taken into account, public-sector workers earn less, on average, than their private-sector counterparts.[69]

The introduction of these anti-union bills, and their passage in Wisconsin and Ohio, lit a fire under the feet of the U.S. labor movement, unleashing a historic wave of popular protest in defense of public-sector workers' collective bargaining rights. As many as 100,000 workers, students, and other allies converged on the streets of Madison, and several thousands more took over the capitol building in Wisconsin. Thousands more protested in Ohio's state capital. Union activists throughout the country also organized a series of protests and rallies in solidarity with Wisconsin's public-sector workers. The legality of denying public-sector workers their collective bargaining rights, and the process through which the Wisconsin law was passed, are being contested in the court system at the time of this writing. Wisconsin activists on both sides of the budget debate also launched an unprecedented wave of recall campaigns against sixteen state senators (eight Republicans and eight Democrats) in 2011—everyone legally eligible for recall that year.[70] These recall campaigns provide an important opportunity for union and community activists to directly engage with voters, raising their concerns about workers' rights and proposed budget cuts. Meanwhile, Ohio public-sector workers and their allies hope to win back public employees' collective bargaining rights through a ballot initiative.

How these sweeping attacks on public spending and public-sector workers' collective bargaining rights will affect the U.S. welfare rights movement remains to be seen. On the one hand, attacks on public-sector workers' collective bargaining rights have helped to galvanize into action not only public employees but the broader U.S. labor movement. Likewise, efforts to defend public education and other services against cutbacks has sparked a new wave of activism and expanded coalitions between students, workers, immigrants, and a wide variety of social service clients. On the other hand, such activism has historically fragmented across sectors and communities, and thus across race, class, and gender lines. While there are many exceptions, the providers and clients of all sorts of public social services—from public higher education and libraries to health clinics and in-home supportive services—have often focused narrowly on defending their own rights and funding rather than supporting each others' struggles. Nevertheless, the breadth and depth of the attacks on public services and workers' rights presents a historic opportunity to mobilize voters and the broader public and to shape the debates about government spending, public services, and workers' rights in more constructive ways. This moment also provides the opportunity to mobilize and unite a wide range of constituents around broader political goals that could help to reverse this era of welfare and public-sector retrenchment. Such goals might include increasing taxes among corporations and wealthy families; eliminating corporate welfare; preventing home foreclosures (which drain revenues from local governments); democratizing and making transparent budgetary decisions; and defunding the ever-expanding military, security state, and prison system. These goals would also help raise the revenues needed to address governmental deficits, to create jobs, and to expand and improve welfare and other vital social services.

Revitalizing the Struggle for Welfare Rights

Scholars have suggested various worthwhile ways to strengthen progressive forces in U.S. politics in order to push forward more humane policies for families and working-class people. For example, Skocpol advocates revitalizing the Democratic Party and the labor movement and creating a national network of parent associations that engage parents through the "occasions, places, and networks in which they are already involved with one another."[71] Other scholars emphasize the importance of building power at the local and regional levels before scaling up to the national level.

As Manuel Pastor Jr., Chris Benner, and Martha Matsuoka argue, a new movement for regional equity has been emerging. The rise of regional organizing in the labor movement, the greater role played by central labor councils, and new regional organizing by community and faith-based organizations have contributed to the growth of this movement. They document how various regional campaigns have built alliances across race, class, and geography around shared interests for "economic prosperity and social inclusion," sustainable development, and improvements in social infrastructure.[72] These campaigns have led to living-wage policies, community benefit agreements, workforce development programs, affordable housing ordinances, and improvements in public transit systems.

Bill Fletcher Jr. and Fernando Gapasin, two veteran labor organizers, similarly emphasize the importance of organizing at the regional level given the enormous challenges of shifting national-level politics. They advocate the creation of regional "working-class assemblies," as a way to strengthen the organizational capacity of working-class communities. Such assemblies would bring together local community and labor activists to develop and promote common policy agendas. Were they to form, such assemblies could form the basis for a vibrant mass-based national network. Fletcher and Gapasin also advocate the spread of "social-justice unionism," rooted in a long-term commitment to achieve social justice for the entire working class. Social-justice unionism would help to ensure that alliances between organized labor and community groups were not simply formed to strengthen the aims of already unionized workers.[73] For the progressive movement to really gain ground, broader and deeper alliances among working-class people and their allies and organizations are certainly needed. Coalitions between the anti-poverty movement and other progressive movements—especially the labor movement and the immigrant rights movement—have been growing. These alliances have generally been tactical ones, focused around particular kinds of demands or industries. As a result, the progressive and left movements remain far too weak and fragmented to carry much weight in national politics. The immigrant rights and labor movements are also weakened by serious internal divisions over goals and strategies that must be addressed if these movements are to gain ground.[74]

The formation of local "working-class assemblies," or strong regional alliances between labor and community groups, including parents' associations, could help to overcome the existing fragmentation among progressive forces and help to spur national-level mobilization. Pastor, Benner, and Matsuoka argue that "regional equity organizing might be one powerful stream of an emerging progressive national movement." They point to various national networks and organizations that could help to create "a national regional equity social movement," which they envision as a "cohesive network of cross-constituency organizations focused on building regional equity."[75]

Already, participation in the U.S. Social Forum has helped to strengthen collaboration among working-class and poor people's organizations. Inspired by the World Social Forum process, in 2007 the first U.S. Social Forum in Atlanta, Georgia, drew together more than ten thousand activists from a variety of social movements to exchange ideas, coordinate actions, and expand and strengthen the ties between various social-justice organizations; in 2010, the second U.S. Social Forum drew an estimated eighteen thousand social-justice activists. At the 2007 U.S. Social Forum, a new network of domestic worker organizations was formed.

Grassroots activists and organizations affiliated with the Economic Human Rights Network, Jobs with Justice, and the Right to the City Alliance also used the meetings to strengthen their ties across cities and to expand their reach. During the 2010 U.S. Social Forum, union and community activists launched the Excluded Workers Congress, bringing a host of low-wage, non-traditional workers who were not covered by existing labor laws—including domestic workers, taxi drivers, day laborers, and restaurant employees—to demand greater protection of their rights as workers.[76]

Building even broader and more sustained interest in workers' rights and welfare issues requires more than simply building coalitions, however; it requires an expanded vision for economic justice. As Theda Skocpol points out, there is a "missing middle" in the U.S. welfare system. Most working-age people are not served through government social programs because they are too old, too young, or just not poor enough to qualify. There are millions of working families in the U.S. that struggle to pay for basic necessities such as housing, utilities, child care, and health insurance but who do not qualify for government assistance or have access to private employer-provided benefits.[77] With household incomes above, and sometimes just below, the federal poverty line, they earn too much to qualify for TANF and other forms of public assistance.[78] Research shows that middle-income households tend to have access to the least amount of social benefits since public benefits are more accessible to the lowest income households, while private benefits are most accessible to the highest income households.[79]

Along with class divisions, gender and racial divisions continue to shape policy responses to poverty and unemployment. This was evident even during the recent economic recession. While Congress authorized a series of social insurance extensions for unemployed workers, many of whom were white men, it failed to adopt a federal moratorium on time limits or renew emergency funds for TANF recipients, mostly women of color. Likewise, although thousands of unemployed workers joined new organizations, sometimes with union support, they rarely made common cause with public assistance recipients. The means-tested and categorical nature of the U.S. welfare state, in combination with the politics of class, race, and gender that animates it, has encouraged such fragmentation.

What is needed to overcome such divisions and to truly improve the lives of most workers and their families is a far more universal welfare system that provides all residents with basic income and services, including health care, child care, elder care, and housing assistance. Expanding these social services would also help to create more jobs for underemployed workers; Marcia Meyers argues, "Our challenge is to design antipoverty policies that are not about 'poverty' but about economic security . . ."[80] As cross-national research shows, universal programs provide a broader base of support for welfare rights than means-tested categorical ones, which tend to marginalize and divide the poor. The cost of providing such goods and services would certainly be expensive, but it is not beyond the nation's fiscal capacity. Funding a more far-reaching welfare state would require a major restructuring of our tax system, reversing several decades of tax cuts to corporations and the wealthy and significantly reducing the nation's military spending. The fight against poverty also requires greater protection of workers' rights to unionize and to bargain collectively with employers, as well as the expansion of such rights to independent contractors and temporary workers, a rapidly growing sector of the workforce. Such policies would go far to address the needs of the millions of Americans, not just the very poor, who yearn for greater economic security and a better quality of life. How a broad-based, militant national movement capable of moving forward such an agenda can grow and flourish in an era of deepening retrenchment and corporate-dominated politics remains the key question of the day.

Appendix

Data and Methods

My research is based on multiple data and methods. I interviewed a total of 110 people between 1998 and 2008. These included forty-four people in California and sixty-six people in Wisconsin. Most of these interviews took place in Los Angeles and Milwaukee and were with organizers, staff members, or leaders of grassroots welfare rights groups, advocacy organizations, unions, and service agencies that were involved in various welfare rights campaigns, although a few of these interviews were with rank-and-file members. To better understand some of the problems confronting low-income people and welfare politics, I also interviewed seven former welfare recipients and several staff of homeless shelters, four local policymakers, and a staff member at the Wisconsin Legislative Audit Bureau.

Interviews with welfare rights advocates focused on their views on welfare reform, how their organizations tried to influence state or local welfare policies, their collaboration with other groups, and the results of their efforts. Interviews typically lasted about an hour, with some interviews lasting several hours. Most of these interviews were audio-taped and later transcribed in whole or in part. Six informants from Milwaukee and one informant from Los Angeles were interviewed multiple times in order to follow up on the results of various campaigns and to update my information.

Whenever possible, my interviews were supplemented with field research. My interest in this book initially grew out of my observation of a public forum on welfare reform that took place in Los Angeles in 1997 and my volunteer work for the Los Angeles office of the Association of Community Organizations for Reform Now (ACORN), which I began doing in 1998. At that time, ACORN was organizing General Relief recipients as workfare workers and calling for improvements in their labor and employment rights. This volunteer work quickly drew me into other welfare rights events taking place in California. I participated in countless meetings, public forums, conference calls, rallies, demonstrations, and sit-in protests organized by various welfare rights groups in Los Angeles between 1997 and 2007. I also observed activists' coalition meetings and organizational membership meetings and listened to testimonies at various public hearings. Through this participation I talked with both organizers and rank-and-file members of various campaigns as I sat beside them on the bus en route to a rally or protest, stood next to them at various events and meetings, offered rides to members, or participated in conference calls. These conversations deepened my understanding of these campaigns and the organizations involved in them and helped to fill gaps in my knowledge.

Given my time and budget constraints, I was unable to conduct nearly as much field research in Milwaukee as I was able to do in Los Angeles. The only events and meetings that I was able to observe were those that coincided with my research visits to Milwaukee. These included a protest organized by Welfare Warriors, several meetings of the Wisconsin Works monitoring committee, a public forum about a job creation proposal, and a taskforce meeting organized by members of Hope Offered through Shared Ecumenical Action. To overcome my lack of field research in Wisconsin, I interviewed more people there. I also conducted eleven follow-up interviews in order to update my information.

For both California and Wisconsin, I examined accounts of welfare rights campaigns that were contained in newspaper articles, organizational literature, and other reports. Through my interviews and field research, I gathered organizational literature, including newsletters, flyers, meeting minutes, and other literature produced by welfare rights activists that described their campaigns. I also drew on relevant newspaper articles and research reports focusing on the administration of local welfare programs, welfare policy debates, and changes in welfare policies. Reports by journalists and researchers helped to verify activists' recollections of events, to update my research on ongoing campaigns, and to compare activists' perspectives with those of policymakers and opponents.

Notes

Chapter 1

1. Parts of this chapter are contained in Reese (2005a, 2007a, 2007b) and Krinsky and Reese (2006). They are reprinted with permission of the publishers.
2. See Pierson (1994); Stefancic and Delgado (1996); Teles (1996); and Weaver (2000).
3. Brock (2008); Mink (1998); Hays (2003a); Gilens (1999); Neubeck and Cazenave (2001); Fording, Soss, and Schram (2007).
4. Pierson (1994, 1996, 2001a, 2001b, 2001c).
5. These figures are for Temporary Assistance for Needy Families (Brown 2010).
6. Albelda (2001); Hays (2003a, 55; 2003b); Legal Momentum (2011); Loprest (1999); Savner, Strawn, and Greenberg (2002, 4); Weicher (2001, 19).
7. Legal Momentum (2010).
8. Gornick and Meyers (2003, 75); Neubeck (2006). These international measures of the poverty rate are based on the percentage of the population that earns 50 percent or less of the country's median income.
9. Christopher (2002).
10. The poverty rate was 20.7 percent for all persons below eighteen years of age (DeNavas-Walt, Proctor, and Smith 2010).
11. For 2009, the poverty rate was 35.4 percent among African American children and 33.1 percent among Latino children (U.S. Census Bureau 2010a).
12. U.S. Census Bureau (2010b).
13. U.S. Census Bureau (2010a, 2010b).
14. The federal government's two official measures of poverty—the poverty threshold and the poverty guideline—were developed in the 1960s. These measures are based on two slightly different estimates of the annually adjusted cost of a minimally sufficient diet for a family of a given size. These estimates are then multiplied by three. This multiplier was chosen based on consumption patterns found in the 1950s, which suggested that families

spent about one-third of their household income on food. Since the 1950s, the real prices of many goods and services have increased markedly, including the cost of housing, health insurance, child care, and transportation. The cost of living also varies greatly across U.S. cities and between urban and rural areas.

15. In other words, these scholars suggest that the poverty guideline for a family of three in 2008 should be *at least* $35,200, rather than the federal government's figure of $17,600; this latter figure would place most female-headed households in poverty (Cauthen and Fass 2008).

16. Compared to welfare states in most other highly industrialized democratic nations, the U.S. welfare state is a residual one (Esping-Anderson 1990).

17. It required states to have at least 50 percent of single adult TANF recipients engaged in at least thirty hours of "work activities" (twenty hours of which should be actual work) and provided credit toward this goal for caseload reductions. Able-bodied adult recipients of food stamps (ages eighteen to forty-nine) with no dependent children were denied assistance after three months if they did not work at least twenty hours per week or meet their state's welfare-to-work requirements, unless they were exempt because of their area's job shortages, high unemployment rates, or other reasons. Recipients were required to work at least twenty hours per week or participate in a workfare program for the number of hours it would take for them to earn their benefits if they were paid the federal or state minimum wage (whichever was higher).

18. Polls taken in 1993 and 1994 show that most respondents believed that recipients should be allowed to receive benefits at the end of their time limit if they worked for them. A 1993 survey found that more than 70 percent of voters were willing to make exceptions for the two-year consecutive time limit for mothers with preschool children and those working part-time at low wages. Approximately 60 percent of respondents did not think that work requirements should be applied to mothers of infants (Weaver 2000, 181–84; Garin, Molyneux, and DiVall 1994).

19. Mettler (2000); Schram (2006).

20. Polls taken in the 1990s also showed high levels of public support for job training for welfare recipients, with most respondents indicating a willingness to pay more in taxes to provide it (Weaver 2000, 181; Weaver, Shapiro, and Jacobs 1995, 620). The work-first approach was encouraged by PRWORA's stipulation that states only allow education to count as a work activity for 20 percent of their caseload (Gordon 2001, 13). The policy was later revised so that 30 percent of recipients in each state are allowed to participate in educational activities as part of their mandatory welfare-to-work hours.

21. The number of state General Relief programs declined from twenty-five to thirteen (Gallagher 1999, 5–6).

22. Sparks (2003).

23. Brown (2010).
24. Albert and King (2001); Hays (2003a, 58; 2003b); Rogers-Dillon (2001, 8–9); Weicher (2001, 19); Loprest and Wissoker (2002). The expansion of the Earned Income Tax Credit, child care services, publicly subsidized health insurance, and minimum-wage increases in the 1990s also made it easier for poor mothers to leave welfare for work (Savner, Strawn, and Greenberg 2002, 3–5).
25. Brown (2010); Loprest (2003); Savner, Strawn, and Greenberg (2002, 3–5); *New York Times* (2002). An Urban Institute survey found that "thirty-two percent of welfare recipients were in paid jobs in 1999. That number dropped to 28 percent by 2002. Employment also declined among those who had just come off of the welfare rolls, slipping from 50 percent in 1999 to 42 percent in 2002" (Zedlewski and Loprest 2003, 9).
26. Brown (2010).
27. Loprest (1999); Rogers-Dillon (2001); Urban Institute (2001); Savner, Strawn, and Greenberg (2002, 3).
28. Studies of former welfare recipients who found employment showed that most were earning between $7.00 and $7.50 per hour in the late 1990s, and most did not work full-time and year-round (Albelda 2001; Hays 2003a, 55, 2003b; Weicher 2001, 19). Another review of more than thirty recent state-level "leaver studies" found that median wages ranged from $6.00 to $8.47 an hour, while a national survey by the Urban Institute found that the national median hourly wage for welfare leavers was $6.61 in 1997 and $7.15 in 1999 (Savner, Strawn, and Greenberg 2002, 4; Loprest 1999, chart 7). See also Legal Momentum (2011).
29. Burnham (2001); Legal Momentum (2011); Loprest (1999); Hays (2003a, 226).
30. Hays (2003a, 59).
31. This philosophy, associated with the welfare reform program adopted in Riverside, California, quickly spread across U.S. states and shaped policy debates in Western Europe, Canada, and Australia (Peck 2001).
32. Jones-DeWeever and Gault (2006); Legal Momentum (2011).
33. Legal Momentum (2011).
34. Peck and Theodore (1999, 6); see also Peck (2001).
35. Carroll (2001, online).
36. Cook (1998).
37. Heuler Williams (1998).
38. Citizens for Workfare Justice (1998); Krinsky and Reese (2006).
39. Falcocchio (2001).
40. Work exemption rules varied across states but commonly included welfare recipients with disabilities and victims of domestic violence (Pear 2002). On the impact of caseload reduction credits, flexibility in the use of

federal "Maintenance of Effort" funds, the use of state funds to provide assistance to TANF recipients, and other administrative practices on the implementation of welfare-to-work requirements, see DeParle (2004, 220) and Brown (2010, 10–13).

41. Handler (1995); Handler and Hasenfeld (1991, 40).
42. Post (1997, 35); Tilly (1996).
43. Business groups tried to cut labor costs even further by seeking exemptions from minimum-wage and other labor laws for welfare-to-work participants, though they were not successful (DeParle 1997; Post 1997, 27; Rector 1997).
44. Schram (2006); Wacquant (2009).
45. Legal Momentum (2011).
46. Rowe and Murphy (2006, 70–71).
47. This is the most recent General Accounting Office analysis available (Brown 2010).
48. Legal Momentum (2011).
49. Brown (2010).
50. Zedlewski et al. (2002).
51. Legal Momentum (2010); U.S. Congressional Budget Office (2005).
52. Zedlewski et al. (2008).
53. These latter women were particularly vulnerable; they were abused as children, had children at an early age, did not finish high school, had little or no job experience, were currently involved with abusive men, and sometimes suffered from drug addictions (Scott, London, and Myers 2002).
54. Burnham (2001, 40–41).
55. U.S. Conference of Mayors (2009).
56. Farrell et al. (2008, 112).
57. Patriquin (2001, 87); Gordon (2001, 4).
58. Farrell et al. (2008, 93, 112).
59. Schott and Finch (2010).
60. Legal Momentum (2011).
61. Collins and Mayer (2010); Dohan (2003); Edin and Lein (1997); Legal Momentum (2011).
62. Legal Momentum (2011, 7).
63. Bronfenbrenner (2009).
64. Greenhouse (2008, 5).
65. Greenhouse (2008, 9).
66. DeNavas-Walt, Proctor, and Smith (2010).

67. Brown (2010).

68. Collins and Mayer (2010).

69. *New York Times* (2009).

70. Realty Trac (2010).

71. U.S. Bureau of Labor Statistics (2010a).

72. Anderson (2011); Williams and Hegewisch (2011).

73. Center on Budget and Policy Priorities (2009, 2010).

74. DeVerteuil, Marr, and Snow (2009) identify four forms of resistance by homeless people to anti-homeless ordinances and displacement: exit, adaptation, persistence, and voice. Only the last involves collective action; the former three forms refer to individual responses.

75. DeParle (2004, 16).

76. DeParle (2004, 59).

77. For a good review of these reforms, see DeParle (2004, 165–70) and Collins and Mayer (2010, 57–58).

78. Hein (2002, para. 8).

79. Collins and Mayer (2010, 56–57).

80. Collins and Mayer (2010, 59); Wilayto (1997); Hudson Institute (2002).

81. Manhattan Institute for Policy Research (2002); Stefancic and Delgado (1996, 86); Rector (1997).

82. Handler (2004); Reese (2007a).

83. Flaherty (1997); Sharma-Jensen (1997).

84. Carleton (1998); Dresang (1998a); Hein (2002); Mayers (1999a, 1999b).

85. Hein (2002).

86. *Cairns Post* (2000); Mendes (2003, 42).

87. U.S. General Accounting Office (2000).

88. In total, forty-two out of fifty states deny recipients' entire benefit or close the case as the most severe form of sanction when recipients are not compliant with program rules. However, most states do this for only a limited time period, ranging between one and twelve months (Rowe and Murphy 2006).

89. California, along with twenty-four states, exempts from work requirements mothers of infants that are less than twelve months old. Like only twelve other states, Wisconsin only exempts mothers with infants who are three months old or less. Unlike Wisconsin, California exempts ill or incapacitated recipients (like eleven other states), those caring for an ill or incapacitated person (like nine other states), those sixty years or more in age (like seven other states), and victims of domestic violence (like thirteen other states). California also extends the time limit for all of these

groups, whereas Wisconsin does not. The only time limit exemption that Wisconsin has authorized that California has not is an exemption for recipients caring for an infant three months or less in age. Wisconsin, unlike California, also extends the time limit for recipients who are cooperating with welfare regulations but are unable to find employment (Rowe and Murphy 2006). In practice, however, recipients, especially those in Milwaukee, were frequently denied welfare if they were deemed "job-ready," even if they had no employment offer.

90. Collins and Mayer (2010, 65).
91. Collins and Mayer (2010, 23).
92. Peck (2001).
93. Collins and Mayer (2010, 29).
94. Milkman (2006).
95. Staggenborg (1986, 375).
96. Amenta, Halfmann, and Young (1999, 6–7; see also Amenta and Young 1999).

Chapter 2

1. For example, see Noble (1997) and Lieberman (1998).
2. Marston (2000).
3. Lipset (1950).
4. Jenness, Meyer, and Ingram (2005, 300). As Deleon (1999) points out, these phases have been conceptualized differently by various scholars. Laswell (1971) initially distinguished seven stages in the policy process (intelligence, promotion, prescription, invocation, application, termination, and appraisal), which were later condensed by Brewer (1974) to six stages: initiation, estimation, selection, implementation, evaluation, and termination.
5. Deleon (1999, 23).
6. Sabatier (1999).
7. For example, see Hicks (1999); Noble (1997); Quadagno (1984, 1985, 1994); Piven and Cloward (1993 [1971], 1977b); Peck (2001).
8. Reese (2005a).
9. Collins and Mayer (2010); Peck (2001); Peck and Theodore (1999); Tilly (1996); Wacquant (2009).
10. Ridzi (2009).
11. Brown (1999); Fording (1997); Fording, Soss, and Schram (2007); Gilens (1999); Gooden (1995); Gordon (1994); Lieberman (1998); Mettler (1998); Mink (1998); Neubeck and Cazenave (2001); Quadagno (1994).

12. Reese (2005a).
13. Reese (2005a).
14. Wacquant (2009).
15. Albelda (2001, 71); Institute for Women's Policy Research (1994); Duncan (2000, 435); Reese (2005a, chapter 1).
16. One exception to this is the higher rate of Supplemental Security Income usage among immigrants, especially Asian refugees, in 1989 (Bean, Van Hook, and Glick 1997, 448). Blau (1984); Chang (2000, 21–32); Jensen (1988); Kposowa (1998, 147–59); Tienda and Jensen (1986); Clark and Passel (1993), cited in Calavita (1996, 290); National Research Council of the National Academy of Sciences, cited in Moore (1998); Suárez-Orozco and Suárez-Orozco (1995, 28–35).
17. Gilens (1999); Hondagneu-Sotelo (1995); Neubeck and Cazenave (2001); Schram, Soss, and Fording (2003).
18. By 1995, 63.5 percent of married women (with husbands present) with children under age six were employed—more than double the figure for 1970 (U.S. Census Bureau 2001). Polls taken in the mid-1990s found that most respondents supported time limits for welfare and work requirements for mothers with children under age three (Weaver 2000, 177–83).
19. Skocpol (1992).
20. Piven and Cloward (1977b); Amenta (1998).
21. Amenta (1998, 2006).
22. Steensland (2008); Quadagno (2005).
23. Kornbluh (1997); Nadasen (2005); Piven and Cloward (1977b); Quadagno (1994); West (1981).
24. Amenta (2006).
25. De Jong et al. (2006).
26. Mettler (2000).
27. Gonzales (2007, 190–92).
28. Gonzales (2007, 190–92).
29. Anheier (2009, 1092).
30. Aiken and Bode (2009); Harris and McDonald (2000); Gonzales (2007).
31. Gonzales (2007, 197–98).
32. Anheier (2009, 1088).
33. Andrew (2006).
34. Fording (2003) finds that tougher time limits were more likely to be adopted when higher shares of states' caseloads were black or Latino (see also Brock 2008). States were significantly more likely to adopt tougher sanctions and family caps when a higher share of their caseload was black

but not Latino (Soss et al. 2001; Gais and Weaver 2002). Survey research also shows that public support for more welfare spending is significantly lower in states where higher proportions of recipients are black (Johnson 2003, 157; Fox 2004). However, consistent with the "contact hypothesis," research shows that whites who live in areas with small numbers of Latinos are more likely than those from areas where Latinos are more prevalent to stereotype Latinos as lazy, to want to decrease spending on welfare, and to let their negative stereotypes about Latinos influence their welfare-spending preferences (Fox 2004).

35. Fording (2003, 81–88); Soss et al. (2001).
36. Fording (2003, 81–88); Gais and Weaver (2002);
37. Cauthen and Amenta (1996); Fording (2003, 81–88); Soss et al. (2001); Gais and Weaver (2002).
38. Mettler (2000).
39. Analyzing administrative data from Florida, Fording, Soss, and Schram (2007, 306) found "that [TANF] sanctioning is lower in areas with a large minority population," which could be due to "indirect pressure that members of minority populations exert on TANF officials" or greater representation of minorities among TANF case managers and administrators. Keiser, Mueser, and Choi's (2004) analysis of the implementation of welfare sanctions in Missouri counties suggests that there is a curvilinear relationship between the implementation of welfare sanctions and racial context; they found that, controlling for other factors, sanction rates increased along with the minority population share until that share reached 16 percent of the total population; after that point, the sanction rate declined. These studies also reveal that higher sanction rates are found in more politically conservative areas.
40. Lipsky (2010).
41. Ridzi (2004); Ridzi and London (2006).
42. Korteweg (2006, 329).
43. Korteweg (2006, 330).
44. Hays (2003a).
45. Ridzi (2009).
46. Heath (2009, 44).
47. This research was produced by Susan Gooden, cited in Burnham (2001, 44).
48. Korteweg (2006, 327).
49. Banerjee and Ridzi (2008).
50. Ridzi (2004); Ridzi and London (2006).
51. Ridzi (2004); Ridzi and London (2006).
52. Heath (2009).

53. For example, see Bhargava (2002); Daniel (2002); Hall and Strege-Flora (2002); Kingfisher (1996); Krajcer and Delgado (2002); Miewald (2003); Neubeck (2006); Abramovitz (2000); Baptist and Bricker-Jenkins (2002).
54. Lipsky (2010).
55. McAdam (1999 [1982], 25).
56. Tarrow (1998).
57. Betz (1974); Jackson and Johnson (1974); Swank and Hicks (1984).
58. Gerhards and Rucht (1992); Jones et al. (2001); Jenkins and Perrow (1977); McAdam, McCarthy, and Zald (1988, 1996, 13); McAdam (1999 [1982]); Reese (2005b); Shearer (1982); Shaw (1999); Staggenborg (1986).
59. Prunty (1984); Epstein (1996); Taylor (1996).
60. Diani (1997); Gamson (1975).
61. For example, see Gerhards and Rucht (1992); Jenkins and Perrow (1977); Jones et al. (2001); Reese (2005b); Shaw (1999); Shearer (1982); Staggenborg (1986).
62. Tarrow (1998, 103–4, 152).
63. Zald and McCarthy (1980); Kleidman and Rochon (1997); Hathaway and Meyer (1997, 61–67); Staggenborg (1986).
64. Arnold (1995); Gitlin (1995, 116–25); Rose (2000).
65. McAdam (1999 [1982]).
66. Piven and Cloward's (1977a, 1977b) theory has been rightly criticized for overlooking the role of organizations and organizational resources, such as money, staff, and leaders, in shaping the mobilization of low-income people (Jenkins and Perrow 1977; Cress and Snow 2000; Valocchi 1990).
67. Imig (1996); Jenkins and Eckert (1986); McAdam (1999 [1982]); Cress and Snow (1996).
68. Fletcher and Gapasin (2008).
69. Amenta (1998); Amenta, Carruthers, and Zylan (1992); Cress and Snow (2000).
70. Schneider and Ingram (1993, 334).
71. Schneider and Ingram (1993, 344).
72. My argument here borrows insights from the political process model of social movements, which suggests that activists' incentives to overcome their differences and such challenges for cooperation increase in response to new political opportunities or threats. New opportunities and threats not only create a sense of urgency among organizers, they tend to mobilize constituents and donors, which reduces the scarcity of—and competition for—organizational resources (see Hathaway and Meyer 1997; Kleidman and Rochon 1997; Staggenborg 1986). Various studies examine the relative importance of threat and opportunity for

the formation of various kinds of social movement coalitions. For example, see McCammon and Campbell (2002), Van Dyke and Soule (2002), and Van Dyke (2003). Almeida's (2003) case study of El Salvador explores how threat and opportunity operated *sequentially* to produce two distinct protest waves.

73. Gordon (2001, 13); United States Student Association (2002, 5).
74. Kornbluh (1998); Miewald (2003).
75. Wheeler (2002).
76. Abramovitz (2000, 147).
77. Daniel (2002); Krajcer and Delgado (2002).
78. Reese and Ramirez (2002a, 2002b).
79. Some of these groups worked with the Applied Research Center's Welfare Advocacy Research Project (WARP) and the Northwest Federation of Community Organizations (Krajcer and Delgado 2002).
80. Krajcer and Delgado (2002).
81. Neubeck (2006, chapter 8); Abramovitz (2000, 144–46); Baptist and Bricker-Jenkins (2002, 206–7).
82. Naples (1997).
83. Abramovitz (2000, 145–46).
84. Liu (1999); Defranco (1999).
85. A similar campaign in Montana was more successful in gaining allies and making policy gains. There, members of Working for Economic Equality and Liberation and their allies successfully urged state lawmakers to allow low-income parents to receive child care subsidies for taking care of their own children (Bhargava 2002).
86. Abramovitz (2000, 145–46).
87. The American Federation of State, County, and Municipal Employees (AFSCME) formed a temporary organizing partnership with A Job Is a Right in New York City; Service Employees International Union (SEIU) invested in several workfare organizing projects, in collaboration with People Organized to Win Employment Rights (POWER) in San Francisco and Action for Grassroots Empowerment and Neighborhood Development Alternatives (AGENDA) in Los Angeles; Communications Workers of America (CWA) formed an organizing partnership with the Association of Community Organizations for Reform Now (ACORN) in New Jersey and in Milwaukee; and the American Federation of Labor and Congress of Industrial Organizations (AFL-CIO) supported a workfare organizing project in Baltimore (Krinsky and Reese 2006; Simmons 2002).
88. Worthen, Edwards, and Stokes (2002).
89. Simmons (2002, 73–78).
90. Tait (2005).

91. Reese and Newcombe (2003); West (1981).
92. Ridzi (2007).
93. Clawson (2003); Isaac and Christiansen (2002, 723–25); Katznelson (1981, 2005); Stepan-Norris and Zeitlin (2003); Tait (2005).
94. Fantasia and Voss (2004); Levi (2001); Nissen (2003a, 2003b); Voss and Sherman (2000).
95. Ness (1998); Nissen (2003b, 138–41); Robinson (2000); Rose (2000); Tait (2005).
96. Simmons (2002).
97. Dreiling (1998); Johnston (2000); Obach (2004); Robinson (2000); Nissen (2003a, 2003b); Scipes (1992); Voss and Sherman (2000).
98. Nissen (2003a, 2003b, 2004); Voss and Sherman (2000).
99. Johnston (2000); Robinson (2000); Rose (2000, 99–102); Voss and Sherman (2000).
100. Bronfenbrenner et al. (1998); Clawson (2003); Nissen (1995, 2004); Brecher and Costello (1990).
101. Clawson (2003); Eimer (1999); Matejka (2000); Ness and Eimer (2001); Reynolds (1999); Obach (2004).
102. Heredia (2008); Reese (2005a).
103. The measure was overturned through a court ruling in 1997, and the state's appeal of this ruling was dropped in 1998 under Governor Gray Davis.
104. Diaz (2010); Heredia (2008).
105. Diaz (2010); Heredia (2008).
106. Bhargava (2002, 208).
107. As of 2006, only one state (New Hampshire) used a standard of need above the federal poverty guideline, while thirty-four other U.S. states set their income ceilings *below* the federal poverty guideline to determine eligibility for TANF—a guideline that many experts consider to be set too low. Twelve states used the federal poverty guideline to determine the maximum monthly earnings a family can have and be eligible for TANF (Rowe and Murphy 2006, 70–71).
108. In part, this was the outcome of prior welfare rights campaigns involving particular groups of low-income people or their advocates, such as the elderly, veterans, unemployed workers, and maternalist social reformers concerned about the plight of low-income single mothers (Amenta 1998); Skocpol (1992); Goldberg (2007); Piven and Cloward (1977a, 1977b); Gordon (1994).
109. Nelson (2006).
110. This group was initially organized by the Unitarian Universalist Service Committee (Abramovitz 2000, 148).
111. Miewald (2003).

112. Daniel (2002).
113. Atlas and Dreier (2009). On coverage of Rathke and his brother's misuse of funds, see Strom (2008).
114. Krajcer and Delgado (2002).
115. Hall and Strege-Flora (2002, 193).
116. For example, in Maine, the Maine Equal Justice Project and the Maine Association of Interdependent Neighborhoods and their allies celebrated when state legislators authorized funds for a "Parents as Scholars" program that allowed two thousand welfare recipients to attend school and be exempt from time limits (Bhargava 2002, 203). In Kentucky, state policymakers, pressed by activists, agreed to increase the supportive services available to recipients enrolled in school, to allow twenty-four months of college education without additional work requirements for full-time students, to allow students to count ten hours per week of class time toward their thirty-hour weekly work requirement, to create additional work-study placements for them, and to give any participant a $250 bonus for completing an educational program (Miewald 2003, 176–78).
117. Krinsky and Reese (2006); Reese, Giedraitis, and Vega (2006).
118. Kingfisher (1996); Miewald (2003).

Chapter 3

1. This chapter was written with help from Elvia Ramirez. Sections of it have been published in Reese and Ramirez (2002a) and Reese (2005a, 2005b) and appear in Reese and Ramirez (2002b). They are reprinted with permission of the publishers.
2. The first epigraph is cited in Hernandez (1996, 14). The second quote is from Morain (1997, A19). The third quote is from McDonnell (1997a, 1).
3. The "qualified" immigrant category includes lawful permanent residents; refugees, asylees, and persons granted withholding of deportation or removal; Cuban and Haitian immigrants; those with Immigration and Naturalization Service parole for at least one year; conditional entrants; and those identified as victims of domestic violence and their dependents. "Unqualified" legal immigrants include those without green cards but who are nevertheless in the United States legally, as well as immigrants who entered the country legally on or after August 22, 1996 (the day the law was passed). Recent immigrants are ineligible for the first five years that they are in the United States. Legal immigrants are ineligible unless they are veterans, are refugees, or can prove they worked in the U.S. for ten years or more (McDonnell 1996; National Immigration Law Center 2002, 3).
4. Chang (2000); Fragomen (1997, 441); McBride (1999, 299).
5. Zimmerman and Tumlin (1999, 11).

6. Boggs (2000, 30–31); Piven and Cloward (2000); Ramakrishnan and Espenshade (2001).
7. Schneider and Ingram (1993).
8. *Wisconsin State Journal* (1997).
9. This sharp rise was part of a longer-term rise in the number of immigrants naturalizing. Other factors that contributed to this rise were (1) the decision of some Latin American governments to allow immigrants to have dual nationality, (2) the Immigration and Naturalization Service's decision to lower the relative cost of naturalization compared to replacing a green card, and (3) the fact that many undocumented immigrants granted permanent resident status in 1986 under the Immigration Reform and Control Act became eligible for naturalization in the 1990s (Ramakrishnan 2001).
10. Ramakrishnan (2001).
11. Zimmerman and Tumlin (1999).
12. National Immigration Law Center (2002).
13. On "welfare racism," see Neubeck and Cazenave (2001) and Schram, Soss, and Fording (2003).
14. Fox (2009).
15. Beginning in 1931, federal agents and local welfare officials deported, threatened to deport, and urged Mexicans and Mexican Americans to leave the country voluntarily, even if they were legal residents or citizens of the United States. They even offered to subsidize their return trip back to Mexico. Between 1930 and 1934, well over 400,000 Mexican immigrants and Mexican Americans left the United States for Mexico, and by 1940, the U.S. Mexican population was about half as large as it was in 1930. While these programs supposedly targeted male migrants, entire families were repatriated, and women made up as many as two-thirds of deportees between 1931 and 1933 (Guerin-Gonzales 1996, 77–114; Gann and Duignan 1986, 51; Hondagneu-Sotelo 1995, 174–76; Samora and Simon 1977, 137).
16. Fox (2009).
17. Fox (2009).
18. Chang (2000, 61).
19. Fox (2009).
20. Lindsley (2002); Hondagneu-Sotelo (1995).
21. Brugge (1995, 5); see also Chang (2000, 21–53).
22. Cited in Weinberg (1998, 66).
23. Fujiwara (1999, 7, 96, 158).
24. Fujiwara (1999, 14, 32).
25. Yoo (2001, 57).

26. Fujiwara (1999, 164).

27. Fujiwara (1999, 135).

28. On immigrants' relatively low rates of welfare usage, see Blau (1984); Chang (2000, 21–32); Jensen (1988); Kposowa (1998, 147–59); Tienda and Jensen (1986); Clark and Passel (1993), cited in Calavita (1996, 290); Suárez-Orozco and Suárez-Orozco (1995, 28–35).

29. National Research Council of the National Academy of Sciences, cited in Moore (1998).

30. Lapinski et al. (1997, 365). Nativism is more common among whites but not confined to them. For example, a 1992 *Business Week*/Harris Poll found that 69 percent of non-blacks and 53 percent of blacks thought that present-day immigration was bad for the country. Racial and ethnic minorities often fear immigrants will increase competition for unskilled or semi-skilled jobs or resent "middle-man minorities" who do employers' dirty work (Brugge 1995, 6; Sanchez 1997; Jaret 1999, 14; Bonacich and Appelbaum 2000).

31. Lapinski et al. (1997, 372–73); Jaret (1999, 10).

32. Lapinski et al. (1997, 360–63).

33. Shaw and Shapiro (2002, 118–19).

34. Mehan (1997, 263).

35. Armbruster, Geron, and Bonacich (1995, 661).

36. Weaver (2000, 231).

37. Rector and Lauber (1995).

38. Stein (1995, 448).

39. Shapiro (1997, 1).

40. Cited in Shogren (1994b, A1).

41. Shogren (1994a).

42. Weaver (2000, 246, 291).

43. Cited in Shogren (1994b, A1).

44. National Immigration Law Center (2002).

45. Chang (2000, 61); Kilty and de Haymes (2000, 11–12); McBride (1999); Newton (2005); Parenti (1999, 139–60); Ramakrishnan (2001); Schneider (2000).

46. Burnham (2001, 46).

47. Chang (2000); Newton (2005); Reese and Ramirez (2002a).

48. Hein (2006).

49. *City News Service* (1996).

50. Emma Lazarus Fund (1996).

51. Ong (1999, 262).

52. Chang (2000, 36).
53. Chang (2000, 36); Kelsey (1994).
54. Coalition for Humane Immigrants Rights (CHIRLA) staff member, personal interview, Los Angeles, August 9 and August 13, 2001; Asian Pacific American Legal Center (APALC) staff member, personal interview, Los Angeles, July 17, 2001.
55. APALC staff member, personal interview.
56. McDonnell (1997b, 3).
57. CHIRLA staff member, personal interview; Los Angeles Coalition to End Hunger and Homelessness (LACEH&H) staff, personal interview, Los Angeles, July 17, 2001.
58. Whether or not this elite patronage moderated the goals and tactics of the welfare and immigrant rights movements is an interesting research question but beyond the scope of this study.
59. Moody (1997).
60. Zimmerman and Tumlin (1999).
61. *Fresno Bee* (1997).
62. Unz (1994).
63. Qualified immigrants included refugees, asylees, and persons granted withholding of deportation or removal, as well as Cuban and Haitian immigrants.
64. McDonnell (1996); National Immigration Law Center (2002, 3).
65. Zimmerman and Tumlin (1999).
66. Fujiwara (1999, 160–86, 203–24).
67. Reese and Ramirez (2002b).
68. Hero and Preuhs (2006, 2007).
69. The other state was Maine, home to very few immigrants (National Immigration Law Center 2002).
70. Capps (1997a, A5).
71. *Fresno Bee* (1997); APALC staff, personal interview; LACEH&H staff, personal interview; *Los Angeles Times* (1996); McDonnell (1997c).
72. Ellis (1997a); *San Francisco Examiner* (1997); Morain (1997).
73. This figure was based on the average number of legal immigrants that entered the state between 1990 and 1998 (State of California Department of Finance 2000); Zimmerman and Tumlin (1999, 57).
74. Fagan (1996).
75. Ramakrishnan (2001, 8).
76. Nakao (1996); Sample (1996).

77. Jacobs (1996). This is the number of legal immigrants actually receiving these benefits at the time and does not take into consideration the number that qualify for them after naturalizing (Wolch and Sommer 1997).
78. This was the Asian Pacific Policy and Planning Council (AP3CON) in Los Angeles (AP3CON staff member, personal interview, Los Angeles, July 17, 2001).
79. This list was based on information from newspaper reports of this issue during the first year after PRWORA's passage and our interviews.
80. Doyle (1997, A10).
81. Fujiwara (1999, 215–23).
82. Fujiwara (1999, 196).
83. Fujiwara (1999, 215–16).
84. Albano (1997).
85. Fujiwara (1999, 195–96). Journalists, by contrast, claim that only about 1,200 people participated in the second event (Bee 1997).
86. Fujiwara (1999, 197).
87. *Press Enterprise* (1996).
88. Minton (1997).
89. Pyle, McDonnell, and Tobar (1998).
90. National Association of Latino Elected Officials Educational Fund (1997).
91. LACEH&H staff member, personal interview, 2001; APALC staff member, personal interview, 2001.
92. Albano (1997).
93. Ellis (1997b, A1).
94. California State Assembly (1997); Ellis (1997b); Jacobs (1997); Mendel (1997).
95. California Immigrant and Welfare Collaborative (CIWC) staff member, personal interview, Sacramento, September 17, 2001.
96. Rodriguez (1997).
97. APALC staff member, personal interview; AP3CON staff member, personal interview; LACEH&H staff member, personal interview, 2001; CHIRLA staff member, personal interview; People's Community Organization for Reform and Empowerment staff member, personal interview, Los Angeles, August 9, 2001.
98. CIWC staff member, personal interview; LACEH&H staff member, personal interview; CHIRLA staff member, personal interview; APALC staff member, personal interview.
99. Morgan (1996); Griswold (1998).
100. McCarthy (1997, B1).
101. Bier (1998, A1).

102. Fujiwara (1999).
103. Wisconsin Immigrant and Refugee Coalition (1997); Martin and Schubert (1998).
104. Blumenfeld (1998); Wisconsin Immigrant and Refugee Coalition (1997).
105. Wisconsin Immigrant and Refugee Coalition leader, personal interview, Madison, Wisconsin, September 20, 2002.
106. Blumenfeld (1997a, 1997b, 1997c); Wisconsin Immigrant and Refugee Coalition (1997); Wisconsin Immigrant and Refugee Coalition leader, personal interview.
107. Wisconsin Immigrant and Refugee Coalition leader, personal interview.
108. Wisconsin Immigrant and Refugee Coalition leader, personal interview; Hmong American Friendship Association staff member, personal interview, Milwaukee, August 19, 2002.
109. Wisconsin Immigrant and Refugee Coalition and Wisconsin Child Nutrition Alliance (1998, 1).
110. Hall (1998).
111. Blumberg and Huebscher (1998).
112. Blumenfeld (1998).
113. Cioni (1998).
114. *Capital Times* (1997).
115. Cioni (1998).
116. Wisconsin Immigrant and Refugee Coalition leader, personal interview.
117. Balousek (1997).
118. Balousek (1997); Callender (1998a, 1998b); Pommer (1998); *Wisconsin State Journal* (1998a); Wisconsin Immigrant and Refugee Coalition (1997).
119. Hall (1998); Martin and Schubert (1998).
120. Wisconsin Immigrant and Refugee Coalition (1997); *Wisconsin State Journal* (1998a).
121. *Sheboygan Press* (1997).
122. Callender (1998b, 6A).
123. Callender (1998c).
124. Jones (1998); Rinard (1998); Walters (1998).
125. Jones (1998).
126. *Wisconsin State Journal* (1998a).
127. Rinard (1998).
128. Pommer (1998).
129. Jones (1998, online).

130. Reese and Ramirez (2002b).
131. Reese and Ramirez (2002b).

Chapter 4

1. This chapter was written with research assistance from Vincent Giedraitis and Eric Vega. Parts of this chapter are contained in Reese, Giedraitis, and Vega (2005, 2006). They are reprinted with permission of the publishers. See also Reese (2002a).
2. Gonzales (2007, 199–200).
3. Andrew (2006); Gonzales (2007); Harris and McDonald (2000).
4. Gonzales (2007, 202).
5. Harris and McDonald (2000, 58).
6. Andrew (2006, 323).
7. Rummery (2010, 295).
8. Gonzales (2007, 199).
9. Andrew (2006); Anheier (2009); Aiken and Bode (2009).
10. Gonzales (2007, 203).
11. Andrew (2006, 318).
12. Anheier (2009, 1092).
13. Winston et al. (2002); see also Brodkin, Fuqua, and Thoren (2002).
14. American Federation of State, County, and Municipal Employees (AFSCME) (2006); Reese, Giedraitis, and Vega (2005, 2006).
15. Janison (2000).
16. Probably, this was done in order to increase its job placement rates since these were calculated as a ratio of the total number of clients, creating an incentive to minimize the number of clients (Zullo 2000, 11–14).
17. Brodkin, Fuqua, and Thoren (2002).
18. Nilsen (2002, 26).
19. Nilsen (2002, 3); see also Sanger (2003, 105).
20. AFSCME (1998a, 2006); Reese, Giedraitis, and Vega (2005, 2006).
21. Alquist (1997); see also AFSCME (2006).
22. Anheier (2009, 1084).
23. Andrew (2006, 321).
24. Andrew (2006).
25. Aiken and Bode (2009).
26. Rummery (2010).
27. Rummery (2010).

28. Rummery (2010, 296); see also Andrew (2006).
29. Anheier (2009); Gonzales (2007, 193–95).
30. This amount includes state maintenance-of-effort funds.
31. Nilsen (2002).
32. Sanger (2003, 46).
33. AFSCME (2006).
34. Hartung and Washburn (1998); Murray (1999); DeParle (2004, 230–50).
35. Sanger (2003, 73).
36. Sanger (2003, 73).
37. Lockheed Martin IMS was sold to Affiliated Computer Services in 2001 (Sanger 2003, 74).
38. Harris (1988); Roderick (1988); Wood (1988, 10–25, 12–20).
39. Wood (1988, 10–25); Roderick (1988).
40. Wood (1988, 12–20, 10–25); Varga (2001).
41. Kyle, Savage, and Diaz (1991).
42. Riccardi (2000a).
43. Riccardi (2000a).
44. SEIU 660 staff member, personal interview, Los Angeles, September 2001; Riccardi (2000a).
45. SEIU 660 staff member, personal interview, Los Angeles, September 2001.
46. SEIU 660 staff member, personal interview, 2001.
47. Martinez (1998).
48. ACORN-LA (1998a); author's fieldnotes, Los Angeles, March 26, 1998.
49. Author's fieldnotes, Los Angeles, June 16, 2000.
50. Author's fieldnotes, Los Angeles, January 29, 2002; personal correspondence with SEIU staff, March 6, 2002; Riccardi (2000a, 2000b).
51. Riccardi (2000a, 2000b).
52. Maximus's bid was not the lowest although the county officials held that the company was the most qualified and thus recommended its approval.
53. Riccardi (2000b).
54. Riccardi (2000b, B1).
55. Riccardi (2000b).
56. Keating (2000).
57. Berg (2000); Keating (2000).
58. Keating (2000).
59. SEIU 660 staff member, personal interview, 2001.

60. SEIU 660 staff member, personal interview, 2001.
61. Personal email correspondence with Tanya Akel, January 22, 2001; Dobuzinskis (2002); Zahniser (2002).
62. SEIU 660 (2001).
63. Los Angeles Coalition to End Hunger and Homelessness staff member, personal interview, Los Angeles, July 17, 2001.
64. SEIU 660 staff member, personal interview, 2001.
65. Wahla (2001); Reese (2002a).
66. Author's fieldnotes, Los Angeles, January 29, 2002; personal correspondence with SEIU staff, March 6, 2002.
67. Los Angeles County Office of Education was awarded a two-year, $20.5 million contract, with an option for three one-year extensions (Dobuzinskis 2002; Zahniser 2002).
68. Personal email correspondence with SEIU staff, March 11, 2001; Dobuzinskis (2002); Zahniser (2002).
69. SEIU 660 staff member, personal interview, 2001.
70. Krinsky and Reese (2006); Reese (2002b); Reese and Ramirez (2002b).
71. Some provided case management services for these counties' Greater Avenues for Independence (GAIN) program (California's welfare-to-work program for low-income parents). Others processed applications for Supplemental Security Income (SSI). On average, Maximus employees were employed with the company for 35 months and Lockheed employees were employed with the company for 8.5 months. Eight of these employees had been employed with Maximus, while five were employed with Lockheed. Four were employed in Orange County, while ten were employed in Los Angeles County (one was employed in both counties). Most interviews lasted thirty to forty minutes and focused on employees' concerns about the company's service delivery and reporting practices (Reese 2002a).
72. I interviewed a smaller number of former Lockheed employees than former Maximus employees, making it difficult to accurately compare the magnitude of these problems across these companies (Reese 2002a).
73. All of these above quotes are cited in Reese (2002a, 12–16).
74. Wahla (2001).
75. Between October 2000 and June 2001, Maximus was faulted for this in three out of nine monthly reviews, while Lockheed was faulted for it in four out of nine monthly reviews.
76. Maximus was faulted for this in seven out of nine monthly reviews, while Lockheed was faulted for this in six out of nine monthly reviews.
77. Between October 2000 and June 2001, Maximus was faulted for this in four out of nine monthly reviews, while Lockheed was faulted for it in seven out of nine monthly reviews (Milton, "On-Site Case Review Findings.").

78. Collins and Mayer (2010, 62).
79. Winston et al. (2002).
80. Nilsen (2002); AFSCME (2006); Winston et al. (2002).
81. Sanger (2003).
82. AFSCME District Council 48 staff member, personal interview, Milwaukee, August 24, 2002; AFSCME District Council 48 official, personal interview, Milwaukee, August 21, 2002; AFSCME Local 594 official, personal interview, Milwaukee, June 15, 2001; Smith Nightingale and Mikelson (2000, 4).
83. Between September of 1997 and December of 1999, the contracts awarded were: Employment Solutions ($112.4 million), Maximus ($58.3 million), Opportunities Industrialization Center of Greater Milwaukee ($57.2 million), United Migrant Opportunity Services ($50.9 million), and YW Works ($40.0 million; Wisconsin Joint Legislative Audit Committee 1999).
84. DeParle (2004, 231).
85. Schultze (2000f).
86. Elke (1998); Flaherty (1998).
87. AFSCME (1998a, 1).
88. Pat Gowens, personal interview, Milwaukee, July 1999, and August 2000; Dresang (1998a); 9to5 members, personal interview, Milwaukee, June 20, 2001; Welfare Mothers' Voice (2001a, 2001b, 2001c).
89. DeParle (2004, 230–50).
90. AFSCME District Council 48 staff member, personal interview.
91. AFSCME District Council 48 staff member, personal interview; AFSCME Local 594 official, personal interview; see also DeParle (2004, 230–50).
92. Coalition to Save Our Children member, personal interview, Milwaukee, September 18, 2000.
93. Coalition to Save Our Children member, personal interview.
94. Dresang (1998a); Pat Gowens, personal interview, 1999, 2000; HOSEA Welfare Reform Task Force member, personal interview, Milwaukee, June 2001; 9to5 members, personal interview; Welfare Mothers' Voice (2001b, 2001c); Legal Aid staff attorney, personal interview, Milwaukee, 2005.
95. AFSCME District Council 48 official, personal interview.
96. AFSCME District Council 48 staff member, personal interview; AFSCME 594 official, personal interview.
97. Cited in Cotant (1996).
98. AFSCME District Council 48 staff member, personal interview; AFSCME 645 official, personal interview.
99. Milwaukee Central Labor Council official, personal interview, Milwaukee, September 2000.

100. AFSCME 594 official, personal interview; Milwaukee Central Labor Council official, personal interview.
101. AFSCME 645 official, personal interview.
102. He attributed the high turnover to welfare contractors' bad managerial styles, the de-professionalization of social work, and failure to provide its employees with good benefits (AFSCME 645 official, personal interview).
103. AFSCME Local 645 official, personal interview; AFSCME District Council 48 official, personal interview.
104. AFSCME 594 official, personal interview.
105. Silas-Green (1997).
106. AFSCME Local 594 official, personal interview.
107. Kertscher (2001); Welfare Mothers' Voice (2000).
108. Welfare Warriors (2000); Pat Gowens, personal interview; 9to5 members, personal interview; Kertscher (2001).
109. DeParle (2004, 238–40).
110. They claimed that the agency cut families off assistance without notification, took too long to return calls from applicants, and advised participants poorly (Dresang 1997).
111. 9to5 members, personal interview, 2001.
112. DeParle (2004); see also Ridzi (2007) on similar dynamics in New York.
113. Collins and Mayer (2010, 72); Sanger (2003, 44); According to DeParle, "unrestricted profits were capped at 7 percent of the contract. . . . After that, the agencies kept only 10 percent of leftover funds" (2004, 244).
114. Sanger (2003, 87–88).
115. 9to5 members, personal interview. Between 2002 and 2004, Maximus used $700,000 for employee bonuses (AFSCME 2006, 14).
116. Nilsen (2002, 29).
117. Collins and Mayer (2010, 63).
118. Institute for Wisconsin's Future (1999c); Wisconsin Legislative Audit Bureau (2000).
119. According to DeParle, the state required W-2 caseworkers (Financial Employment Planners) to serve no more than fifty-five clients, but Maximus's caseworkers sometimes served more than twice this number (2004, 234).
120. AFSCME (1998b); 9to5 members, personal interview.
121. Norman (1999a, 1999b, 1999c).
122. Hunger Action Task Force staff member, personal interview, Milwaukee, 2000; HOSEA Welfare Reform Task Force member, personal interview; Schultze (2000a); Wisconsin Legislative Audit Bureau (2000).

123. Sanger (2003, 57).
124. Mendel-Clemens (2002); Wisconsin Department of Children and Families (2008); Schultze (2000a); Wisconsin Legislative Audit Bureau (2000).
125. Collins and Mayer (2010, 75).
126. Collins and Mayer (2010, 81).
127. Collins and Mayer (2010, 63–64); Marley (2010).
128. Causey (2009); Collins and Mayer (2010, 63–64).
129. Hmong American Friendship Association, personal interview, 2002.
130. State welfare officials and legislative auditors found racial disparities in sanction rates, although they were less pronounced in Milwaukee than in the rest of the state (Wisconsin Legislative Audit Bureau 2005, 95–96). See also Mulligan-Hansel and Fendt (2002); Wisconsin Legislative Audit Bureau (2001, 8).
131. AFSCME District Council 48, personal interview; HOSEA Welfare Reform Task Force member, personal interview.
132. Collins and Mayer (2010, 73); Wisconsin Legislative Audit Bureau (2001, 2005). As an outcome of that federal civil rights investigation, the Wisconsin Department of Children and Families agreed to ensure equal opportunities to participate in the TANF program (U.S. Department of Health and Human Services 2010).
133. HOSEA Welfare Reform Task Force member, personal interview.
134. Legal Aid staff attorney, personal interview.
135. Dresang (1998a).
136. Pat Gowens, personal interview, 1999.
137. 9to5 members, personal interview, 2001.
138. Welfare Mothers' Voice (2001b).
139. AFSCME (1998b).
140. Huston (1998g).
141. Coalition to Save Our Children member, personal interview, 2000; W-2 Monitoring Task Force (2000); D'Alessio (2001).
142. AFSCME District Council 48 staff member, personal interview; Women in Poverty Public Education Initiative staff member, personal interview, Chicago, August 18, 2002.
143. Millard (2000); AFSCME District Council 48 staff member, personal interview.
144. Even while it was under investigation for improper spending, Maximus was given a $15 million contract for collecting unclaimed federal human-service money for Wisconsin (Schultze 2000b).
145. Price (2000a, 2000b); Schultze (2000c, 2000d, 2000f, 2000g); Wisconsin Department of Workforce Development (2000); Nilsen (2002, 29–30). The

company paid back $500,000 to the state and agreed to spend the rest on services to the poor (Schultze 2001a). See also DeParle (2004, 245–46).

146. Schultze (2000d, 2000e, 2001a, 2001b).
147. DeParle (2004, 243).
148. DeParle (2004, 243–45).
149. DeParle (2004, 245).
150. Both HOSEA and MICAH were involved in this effort (HOSEA 2000a; HOSEA staff member, personal interview).
151. HOSEA (2000b).
152. HOSEA Welfare Reform Task Force member, personal interview; Evans (2001); Schultze (2000h).
153. Welfare Warriors (2000, 2001).
154. Welfare Mothers' Voice (2001a); Welfare Warriors (2001).
155. Welfare Mothers' Voice (2001b).
156. Welfare Mothers' Voice (2001c).
157. Collins and Mayer (2010, 74).
158. Hmong American Friendship Association, personal interview, 2002.
159. Schultze (2005); Wisconsin Legislative Audit Bureau (2005, 12).
160. Schultze (2009).

Chapter 5

1. This chapter was written with help from John D. Krinsky. Some of the material for this chapter was previously published in Reese (2005a, 2002b) and is included in Krinsky and Reese (2006). They are reprinted with permission of the publishers.
2. The first epigraph comes from an ACORN protest in 1998 in Los Angeles, which was filmed by Ernest Savage for "The Price of Poverty." The second epigraph comes from a testimony at an impromptu public hearing at the Los Angeles Board of Supervisors in 1998 that was held in response to a disruptive protest earlier that day. The third epigraph is cited in 9to5 (2001, 2); the fourth epigraph comes from A Job Is a Right Campaign (1998b, 1).
3. Krinsky and Reese (2006); Tait (1998).
4. Goldberg (2001).
5. Rathke and Schur (1999, 3).
6. Although ACORN initially focused on welfare rights, it later shied away from welfare issues because organizers believed they were too controversial to gain broad support among low- and moderate-income people. In 1971, ACORN formed an Unemployed Workers' Organizing Committee in

Arkansas. In 1977, it helped to organize "Jobs and Justice" campaigns, which organized participants in federal job training programs and welfare-to-work programs around demands for better training, employment opportunities, and speedier job placements (Delgado 1986, 46, 57, 104–5, 112–13; Piven and Cloward 1979, 40–43). In the 1980s and 1990s, ACORN chapters sought, and often won, local "living-wage" ordinances and "first-source" hiring agreements that prioritized the hiring of local unemployed residents by developers (ACORN-LA, n.d.)

7. For example, see Quadagno (1994).
8. CWA staff member, personal interview, Milwaukee, July 1999; New Jersey ACORN staff member, personal correspondence, June 2000.
9. Fletcher and Gapasin (2008); Tait (2005).
10. Tilly (1996); Collins and Mayer (2010, 153).
11. Collins and Mayer (2010).
12. Collins and Mayer (2010, 132–38).
13. Pastor, Benner, and Matsuoka (2009, 79–86).
14. In contrast, the University Wisconsin's Center for Economic Development found that in 2002, nearly 60 percent of working-age black men were jobless (measured by unemployment in the working-age population according to the Bureau of Labor Statistics) and that this was the highest rate of joblessness in the nation (Collins and Mayer 2010, 45).
15. About 59 percent of Milwaukee's W-2 participants who left the program in 1998 found paid employment within the first year, but employment rates declined to almost 42 percent by 2003 (Wisconsin Legislative Audit Bureau 2001, appendix 13-3; 2005, appendix 13). Employment rates for former and current welfare-to-work participants in Los Angeles rose to 42 percent in 1998 but then declined to 23 percent in 2001 (Burns et al. 2003, 10–12). For even later outcomes in Milwaukee, see Collins and Mayer (2010).
16. Los Angeles Coalition to End Hunger and Homelessness (1998).
17. Wisconsin Legislative Audit Bureau (2001, appendix 13-2; 2005, 60). Drayse, Flaming, and Force (2000, 27–28); see also Burns et al. (2003, 1, 46, 141–45); Smith Nightingale and Mikelson (2000, 28–32); Institute for Wisconsin's Future (1999a, 1999b); Collins and Mayer (2010, 67).
18. Burns et al. (2003, 141).
19. Burns et al. (2003, 145); Kao (2002).
20. By comparison, 12.7 percent of adults between eighteen and fifty-four lacked a high school diploma or a GED. A study conducted in urban Michigan in 1997 found that only 39 percent of welfare mothers without a high school degree worked at least twenty hours per week, compared to 66 percent of those with high school degrees (Goldberg 2002, 4, 7). Higher education also significantly improves employment outcomes for former welfare recipients (United States Student Association 2002, 17).

National studies also indicate that welfare-to-work programs that emphasize job quality rather than initial employment lead to better employment outcomes (Savner, Strawn, and Greenberg 2002, 5).

21. When labor market conditions worsened in 2005, less than 50 percent of participants were in community service jobs or workfare (Collins and Mayer 2010, 65).
22. Institute for Wisconsin's Future (1998b, 11).
23. ACORN's W-2 Workers' Organizing Committee (1997, 1).
24. Collins and Mayer (2010).
25. 9to5 members, personal interview.
26. Collins and Mayer (2010, 18).
27. Milwaukee Women and Poverty Public Education Initiative (2000, 8).
28. Collins and Mayer (2010, 81).
29. Moore and Selkowe (1999, ii, 11).
30. 9to5 members, personal interview.
31. Institute for Wisconsin's Future (1998a, 4).
32. Ad Hoc W-2 coalition member, personal interview in Milwaukee, Wisconsin, 2000; Huston (1998h).
33. Burns et al. (2003, 3, 14).
34. Most welfare-to-work participants receiving education and training were in classes to learn English or to prepare for the GED. Others were in vocational education or community college courses.
35. Burns et al. (2003, 47–48).
36. ACORN staff member, interview with Ernest Savage, Los Angeles, 1998; Los Angeles Coalition to End Hunger and Homelessness (1998).
37. Interview with welfare mother at 2001 Mothers' Day Protest by Ernest Savage, Los Angeles, 2001; Ernest Savage, "The Price of Poverty" raw footage.
38. Mulligan-Hansel and Fendt (2002); Wisconsin Legislative Audit Bureau (2001, 8).
39. Burns et al. (2003, 44–46).
40. AFSCME District Council 48 staff member, personal interview.
41. Citizens for Workfare Justice (1998).
42. Drayse, Flaming, and Force (2000, 27–28).
43. Because General Relief workers' hours are based on the minimum wage and tied to their $221-per-month benefits, they are only engaged in welfare-to-work activities up to forty hours per month (Citizens for Workfare Justice 1998).

44. Wisconsin Legislative Audit Bureau (2001, 23).
45. SEIU 660 (n.d.).
46. SEIU 660 (2001); Citizens for Workfare Justice (1998).
47. SEIU 660 (1998); This figure is from a monthly report from 2002 (Burns et al. 2003, 46).
48. ACORN-LA organizer, personal interview, Los Angeles, December 12, 2002; SEIU 660 (1997).
49. There were multiple reasons for this: the higher demand for unskilled labor, the administration of W-2 by private agencies, AFSCME's lobbying against public-sector work assignments, and the city's living-wage ordinance for municipal workers (AFSCME District Council 48 official, personal interview; AFSCME District Council 48 staff member, personal interview).
50. Heuler Williams (1998); Institute for Wisconsin's Future (1998a, 1998b); Collins and Mayer (2010).
51. Collins and Mayer (2010, 117).
52. 9to5 organizer, personal interview, Milwaukee, August 23, 2002; Hmong American Friendship Association staff and members, personal interviews, 2002; Repairers of the Breach day shelter clients, personal interviews, Milwaukee, August 23, 2002; Federation for Civic Action staff member, personal interview, Milwaukee, August 23, 2002; see also Collins and Mayer (2010).
53. Author's fieldnotes, Los Angeles, May 1, 1998.
54. Aurelio (1998); ACORN-LA (1998b); Citizens for Workfare Justice (1998).
55. Aurelio (1998, A8).
56. Savage, "The Price of Poverty," raw footage: December 17, 1997.
57. Rivera (1997).
58. Kaufman (1997); Linares (1997); Moore and Boxall (1997); Rivera (1997).
59. ACORN-LA (n.d.).
60. ACORN-LA (1998c); De la Cruz (1997).
61. Aubry (1998).
62. Workfare workers were to be given first priority only after agreements to rehire laid off and transferred union employees were met.
63. Henry (1998); Savage, December 17, 1997.
64. ACORN-LA (1998c); Amy Schur and John Jackson, personal communication, 1999.
65. ACORN organizer, personal communication, June 29, 1999.
66. Pat Knauss, personal interview, Los Angeles, January 1999.
67. Pat Knauss, personal interview.

68. Urevich (1998).
69. Author's fieldnotes, Los Angeles, June 18, 1998.
70. ACORN-Workfare Workers Organizing Committee (1998).
71. Bitton (1998).
72. Author's fieldnotes, Los Angeles, June 23, 1998.
73. Author's fieldnotes, Los Angeles, July 1, 1998.
74. This program was partly funded through a federal grant (Crogan 1998; Lee 1998; Los Angeles Coalition to End Hunger and Homelessness staff member, personal interview, Los Angeles, October 10, 2000).
75. SEIU 347 staff member, personal interview, Los Angeles, January 2003; SEIU 660 staff member, personal interview, Los Angeles, September 2001.
76. DeParle (1997). Despite the Department of Labor's determination that workfare workers should be covered by the Fair Labor Standards Act, California's governor, Pete Wilson, sent a policy memo to all counties in 1998, allowing them to place TANF recipients into work experience programs at a rate below the minimum wage (ACORN-LA 1998d; Klabin 1999).
77. National Campaign for Jobs and Income Support Staff, personal communication, April 12, 2003; ACORN-LA organizer, personal interview.
78. ACORN-LA organizer, personal interview.
79. AGENDA stands for Action for Grassroots Empowerment and Neighborhood Development Alternatives.
80. ACORN-LA organizer, personal interview; SEIU 660 (1997).
81. SEIU 660 staff member, personal interview, 1999.
82. SEIU 660 staff member, personal interview, 1999; SEIU 347 staff member, personal interview.
83. SEIU 347 staff member, personal interview.
84. SEIU 660 (1999).
85. SEIU 347, SEIU 660, and AGENDA staff members, personal interviews, Los Angeles, 1998.
86. SEIU 660 (2001).
87. SEIU 347 staff, personal interview.
88. SEIU 347, SEIU 660, and AGENDA staff members, personal interviews.
89. AGENDA organizer, personal interview, Los Angeles, March 2000; SEIU 347 staff member, personal interview.
90. SEIU 660, SEIU 347, and AGENDA staff, personal interview.
91. Organizers recruited welfare-to-work participants, with help from union stewards and members, through worksite visits, home visits, and door-to-door canvassing and meetings in high-poverty neighborhoods (SEIU 660, SEIU 347, and AGENDA staff member, personal interview).

92. SEIU 347 staff member, personal interview; SEIU 660 staff member, personal interview, 2001; AGENDA organizer, personal interview.
93. AGENDA organizer, personal interview; SEIU 347 staff member, personal interview; SEIU 660 staff member, personal interview, 2001.
94. SEIU 660 staff member, personal interview, 2001.
95. AGENDA organizer, personal interview; Department of Public Social Services GAIN Division (2000).
96. AGENDA organizer, personal interview; SEIU 660 staff member, personal interview, 2001.
97. Heckenlively (1997, 23).
98. A Job Is a Right Campaign (1997).
99. The Nation of Islam and the Wisconsin Injured Workers' Network collaborated with A Job Is a Right in this effort.
100. Davidoff (1997); Heckenlively (1997); A Job Is a Right Campaign (1997); Pfeifer (1997).
101. Cited in Pfeifer (1997, 3).
102. A Job Is a Right Campaign (1997).
103. Heckenlively (1997).
104. Wichman (1997, 6).
105. W-2 Workers United (1997, 1).
106. Jones (1997).
107. A Job Is a Right Campaign (1997).
108. AFSCME District Council 48 official, personal interview; AFSCME Local 645 official, personal interview, Milwaukee, June 2001; W-2 Advisory Board member, personal interview, Milwaukee, September 2000.
109. Milwaukee Women and Poverty Public Education Initiative (2000); Silas-Green (1997); Center for Wisconsin Strategy (2002).
110. Personal communication with A Job Is a Right Campaign organizer, June 2000; A Job Is a Right Campaign volunteer, personal interview, Milwaukee, August 1999.
111. For example, see Jones (1997); A Job Is a Right Campaign (1998a).
112. Krinsky and Reese (2006).
113. Collins and Mayer (2010, 68).
114. W-2 Advisory Board member, personal interview.
115. Davidoff (1997).
116. AFSCME District Council 48 official, personal interview.
117. AFSCME District Council 48 staff member, personal interview.
118. W-2 Advisory Board member, personal interview.

119. AFSCME District Council 48 official, personal interview.
120. Huston (1997); A Job Is a Right Campaign (1998a; 1998c, 1).
121. A Job Is a Right Campaign (1998a, 1).
122. A Job Is a Right Campaign (1998a, 1).
123. McBride, Garza, and Huston (1997); McBride (1997).
124. Derus (1998).
125. These organizations were Repairers of the Breach and Women and Poverty Public Education Initiative.
126. A Job Is a Right Campaign (1998d, 1999).
127. Personal communication with A Job Is a Right organizer, June 2000; A Job Is a Right Campaign volunteer, personal interview.
128. Dresang (1998a); Sloan (1998).
129. AFSCME District Council 48 official, personal interview.
130. The organizer was paid by the CWA.
131. ACORN and CWA (1998).
132. CWA staff supervisor, personal interview, Milwaukee, August 2002.
133. Rose (2000).
134. CWA organizer, personal interview; CWA staff supervisor, personal interview.
135. ACORN and CWA staff worked together to identify job sites for a union-organizing drive using ACORN's membership list, communicating with W-2 participants outside of W-2 agencies and an outdated list of job sites provided by the county's W-2 task force (ACORN and CWA 1998; CWA organizer, personal interview).
136. Dresang (1998b); United States of ACORN (1998).
137. Bronfenbrenner (1994); Hurd and Uehlein (1994); Beaumont (1992, 46); Johnston (1994).
138. CWA organizer, personal interview.
139. CWA organizer, personal interview.
140. CWA staff supervisor, personal interview; CWA organizer, personal interview; ACORN National staff member, personal communication, July 1999.
141. CWA organizer, personal interview.
142. CWA organizer, personal interview.
143. CWA staff supervisor, personal interview.
144. Chilsen (1998).
145. Schultze (2009).
146. Krinsky and Reese (2006).

147. Collins and Mayer (2010, 157).
148. Collins and Mayer (2010, 138).
149. Collins and Mayer (2010); Fletcher and Gapasin (2008).

Chapter 6

1. Parts of this chapter are contained in Reese (2010) and are reprinted with permission of the publisher.
2. The first two quotes come from interviews that I conducted in Los Angeles in April 2002. The third comes from Pat Gowens, personal interview, 1999.
3. Naples (1997).
4. Funding for subsidized child care was also expanded through the Child Care and Development Fund, and Head Start programs were expanded to serve children as young as six months and to provide full-time care for longer periods (News Service Reports 1997). In 1997, an estimated 3.5 million additional children were expected to need subsidized child care because of the implementation of welfare reform, in addition to the 7 million already receiving it (Healy and Lesher 1997).
5. Marcucci (2002b). A federal audit of nine states found that, while TANF caseloads fell dramatically, child care spending rose significantly between 1995 and 2000, then rose more gradually from 2000 to 2004 (Bellis and Czerwinski 2006).
6. Whitebook (2001).
7. Ridzi (2007).
8. Boris and Klein (2008).
9. Ridzi (2009); Ridzi and London (2006); Korteweg (2006).
10. Collins and Mayer (2010).
11. Morris (2002); see also Rothstein (2002).
12. Duncan, Huston, and Weisner (2007).
13. Collins and Mayer (2010).
14. Collins and Mayer (2010, xii).
15. Rowe and Murphy (2006).
16. Cited in Capps (1997b, A1).
17. Center for Law and Social Policy and Center on Budget and Policy Priorities (2000).
18. The International Wages for Housework Campaign was formed in 1972 and promoted the demand for wages for women's unpaid domestic work, seen as critical to women's liberation and the subversion of capital (Malos 1978; Kawan and Weber 1981, 430).

19. Author's fieldnotes, Los Angeles, November 27, 2001.
20. International Wages for Housework Campaign (2001, 1).
21. Every Mother Is a Working Mother (2001, 1).
22. Mink (1995).
23. On the "wages for housework" movement, see Malos (1978) and Kawan and Weber (1981). On the NWRO's critique of work requirements for welfare mothers, see West (1981).
24. This campaign was organized by the People's Network for a New Safety Net (EMWM n.d.a).
25. This was a slogan used for a sign during the Global Women's Strike (*Los Angeles Times* 2001, B2).
26. Author's fieldnotes, Los Angeles, December 1, 2001.
27. Every Mother Is a Working Mother (2001, 2).
28. Kabler (2001, 11); see also Every Mother Is a Working Mother (2001).
29. Naples (1997).
30. Every Mother Is a Working Mother (n.d.b).
31. Collins and Mayer (2010, 23).
32. Parents with partial disabilities or caring for disabled children were placed into the "W-2 Transitions" program. They were only expected to work up to twenty-eight hours per week but were given lower benefits because they worked less than other W-2 recipients (Institute for Wisconsin's Future 1998b; Swartz et al. 1999).
33. Wisconsin also failed to recognize five other types of work exemptions for adult TANF recipients that were adopted by twenty or more other states (Center for Law and Social Policy and Center on Budget and Policy Priorities 2000).
34. Coalition to Save Our Children member, personal interview; Pat Gowens, personal interview, 1999.
35. Coalition to Save Our Children member, personal interview.
36. Cited in Milwaukee Women and Poverty Public Education Initiative (1998, 5).
37. Coalition to Save Our Children member, personal interview.
38. Wisconsin Council for Children and Families staff member, personal interview, Milwaukee, June 20, 2001.
39. Coalition to Save Our Children member, personal interview.
40. Dembski (2005).
41. Weier (2003). Amy Stear from 9to5 pointed out that the savings could be even higher than this since infant care tends to be more expensive than other types of child care (Price 2003).
42. Pommer (2003a).

43. Antlfinger (2004); Schultze (2004).
44. Davidoff (2008); Schultze (2009).
45. Pommer (2003a, 2003b).
46. Pommer (2003b, 4A).
47. Ross (2003, online).
48. Simms (2005); Callender (2005); Marley and Walters (2007); Davidoff (2008).
49. Schultze (2009).
50. Wisconsin Council for Children and Families staff member, personal interview, 2002.
51. Wisconsin Council on Developmental Disabilities staff member, personal interview, Madison, August 25, 2002.
52. Wisconsin Council on Developmental Disabilities, personal interview.
53. Wisconsin Council on Developmental Disabilities, personal interview.
54. McBride (1998).
55. Milfred (1999).
56. Wisconsin Council on Developmental Disabilities, personal interview.
57. Wisconsin Council on Developmental Disabilities, personal interview.
58. Wisconsin Council on Developmental Disabilities, personal interview.
59. Institute for Wisconsin's Future (1998a); Swartz et al. (1999).
60 Wisconsin Council on Developmental Disabilities, personal interview.
61. Wisconsin Council on Developmental Disabilities, personal interview.
62. Wisconsin Council on Developmental Disabilities, personal interview.
63. Naples (1997); Ridzi (2009) calls this the "new common sense of employment."
64. EMWM (n.d.b).
65. Whitebook (2001).
66. Giannarelli and Barsimantov (2000).
67. Giannarelli and Barsimantov (2000); Savner, Strawn, and Greenberg (2002, 6, 9).
68. Schulman and Blank (2008).
69. Schulman and Blank (2008, 2010).
70. Whitebook, Howes, and Phillips (1990); Whitebook et al. (2001), cited in Brooks (2003, 3).
71. Whitebook (2001, 45).
72. Official labor statistics show that in 2000, of the 2.3 million workers paid to care for a child age five or younger in the U.S., 28 percent were family-based providers, while 35 percent were paid relatives (Center for the Child Care Workforce and Human Services Policy Center 2002, 2).

73. These figures exclude preschool teachers and teacher assistants (U.S. Bureau of Labor Statistics 2010b).
74. Schulman and Blank (2010).
75. Dickerson (1998).
76. Brooks (2005).
77. Whitebook (2001, 44–45).
78. Keystone Research Center (2006, 1).
79. Chalfie, Blank, and Entmacher (2007, 6).
80. Whitebook (2001).
81. Brooks (2003, 2005).
82. Chalfie, Blank, and Entmacher (2007, 6).
83. Whitebook (2001); Keystone Research Center (2006); Brooks (2003, 2005).
84. Keystone Research Center (2002); Boris and Klein (2007, 2008).
85. Chalfie, Blank, and Entmacher (2007).
86. According to this agreement, SEIU would organize child care workers in Arizona, Colorado, Connecticut, Louisiana, Massachusetts, Maryland, North Carolina, and Rhode Island. AFSCME would organize them in Hawaii, Michigan, Oklahoma, New Jersey, New Mexico, New York, Ohio, and Wisconsin.
87. Keystone Research Center (2006, 3–4); Chalfie, Blank, and Entmacher (2007, 12).
88. Whitebook (2001).
89. Both AFSCME and SEIU also organized child care centers, aggregating them across sites through the formation of unionized professional employee organizations. In that model, the professional employer organization (PEO) becomes the employer of record for agencies contracted with it; it provides them with benefits and processes their payroll (Keystone Research Center 2006, 2–4).
90. Chalfie, Blank, and Entmacher (2007); Blank, Campbell, and Entmacher (2010).
91. See also Boris and Klein (2008).
92. McDonald and Merrill (2002); Cobble (2010). The term "ethic of care" was coined by Carol Gilligan and revived by Joan Tronto in her 1993 book, *Moral Boundaries: A Political Argument for an Ethic of Care* (personal communication with Dorothy Sue Cobble, July 1, 2004).
93. McDonald and Merrill (2002).
94. McDonald and Merrill (2002).
95. Keystone Research Center (2002); Boris and Klein (2007, 2008).

96. A 2001 study showed that California was more liberal in terms of its eligibility rules for subsidized child care compared to four other large states (New York, Texas, Illinois, and Florida) in terms of covering children up to age thirteen, having a higher income ceiling for eligibility, and requiring lower fees (*Alameda Times-Star* 2001).
97. Graves (2005, 7).
98. Graves (2005, 5–6).
99. Marcucci (2001a).
100. Klabin (1999); Klabin and Weinstein (2000).
101. Barfield (1999).
102. Farwell (2000).
103. Coleman (1999, A1).
104. Anderson (2001); Klabin (1999); Klabin and Weinstein (2000).
105. Riccardi (1999); Rivera (2000); *Daily News* (1999); author's fieldnotes, Los Angeles, June 22, 2000.
106. EMWM (n.d.b).
107. Asian Pacific Policy and Planning Council staff member, personal interview.
108. Wilson (1998).
109. Matlosz (2000).
110. Reportedly, staff from the Welfare Reform Coalition felt that ACORN was "taking over their territory," especially when it attempted to distribute flyers at its parents' convention. ACORN, however, believed that there were more than enough child care providers for both groups to organize and initially focused on organizing license-exempt providers, which were not the Welfare Reform Coalition's focus (personal communication, ACORN staff, September 1, 2000).
111. Welfare Reform Coalition staff member, personal interview, Los Angeles, April 18, 2000, and August 31, 2000.
112. Welfare Reform Coalition staff member, personal interview.
113. Klabin (1999); Klabin and Weinstein (2000).
114. Welfare Reform Coalition staff member, personal interview.
115. Author's fieldnotes, Los Angeles, August 31, 2000; ACORN-USA (2001).
116. Cited in ACORN-LA (2000, 1).
117. Author's fieldnotes, May 18, 2000.
118. Author's fieldnotes, October 15, 2001, and March 17, 2001.
119. Author's fieldnotes, April 5, 2002.
120. Author's fieldnotes, March 17, 2001; ACORN-LA (2001b).

121. ACORN-USA (2001).
122. Klabin (1999).
123. Every Mother Is a Working Mother (n.d.b).
124. At first the county contracted with ten agencies but later with twelve.
125. ACORN-LA (2001a).
126. Author's fieldnotes, March 17, 2001, January 31, 2002, February 7, 2000; ACORN-LA (2001b).
127. State and federal funding for child care in California declined in inflation-adjusted dollars by 4.3 percent between 2001 and 2005 (Graves 2005, 6–8).
128. Marcucci (2001a).
129. Author's fieldnotes, March 17, 2001.
130. California ACORN (2001).
131. Marcucci (2001b, 2001c).
132. Hill (2002a, A1).
133. Hill (2002a, 2002b).
134. Marucci (2002a, online).
135. The proposed rules would lower the age limit for receiving care from thirteen to twelve, lower the income ceiling for eligibility, and eliminate the preference for serving former welfare families.
136. Marcucci (2002a); Hill (2002a).
137. California Center for Research on Women and Families (2002).
138. Boudreau (2002).
139. Brown (2002a, 2002b).
140. Personal communication with member of Child Development Policy Advisory Committee, April 7, 2002.
141. Personal communication, ACORN organizer, April 5, 2002.
142. de Sá (2002, A17).
143. Hill (2002b).
144. Whitney (2003a, 2003b).
145. Hernandez (2003).
146. Whitney (2003b).
147. Author's fieldnotes, Los Angeles, March 25, 2004.
148. Author's fieldnotes, June 27, 2004.
149. SEIU staff member, personal interview, Los Angeles, April 9, 2005.
150. SEIU staff member, phone interview, April 24, 2006.
151. AFSCME staff member, phone interview, May 23, 2006.

152. Personal communication with SEIU organizer, 2006.

153. ACORN Child Care Providers for Action (2003).

154. Author's fieldnotes, Los Angeles leadership meeting of Child Care Providers United, June 21, 2008.

155. The plan included new three-year time limits for child care subsidies for former welfare recipients, a 40 percent reduction in payments to relatives caring for children, and increases in parents' fees that would affect more than seventy-seven thousand families. Other proposals would cut off subsidies for eleven- and twelve-year-olds unless they could not be served by an after-school program (Marcucci 2004a, 2004b).

156. Graves (2005, 11–12).

157. *Monterey County Herald* (2004).

158. Grippi (2004).

159. Sheehan (2004).

160. Marcucci (2004b).

161. Marimow and Gladstone (2004).

162. Bluth (2004).

163. Nugent (2006).

164. Benson (2006).

165. Associated Press (2002).

166. Johnson (2002).

167. Nichols (2006).

168. Lowest-performing schools were those performing in the bottom 30 percent in terms of the statewide Academic Performance Index (Geissinger 2006).

169. *Inside Bay Area* (2006).

170. SEIU staff member, phone interview; SEIU staff member, phone interview, February 3, 2007.

171. Cited in Huston (1998a, online); see also DeParle (2004).

172. Stewart (1997); Huston (1998b).

173. Callender (1998d).

174. Norman (2000).

175. Ridzi (2009).

176. Milfred (1998); Huston (1998c, 1998d, 1998f).

177. Community Advocates staff member, personal interview, Milwaukee, June 27, 2001.

178. Mendel-Clemens (2002); Wisconsin Department of Children and Families (2008); Schultze (2000a); Wisconsin Legislatiave Audit Bureau (2000).

179. Huston (1997, 1998b).
180. Piliavin, Courtney, and Dworsky (2000).
181. This research was conducted by the office of a state representative from Milwaukee (Dembski 2002).
182. Bleidorn (1998).
183. Huston (1998b, 1998d).
184. 9to5 staff member, personal interview.
185. Price (2001a, 2001b).
186. Mapp (2000).
187. Huston (1998b).
188. Providers Taking Action leader, phone interview, July 2007.
189. McDonald and Merrill (2002); Cobble (2010); see note 92.
190. South Central Federation of Labor (2000, 2).
191. *Wisconsin State Journal* (1998b); Ad Hoc W-2 Coalition member, personal interview, Milwaukee, September 20, 2000.
192. *Wisconsin State Journal* (1998c).
193. Huston (1998e).
194. Callender (1998a).
195. Schneider and Callender (1998).
196. 9to5 staff member, personal interview.
197. Callender (1998d).
198. Milfred (1999); *Wisconsin State Journal* (2000).
199. 9to5 staff member, personal interview.
200. Abdul-Alim (2003)
201. Groves (2005).
202. Providers Taking Action leader, phone interview.
203. Wisconsin Executive Order, supra note 26, para.2, cited in Chalfie, Blank, and Entmacher (2007, 19).
204. Chalfie, Blank, and Entmacher (2007, 19); Early Childhood Focus (2006).
205. Blank, Campbell, and Entmacher (2010).
206. Blank, Campbell, and Entmacher (2010, 20).
207. Davidoff (2007a, C1).
208. Walters (2007).
209. Davidoff (2007b).
210. This latter policy was initially rescinded by the legislature but this ban on attendance-based reimbursement was then line-item vetoed by the gov-

ernor. Although the governor rejected the policy through the 2007 to 2008 fiscal year, state officials retained the authority to reinstate it, although they had not done so as of May 2009 (Blank, Campbell, and Entmacher 2010, 223).

211. Rutledge (2009, online).

212. Richmond (2009).

213. Rutledge (2010, online).

214. Prior to January 26, 2009, the state was recouping overpayments at the rate of 50 percent of providers' biweekly payments, regardless of cause. According to the new policy, if overpayment was the result of caseworker error, providers were required to pay the amount back at a rate of 10 percent of a provider's biweekly payment, and 25 percent if it was the result of an unintended error by the provider (Blank, Campbell, and Entmacher 2010, 20–23).

215. Whitebook (2001).

216. Cobble (forthcoming).

217. Blank, Campbell, and Entmacher (2010, 35).

218. This is revealed in the case studies above. Also see Brooks (2003, 2005).

Chapter 7

1. Collins and Mayer (2010); Noble (1997); Peck (2001); Peck and Theodore (1999); Piven and Cloward (1993 [1971]); Tilly (1996); Wacquant (2009).
2. Ridzi (2009).
3. For example, see Gordon (1994); Lieberman (1998); Mink (1995); Neubeck and Cazenave (2001); Quadagno (1994).
4. Gilens (1999); Mink (1998); Neubeck and Cazenave (2001); Reese (2005a).
5. Fording, Soss, and Schram (2007); Keiser, Mueser, and Choi (2004).
6. Lipsky (2010).
7. Hays (2003a); Heath (2009); Ridzi (2004, 2007, 2009); Korteweg (2006).
8. Schneider and Ingram (1993).
9. Ridzi (2004, 2009); Hays (2003a); Korteweg (2006).
10. Imig (1996).
11. Marston (2000).
12. Imig (1996).
13. McDonald and Merrill (2002); Cobble (forthcoming).
14. Krinsky and Reese (2006).
15. Collins and Mayer (2010, 157).

16. Collins and Mayer (2010, 138).
17. Gonzales (2009).
18. Unions and their political action committees mobilized more than thirteen million voters and spent nearly $450 million on the 2008 presidential election (Tilly 2011).
19. Estimates of the cost of assisting financial institutions vary. The Real Economy Project of the Center for Media and Democracy estimates that, as of September 2010, a total of $4.72 trillion was disbursed, an estimate that has been peer-reviewed by economists at the Center for Economic and Policy Research (The Real Economy Project 2010). Economists Nomi Prins and Krisztina Ugrin estimate that $3.5 trillion was distributed to Wall Street institutions, plus an additional $2.8 trillion to government-sponsored enterprises, as of October 2010 (Prins and Ugrin 2010).
20. *New York Times* (2009).
21. Heath (2011).
22. Schmit (2011a).
23. Schmit (2011b).
24. U.S. Department of Health and Human Services (2009); Collins and Mayer (2010).
25. Pavetti, Schott, and Lower-Basch (2011).
26. Collins and Mayer (2010, xii). Employers, seeking to avoid paying their share of these benefits, increasingly challenged unemployment claims, arguing that employees were laid off for performance reasons (Whoriskey 2009).
27. Wentworth (2011).
28. Dreier and Gitlin (2009, 3).
29. Zeese (2011).
30. Moberg (2009, 1).
31. Piven and Cloward (1977b); Tilly (2011).
32. Tilly (2011); see also Fletcher and Gapasin (2008).
33. Dreier (2009).
34. Tilly (2011).
35. Skocpol (2000, 53).
36. Imig (1996, 10–13).
37. Imig (1996, 38, 115).
38. Center on Budget and Policy Priorities (2009, 2010, 2011).
39. Leachman, Williams, and Johnson (2011).
40. Center on Budget and Policy Priorities (2009, 2010, 2011).

41. Brown (2010).
42. Broder (2007).
43. Watanabe (2010).
44. California Budget Project (2009, 2010).
45. Mothers of children under three years and those with two or more children under age six were exempt from welfare-to-work requirements through July 2011.
46. California Legislative Analyst's Office (2009).
47. Buchanan (2009).
48. California Budget Project (2010).
49. Dolan and Goldmacher (2010).
50. Dolan and Goldmacher (2010).
51. Community Voices L.A. (2011); de Brito (2010).
52. Decker (2010).
53. Herald and Bartholow (2011).
54. The CalWorks benefit reductions included an 8 percent cut in the maximum grant levels and reductions of up to 15 percent for child-only grants. Child-only grant reductions would be implemented over time, with a 5 percent cut introduced after sixty months of aid, 10 percent after seventy-two months, and 15 percent after eighty-four months (California Budget Project 2011).
55. Baldassare et al. (2011a, 2011b).
56. USC News (2011).
57. Some of the state funds for these programs came from tighter regulation of the state's subsidized child care program (Peacock 2009a).
58. Peacock (2009b). On reasons behind the change in the time limit policy, see Wisconsin Legislative Fiscal Bureau (2009).
59. Schultze (2009). However, legislators rejected Governor Doyle's proposal to eliminate the "learnfare" program that sanctioned W-2 families when children were repeatedly truant, despite research showing the program was administratively burdensome and ineffective in improving school attendance (Peacock 2009b).
60. Blank, Campbell, and Entmacher (2010).
61. Peacock (2009c).
62. Peacock (2009b, 3).
63. Peacock (2010, 3).
64. *Wisconsin State Journal* (2009).
65. Marley (2010).
66. Wisconsin Budget Project (2011); Zemlicka (2011).

67. Verberg (2011).
68. Greenhouse (2011).
69. Schmitt (2010).
70. Gilbert (2011).
71. Skocpol (2000, 170).
72. Pastor, Benner, and Matsuoka (2009, 21).
73. Fletcher and Gapasin (2008).
74. Fletcher and Gapasin (2008).
75. Pastor, Benner, and Matsuoka (2009, 213). These groups include the Gamaliel Foundation (a faith-based network), the Partnership for Working Families (a national network founded by union activists), the Pushback Network (a network of community-based organizations engaged in grassroots electoral organizing), and the Right to the City Alliance (a network of community-based organizations, many of which are engaged in antigentrification struggles). Regional campaigns have also been initiated by unions and central labor councils as well as national organizations—namely Jobs with Justice, Association of Community Organizations for Reform Now, and the Industrial Areas Foundation.
76. Reese et al. (forthcoming).
77. Skocpol (2000); see also Meyers (2007).
78. As of 2006, only one state (New Hampshire) used a standard of need above the federal poverty guideline, while the thirty-four other U.S. states set their income ceilings *below* the federal poverty guideline to determine eligibility for TANF, a guideline that many experts consider to be set too low. Twelve U.S. states used the federal poverty guideline to determine the maximum monthly earnings a family can have and be eligible for TANF (Rowe and Murphy 2006, 70–71).
79. Meyers (2007).
80. Meyers (2007, 61).

References

9to5. 2001. *Welfare as We Know It: The Case for Reforming TANF*. Milwaukee, Wisc.: 9to5, National Association of Working Women.

Abdul-Alim, Jamaal. 2003. "Child Care Providers Face Reimbursement Cut." *Milwaukee Journal Sentinel*. February 18. Available at: Lexis Nexis Academic Universe (accessed September 29, 2007).

Abramovitz, Mimi. 2000. *Under Attack, Fighting Back: Women and Welfare in the United States*. New York: Monthly Review Press.

ACORN Child Care Providers for Action. 2003. "Survey of Members." Los Angeles: ACORN Child Care Providers for Action.

ACORN and Communications Workers of America (CWA). 1998. "An Organizing Partnership Agreement between Milwaukee ACORN and CWA." Electronic communication from Madeline Talbot to Seth Rosen, June 4.

ACORN-LA. n.d. "Workfare Workers on the Move." Leaflet provided by ACORN-LA.

———. 1998a. Flyer for Lockheed Martin I.M.S. protest, March 26.

———. 1998b. "Action Agenda," Flyer, June 16.

———. 1998c. "County Workfare Participant Hiring Initiative," Flyer, September.

———. 1998d. "Workfare and Minimum Wage in Los Angeles County," Flyer, October.

———. 2000. Press Release, May 18.

———. 2001a. "Los Angeles Childcare Providers Organize." Newsletter, July 9.

———. 2001b. Los Angeles ACORN. Newsletter, October.

ACORN-USA. 2001. National newsletter, August 31.

ACORN's W-2 workers' organizing committee member. 1997. Testimony for the workers' rights board hearing on W-2. Milwaukee, Wisconsin (December).

ACORN-Workfare Workers Organizing Committee. 1998. "The County Must Stop Using Temp Agencies!" *At Work in Los Angeles*. Newsletter, July.

Aiken, Mike, and Ingo Bode. 2009. "Killing the Golden Goose? Third Sector Organizations and Back-to-Work Programmes in Germany and the U.K." *Social Policy & Administration* 43(3): 209–25.

A Job Is a Right Campaign. 1997. "Why W-2 Workers Need a Union." Flyer.

———. 1998a. *A Job Is a Right!* Newsletter, March-April (Milwaukee).

———. 1998b. "Why We Are Marching Today." *A Job Is a Right!* Newsletter. April 4, special edition (Milwaukee).

———. 1998c. *A Job Is a Right!* Newsletter, May–June (Milwaukee).

———. 1998d. *A Job Is a Right!* Newsletter, November–December (Milwaukee).

———. 1999. *A Job Is a Right!* Newsletter, January–February (Milwaukee).

Alameda Times-Star. 2001. "Governor Davis Is Trying to Expand Child Care, Not Cut It." Editorial, December 16. Available at: Lexis Nexis Academic Universe (accessed June 28, 2011).

Albano, Leilani. 1997. "Up in Arms Over Welfare Reform: 2000 Attend Rally to Protest Cuts in Aid to Immigrants." *Daily News of Los Angeles*. March 10: N4. Available at: Lexis Nexis Academic Universe (accessed June 29, 2011).

Albelda, Randy. 2001. "Fallacies of Welfare-to-Work Policies." *The Annals of the American Academy of Political and Social Science* 577(September): 66–78.

Albert, Vicky N., and William C. King. 2001. "The Impact of the Economy and Welfare Policy on Welfare Accessions: Implications for Future Reforms." *Journal of Sociology and Social Welfare* 28(3): 5–27.

Almeida, Paul D. 2003. "Opportunity Organizations and Threat-Induced Contention: Protest Waves in Authoritarian Settings." *American Journal of Sociology* 109(2): 345–400.

Alquist, Elaine. 1997. "Statement of Assemblywoman Elaine Alquist." Hearing of the California Joint Legislative Audit Committee, May 20. Sacramento: California Legislature.

Amenta, Edwin. 1998. *Bold Relief: Institutional Politics and the Origins of the Modern American Social Policy*. Princeton, N.J.: Princeton University Press.

———. 2006. *When Movements Matter: The Townsend Plan and the Rise of Social Security*. Princeton, N.J.: Princeton University Press.

Amenta, Edwin, Bruce G. Carruthers, and Yvonne Zylan. 1992. "A Hero for the Aged? The Townsend Movement, the Political Mediation Model, and the U.S. Old-Age Policy, 1934–1950." *American Journal of Sociology* 98(2): 308–39.

Amenta, Edwin, Drew Halfmann, and Michael P. Young. 1999. "The Strategies and Contexts of Social Protest: Political Mediation and the Impact of the Townsend Movement in California." *Mobilization* 4(1):1–24.

Amenta, Edwin, and Michael P. Young. 1999. "Making an Impact: Conceptual and Methodological Implication of the Collective Goods Criterion." In *How Movements Matter: Theoretical and Comparative Studies on the Consequences of Social Movements*, edited by Marco Giugni, Doug McAdam, and Charles Tilly. Minneapolis: University of Minnesota Press.

American Federation of State, County, and Municipal Employees (AFSCME). 1998a. *Private Profits, Public Needs: The Administration of W-2 in Milwaukee*. Milwaukee: AFSCME.

———. 1998b. Letter to Welfare Advocates Group from Marie Monrad, director of public policy department.

———. 2006. *Safety Net for Sale: The Dangers of Privatization*. Washington, D.C.: AFSCME.

Anderson, Alissa. 2011. "Recession and State Budget Cuts Dealt a Double Blow to Many Single Parents." Sacramento: California Budget Project. Available at: http://californiabudgetbites.org/2011/04/20/recession-and-state-budget-cuts-dealt-a-double-blow-to-many-single-parents/ (accessed June 9, 2011).

Anderson, Barbara. 2001. "Child-Care Aid Lacking: Report Says Group Says Quality Care Is a Way to Reduce Juvenile Crime." *Fresno Bee*. March 15. Available at: Lexis Nexis Academic Universe (accessed September 7, 2007).

Andrew, Merrindahl. 2006. "Learning to Love (the State) Again? Money, Legitimacy, and Community Sector Politics." *Australian Journal of Social Issues* 41(3): 313–26.

Anheier, Helmut. 2009. "What Kind of Nonprofit Sector, What Kind of Society? Comparative Policy Reflections." *American Behavioral Scientist* 52(7): 1082–94.

Antlfinger, Carrie. 2004. "DWD Wants to Revamp Jobs Program, Double Maternity Leave." Associated Press. November 12. Available at: Lexis Nexis Academic Universe (accessed July 30, 2007).

Armbruster, Ralph, Kim Geron, and Edna Bonacich. 1995. "The Assault on California's Latino Immigrants: The Politics of Proposition 187." *International Journal of Urban and Regional Research* 19(4): 655–63.

Arnold, Gretchen. 1995. "Dilemmas of Feminist Coalitions: Collective Identity and Strategic Effectiveness in the Battered Women's Movement." In *Feminist Organizations: Harvest of the New Women's Movement,* edited by Myra Max Ferree and Patricia Yancey Martin. Philadelphia: Temple University Press.

Associated Press. 2002. "L.A. to Spend Smoke Tax on Schools." August 9. Available: Lexis Nexis Academic Universe (accessed September 8, 2007).

Atlas, John, and Peter Dreier. 2009. "ACORN Scandal Offers Key Lessons to All Charities." *Huffington Post.* December 9. Available at: http://www.huffingtonpost.com/john-atlas/acorn-scandal-offers-key_b_386064.html (accessed June 9, 2011).

Aubry, Erin J. 1998. "Welfare's Phantom Workers: Coalition Challenges Unfair Workfare." *LA Weekly.* February 13.

Aurelio, Mary Lou. 1998. "Workfare Workers Protesting." *Long Beach Press.* May 2.

Baldassare, Mark, Dean Bonner, Sonja Petek, and Jui Shrestha. 2011a. "Californians and Their Government." San Francisco: Public Policy Institute of California, in Collaboration with the James Irvine Foundation. Available at: http://www.ppic.org/content/pubs/survey/S_311MBS.pdf (accessed June 9, 2011).

———. 2011b. "Californians and Education." San Francisco: Public Policy Institute of California, in collaboration with the James Irvine Foundation. Available at: http://www.ppic.org/content/pubs/survey/S_411MBS.pdf (accessed June 9, 2011).

Balousek, Mary. 1997. "County Supervisors Support Safety Net for Legal Immigrants." *Wisconsin State Journal.* June 20: 1C, 2C. Available at: Lexis Nexis Academic Universe (accessed June 29, 2011).

Banerjee, Payal, and Frank Ridzi. 2008. "Indian IT Workers and Black TANF Clients in the New Economy: A Comparative Analysis of the Racialization of Immigration and Welfare Policies in the U.S." *Race, Gender, and Class* 15(1–2): 98–114.

Baptist, Willie, and Mary Bricker-Jenkins. 2002. "A View from the Bottom: Poor People and Their Allies Respond to Welfare Reform." In *Lost Ground: Welfare Reform, Poverty, and Beyond.* Cambridge, Mass.: South End Press.

Barfield, Chet. 1999. "Need Day Care? Get in Line: In San Diego, One Slot Is Available for Every 3.9 Children." *San Diego Union-Tribune.* December 8. Available at: Lexis Nexis Universe (accessed September 5, 2007).

Bean, Frank D., Jennifer V. W. Van Hook, and Jennifer Glick. 1997. "Country of Origin, Type of Public Assistance, and Patterns of Welfare Recipiency Among U.S. Immigrants and Natives." *Social Science Quarterly* 78(2): 432–51.

Beaumont, Phil B. 1992. *Public Sector Industrial Relations.* London, New York: Routledge.

Bee, Pamela J. 1997. "Immigrants Lobby State to Address Welfare Losses; Protesters Urge Lawmakers to Restore Key Benefits at Capitol Rally." *Fresno Bee.* May 29: B1. Available at: Lexis Nexis Academic Universe (accessed February 1, 2001).

Bellis, David D., and Stanley J. Czerwinski. 2006. "Better Information Needed to Understand Trends in States' Use of the TANF Block Grant." Report no. GA-06-414. March 3. Washington: General Accounting Office. Available at: http://www.gao.gov/new.items/d06414.pdf (accessed June 9, 2011).

Benson, Clea. 2006. "Advocacy Groups to Seek a Slice of $4 Billion Windfall." *Sacramento Bee.* May 8. Available at: Lexis Nexis Academic Universe (accessed September 1, 2007).

Berg, Emmett. 2000. "County to Employ Two Private Firms to Oversee Portion of Welfare Program." *City News Service.* Available at: Lexis Nexis Academic Universe (accessed July 18, 2002).

Betz, Michael. 1974. "Riots and Welfare: Are They Related?" *Social Problems* 21(3): 345–55.

Bhargava, Deepak. 2002. "Progressive Organizing on Welfare Policy." In *From Poverty to Punishment: How Welfare Reform Punishes the Poor,* edited by Applied Research Center. Oakland, Cal.: Applied Research Center.

Bier, Jerry. 1998. "Judge Denies Petition to Reinstate Hmong Food Stamps: Plaintiff Left with $900 a Month to Support Wife, Mother and 11 Children." *Fresno Bee.* March 7: A1. Available at: Lexis Nexis Academic Universe (accessed June 29, 2011).

Bitton, Michael. 1998. "Church Groups Say County Can't Dump Needy." *Antelope Valley Press.* May 27: A1, A8.

Blank, Helen, Nancy Duff Campbell, and Joan Entmacher. 2010. "Getting Organized: Unionizing Home-Based Child Care Providers: 2010 Update." Washington, D.C.: National Women's Law Center. Available at: http://www.irle.berkeley.edu/cscce/wp-content/uploads/2010/09/gettingorganizedupdate2010.pdf (accessed June 9, 2011).

Blau, Francine D. 1984. "The Use of Transfer Payments by Immigrants." *Industrial and Labor Relations Review* 37(2): 222–39.

Bleidorn, K. Joan. 1998. "W-2 Needs Humane Replacement." *Milwaukee Journal Sentinel.* June 16. Available at: Lexis Nexis Academic Universe (accessed May 5, 2007).

Blumberg, Michael, and John Huebscher. 1998. "Religious Groups Urge Addition of Food Stamps for Immigrants to Budget Bill." Press release. April 24.

Blumenfeld, Michael. 1997a. "Memo to WIRC members from WIRC Chair, Re: Update." April 24.

———. 1997b. "Memo to WIRC members from WIRC Chair, Re: Update." May 15.

———. 1997c. "Memo to WIRC members from WIRC Chair, Re: Action Alert." July 9.

———. 1998. "Memo to Senate Committee on Health and Human Services. Re: Senate Bill 419 from the Chair of the Wisconsin Immigrant and Refugee Coalition." February 11.

Bluth, Alexa H. 2004. "Revised Budget Backs Off Cuts: $103 Billion Plan Mostly Spares Health Services." *Sacramento Bee*. May 14. Available at: Lexis Nexis Academic Universe (accessed September 3, 2007).

Boggs, Carl. 2000. *The End of Politics: Corporate Power and the Decline of the Public Sphere*. New York: The Guilford Press.

Bonacich, Edna, and Richard P. Appelbaum. 2000. *Behind the Label: Inequality in the Los Angeles Apparel Industry*. Berkeley, Cal.: University of California Press.

Boris, Eileen, and Jennifer Klein. 2007. " 'We Were the Invisible Work Force': Unionizing Home Care." In *The Sex of Class: Women Transforming American Labor*, edited by Dorothy Sue Cobble. Ithaca, N.Y.: ILR Press.

———. 2008. "Labor on the Home Front: Unionizing Home-Based Care Workers." *New Labor Forum* 17(2): 32–41.

Boudreau, John. 2002. "State Budget Cuts Draining Non-Profits." *San Jose Mercury News*. March 15. Available at: Lexis Nexis Academic Universe (accessed September 10, 2007).

Brecher, Jeremy, and Tim Costello, eds. 1990. *Building Bridges: The Emerging Grassroots Coalition Between Labor and Community*. New York: Monthly Review Press.

Brewer, Gary D. 1974. "The Policy Sciences Emerge: To Nurture and Structure a Discipline." Rand Corporation Paper Series. Santa Monica, California: Rand Corp. Available at: http://www.rand.org/pubs/papers/2008/P5206.pdf (accessed June 9, 2011).

Brock, Nailah R. 2008. "African Americans and Welfare Time Limits: Comparative Analysis of State Time Limit Policies Under the Personal Responsbility and Work Opportunity Reconciliation Act of 1996." *Journal of Black Studies* 39(6): 1–12.

Broder, Tanya. 2007. "State and Local Policies on Immigrant Access to Services: Promoting Integration or Isolation?" Washington, D.C.: National Immigration Law Center. Available at: http://www.nilc.org/immspbs/sf_benefits/state localimmpolicies06-07_2007-05-24.pdf (accessed June 9, 2011).

Brodkin, Evelyn Z., Carolyn Fuqua, and Katarina Thoren. 2002. "Contracting Welfare Reform: Uncertainties of Capacity-Building Within Disjointed Federalism." Project on the Public Economy of Work. Working paper. Chicago: University of Chicago. Available at: http://www.northwestern.edu/ipr/jcpr/workingpapers/wpfiles/brodkin_fuqua_thoren.pdf (accessed June 9, 2011).

Bronfenbrenner, Kate. 1994. "Employer Behavior in Certification Elections and First Contracts: Implications for Labor Law Reform." In *Restoring the Promise of American Labor Law*, edited by Sheldon Friedman, Richard Hurd, Rudy Oswald, and Ronald Seeber. Ithaca, N.Y.: ILR Press.

———. 2009. "No Holds Barred: The Intensification of Employer Opposition to Organizing." Economic Policy Institute. Briefing paper no. 235. May 20. Available at: http://www.epi.org/page/-/pdf/bp235.pdf?nocdn=1 (accessed June 9, 2011).

Bronfenbrenner, Kate, Sheldon Friedman, Richard W. Hurd, Rudolph A. Oswald, and Ronald L. Seeber, eds. 1998. *Organizing to Win: New Research in Union Strategies*. Ithaca, N.Y.: ILR Press.

Brooks, Fred P. 2003. "What Differences Unionizing Teachers Might Make on Child Care in the USA: Results from an Exploratory Study." *Child & Youth Care Forum* 32(1): 3–22.

———. 2005. "New Turf for Organizing: Family Child Care Providers." *Labor Studies Journal* 29(4): 45–64.

Brown, Kay E. 2010. "Temporary Assistance for Needy Families: Implications of Caseload and Program Changes for Families and Program Monitoring." Statement of Kay E. Brown, Director of Education, Workforce, and Income Security for the U.S. Senate Committee on Finance. Available at: http://www.gao.gov/new.items/d10815t.pdf (accessed June 9, 2011).

Brown, Mareva. 2002a. "Child Care Subsidy at Risk Some Families Would Lose Aid Under the Governor's Plan to Shift Help to Those with Lower Incomes." *Sacramento Bee.* April 21. Available at: Lexis Nexis Academic Universe (accessed September 8, 2007).

———. 2002b. "Child-Case Subsidy Changes Dropped But a Proposal to Alter the Rules and Make Some Parents Pay Fees Could Pop Up Again." *Sacramento Bee.* May 26. Available at: Lexis Nexis Academic Universe (accessed September 8, 2007).

Brown, Michael K. 1999. *Race, Money, and the American Welfare State.* Ithaca, N.Y.: Cornell University Press.

Brugge, Doug. 1995. "The Anti-immigrant Backlash." *Public Eye Magazine* 9(2): 1–13.

Buchanan, Wyatt. 2009. "Governor Signs, Slashes Budget." *San Francisco Chronicle.* July 29: A1.

Burnham, Linda. 2001. "Welfare Reform, Family Hardship, and Women of Color." *The Annals of the American Academy of Political and Social Science* 577(September): 39–47.

Burns, Patrick, Mark Drayse, Daniel Flaming, and Brent Haydamack. 2003. "Prisoners of Hope: Welfare-to-Work in Los Angeles." Los Angeles: Economic Roundtable. Available at: http://www.economicrt.org/download/prisoners_of_hope.html (accessed June 9, 2011).

Cairns Post. 2000. "Active Role for Jobless in Reforms." December 15: 11. Available at: Lexis Nexis Academic Universe (accessed June 30, 2011).

Calavita, Kitty. 1996. "The New Politics of Immigration: Balanced-Budget Conservativism and the Symbolism of Proposition 187." *Social Problems* 43(3): 284–305.

California ACORN. 2001. Electronic newsletter. May 29.

California Budget Project. 2009. "An Overview of Recent Cuts to California's Safety Net." Sacramento: California Budget Project. Available at: http://www.cbp.org/pdfs/2009/090821_Post_Webinar_Slides.pdf (accessed June 24, 2011).

———. 2010. "Searching for Balance: An Analysis of Key Provisions of the 2010–11 Budget Agreement." October 20. Sacramento: California Budget Project. Available at: http://www.cbp.org/pdfs/2010/100618_Budget_Comparision.pdf (accessed October 20, 2011).

———. 2011. "Back to the Future: How Do the Budget Plans Compare?" March 22. Sacramento: California Budget Project. Available at: http://www.cbp.org/pdfs/2011/110225_Budget_Plans_Compare.pdf (accessed June 9, 2011).

California Center for Research on Women and Families. 2002. "The California Working Families Policy Summit 2002: An Inside Look at the Issues Facing the Working Poor." PR Newswire. January 17. Available at: Lexis Nexis Academic Universe (accessed September 8, 2007).

California Legislative Analyst's Office. 2009. "July 2009 Budget Package." Sacramento: Legislative Analyst's Office. Available at: http://www.lao.ca.gov/2009/bud/july_09_budget_package/july_2009_budget_package_072909. pdf (accessed June 9, 2011).

California State Assembly. 1997. "Roll Call Votes for Assembly Bill 1576." Assembly record. Sacramento: California State Government.

Callender, David. 1998a. "Child Care Providers Want W-2 Fees Cut." *Capital Times.* April 22. Available at: Lexis Nexis Academic Universe (accessed May 5, 2007).

———. 1998b. "Refugee Kids Won't Get Help." *Capital Times.* May 1. Available at: Lexis Nexis Academic Universe (accessed June 29, 2011).

———. 1998c. "Assembly Republicans Reject Food Stamps for Immigrants." *Capital Times.* May 7. Available at: Lexis Nexis Academic Universe (accessed June 29, 2011).

———. 1998d. "Child Care Availability Under W-2 Rated Low" (1st ed.); "Child Advocates Rip Provision of Care Under W-2" (2d ed). *Capital Times.* June 3. Available at: Lexis Nexis Academic Universe (accessed May 5, 2007).

———. 2005. "Dem Calls Cuts 'War on the Poor': $24 Million Out of Budget." *Capital Times.* May 20. Available at: Lexis Nexis Academic Universe (accessed May 5, 2007).

Capital Times. 1997. "Insurance for Thousands." June 19: 1A. Available at: Lexis Nexis Academic Universe (accessed June 29, 2011).

Capps, Steven A. 1997a. "Wilson Identifies Cuts for Illegal Immigrants; 200 Public Programs Will Now Require Legal Residence Proof." *San Francisco Examiner.* March 26: A5. Available at: Lexis Nexis Academic Universe (accessed February 9, 2011).

———. 1997b. "State Demos Unveil Welfare Plan; Counterproposal to Wilson's Boosts Funds for Job Training, Child Care, Monthly Grants." *San Francisco Examiner.* May 8: A1. Available at: http://www.sfgate.com/cgi-bin/article.cgi?f=/e/a/1997/05/08/NEWS6815.dtl (accessed June 28, 2011).

Carleton, Gwen. 1998. "British Leader Sets Welfare Talk." *Capital Times.* March 14: 4A. Available at: Lexis Nexis Academic Universe (accessed June 29, 2011).

Carroll, Rodney J. 2001. "Testimony for the Work Requirements on the TANF Cash Welfare Program Hearing." Subcommittee on Human Resources of the Committee on Ways and Means, House of Representatives. 107th Cong. April 3. Serial 107-10. Available at: http://www.waysandmeans.house.gov/legacy/humres/107cong/4-3-01/107-10final.htm#carroll (accessed October 7, 2011).

Causey, James E. 2009. "Poverty: W-2 Is Not Equipped to Help the State's Neediest." *Milwaukee Journal Sentinel.* May 24. Available at: http://www.allbusiness.com/society-social/families-children-family/14659975-1.html (accessed June 27, 2011).

Cauthen, Nancy, and Edwin Amenta. 1996. "Not for Widows Only: Institutional Politics and the Formative Years of Aid to Dependent Children." *American Sociological Review* 61(3): 427–48.

Cauthen, Nancy, and Sarah Fass. 2008. "Measuring Poverty in the United States." New York: National Center for Children in Poverty, Mailman School of Public Health, Columbia University. Available at: http://www.nccp.org/publications/pdf/text_825.pdf (accessed June 9, 2011).

Center for the Child Care Workforce and Human Services Policy Center. 2002. "Estimating the Size and the Components of the U.S. Child Care Workforce and Caregiving Population." Washington, D.C.: Center for Child Care Workforce. Available at: http://www.ccw.org/storage/ccworkforce/documents/publications/ccw_exec_final.pdf (accessed June 10, 2011).

Center for Law and Social Policy and Center on Budget and Policy Priorities. 2000. "Work Requirements: Exemptions (as of October 1999)." Available at: http://www.sddp.org/tanf/exemptions.pdf (accessed September 20, 2007).

Center for Wisconsin Strategy. 2002. "The Milwaukee Jobs Initiative." Available at: http://www.cows.org/pdf/ov-mji-2.pdf (accessed June 21, 2011).

Center on Budget and Policy Priorities. 2009. "An Update on State Budget Cuts." Washington, D.C.: Center on Budget and Policy Priorities. Available at: http://www.cbpp.org/files/3-13-08sfp.pdf (accessed January 10, 2010).

———. 2010. "An Update on State Budget Cuts." Washington, D.C.: Center on Budget and Policy Priorities. Available at: http://www.cbpp.org/files/3-13-08sfp.pdf (accessed November 5, 2010).

———. 2011. "An Update on State Budget Cuts: At Least 46 States Have Imposed Budget Cuts." Washington, D.C.: Center on Budget and Policy Priorities. Available at: http://www.cbpp.org/files/3-13-08sfp.pdf (accessed June 9, 2011).

Chalfie, Deborah, Helen Blank, and Joan Entmacher. 2007. "Getting Organized: Unionizing Home-Based Child Care Providers." Washington, D.C.: National Women's Law Center. Available at: http://www.nwlc.org/sites/default/files/pdfs/GettingOrganized2007.pdf (accessed June 10, 2011).

Chang, Grace. 2000. *Disposable Domestics: Immigrant Women Workers in the Global Economy.* Cambridge, Mass.: South End Press.

Chilsen, Jim. 1998. "Governor Announces Job Training Program." The Associated Press, State and Local Wire. September 9. Available at: Lexis Nexus Academic Universe (accessed August 30, 2011).

Christopher, Karen. 2002. "Single Motherhood, Employment, or Social Assistance: Why Are U.S. Women Poorer than Women in Other Affluent Nations?" *Journal of Poverty* 6(2): 61–80.

Cioni, Tom. 1998. "Advocate for Hmong Says Suicide Threats State Trend." *Press Gazette.* February 21. Available at: Lexis Nexis Academic Universe (accessed May 20, 2001).

Citizens for Workfare Justice. 1998. "When Work Doesn't Pay: 'Workfare' in Los Angeles County." February 13. Los Angeles: Citizens for Workfare Justice.

City News Service. 1996. "Midnight Headlines." October 11. Available at: Lexis Nexis Academic Universe (accessed June 29, 2011).

Clawson, Dan. 2003. *The Next Upsurge: Labor and New Social Movements.* Ithaca, N.Y.: ILR Press.

Cobble, Dorothy Sue. 2010. "More Intimate Unions." In *Intimate Labors: Interdisciplinary Perspectives on Care, Sex, and Domestic Work,* edited by Eileen Boris and Rhacel Salazar Parrenas. Stanford, Cal.: Stanford University Press.

Coleman, Donald E. 1999. "County Outlines Child-Care Deficiencies: Central Fresno Is One of the Areas Hardest Hit by a Shortage of Care." *Fresno Bee.* June 21. Available at: Lexis Nexis Academic Universe (accessed September 9, 2007).

Collins, Jane L., and Victoria Mayer. 2010. *Both Hands Tied: Welfare Reform and the Race to the Bottom in the Low-Wage Labor Market.* Chicago and London: University of Chicago Press.

Community Voices L.A. 2011. "Big Victory for Thousands of Working Families and Small Businesses." January 14. Available at: http://www.communityvoicesla.blogspot.com (accessed June 10, 2011).

Cook, Christopher D. 1998. "Plucking Workers: Tyson Foods Looks to the Welfare Rolls for a Captive Labor Force." *Progressive* (August): 28–31.

Cotant, Pamela. 1996. "500 Bused in to Blast Gov's Welfare Plan." *Capital Times.* January 4. Available at: Lexis Nexis Academic Universe (accessed December 11, 2001).

Coughlin, Teresa, Joshua M. Weiner, Jill A. Marsteller, David G. Stevenson, Susan Wallin, and Debra J. Lipson. 1998. "Health Policy for Low-Income People in Wisconsin." State report. Washington, D.C.: The Urban Institute. Available at: http://www.urban.org/uploadedPDF/wischeal.pdf (accesed August 2, 2011).

Council of State Governments. 1998. *The Book of the States, 1996–1997 Edition, Vol. 31.* Lexington, Ky: The Council of State Governments.

Cress, Daniel M., and David A. Snow. 1996. "Mobilization at the Margins: Resources, Benefactors, and the Viability of Homeless Social Movement Organizations." *American Sociological Review* 61(6): 1089–109.

———. 2000. "The Outcomes of Homeless Mobilization: The Influence of Organization, Disruption, Political Mediation, and Framing." *American Journal of Sociology* 105(4): 1063–104.

Crogan, Jim. 1998. "L.A. County's Poorest Catch a Break." *LA Weekly.* August 12: 16. Available at: http://www.laweekly.com/1998-08-20/news/l-a-county-s-poorest-catch-a-break/ (accessed June 29, 2011).

D'Alessio, John. 2001. Letter to Governor Tommy G. Thompson from Deacon John D'Alessio. HOSEA President. August 18, 2001.

Daily News. 1999. "After-School Plan Ok'd by Supervisors." May 12. Available at: Lexis Nexis Academic Universe (accessed June 29, 2011).

Daniel, Vanessa. 2002. "The New World of Welfare Meets the New Welfare Rights Movement." In *From Poverty to Punishment: How Welfare Reform Punishes the Poor,* edited by Applied Research Center. Oakland: Applied Research Center.

Davidoff, Judith. 1997. "W-2's Last Critics." *Isthmus* 22(42): 9–10.

———. 2007a. "Child Care Programs Face Huge Deficit: W-2 Problems Create Budget Challenge for Doyle." *Capital Times.* January 24. Available at: Lexis Nexis Academic Universe (accessed September 14, 2007).

———. 2007b. "Child Care Subsidies Get Boost: Joint Finance Panel Closes Funding Gap." *Capital Times.* May 23. Available at: Lexis Nexis Academic Universe (accessed July 31, 2007).

———. 2008. "Working Hard for the Money: Lawton Claims Gains in Women's Economic Status." *Capital Times.* June 4: 9. Available at: Lexis Nexis Academic Universe (accessed July 29, 2010).

de Brito, Deia. 2010. "Deep Cuts to Child Care Delayed." California Watch, Daily Report. November 18. Available at: http://californiawatch.org/dailyreport/deep-cuts-child-care-delayed-6790 (accessed June 10, 2011).

Decker, Cathleen. 2010. "GOP Bid for Governor Becomes a Brawl." *Los Angeles Times.* May 16: A37. Available at: Lexis Nexis Academic Universe (accessed October 8, 2010).

Defranco, Kim. 1999. "Put a Time Limit on Poverty, Not on Welfare!" *Fight Back* 2(4). Available at: http://www.fightbacknews.org/1099/mntime.html (accessed August 4, 2006).

De Jong, Gordon F., Deborah Roempke Graefe, Shelley K. Irving, and Tanja St. Pierre. 2006. "Measuring State TANF Policy Variations and Change After Reform." *Social Science Quarterly* 87(4): 755–81.

De la Cruz, Elena. 1997. "Trabajadores de Asistencia General Demanden Empleos Reales." *La Opinion.* August 29: 1B, 2B.

Deleon, Peter. 1999. "The Stages Approach to the Policy Process." In *Theories of the Policy Process,* edited by Paul A. Sabatier. Boulder, Colo.: Westview Press.

Delgado, Gary. 1986. *Organizing the Movement: The Roots and Growth of ACORN.* Philadelphia: Temple University Press.

Dembski, Barbara. 2002. "Cleaning Up: Candidates for County Executive Address the Issues." *Milwaukee Journal Sentinel.* March 24. Available at: Lexis Nexis Academic Universe (accessed July 27, 2007).

———. 2005. "It's More Than Economics." *Milwaukee Journal Sentinel.* March 25. Available at: Lexis Nexis Academic Universe (accessed July 30, 2007).

DeNavas-Walt, Carmen, Bernadette D. Proctor, and Jessica C. Smith. 2010. "Income, Poverty, and Health Insurance Coverage in the United States: 2009." Table 4. Washington: U.S. Census Bureau. Available at: http://www.census.gov/prod/2010pubs/p60-238.pdf (accessed June 10, 2011).

DeParle, Jason. 1997. "White House Calls for Minimum Wage in Workfare Plan." *New York Times.* May 16: A1. Available at: Lexis Nexis Academic Universe (accessed June 29, 2011).

———. 2004. *American Dream: Three Women, Ten Kids, and a Nation's Drive to End Welfare.* New York: Viking.

Department of Public Social Services GAIN Division. 2000. "Grounds Maintenance Helper Pilot Program: Design and Implementation Plan." Memo, May 25.

Derus, Michele. 1998. "W-2 Families Squeeze in Together: Welfare Changes Have Some Doubling, Tripling Up in Rental Units." *Milwaukee Journal Sentinel.* January 18: Real Estate, 1. Available at: Lexis Nexis Academic Universe (accessed May 10, 2001).

de Sá, Karen. 2002. "Health Care Would Be Hardest Hit by New Plan, Social Services." *San Jose Mercury News.* May 15. Available at: Lexis Nexis Academic Universe (accessed September 8, 2007).

DeVerteuil, Geoffrey, Matthew Marr, and David Snow. 2009. "Any Place Left? Homeless Resistance by Place-Type in Los Angeles County." *Urban Geography* 30(6): 633–51.

Diani, Mario. 1997. "Social Movements and Social Capital: A Network Perspective on Movement Outcomes." *Mobilization* 2(2): 129–47.

Diaz, Jesse Jr. 2010. *Organizing the Brown Tide: La Gran Epoca Primavera 2006 en Los Angeles, An Insider's Story*. Ph.D. Dissertation. Department of Sociology, University of California, Riverside.

Dickerson, Marla. 1998. "A New Army of Child-Care Workers: Welfare Recipients Are Being Trained to Help Ease Critical Shortage, Transition Is Not Expected to Be Easy." *Los Angeles Times*. August 12. Available at: Lexis Nexis Academic Universe (accessed February 27, 2002).

Dobuzinskis, Alex. 2002. "Job Training." *City News Service*. Available at: Lexis Nexis Academic Universe, U.S. News (accessed July 18, 2002).

Dohan, Daniel. 2003. *The Price of Poverty: Money, Work, and Culture in the Mexican American Barrio*. Berkeley and Los Angeles: University of California Press.

Dolan, Jack, and Shane Goldmacher. 2010. "Governor's Veto Ax Falls Heavily on Welfare, Child Care, and Special Education Programs." *Los Angeles Times*. October 9: AA1. Available at: http://articles.latimes.com/2010/oct/09/local/la-me-budget-vetoes-20101009 (accessed June 27, 2011).

Doyle, Michael. 1997. "Hmong Vet Leads Gight to Regain Aid." *Modesto Bee*. March 3: A10. Available at: Lexis Nexis Academic Universe (accessed June 29, 2011).

Drayse, Mark, Daniel Flaming, and Peter Force. 2000. *The Cage of Poverty*. Los Angeles: Economic Roundtable. Available at: http://www.economicrt.org/publications.html#Human_Services_Pub (accessed June 10, 2011).

Dreier, Peter. 2009. "We Need More Protest to Make Reform Possible." *The Nation*. August 6. Available at: http://www.thenation.com/article/we-need-more-protest-make-reform-possible (accessed June 11, 2011).

Dreier, Peter, and Todd Gitlin. 2009. "Demonstrations at CEO Mansions? Ho Hum." *Columbia Journalism Review*. October 5. Available at: http://www.cjr.org/behind_the_news/demonstrations_at_ceo_mansions.php (accessed June 11, 2011).

Dreiling, Michael. 1998. "From Margin to Center: Environmental Justice and Social Unionism as Sites for Intermovement Solidarity." *Race, Gender & Class* 6(1): 51–69.

Dresang, Joel. 1997. "State to Check Alleged W-2 Flaws; For-Profit Agency Says Some Mistakes Have Already Been Fixed." *Milwaukee Journal Sentinal*. December 13. Available at: Lexis Nexis Academic Universe (accessed May 28, 2002).

———. 1998a. "Demonstration Shuts Down W-2 Agency: 2 Protestors Arrested; Protestors Say Guards Used Pepper Spray." *Milwaukee Journal Sentinel*. February 27. Available at: Lexis Nexis Academic Universe (accessed December 22, 2001).

———. 1998b. "Activists March for W-2 Participants." *Milwaukee Journal Sentinel*. July 28: 1–2. Available at: Lexis Nexis Academic Universe (accessed December 22, 2001).

Duncan, Greg J., Aletha C. Huston, and Thomas S. Weisner. 2007. *Higher Ground: New Hope for the Working Poor and Their Children*. New York: Russell Sage Foundation.

Duncan, Kevin. 2000. "Incentives and Work Decisions of Welfare Recipients: Evidence from the Panel Survey of Income Dynamics, 1981–1988." *American Journal of Economics and Sociology* 59(3): 433–49.

Early Childhood Focus. 2006. "WI-Child Care Union Forms." November 15. Available at: http://www.earlychildhoodfocus.org/modules.php?name=News&file=article&sid=3318 (accessed July 31, 2007).

Edin, Kathryn, and Laura Lein. 1997. *Making Ends Meet.* New York: Russell Sage Foundation.

Eimer, Stuart. 1999. "From 'Business Unionism' to 'Social Movement Unionism': The Case of the AFL-CIO Milwaukee County Labor Council." *Labor Studies Journal* 24(2): 63–81.

Elke, Gretchen. 1998. "Tax Savings Seen by Privatizing State Operations." Associated Press. August 9. Available at: Lexis Nexis Academic Universe (accessed February 18, 2002).

Ellis, Virginia. 1997a. "Democrats Propose Welfare Package Aid: Plan Calls for State to Help Legal Immigrants Whose Benefits Will Be Cut Off Under New U.S. Rules." *Los Angeles Times.* May 9: A3. Available at: Proquest-Los Angeles Times (current; accessed June 27, 2011).

———. 1997b. "State Democrats Call Immigrant Aid Top Budget Issue." *Los Angeles Times.* July 22: A1. Available at: Proquest-Los Angeles Times (current; accessed June 27, 2011).

Emma Lazarus Fund. 1996. "Soros Pledges $50 Million to Aid Legal Immigrants; Emma Lazurus Fund Available Immediately." Available at: http://www.soros.org/emma/html/50million.html (accessed July 31, 2002).

Epstein, Steven. 1996. *Impure Science: AIDS, Activism, and the Politics of Knowledge.* Berkeley, Cal.: University of California Press.

Esping-Anderson, Gosta. 1990. *The Three Worlds of Welfare Capitalism.* Princeton, N.J.: Princeton University Press.

Evans, Frank. 2001. Letter to Milwaukee Area Legislators from MICAH Jobs and Economic Development Committee Chair. June 11.

Every Mother Is a Working Mother (EMWM). 1998. "Afterschool Care Based on School Campuses." Published leaflet.

———. 2001. "Value Daring Work in Welfare Benefits." Published leaflet.

———. n.d.a. "Every Mother is a Working Mother Network." Published leaflet.

———. n.d.b. "Commitments by L.A. Department of Public Social Services from the Community Dialogues on Welfare Reform and Childcare Coordinated by the Every Mother Is a Working Mother Network." Published leaflet.

Fagan, Kevin. 1996. "Welfare Limbo Reigns as New Reform Kicks In." *San Francisco Chronicle.* October 2: A1. Available at: Lexis Nexis Academic Universe (accessed June 29, 2011).

Falcocchio, Lisa. 2001. "New York City Parks Department, Testimony Before the Subcommittee on Human Resources of the Committee on Ways and Means." Hearing on Work Requirements on the TANF Cash Welfare Program, House of Representatives. 107th Cong., 1st sess. Serial 107-10. April 3. Available at: http://waysandmeans.house.gov/legacy/humres/107Cong/4-3-01/107-10final.htm (accessed June 25, 2011).

Fantasia, Rick, and Kim Voss. 2004. *Hard Work: Remaking the American Labor Movement.* Berkeley and Los Angeles: University of California Press.

Farrell, Mary, Sarah Rich, Lesley Turner, David Seith, and Dan Bloom. 2008. "Welfare Time Limits: An Update on State Policies, Implementation, and Effects on Families." The Lewin Group and MDRC. Available at: http://www.mdrc.org/publications/481/full.pdf (accessed June 22, 2011).

Farwell, Scott. 2000. "Someone to Watch Over Them: A Working Parent's Distress." *The Press-Enterprise.* October 1, 2000. Available at: Lexis Nexis Academic Universe (accessed September 5, 2007).

Flaherty, Mike. 1997. "The World Watches as Welfare Wheel Turns." *Wisconsin State Journal.* November 23: 1C. Available at: Lexis Nexis Academic Universe (accessed June 29, 2011).

———. 1998. "Privatizing Welfare Saves Bucks for State, Study Says." *Wisconsin State Journal.* January 30. Available at: Lexis Nexis Academic Universe (accessed February 18, 2002).

Fletcher, Bill Jr., and Fernando Gapasin. 2008. *Solidarity Divided: The Crisis in Organized Labor and a New Path Toward Social Justice.* Berkeley: University of California Press.

Fording, Richard C. 1997. "The Conditional Effect of Violence as a Political Tactic: Mass Insurgency, Welfare Generosity, and Electoral Context in the American States." *American Journal of Political Science* 41(1): 1–29.

———. 2003. " 'Laboratories of Democracy' or Symbolic Politics? The Racial Origins of Welfare Reform." In *Race and the Politics of Welfare Reform,* edited by Sanford F. Schram, Joe Soss, and Richard C. Fording. Ann Arbor: University of Michigan Press.

Fording, Richard C., Joe Soss, and Sanford F. Schram. 2007. "Devolution, Discretion, and the Effect of Local Political Values on TANF Sanctioning." *Social Service Review* 81(2): 285–316.

Fox, Cybelle. 2004. "The Changing Color of Welfare? How Whites' Attitudes Towards Latinos Influence Support for Welfare." *American Journal of Sociology* 110(3): 580–625.

———. 2009. "A New Nativism or an American Tradition? Federal Citizenship and Legal Status Restrictions for Medicaid and Welfare." Paper presented at the annual meeting of the American Sociological Association, San Francisco, California (August 7–11).

Fragomen, Austin T., Jr. 1997. "The Illegal Immigration Reform and Immigration Responsibility Act of 1996: An Overview." *International Migration Review* 31(summer): 438–60.

Fresno Bee. 1997. "Fixing Congress' Callousness." February 10: B4. Available at: Lexis Nexis Academic Universe (accessed June 29, 2011).

Fujiwara, Lynn H. 1999. "Sanctioning Immigrants: Asian Immigrant and Refugee Women and the Racial Politics of Welfare Reform." Ph.D. Dissertation. Department of Sociology, University of California, Santa Cruz.

Gais, Thomas, and R. Kent Weaver. 2002. "State Policy Choices Under Welfare Reform." Welfare Reform and Beyond policy brief no. 21. Washington, D.C.: Brookings Institution. Available at: http://www.brookings.edu/~/media/Files/rc/papers/2002/04welfare_gais/pb21.pdf (accessed June 11, 2011).

Gallagher, Jerome. 1999. "A Shrinking Safety Net: General Assistance from 1989 to 1998." Washington, D.C.: The Urban Institute. Available at: http://www.urban.org/UploadedPDF/anf_a36.pdf (accessed June 11, 2011).

Gamson, William A. 1975. *The Strategy of Social Protest.* Homewood, Ill.: Dorsey Press.

Gann, Lewis. H., and Peter J. Duignan. 1986. *The Hispanics in the United States: A History.* Boulder, Colo.: Westview Press.

Garin, Geoffrey, Guy Molyneux, and Linda DiVall. 1994. "Public Attitudes Toward Welfare Reform." *Social Policy* 25(2): 44–49.

Geen, Rob, Wendy Zimmermann, Toby Douglas, Sheila Zedlewski, and Shelley Waters. 1998. "Income Support and Social Services for Low-Income People in California." State report. Washington, D.C.: The Urban Institute. Available at: http://www.humanservices.ucdavis.edu/resource/uploadfiles/Income and support CA.pdf (accessed August 2, 2011).

Geissinger, Steve. 2006. "$50 Million OK'd for Neediest Preschools." *Whittier Daily News.* September 7. Available at: Lexis Nexis Academic Universe (accessed September 1, 2007).

Gerhards, Jurgen, and Dieter Rucht. 1992. "Mesomobilization: Organizing and Framing in Two Protest Campaigns in West Germany." *American Journal of Sociology* 98(3)–95.

Giannarelli, Linda, and James Barsimantov. 2000. "Child Care Expenses of America's Families." Occasional paper number 40. Washington, D.C.: The Urban Institute. Available at: http://www.urban.org/UploadedPDF/310028_occa40.pdf (accessed June 11, 2011).

Gilbert, Craig. 2011. "Recall Drives Could Make History." *Journal Sentinel Online.* March 6. Available at: http://www.jsonline.com/news/statepolitics/117501513.html (accessed June 25, 2011).

Gilens, Martin. 1999. *Why Americans Hate Welfare: Race, Media, and the Politics of Antipoverty Policy.* Chicago and London: University of Chicago Press.

Gitlin, Todd. 1995. *The Twilight of Common Dreams: Why America Is Wracked by Culture Wars.* New York: Metropolitan Books.

Goldberg, Chad. 2001. "Welfare Recipients or Workers? Contesting the Workfare State in New York City." *Sociological Theory* 19(2): 187–218.

———. 2007. *Citizens and Paupers: Relief, Rights, and Race, From the Freedman's Bureau to Workfare.* Chicago: University of Chicago Press.

Goldberg, Heidi. 2002. "Improving TANF Program Outcomes for Families with Barriers to Employment." Washington, D.C.: Center on Budget and Policy Priorities. Available at: http://www.cbpp.org/archiveSite/1-22-02tanf3.pdf (accessed June 11, 2011).

Gonzales, George. 2009. "Thematic Session: The Future of Community Organizing During an Obama Presidency." Presentation at the annual meeting of the American Sociological Association, San Francisco, California (August 9).

Gonzales, Vanna. 2007. "Globalization, Welfare Reform and the Social Economy: Developing an Alternative Approach to Analyzing Social Welfare Systems in the Post-Industrial Era." *Journal of Sociology & Social Welfare* 34(2): 187–211.

Gooden, Susan T. 1995. "Local Discretion and Welfare Policy. The Case of Virginia (1911–1970)." *Southern Studies* 6(4): 79–110.

Gordon, Linda. 1994. *Pitied But Not Entitled: Single Mothers and the History of Welfare.* New York: The Free Press.

Gordon, Rebecca. 2001. *Cruel and Unusual: How Welfare 'Reform' Punishes Poor People*. Oakland, Cal.: Applied Research Center.

Gornick, Janet C. and Marcia K. Meyers. 2003. *Families That Work: Policies for Reconciling Parenthood and Employment*. New York: Russell Sage Foundation.

Graves, Scott. 2005. "California's Child Care and Development System Budget Backgrounder: Making Dollars Make Sense." Sacramento: California Budget Project. Available at: http://www.cbp.org/pdfs/2005/0504bb_childcare.pdf (accessed June 21, 2011).

Greenhouse, Steven. 2008. *The Big Squeeze*. New York: Alfred A. Knopf.

———. 2011. "In Indiana, Clues to Future of Wisconsin Labor." *New York Times*. February 26. Available at: http://www.nytimes.com/2011/02/27/business/27collective-bargain.html?_r=1&ref=todayspaper (accessed June 24, 2011).

Grippi, Tamara. 2004. "County Greets Budget with Doom, Gloom; Supervisors Contemplate How." *Tri-Valley Herald*. January 14. Available at: Lexis Nexis Academic Universe (accessed September 3, 2007).

Griswold, Lewis. 1998. "Two Resolutions Supportive of Hmong War Vets; Visalia and Tulare County Express Gratitude Following Recent Reunion." *Fresno Bee*. March 18: B2. Available at: Lexis Nexis Academic Universe (accessed June 29, 2011).

Groves, Ethnie. 2005. "Governor Doyle Signs State Budget." Press Release. July 25. Available at: http://www.wisgov.state.wi.us/journal_media_detail.asp?prid=1241 (accessed January 27, 2010).

Guerin-Gonzales, Camille. 1996. *Mexican Workers and American Dreams: Immigration, Repatriation, and California Farm Labor, 1900–1939*. New Brunswick, N.J.: Rutgers University Press.

Hall, Dee J. 1998. "A Tearful Plea for Food in Wisconsin." *Wisconsin State Journal*. February 12: 1B. Available at: Lexis Nexis Academic Universe (accessed June 29, 2011).

Hall, LeeAnn, and Carson Strege-Flora. 2002. "Access Denied." In *From Poverty to Punishment: How Welfare Reform Punishes the Poor*, edited by Applied Research Center. Oakland, Cal.: Applied Research Center.

Handler, Joel. 1995. *The Poverty of Welfare Reform*. New Haven, Conn.: Yale University Press.

———. 2004. *Social Citizenship and Workfare in the United States and Western Europe: The Paradox of Inclusion*. Cambridge: Cambridge University Press.

Handler, Joel, and Yeheskel Hasenfeld. 1991. *The Moral Construction of Poverty: Welfare Reform in America*. Newbury Park, Cal.: Sage Publications.

Harris, John, and Catherine McDonald. 2000. "Post-Fordism, the Welfare State and the Personal Services: A Comparison of Australia and Britain." *British Journal of Social Work* 30: 51–70.

Harris, Scott. 1988. "Row with State Threatens County Workfare Project." *Los Angeles Times*. Available at: Lexis Nexis Academic Universe, U.S. News (accessed July 18, 2002).

Hartung, W. D., and J. Washburn. 1998. "Lockheed Martin: From Warfare to Welfare." *The Nation*. March 2: 11–16.

Hathaway, Will, and David S. Meyer. 1997. "Competition and Cooperation in Movement Coalitions: Lobbying for Peace in the 1980s." In *Coalitions and Political Movements: The Lessons of the Nuclear Freeze,* edited by Thomas R. Rochon and David S. Meyer. Boulder & London: Lynne Rienner Publishers.

Hays, Sharon. 2003a. *Flat Broke With Children: Women in the Age of Welfare Reform.* New York: Oxford University Press.

———. 2003b. "Off the Rolls: The Ground-Level Results of Welfare Reform." *Dissent* 50(4): 48–53.

Healy, Melissa, and David Lesher. 1997. "Child Care Major Pitfall in Welfare Reform." *Los Angeles Times.* May 4. Available at: Proquest-Los Angeles (current; accessed June 27, 2011).

Heath, Brad. 2011. "Complaints Showed Flaws in Mortgage Relief Plan." *USA Today.* April 12. Available at: http://www.usatoday.com/money/economy/housing/2011-04-12-mortgage-borrowers-letters.htm (accessed June 27, 2011).

Heath, Melanie. 2009. "State of Our Unions: Marriage Promotion and the Contested Power of Heterosexuality." *Gender & Society* 23(1): 27–48.

Heckenlively, John. 1997. "Activist: Program Threatens Workers." *Racine Labor.* August 29: 23, 26.

Hein, Jay F. 2002. "Ideas as Exports; The National and International Welfare Reform Efforts of the Past Decade Got Their Start in Madison, Wisconsin." *American Outlook* (summer). Available at: http://www.sagamoreinstitute.org/article/ideas-as-exports (accessed October 7, 2011).

Hein, Jeremy. 2006. *Ethnic Origins: The Adaptation of Cambodian and Hmong Refugees in Four American Cities.* New York: Russell Sage Foundation.

Henry, Michael J. 1998. "Memo to All Department Heads from Michael J. Henry, Director of Personnel, County of Los Angeles Department of Human Resources." January 12. ACORN-LA files.

Herald, Michael, and Jessica Bartholow. 2011. "The Foreseeable Harm from Governor Brown's Proposal to Reduce CalWorks Grants for Children." Sacramento: Western Center on Law and Poverty. Available at: http://healthjusticenetwork.wordpress.com/2011/03/04/the-foreseeable-harm-from-governor-brown%E2%80%99s-proposal-to-reduce-calworks-grants-for-children/ (accessed June 21, 2011).

Heredia, Luisa. 2008. *Faith in Action: The Catholic Church and the Immigrant Rights Movement, 1980–2007.* Ph.D. Dissertation. Department of Sociology, Harvard University.

Hernandez, Roberto. 2003. "Plans to Cut Day-Care Hit: INLAND: Parents Protest Possible State Budgets Cuts Affecting 800 Children at 14 YMCA-Affiliated Sites." *The Press Enterprise.* March 4. Available at: Lexis Nexis Academic Universe (accessed September 8, 2007).

Hernandez, Sandra. 1996. "Where's Riordan? Our Man in New York; N.Y. Mayor Carries L.A. Challenge to Federal Rules." *LA Weekly.* September 20: 14.

Hero, Rodney E., and Robert R. Preuhs. 2006. "From Civil Rights to Multiculturalism and Welfare for Immigrants: An Egalitarian Tradition Across the American States." *Du Bois Review* 3(2): 317–340.

———. 2007. "Immigration and the Evolving American Welfare State: Examining Policies in the U.S. States." *American Journal of Political Science* 51(3): 498–517.

Heuler Williams, Lisa. 1998. *Study and Evaluation of W2 Workers and Temporary Employment in Milwaukee, Wisconsin.* Milwaukee: 9to5, National Association of Working Women.

Hicks, Alexander. 1999. *Social Democracy and Welfare Capitalism: A Century of Income Security Politics.* Ithaca, N.Y.: Cornell University Press.

Hill, John. 2002a. "Davis Budget: A Balancing Act." *Sacramento Bee.* January 11. Available at: Lexis Nexis Academic Universe (accessed September 8, 2007).

———. 2002b. "Davis: $10 billion in Cuts, Schools, Roads, the Elderly: No Group Is Left Unscathed." *Sacramento Bee.* December 7. Available at: Lexis Nexis Academic Universe (accessed September 10, 2007).

Hondagneu-Sotelo, Pierette. 1995. "Women and Children First: New Directions in Anti-Immigrant Politics." *Socialist Review* 25(1): 169–90.

Hudson Institute. 2002. "Research and Projects." Washington, D.C.: Welfare Policy Center of the Hudson Institute. Available at: http://www.welfarereformer.org (accessed February 18, 2002).

Hope Offered Through Shared Ecumenical Action (HOSEA). 2000a. Letter from Deacon John D'Alessio to Governor Thompson. August 18.

———. 2000b. "HOSEA/MICAH Call on Governor Thompson to Ensure Accountability for Maximus, Inc. and All Other W-2 Providers in Milwaukee County." Press Conference. August 21.

Hurd, Richard W. and Joseph B. Uehlein. 1994. "Patterned Responses to Organizing: Case Studies of the Union-Busting Convention." In *Restoring the Promise of American Labor Law,* edited by Sheldon Friedman, Richard Hurd, Rudy Oswald, and Ronald Seeber. Ithaca N.Y.: ILR Press.

Huston, Margo. 1997. "W-2 Work or Else; County Falls Far Behind on W-2 Child-Care Aid." *Milwaukee Journal Sentinel.* November 25. Available at: Lexis Nexis Academic Universe (accessed April 30, 2007).

———. 1998a "Clinton Proposes Child-Care Package $21.7 Billion; Will Be Big Help to W-2 Families, State Leaders Say." *Milwaukee Journal Sentinel.* January 8. Available at: Lexis Nexis Academic Universe (accessed May 5, 2007).

———. 1998b. "Less than 40% of W-2 Families Use Child-Care Subsidies. New Study Asks Businesses to Play Greater Role in Helping County's Children." *Milwaukee Journal Sentinel.* June 8. Available at: Lexis Nexis Academic Universe (accessed May 5, 2007).

———. 1998c. "W-2 Work or Else: Country's Faulty Subsidy System Hurts Child Care, Providers Say." *Milwaukee Journal Sentinel,* February 4. Available at: Lexis Nexis Academic Universe (accessed May 5, 2007).

———. 1998d. "W-2 Work or Else; Payment Backlog Freezes Child Care; Some Centers, Stung by County's Delay, Reject Children of W-2 Clients." *Milwaukee Journal Sentinel.* April 20. Available at: Lexis Nexis Academic Universe (accessed May 5, 2007).

———. 1998e. "W-2 Work or Else; Private W-2 Agencies to Share in Profits." *Milwaukee Journal Sentinel.* October 13. Available at: Lexis Nexis Academic Universe (accessed February 18, 2002).

———. 1998f. "Group Seeks Forums on W-2 Surplus." *Milwaukee Journal Sentinel.* October 14. Available at: Lexis Nexis Academic Universe (accessed February 18, 2002).

———. 1998g. "W-2 Work or Else. State Urges Use of Child Care Aid." *Milwaukee Journal Sentinel.* February 25. Available at: Lexis Nexis Academic Universe (accessed May 5, 2007).

———. 1998h. "W-2 Work or Else." *Milwaukee Journal Sentinel,* March 24. Available on Lexis Nexis Academic Universe (accessed May 5, 2007).

Imig, Douglas R. 1996. *Poverty and Power: The Political Representation of Poor Americans.* Lincoln, Neb.: University of Nebraska Press.

Inside Bay Area. 2006. "Opposition to Prop. 82 Duplicitous." June 3. Available at: Lexis Nexis Academic Universe (accessed September 8, 2007).

Institute for Wisconsin's Future. 1998a. *Transitions to W-2: The First Six Months of Welfare Replacement.* Milwaukee: Institute for Wisconsin's Future.

———. 1998b. *The W-2 Job Path: An Assessment of the Employment Trajectory of W-2 Participants in Milwaukee.* Milwaukee: Institute for Wisconsin's Future.

———. 1999a. "The Growing Crisis Among Wisconsin's Poorest Families: A Comparison of Welfare Caseload Declines and Trends in the State's Poverty Population—1986–1997." Report.

———. 1999b. "Life After Welfare: 'Just Barely Making It.' " *W-2 Connection* 2(1).

———. 1999c. "Hunger Task Force of MW Launches Food Stamp Outreach Campaign." *W-2 Connection* 2(1).

Institute for Women's Policy Research. 1994. "Few Women Fit the Stereotypes." *Research-in-Briefs.* Washington, D.C.: Institute for Women's Policy Research.

International Wages for Housework Campaign. 2001. "Statement of Principles, Crossroads Women's Center." Available at: http://www.ourworld.compuserve.com (accessed December 16, 2001).

Isaac, Larry, and Lars Christiansen. 2002. "How the Civil Rights Movement Revitalized Labor Militancy." *American Sociological Review* 67(5): 722–46.

Jackson, Larry R., and William Arthur Johnson. 1974. *Protest by the Poor: The Welfare Rights Movement in New York City.* Lexington, Mass.: Lexington Books.

Jacobs, John. 1996. "The Coming Tidal Wave. What Will Happen When Legal Immigrants Lose Government Services?" *San Diego Tribune.* December 27: Opinion, B-7, 1, 6–8; Ed. B-9, 2–5.

———. 1997. "Bustamante Champions Legal Aliens Assembly Speaker; He Insists the Budget Agreement Include $124 Million in Food Stamps." *Ventura County Star.* July 29: D9.

Janison, Dan. 2000. "Medicaid Contractor Is Faulted by Green; Advocate Says Virginia Firm Fell Short on Client Aid." *Newsday,* Queens Edition. February 24: A28.

Jaret, Charles. 1999. "Troubled by Newcomers: Anti-Immigrant Attitudes and Action During Two Eras of Mass Immigration to the United States." *Journal of American Ethnic History* 18(3): 9–39.

Jenkins, J. Craig, and Craig M. Eckert. 1986. "Channeling Black Insurgency: Elite Patronage and Professional Social Movement Organizations in the Development of the Black Movement." *American Sociological Review* 51(6): 812–29.

Jenkins, J. Craig, and Charles Perrow. 1977. "Insurgency of the Powerless: Farm Worker Movements (1946–1972)." *American Sociological Review* 42(2): 249–68.

Jenness, Valerie, David Meyer, and Helen Ingram. 2005. "Social Movements, Policy, and Democracy: Rethinking the Nexus." In *Routing the Opposition: Social Movements, Public Policy and Democracy,* edited by Helen Ingram, David Meyer, and Valerie Jenness. Minneapolis: University of Minnesota Press.

Jensen, Leif. 1988. "Patterns of Immigration and Public Assistance Utilization, 1970–1980." *International Migration Review* 22(1): 51–83.

Johnson, Jason B. 2002. "Bay Area Tobacco Tax Funds Dip: Most Counties Won't Follow L.A.'s Plan for Free Preschool." *San Francisco Chronicle.* August 18. Available at: Lexis Nexis Academic Universe (accessed September 8, 2007).

Johnson, Martin. 2003. "Racial Context, Public Attitudes, and Welfare Effort in the American States." In *Race and the Politics of Welfare Reform,* edited by Sanford F. Schram, Joe Soss, and Richard C. Fording. Ann Arbor: The University of Michigan Press.

Johnston, Paul. 1994. *Success While Others Fail: Social Movement Unionism and the Public Workplace.* Ithaca, N.Y.: ILR Press.

———. 2000. "The Resurgence of Labor as Citizenship Movement in the New Labor Relations Environment." *Critical Sociology* 26(1–2): 139–60.

Jones, Andrew W., Richard N. Hutchinson, Nella Van Dyke, Leslie Gates, and Michele Companion. 2001. "Coalition Form and Mobilization Effectiveness in Local Social Movements." *Sociological Spectrum* 21(2): 207–31.

Jones, Meg. 1997. "Attracting the Latest Laborers: Holiday Events Include Effort to Involve W-2 Workers." *Milwaukee Journal Sentinel.* September 2: 1, 7.

Jones, Richard P. 1998. "Governor Backs Restoring Food Stamps for Refugees; Thompson to Add Issue to Agenda after Emotional Senate Debate on Hmong." *Milwaukee Journal Sentinel.* May 8: 1. Available at: Lexis Nexis Academic Universe (accessed May 23, 2001).

Jones-DeWeever, Avis A., and Barbara Gault. 2006. *Resilient and Reaching for More: Challenges and Benefits of Higher Education for Welfare Participants and Their Children.* Washington, D.C.: Institute for Women's Policy Research.

Kabler, Deonne. 2001. "Welfare 'Reform' and the Value of Caring Work." *Bay Area Business Woman.* August: 11.

Kao, Dennis. 2002. Testimony of the director of APALC at Los Angeles Coalition to End Hunger & Homelessness' Town Hall meeting on welfare reform. Los Angeles, California (June 15).

Katznelson, Ira. 1981. *City Trenches: Urban Politics and the Patterning of Class in the United States.* Chicago: University of Chicago Press.

———. 2005. *When Affirmative Action Was White: An Untold History of Racial Inequality in Twentieth-Century America.* New York: W. W. Norton.

Kaufman, Leslie. 1997. "Welfare's Labor Pains." *Newsweek.* March 31.

Kawan, Hildegard, and Barbara Weber. 1981 "Reflections on a Theme: The German Women's Movement, Then and Now." *Women's Studies International Quarterly* 4(4): 421–33.

Keating, Gina. 2000. "County Moves to Privatize Welfare Jobs Program." *Daily News of Los Angeles.* Available at: Lexis Nexis Academic Universe, U.S. News (accessed July 18, 2002).

Keiser, Lael R., Peter R. Mueser, and Seung-Whan Choi. 2004. "Race, Bureaucratic Discretion, and the Implementation of Welfare Reform." *American Journal of Political Science* 48(2): 314–27.

Kelsey, Mary E. 1994. "Welfare Policies and Racial Stereotypes: The Structural Construction of a Model Minority." *Explorations in Ethnic Studies* 17(1): 63–78.

Kertscher, Tom. 2001. "Maximus Managers File Complaints: Two Employees Claim Discrimination at Agency." *Milwaukee Journal Sentinel.* June 22. Available at: Lexis Nexis Academic Universe (accessed July 25, 2002).

Keystone Research Center. 2002. "Unions and Child Care—A Brief Summary." Harrisburg, Pa.: Keystone Research Center.

———. 2006. "Brief Summary: Unions in Child Care." Harrisburg, Pa.: Keystone Research Center. Available at: www.earlychildhoodfinance.org/. . ./UnionsECE_Call_Resources_2006.doc (accessed June 21, 2011)

Kilty, Keith M., and Maria Vidal de Haymes. 2000. "Racism, Nativism, and Exclusion: Public Policy, Immigration, and the Latino Experience in the United States." *Journal of Poverty* 4(1–2): 1–25.

Kingfisher, Catherine Pelissier. 1996. "Women on Welfare: Conversational Sites of Acquiescence and Dissent." *Discourse & Society* 7(4): 531–57.

Klabin, Karen. 1999. "First Steps: A Look at Child Care Services Under Welfare Reform in Los Angeles County." Report. Los Angeles: Human Services Network of Los Angeles.

Klabin, Karen, and Vivian Weinstein. 2000. "Where's the Care in Child Care Services?" *Daily News.* Opinion, April 6. Available at: Lexis Nexis Academic Universe (accessed June 29, 2011).

Kleidman, Robert, and Thomas R. Rochon. 1997. "Dilemmas of Organization in Peace Campaigns." In *Coalitions and Political Movements: The Lessons of the Nuclear Freeze,* edited by Thomas R. Rochon and David S. Meyer. Boulder, Colo. & London: Lynne Rienner Publishers.

Kornbluh, Felicia. 1997. "To Fulfill Their 'Rightly Needs': Consumerism and the National Welfare Rights Movement." *Radical History Review* 69(fall): 76–113.

———. 1998. "The Goals of the National Welfare Rights Movement: Why We Need Them Thirty Years Later." *Feminist Studies* 24(1): 65–79.

Korteweg, Anna C. 2006. "The Construction of Gendered Citizenship at the Welfare Office: An Ethnographic Comparison of Welfare-to-Work Workshops in the United States and the Netherlands." *Social Politics: International Studies in Gender, State, and Society* 13(3): 313–40.

Kposowa, Augustine J. 1998. *The Impact of Immigration on the United States Economy.* Lanham, Md.: University Press of America.

Krajcer, Menachem, and Gary Delgado. 2002. "Reframing the Welfare Debate: Racial Equity and Fair Treatment." In *From Poverty to Punishment: How Welfare Reform Punishes the Poor,* edited by Applied Research Center. Oakland, Cal.: Applied Research Center.

Krinsky, John, and Ellen Reese. 2006. "Forging and Sustaining Labor-Community Coalitions: The Workfare Justice Movement in Three Cities." *Sociological Forum* 21(4): 623–58.

Kyle, K., D. Savage, and D. Diaz. 1991. *The Public Cost of Private Contracting* (April). Prepared by the SEIU Local 660 Research Department.

Lapinski, John S., Pia Peltola, Greg Shaw, and Alan Yang. 1997. "Trends: Immigrants and Immigration." *Public Opinion Quarterly* 61(2): 356–83.

Laswell, Harold Dwight. 1971. *Policy Orientation of Political Science.* Agra, India: Lakshmi Narain Agarwal.

Leachman, Michael, Erica Williams, and Nicholas Johnson. 2011. "Governors Are Proposing Further Deep Cuts in Services, Likely Harming Their Economies." Washington, D.C.: Center on Budget and Policy Priorities. Available at: http://www.cbpp.org/cms/?fa=view&id=3389 (accessed June 21, 2011).

Lee, Dan. 1998. "County OKs Welfare Program Overhaul." *San Gabriel Valley Daily Tribune.* December 21: A1, A10.

Legal Momentum. 2010. "TANF Caseloads Fall Again the Second Quarter of 2010." New York: Legal Momentum, The Women's Legal Defense and Education Fund. Available at: http://www.legalmomentum.org/our-work/women-and-poverty/resources—publications/tanf-caseload-declined-again-in.pdf (accessed June 21, 2011).

———. 2011. "Welfare Reform at Age 15: A Vanishing Safety Net for Women and Children." New York: Legal Momentum. Available at: http://www.legalmomentum.org/our-work/women-and-poverty/resources—publications/welfare-reform-15.html (accessed June 21, 2011).

Levi, Margaret. 2001. "Capitalizing on Labor's Capital." In *Social Capital and Poor Communities,* edited by Susan Saegert, J. Phillip Thompson, and Mark R. Warren. New York: Russell Sage Foundation.

Lieberman, Robert C. 1998. *Shifting the Color Line: Race and the American Welfare State.* Cambridge, Mass.: Harvard University Press.

Linares, Jesse J. 1997. "Denuncian Peligrosas Condiciones Laborales." *La Opinion.* May 23: 1B, 2B.

Lindsley, Syd. 2002. "The Gendered Assault on Immigrants." In *Policing the National Body: Sex, Race, and Criminalization,* edited by Jael Silliman and Anannya Bhattacharjee. Cambridge, Mass.: South End Press.

Lipset, Seymour Martin. 1950. *Agrarian Socialism in the Cooperative Commonwealth Federation in Saskatchewan, A Study in Political Sociology.* Berkeley: University of California Press.

Lipsky, Michael. 2010. *Street-Level Bureaucracy: Dilemmas of the Individual in Public Services, 30th Anniversary Edition.* New York: Russell Sage Foundation.

Liu, Caitlin. 1999. "Activists Call for End to Welfare Limits." *Los Angeles Times.* August 19: 3. Available at: Proquest-Los Angeles Times (current; accessed June 27, 2011).

Loprest, Pamela. 1999. "Families Who Left Welfare: Who Are They and How Are They Doing?" Assessing the New Federalism. Discussion papers. Washington, D.C.: The Urban Institute. Available at: http://www.urban.org/UploadedPDF/discussion99-02.pdf (accessed June 21, 2011).

———. 2003. "Fewer Welfare Leavers Employed in Weak Economy." Washington, D.C.: Urban Institute. Available at: http://www.urban.org/uploadedPDF/310837_snapshots3_no5.pdf (accessed June 21, 2011)

Loprest, Pamela, and Douglas Wissoker. 2002. "Employment and Welfare Reform in the National Survey of America's Families." Assessing the New Federalism. Discussion papers. Washington, D.C.: The Urban Institute.

Available at: http://www.urban.org/Uploadedpdf/310440.pdf (accessed June 21, 2011).

Los Angeles Coalition to End Hunger and Homelessness. 1998. "Stop the General Relief Cuts." Flyer. June 16. Los Angeles: Los Angeles Coalition to End Hunger and Homelessness.

Los Angeles Department of Public Social Services. 1998. "Calworks Participants in Welfare-to-Work Activities. Los Angeles County Total." June. Los Angeles: Los Angeles Department of Public Social Services.

Los Angeles Times. 1996. "Kinder Care on Immigrant Aid." Editorial. December 30: B4. Available at: Proquest-Los Angeles (current; accessed June 27, 2011).

———. 2001. "100 Rally for Global Strike by Women." March 9: B2. Available at: Proquest-Los Angeles Times (current; accessed June 27, 2011).

Malos, Ellen. 1978. "Housework and the Politics of Women's Liberation." *Socialist Review* 8(1): 41–71.

Manhattan Institute for Policy Research. 2002. "Manhattan Institute Center for Civic Innovation Program Areas." New York: Manhattan Institute. Available at: http://www.manhattan-institute.org/html/cci.htm (accessed May 25, 2002).

Mapp, Patricia. 2000. "Child Care Should Be Priority." *Wisconsin State Journal.* July 1. Available at: Lexis Nexis Academic Universe (accessed July 27, 2007).

Marcucci, Michele R. 2001a. "Child Care for Poor Placed in Jeopardy: Tri-Valley-Care Program." *Alameda Times-Star.* December 6. Available at: Lexis Nexis Academic Universe (accessed September 7, 2007).

———. 2001b. "Davis Reinstates Threatened Funds to Child Care." *The Daily Review.* May 29. Available at: Lexis Nexis Academic Universe (accessed September 2, 2007).

———. 2001c. "Davis Reinstates Threatened Funds to Child-Care Program." *Alameda Times-Star.* December 6. Available at: Lexis Nexis Academic Universe (accessed September 7, 2007).

———. 2002a. "300,000 of State's Kids Barred from Child Care; Davis Subsidy Remedy Called 'Shell Game.' " *San Mateo County Times.* February 23. Available at: Lexis Nexis Academic Universe (accessed September 8, 2007).

———. 2002b. "Child Care Subsidy Central to Funding Debate; Child Care Subsidy a Necessity for Working Poor." *Tri-Valley Herald.* May 27. Available at: Lexis Nexis Academic Universe (September 8, 2007).

———. 2004a. "Subsidized Child-Care Cutbacks 'Immoral,' Area Lawmakers Say." *Tri-Valley Herald.* March 17. Available at: Lexis Nexis Academic Universe (accessed September 2, 2007).

———. 2004b. "Local Parents Fear the Loss of State Child Care Subsidies." *Oakland Tribune.* May 28. Available at: http://www.insidebayarea.com/archive-search (accessed October 7, 2011).

Marimow, Ann E., and Mark Gladstone. 2004. "Painful Cuts for California; Governor's Plan Slashes, Borrows." *San Jose Mercury News.* January 10. Available at: Lexis Nexis Academic Universe (accessed September 3, 2007).

Marley, Patrick. 2010. "Many Potential Recipients Aren't Getting W-2 Benefits." *Milwaukee Journal Sentinel Online.* January 2. Available at: http://www.jsonline.com/news/statepolitics/80517872.html (accessed June 23, 2011)

Marley, Patrick, and Steven Walters. 2007. "Child Care Ratings Rejected; Budget Committee Proposal Erases Deficit in Aid to Poor." *Milwaukee Journal Sentinel.* May 23. Available at: Lexis Nexis Academic Universe (accessed July 31, 2007.)

Marston, Sallie A. 2000. "The Social Construction of Scale." *Progress in Human Geography* 24(2): 219–42.

Martin, Chuck, and Sunny Schubert. 1998. "Legal Immigrants Deserve Food Aid." *Wisconsin State Journal.* February 27: 11A. Available at: Lexis Nexis Academic Universe (accessed June 29, 2011).

Martinez, Michael. 1998. "Workfare Workers Demand Jobs at Lockheed Martin." *Wave* 80(17): 1, 3.

Matejka, Michael. 2000. "Not in Our Town: A Community-Wide Anti-Racism Program, Labor's Response, and the Community's Response to Labor Within It." *Labor Studies Journal* 25(1): 66–78.

Matlosz, Felicia C. 2000. "Fresno Vigil Draws Attention to $300m Child-Care Subsidy Bill." *Fresno Bee.* April 11. Available at: Lexis Nexis Universe (accessed September 5, 2007).

Mayers, Jeff. 1999a. "British Envoy: Ground Troops Will Be Needed." *Wisconsin State Journal.* May 7: 12A. Available at: Lexis Nexis Academic Universe (accessed June 29, 2011).

———. 1999b. "Wisconsin Strengthening Its Ties to Germany's Hesse: While Hessians Are Interested in W-2, Wisconsin Is Interested in the Thriving Biotechnology Industry." *Wisconsin State Journal.* October 24: 1C. Available at: Lexis Nexis Academic Universe (accessed June 29, 2011).

McAdam, Doug. 1999 [1982]. *Political Process and the Development of Black Insurgency, 1930–1970.* 2d ed. Chicago: University of Chicago Press.

McAdam, Doug, John D. McCarthy, and Mayer N. Zald. 1988. "Social Movements." In *Handbook of Sociology,* edited by Neil J. Smelser. Newbury Park, Cal.: Sage Publications.

———. 1996. "Introduction." In *Comparative Perspectives on Social Movements: Political Opportunities, Mobilizing Structures, and Cultural Framings,* edited by Doug McAdam, John D. McCarthy, and Mayer N. Zald. Cambridge: Cambridge University Press.

McBride, Jessica. 1997. "Fatal Fire Blamed on Space Heater." *Milwaukee Journal Sentinel.* October 30: 1. Available at: Lexis Nexis Academic Universe (accessed June 23, 2004).

———. 1998. "Disabled Boy Dies in Scalding Tub." *Milwaukee Journal Sentinel.* June 16: 1. Available at: Lexis Nexis Academic Universe (accessed June 23, 2004).

McBride, Jessica, Jesse Garza, and Margo Huston. 1997. "3 Children, Man Killed in Two Milwaukee Fires." *Milwaukee Journal Sentinel.* October 29: 1. Available at: Lexis Nexis Academic Universe (accessed June 23, 2004).

McBride, Michael J. 1999. "Migrants and Asylum Seekers: Policy Responses in the United States to Immigrants and Refugees from Central America and the Caribbean." *International Migration* 37(1): 289–314.

McCammon, Holly J., and Karen E. Campbell. 2002. "Allies on the Road to Victory: Coalition Formation Between the Suffragists and the Woman's Christian Teperance Union." *Mobilization* 7(3): 231–51.

McCarthy, Charles. 1997. "Hmong Sues for Aid as CIA Veteran." *Fresno Bee.* November 12: B1. Available at: Lexis Nexis Academic Universe (accessed June 29, 2011).

McDonald, Cameron Lynne, and David A. Merrill. 2002. " 'It Shouldn't Have to Be a Trade': Recognition and Redistribution in Care Work Advocacy." *Hypatia* 17(2): 67–83.

McDonnell, Patrick. 1996. "Legal Advocacy Groups Sue over Food Stamp Changes." *Los Angeles Times.* October 18: A3. Available at: Proquest-Los Angeles Times (accessed June 27, 2011).

———. 1997a. "Immigrants Warned of Impending Aid Cuts." *Los Angeles Times.* February 1: 1. Available at: Proquest-Los Angeles Times (accessed June 27, 2011).

———. 1997b. "INS Backlog Growing as Aid Cutoff Gets Closer." *Los Angeles Times.* February 3: 3. Available at: Proquest-Los Angeles Times (accessed June 27, 2011).

———. 1997c. "Wilson Assails U.S. Plan to Restore Aid to Legal Immigrants." *Los Angeles Times.* February 13: 3. Available at: Proquest-Los Angeles Times (accessed June 27, 2011).

Mehan, Hugh. 1997. "The Discourse of the Illegal Immigration Debate: A Case Study in the Politics of Representation." *Discourse & Society* 8(2): 249–70.

Mendel, Ed. 1997. "Wilson Urged to Back Legal Immigrant Aid." *San Diego Union Tribune.* July 22: A3.

Mendel-Clemens, Amy. 2002. "Incorporating the Informed Choice Philosophy Into W-2." Memo to Economic Support Supervisors, Economic Support Lead Workers, Training Staff, Child Care Coordinators, and W-2 Agencies. July 15. Available at: http://www.dhs.wisconsin.gov/EM/ops-memos/2002/pdf/02-046.pdf (accessed June 21, 2011)

Mendes, Philip. 2003. "Australian Neoliberal Think Tanks and the Backlash Against the Welfare State." *Journal of Australian Political Economy* 51: 29–56.

Mettler, Suzanne. 1998. *Dividing Citizens: Gender and Federalism in New Deal Policy.* Ithaca, N.Y.: Cornell University Press.

———. 2000. "States' Rights, Women's Obligations: Contemporary Welfare Reform in Historical Perspective." *Women & Politics* 21(1): 1–34.

Meyers, Marcia. 2007. "The Institutional Architecture of Antipoverty Policy in the United States: Looking Back, Looking Ahead." *Focus* 25(1): 58–62.

Miewald, Christiana. 2003. "Making Experience Count in Policy Creation: Lessons from Appalacian Kentucky." In *Rediscovering the Other America: The Continuing Crisis of Poverty and Inequality in the United States,* edited by Keith M. Kilty and Elizabeth A. Segal. Binghamton, N.Y.: The Haworth Press, Inc.

Milfred, Scott. 1998. "Where Are the Poorest Children? Child-Care Subsidies Are Going Unused." *Wisconsin State Journal.* February 17. Available at: Lexis Nexis Academic Universe (accessed May 5, 2007).

———. 1999. "Vetoes Called a Setback for W-2 Participants." *Milwaukee State Journal.* November 2. Available at: Lexis Nexis Academic Universe (accessed May 10, 2007).

Milkman, Ruth. 2006. *L.A. Story: Immigrant Workers and the Future of the U.S. Labor Movement.* New York: Russell Sage Foundation.

Millard, Pete. 2000. "State Orders Review of Maximus Complaints." *Milwaukee Business Journal.* March 10: 1, 59.

Milton, Rich. Various dates. "On-Site Case Review Findings." October 2000–June 2001. Los Angeles County Contract Management and Monitoring Division.

Milwaukee Women and Poverty Public Education Initiative. 1998. "W-2 Community Impact Study." Prepared for the Milwaukee County Board of Supervisors. Milwaukee: Milwaukee Women and Poverty Public Education Initiative.

———. 2000. "The Status of Employment Opportunity for W-2 Participants in Central City Milwaukee." July. Milwaukee: Milwaukee Women and Poverty Public Education Initiative.

Mink, Gwendolyn. 1995. *The Wages of Motherhood: Inequality in the Welfare State, 1917–1942.* Ithaca, N.Y.: Cornell University Press.

———. 1998. *Welfare's End.* Ithaca, N.Y.: Cornell University Press.

Minton, T. 1997. "Wilson Postpones Cutoff of Immigrant Food Stamps." *San Francisco Chronicle.* March 21: A30. Available at: Lexis Nexis Academic Universe (accessed June 29, 2011).

Moberg, David. 2009. "Battling Over Employee Free Choice." *In These Times.* May 28. Available at: http://www.inthesetimes.com/article/4450/battling_over_employee_free_choice (accessed June 27, 2011).

Monterey County Herald. 2004. "Panetta Lecture Series Airs Tonight." May 3. Available at: Lexis Nexis Academic Universe (accessed September 3, 2007).

Moody, James. 1997. "George Soros: Financial Wizard With a Halo." *Horizon Magazine.* Available at: http://www.horizonmag.com/1/soros.htm (accessed July 31, 2002).

Moore, Soloman, and Bettina Boxall. 1997. "County Welfare Recipients Seeking to Form a Union." *Los Angeles Times.* February 1: B1, B3. Available at: Proquest-Los Angeles Times (current; accessed June 27, 2011).

Moore, Stephen. 1998. *A Fiscal Portrait of the Newest American.* Washington, D.C.: National Immigration Forum and Cato Institute.

Moore, Thomas, and Vicky Selkowe. 1999. *The Impact of Welfare Reform on Wisconsin's Hmong Aid Recipients.* Milwaukee: The Institute for Wisconsin's Future.

Morain, Dan. 1997. "Estimated Cost of State Food Stamp Plan for Legal Immigrants Quadruples: Panel to Urge States' Congress Members to Seek Restoration of Federal Aid." *Los Angeles Times.* June 14: A19. Available at: Proquest-Los Angeles Times (current; accessed June 27, 2011).

Morgan, Skip. 1996. "Welfare Hearing Attracts Big Crowd." *The Press Enterprise* (Riverside, Cal.). November 26: B1.

Morris, Pamela A. 2002. "The Effects of Welfare Reform Policies on Children." *Social Policy Report* 16(1): 4–19.

Mulligan-Hansel, Kathleen, and Pam Fendt. 2002. "Unfair Sanctions: Does W-2 Punish People of Color?" Milwaukee: Institute for Wisconsin's Future. Available at: http://www4.uwm.edu/ced/publications/race_report.pdf (accessed June 21, 2011).

Murray, Bobbi. 1999. "No Welfare for Lockheed or Maximus." *LA Weekly*. July 23. Available at: www.laweekly.com/1999-07-29/news/no-welfare-for-Lockheed-or-Maximus/ (accessed June 29, 2011).

Nadasen, Premilla. 2005. *Welfare Warriors: The Welfare Rights Movement in the United States*. New York: Routledge.

Nakao, Annie. 1996. "Asian Vote a New Force; Bay Area Seeing Surge in Registration as Impact of Government Becomes Evident." *San Francisco Examiner*. October 20: C1.

Naples, Nancy A. 1997. "The 'New Consensus' on the Gendered Nature of the Welfare State." *Signs* 22(4): 907–45.

National Association of Latino Elected Officials Educational Fund. 1997. *1996 National Directory of Latino Elected Officials*. Washington, D.C.: National Association of Latino Elected Officials Educational Fund.

National Immigration Law Center. 2002. *Guide to Immigrant Eligibility for Federal Programs*. Los Angeles: National Immigration Law Center.

Nelson, Margaret. 2006. "Lessons From Vermont." In *The Promise of Welfare Reform*, edited by Keith M. Kilty and Elizabeth A. Segal. Binghamton, N.Y.: Hayward Press.

Ness, Immanuel. 1998. *Trade Unions and the Betrayal of the Unemployed: Labor Conflicts During the 1990s*. New York: Garland Publishing.

Ness, Immanuel, and Stuart Eimer. 2001. *Central Labor Councils and the Revival of American Unionism: Organizing for Justice in Our Communities*. Armonk, N.Y.: M. E. Sharpe.

Neubeck, Kenneth J. 2006. *When Welfare Disappears: The Case for Economic Human Rights*. New York: Routledge.

Neubeck, Kenneth J., and Noel A. Cazenave. 2001. *Welfare Racism: Playing the Race Card Against America's Poor*. New York and London: Routledge.

New York Times. 2002. "More People on Welfare After Years of Decline." December 31: A16. Available at: Lexis Nexis Academic Universe (accessed May 11, 2003).

———. 2009. "Foreclosures: No End in Sight." June 2: A22. Available at: Lexis Nexis Academic Universe (accessed June 29, 2011).

News Service Reports. 1997. "White House Looking to Boost Head Start." *The Record*. March 26: A17.

Newton, Lina. 2005. " 'It Is Not a Question of Being Anti-Immigration': Categories of Deservedness in Immigration Policymaking." In *Deserving and Entitled: Social Constructions and Public Policy*, edited by Anne Schneider and Helen Ingram. Albany: State University of New York Press.

Nichols, Dana M. 2006. "After-School Expansion Set." *The Record*. August 29. Available at: Lexis Nexis Academic Universe (accessed September 1, 2007).

Nilsen, Sigurd R. 2002. *Welfare Reform: Federal Oversight of State and Local Contracting Can Be Strengthened*. Washington, D.C.: U.S. General Accounting Office. Available at: http://www.eric.ed.gov/PDFS/ED465885.pdf (accessed June 29, 2011).

Nissen, Bruce. 1995. *Fighting for Jobs: Case Studies of Labor-Community Coalitions Confronting Plant Closings*. Albany: State University of New York Press.

———. 2003a. "Contemporary Affairs: What Are Scholars Telling the U.S. Labor Movement to Do?" *Labor History* 44(2): 158–65.

———. 2003b. "Alternative Strategic Directions for the U.S. Labor Movement: Recent Scholarship." *Labor Studies Journal* 28(1): 133–55.

———. 2004. "The Effectiveness and Limits of Labor-Community Coalitions: Evidence from South Florida." *Labor Studies Journal* 29(1): 67–89.

Noble, Charles. 1997. *Welfare as We Knew It: A Political History of the American Welfare State.* New York: Oxford University Press.

Norman, Jack. 1999a. "Thompson Food Stamp Meets Opposition: Proposal Seeks to Privatize Under W-2 Agencies." *Milwaukee Journal Sentinel.* June 3. Available at: Lexis Nexis Academic Universe (accessed January 27, 2002).

———. 1999b. "Food Stamp Use Plunges 32% in State, Federal Report Finds." *Milwaukee Journal Sentinel.* August 4: 1.

———. 1999c. "State Should Be More Involved in Fixing Food Stamp Program, Federal Report Says." *Milwaukee Journal Sentinel.* November 9. Available at: Lexis Nexis Academic Universe (accessed January 27, 2002).

———. 2000. "Number of Working-Poor Children Grows; UWM Report Also Finds Many Don't Get Services." *Milwaukee Journal Sentinel.* May 29. Available at: Lexis Nexis Academic Universe (accessed January 27, 2001).

Nugent, Mary. 2006. "Parenthood Widens His World: In InnerView, Single Dad Mitchell White Learns About Support, and Lends a Hand Too." *Chico-Enterprise-Record.* July 24. Available at: Lexis Nexis Academic Universe (accessed September 1, 2007).

Obach, Brian K. 2004. *Labor and the Environmental Movement: The Quest for Common Ground.* Cambridge, Mass.: MIT Press.

Ong, Aihwa. 1999. "Cultural Citizenship as Subject Making: Immigrants Negotiate Racial and Cultural Boundaries in the United States." In *Race, Identity and Citizenship: A Reader,* edited by Rodolfo D. Torres, Louis F. Mirón, and Jonathan Xavier Inda. Malden, Mass.: Blackwell Publishers.

Parenti, Christian. 1999. *Lockdown America: Police and Prisons in the Age of Crisis.* London: Verso.

Pastor, Manuel Jr., Chris Benner, and Martha Matsuoka. 2009. *This Could Be the Start of Something Big: How Social Movements for Regional Equity Are Reshaping Metropolitan America.* Ithaca, N.Y., and London: Cornell University Press.

Patriquin, Larry. 2001. "The Historical Uniqueness of the Clinton Welfare Reforms: A New Level of Social Misery?" *Journal of Sociology and Social Welfare* 28(3): 71–94.

Pavetti, LaDonna, Liz Schott, and Elizabeth Lower-Basch. 2011. "Creating Subsidized Employment Opportunities for Low-Income Parents: The Legacy of the TANF Emergency Fund." Washington, D.C.: Center on Budget and Policy Priorities. Available at: http://www.cbpp.org/cms/index.cfm?fa=view&id=3400 (accessed June 26, 2011).

Peacock, Jon. 2009a. "An Overview of the 2009-11 Budget." August 28. Madison, Wisc.: Wisconsin Budget Project (an initiative of the Wisconsin Council on Children and Families, Inc.). Available at: http://www.wccf.org/pdf/budget_overview_2009-11_082809.pdf (accessed June 24, 2011).

———. 2009b. "Supports for Low-Income Families." September 3. Madison, Wisc.: Wisconsin Budget Project (an initiative of the Wisconsin Council on Children and Families, Inc.). Available at: http://www.wccf.org/pdf/supports_low-income_families_090309.pdf (accessed June 24, 2011).

———. 2009c. "Pew Report Assessed Budget Challenges, Not the Budget Solution." November 13. Madison, Wisc.: Wisconsin Budget Project (an initiative of the Wisconsin Council on Children and Families, Inc.). Available at: http://www.wccf.org/pdf/pew_report_111309.pdf (accessed June 24, 2011).

———. 2010. "TANF Emergency Fund Helps Cushion Effects of the Recession and Creates Options for State Policymakers." June 22. Madison, Wisc.: Wisconsin Budget Project (an initiative of the Wisconsin Council on Children and Families, Inc.). Available at: http://www.wisconsinbudgetproject.org/TANF_ECF_06-22-10.pdf (accessed June 24, 2011).

Pear, Robert. 2002. "Study by Governors Calls Bush Welfare Plan Unworkable." *New York Times.* April 4: A18. Available at: Lexis Nexis Academic Universe (accessed June 30, 2003).

Peck, Jamie. 2001. *Workfare States.* New York: The Guilford Press.

Peck, Jamie, and Nikolas Theodore. 1999. " 'Dull Compulsion': Political Economies of Workfare." Working paper no. 30. Manchester International Centre for Labour Studies, University of Manchester, Great Britain.

Pfeifer, Bryan G. 1997. " 'The Struggle of Survival': An Interview with W2WU's Janice Thurman." *The UWM Post* [Student weekly newspaper for the University of Wisconsin–Milwaukee]. September 25.

Pierson, Paul. 1994. *Dismantling the Welfare State? Reagan, Thatcher, and the Politics* of Retrenchment. New York: Cambridge University Press.

———.1996. "The New Politics of the Welfare State." *World Politics* 48(2): 143–79.

———, ed. 2001a. *The New Politics of the Welfare State.* New York: Oxford University Press.

———. 2001b. "Introduction: Investigating the Welfare State at Century's End." In *The New Politics of the Welfare State,* edited by Paul Pierson. New York: Oxford University Press.

———. 2001c. "Post-Industrial Pressures on Mature Welfare States." In *The New Politics of the Welfare State,* edited by Paul Pierson. New York: Oxford University Press.

Piliavin, Irving, Mark Courtney, and Amy Dworsky. 2000. "Early Transfers from AFDC to W-2: The Experiences of 100 Dane County Families." University of Wisconsin, Madison: Institute for Research on Poverty. Available at: http://www.irp.wisc.edu/research/welreform/pdfs/dane-co-report.pdf (accessed June 21, 2011).

Piven, Frances F., and Richard Cloward. 1977a. "Dilemmas of Organization Building: The Case of Welfare Rights." *Radical America* 11(5): 39–61.

———. 1977b. *Poor People's Movements: Why They Succeed, Why They Fail.* New York: Vintage Books.

———. 1979. "Who Should Be Organized? 'Citizen Action' vs. 'Jobs and Justice.' " *Working Papers for a New Society* 7(1): 35–43.

———. 1993 [1971]. *Regulating the Poor: The Functions of Public Welfare.* New York: Pantheon Books.

———. 2000. *Why Americans Still Don't Vote and Why Politicians Want It That Way.* Boston: Beacon Press.

Pommer, Matt. 1998. "Gov Asks OK for Food Stamps." *Capital Times*. May 8. Available at: Lexis Nexis Academic Universe (accessed May 16, 2001).

———. 2003a. "Gov: W-2 Shift Good for Babies; Doyle Answers Gard Rap." *Capital Times*. February 20. Available at: Lexis Nexis Academic Universe (accessed July 29, 2007).

———. 2003b. "GOP Rebuffs Doyle on W-2 Moms: It's Back to Work 3 Months after Birth" (1st ed.); "GOP Rejects Maternity Extension for W-2 Moms" (2d ed). *Capital Times*. May 21. Available at: Lexis Nexis Academic Universe (accessed July 29, 2007).

Post, Charles. 1997. "The Capitalist Policy Planning Network and the Welfare Reform Act of 1996." Paper presented at the 1997 annual meeting of the American Sociological Association, Toronto, Canada (August 9–13).

Press Enterprise. 1996. "Welfare Study Says Counties' Costs Not as High as Seen." October 25: A7.

Price, Jenny. 2001a. "Survey Finds W-2 Workers Face Challenges to Staying Employed." Associated Press. November 15. Available: Lexis Nexus Academic Universe (accessed July 27, 2007).

———. 2001b. "Study: 42 Percent of Former W-2 Participants Not Working." Associated Press. December 21. Available at: Lexis Nexis Academic Universe (accessed July 27, 2007).

———. 2003. "Most Women Take 11–12 Weeks Leave, But Six Months Sought for W-2." Associated Press. June 1. Available at: Lexis Nexis Academic Universe (accessed July 29, 2007).

Prins, Nomi and Krisztina Ugrin. 2010. "Bailout Tally Report." October 1. Available at: http://www.nomiprins.squarespace.com/storage/bailouttallyoct2010.pdf (accessed June 21, 2011).

Prunty, Howard. 1984. "Businessmen as Welfare Advocates." In *Community Organizers, Second Edition*, edited by Joan Ecklein. New York: John Wiley & Sons.

Pyle, Amy, Patrick J. McDonnell, and Hector Tobar. 1998. "Latino Voter Participation Doubled Since '94 Primary." *Los Angeles Times*. June 4. Available at: Proquest-Los Angeles Times (current; accessed June 27, 2011).

Quadagno, Jill. 1984. "Welfare Capitalism and the Social Security Act of 1935." *American Sociological Review* 9(5): 632–47.

———. 1985. "Two Developments of Welfare State Development: Reply to Skocpol and Amenta." *American Sociological Review* 50(4): 575–78.

———. 1994. *The Color of Welfare: How Racism Undermined the War on Poverty*. New York: Oxford University Press.

———. 2005. *One Nation Uninsured: Why the U.S. Has No National Health Insurance*. New York: Oxford University Press.

Ramakrishnan, S. Karthick. 2001. "Unpacking the Backlash: Political Threat, Institutional Mobilization, and Immigrant Electoral Participation in the Mid-1990s." Paper presented at the 2001 annual meeting of the American Political Science Association in San Francisco, California.

Ramakrishnan, S. Karthick, and Thomas J. Espenshade. 2001. "Immigrant Incorporation and Political Participation in the United States." *International Migration Review* 35(3): 870–909.

Rathke, Wade, and Amy Schur. 1999. Unpublished paper on workfare worker organizing (in Reese's personal files).

Real Economy Project. 2010. "Total Wall Street Bail Out Cost." Updated September 10. Available at: http://www.sourcewatch.org/index.php?title=Total_Wall_Street_Bailout_Cost (accessed June 28, 2011).

Realty Trac. 2010. "National Real Estate Trends: October 2010 Foreclosure Rate Heat Map." Available at: http://www.realtytrac.com/trendcenter/ (accessed November 12, 2010).

Rector, Robert. 1997. "Washington's Assault on Welfare Reform." Issue Bulletin No. 244. Washington, D.C.: Heritage Foundation. Available at: http://www.heritage.org/research/reports/1997/08/washingtons-assault-on-welfare-reform (accessed June 23, 2011).

Rector, Robert, and William F. Lauber. 1995. "Elderly Non-Citizens on Welfare Will Cost the American Taxpayer $328 Billion Over the Next Decade." The Heritage Foundation. Available at: http://www.heritage.org/library/categories/healthwelf/fyi54.html (accessed September 20, 2001).

Reese, Ellen. 2002a. "Privatization of Welfare Services in Southern California: Employees' Concerns About Service Quality." University of California Institute for Labor and Employment, occasional paper no. 4. Copies of this paper were provided to the Los Angeles County Board of Supervisors in November, 2001.

———. 2002b. "Resisting the Workfare State: ACORN's Campaign to Improve General Relief in Los Angeles." *Race, Gender, and Class* 9(1): 72–95.

———. 2005a. *Backlash Against Welfare Mothers: Past and Present.* Berkeley and Los Angeles: University of California Press.

———. 2005b. "Policy Threats and Social Movement Coalitions: California's Campaign to Restore Legal Immigrants' Rights to Welfare." In *Social Movements, Public Policy and Democracy,* edited by Helen Ingram, David Meyer, and Valerie Jenness. Minneapolis: University of Minnesota Press.

———. 2007a. "Politicians, Think Tanks, and the Global Promotion of the 'Wisconsin Model' of Welfare Reform." In *The Wages of Empire: Globalization, State Transformation, and Women's Poverty,* edited by Amalia Cabezas, Ellen Reese, and Marguerite Waller. Boulder, Colo.: Paradigm Publishers.

———. 2007b. "The Causes and Consequences of U.S. Welfare Retrenchment." *Journal of Poverty* 11(3): 47–64.

———. 2010. "But Who Will Watch the Children? Organizing Child Care Providers in the Wake of Welfare Reform." *In Intimate Labors: Cultures, Technologies, and the Politics of Care,* edited by Eileen Boris and Rhacel Salazar Pareñas. Palo Alto, Calif.: Stanford University Press.

Reese, Ellen, Kadambari Anantram, Linda Kim, Roy Kwon, and Preeta Saxena. (Forthcoming). "Building Labor Solidarity: Unions and Labor Activists at the 2007 US Social Forum." In *A Handbook of World Social Forum Activism,* edited by Jackie Smith, Scott Byrd, Ellen Reese, and Elizabeth Smythe. Boulder, Colo.: Paradigm Publishers.

Reese, Ellen, Vincent Giedraitis, and Eric Vega. 2005. "Mobilization and Threat: Campaigns Against Welfare Privatization in Four Cities." *Sociological Focus* 38(4): 287–307.

———. 2006. "Welfare Is Not for Sale: Campaigns Against Welfare Profiteers in Milwaukee." *Social Justice: A Journal of Crime, Conflict, and World Order* 33(3): 38–53.

Reese, Ellen, and Garnett Newcombe. 2003. "Income Rights, Mothers' Rights, or Workers' Rights? Collective Action Frames, Organizational Ideologies, and the American Welfare Rights Movement." *Social Problems* 50(2): 294–318.

Reese, Ellen, and Elvia Ramirez. 2002a. "The New Ethnic Politics of Welfare: Political Struggles over Immigrants' Rights to Welfare in California." *Journal of Poverty* 6(3): 29–62.

———. 2002b. "The Politics of Welfare Inclusion: Explaining State-Level Restorations of Legal Immigrants' Welfare Rights." Paper presented at the 2002 Society for the Study of Social Problems Conference (Chicago, Illinois).

Reynolds, David. 1999. "Coalition Politics: Insurgent Union Political Action Builds Ties Between Labor and the Community." *Labor Studies Journal* 24(3): 54–76.

Riccardi, Nicholas. 1999. "County to Launch Major Child Care Effort in Schools." Los Angeles Times. May 12: A1, A20.

———. 2000a. "County Nears Private Bids on Welfare Reform." *Los Angeles Times.* February 8. Available at: Proquest-Los Angeles Times (current; accessed June 27, 2011).

———. 2000b. "Political Struggle Centers on Welfare-to-Work contractor." *Los Angeles Times.* June 20. Available at: Proquest-Los Angeles Times (current; accessed June 27, 2011).

Richmond, Todd. 2009. "Day Care Program Paid Improper Subsidies." Associated Press State & Local Wires. June 12. Available at: Lexis Nexis Academic Universe (accessed July 20, 2010).

Ridzi, Frank. 2004. "Making TANF Work: Organizational Restructuring, Staff Buy-In, and Performance Monitoring in Local Implementation." *Journal of Sociology and Social Welfare* 31(2): 27–48.

———. 2007. "Contingent Government Workers and Labor Solidarity: The Case of Contract Welfare-to-Work Staff and Their Clients." *Qualitative Sociology* 30(4): 383–402.

———. 2009. *Selling Welfare Reform: Work-First and the New Common Sense of Employment.* New York: New York University Press.

Ridzi, Frank, and Andrew S. London. 2006. " 'It's Great When People Don't Even Have Their Welfare Cases Opened': TANF Diversion as Process and Lesson." *Review of Policy Research* 23(3): 725–43.

Rinard, Amy. 1998. "Thompson Supports Food Stamps for Hmong." *Milwaukee Journal Sentinel.* May 9: 8. Available at: Lexis Nexis Academic Universe (accessed May 11, 2001).

Rivera, Carla. 1997. "General Relief Workers Say They Face Job Hazards." *Los Angeles Times.* August 19: B1, B2. Available at: Proquest-Los Angeles Times (current; accessed June 27, 2011).

———. 2000 "After-School Plan Gets Mixed Reviews." *Los Angeles Times.* October 5. Available at: Proquest-*Los Angeles Times* (current; accessed June 27, 2011).

Robinson, Ian. 2000. "Neoliberal Restructuring and U.S. Unions: Toward Social Movement Unionism." *Critical Sociology* 26: 109–38.

Roderick, Kevin. 1988. "State Officials Castigate LA County Over GAIN Project." *Los Angeles Times.* Available at: Lexis Nexis Academic Universe (accessed July 18, 2002).

Rodriguez, Robert. 1997. "Welfare Reform Deemed a Failure: Group Observes First Anniversary by Chiding Bustamante, Wilson." *Fresno Bee.* August 23: B1. Available at: Lexis Nexis Academic Universe (accessed June 29, 2011).

Rogers-Dillon, Robin H. 2001. "What Do We Really Know About Welfare Reform?" *Society* 38(2): 7–15.

Rose, Fred. 2000. *Coalitions Across the Class Divide: Lessons from the Labor, Peace, and Environmental Movements.* Ithaca, N.Y.: Cornell University Press.

Ross, J. R. 2003. "Committee Nixes Doyle Proposal to Extend At-Home Stay for W-2 Moms." Associated Press. May 20. Available at: Lexis Nexis Academic Universe (accessed July 29, 2007).

Rothstein, Richard. 2002. "Schoolchildren of Welfare Parents." *New York Times.* June 5: B8. Available at: Lexis Nexis Academic Universe (accessed June 30, 2003).

Rowe, Gretchen, and Mary Murphy. 2006. *Welfare Rules Databook: State TANF Policies as of July 2006.* Washington, D.C.: The Urban Institute. Available at: http://www.urban.org/publications/411686.html (accessed June 23, 2011)/publication.

Rummery, Kirstein. 2010. "Partnerships and Collaborative Governance in Welfare: The Citizenship Challenge." *Social Policy & Society* 5(2): 293–303.

Rutledge, Racquel. 2009. "Child-Care Scam Rake in Thousands: Phantom Caretaking, Fake Jobs Used to Defraud Taxpayer-Funded System." *Milwaukee Journal Sentinel.* January 25. Available at: Lexis Nexis Academic Universe (accessed July 20, 2010).

———. 2010. "Child-Care Fraud Crackdown Saves Wisconsin Taxpayers $45 Million." *Milwaukee Journal Sentinel.* May 21. Available at: Lexis Nexis Academic Universe (accessed July 20, 2010).

Sabatier, Paul A. 1999. "The Need for Better Theories." In *Theories of the Policy Process,* edited by Paul A. Sabatier. Boulder, Colo.: Westview Press.

Samora, Julian, and Patricia Vandel Simon. 1977. *A History of the Mexican-American People.* South Bend, Ind.: University of Notre Dame Press.

Sample, Herbert. 1996. "Republicans Risk Minority Vote Over Immigration, Welfare." *Modesto Bee.* October 28: 4.

Sanchez, George I. 1997. "Face the Nation: Race, Immigration, and the Rise of Nativism in Late Twentieth Century America." *International Migration Review* 31(4): 1009–30.

San Francisco Examiner. 1997. "Welfare Reform Battle." May 9: A2.

Sanger, M. Bryna. 2003. *The Welfare Marketplace: Privatization and Welfare Reform.* Washington, D.C.: Brookings Institution Press.

Savage, Ernest. Video recording. "The Price of Poverty." Documentary film raw footage. Savage City Productions.

Savner, Steve, Julie Strawn, and Mark Greenberg. 2002. "TANF Reauthorization: Opportunities to Reduce Poverty by Improving Employment Outcomes." Center for Law and Social Policy. Available at: http://www.clasp.org/admin/site/publications_archive/files/0075.pdf (accessed June 23, 2011).

Schmit, Julie. 2011a. "Only a Trickle of Homeowners Take Bite of Aid." *USA Today.* February 7. Available at: http://www.usatoday.com/money/economy/housing/2011-02-08-fhaaid08_ST_N.htm (accessed June 26, 2011).

———. 2011b. "Critics Say New Rules on Mortgage Servicers Not Tough Enough." *USA Today*. April 13. Available at: http://m.usatoday.com/article/money/realestate/46054804?preferredArticleViewMode=single (accessed June 26, 2011).

Schmitt, John. 2010. "The Wage Penalty for State and Local Government Employees." Washington, D.C.: Center for Economic and Policy Research. Available at: http://www.cepr.net/documents/publications/wage-penalty-2010-05.pdf (accessed June 24, 2011).

Schneider, Anne, and Helen Ingram. 1993. "The Social Construction of Target Populations: Implications for Politics and Policy." *The American Political Science Review* 87(2): 334–47.

Schneider, Dorothee. 2000. "Symbolic Citizenship, Nationalism, and the Distant State: The United States Congress in the 1996 Debates on Immigration Reform." *Citizenship Studies* 4(3): 255–73.

Schneider, Pat, and David Callender. 1998. "Higher Child Care Co-Pay Under W-2 Threatens Centers." *Capital Times*. March 27. Available at: Lexis Nexis Academic Universe (accessed May 5, 2007).

Schott, Liz, and Ife Finch. 2010. "TANF Benefits Are Low and Have Not Kept Up With Inflation: Benefits Are Not Enough to Meet Basic Needs." Washington, D.C.: Center on Budget and Policy Priorities. Available at: http://www.cbpp.org/files/10-14-10tanf.pdf.

Schram, Sanford F. 2006. "Uncaring Neoliberal Paternalism: A Compassionate Response to the Punitive Turn in Poverty Management." Paper presented at the Symposium on In/Dependence: Disability, Welfare, and Age, sponsored by the Center for the 21st Century Studies, University of Wisconsin, Milwaukee (April 7).

Schram, Sanford F., Joe Soss, and Richard C. Fording, eds. 2003. *Race and the Politics of Welfare Reform*. Ann Arbor: The University of Michigan Press.

Schulman, Karen, and Helen Blank. 2008. "State Child Care Assistance Policies 2008: Too Little Progress for Children and Families." Washington, D.C.: National Women's Law Center. Available at: http://www.nwlc.org/sites/default/files/pdfs/StateChildCareAssistancePoliciesReport08.pdf (accessed June 23, 2011).

———. 2010. "State Child Care Assistance Policies 2010: New Federal Funds Help States Weather the Storm." Washington, D.C.: National Women's Law Center. Available at: http://www.nwlc.org/sites/default/files/pdfs/statechildcareassistancepoliciesreport2010.pdf (accessed June 23, 2011).

Schultze, Steve. 2000a. "Study Paints Rosy Picture of Welfare Reform." *Washington Times*. March 17: A6.

———. 2000b. "Maximus Has No-Bid Contract: Deal Worth $15 Million to Company That's Under Investigation in Two States." *Milwaukee Journal Sentinel*. July 9: 1B. Available at: Lexis Nexis Academic Universe (accessed October 31, 2000).

———. 2000c. "State May Take W-2 Contract from Maximus; $7.6 Million Already Has Been Withheld from Human Service Firm." *Milwaukee Journal Sentinel*. July 26. Available at: Lexis Nexis Academic Universe (accessed February 18, 2002).

———. 2000d. "Cut W-2 from Maximus, Churches Say." *Milwaukee Journal Sentinel.* August 19. Available at: Lexis Nexis Academic Universe (accessed January 19, 2003).

———. 2000e. "State Investigating Improper Welfare Billing." *Milwaukee Journal Sentinel.* August 28. Available at: Lexis Nexis Academic Universe (accessed March 23, 2002).

———. 2000f. "Regulators Accused of Being Easy on W-2 Agencies: Lawmaker Says They Should Share Blame for Maximus' Improper Use of Money." *Milwaukee Journal Sentinel.* September 1. Available at: Lexis Nexis Academic Universe (accessed February 18, 2002).

———. 2000g. "Maximus to Pay Back $500,000; Firm Also Plans Extra Spending for Poor After Audit." *Milwaukee Journal Sentinel.* October 14. Available at: Lexis Nexis Academic Universe (January 6, 2002).

———. 2000h. "Lawmakers Want Maximus Fired." *Milwaukee Journal Sentinel.* October 27. Available at: Lexis Nexis Academic Universe (accessed February 18, 2002).

———. 2001a. "Welfare Money Used for Parties, Soliciting Business, Audit Finds." *Milwaukee Journal Sentinel.* February 17. Available at: Lexis Nexis Academic Universe (February 17, 2002).

———. 2001b. "W-2 Contractor Says It'll Pay Any Fine." *Milwaukee Journal Sentinel.* March 14. Available at: Lexis Nexis Academic Universe (accessed February 17, 2002).

———. 2004. "Doyle Pushes Cut in W-2 Caseloads." *Milwaukee Journal Sentinel.* November 18. Available at: Lexis Nexis Academic Universe (accessed July 30, 2007).

———. 2005. "OIC Money Mess Spreads." *Milwaukee Journal Sentinel.* February 26: B1.

———. 2009. "W-2 Clients Get to Pick Agencies." *Milwaukee Journal Sentinel.* October 16: B1.

Scipes, Kim. 1992. "Understanding the New Labor Movements in the 'Third World': The Emergence of Social Movement Unionism." *Critical Sociology* 19(2): 81–101.

Scott, Ellen K., Andrew S. London, and Nancy A. Myers. 2002. "Dangerous Dependencies: The Intersection of Welfare Reform and Domestic Violence." *Gender & Society* 16(6): 878–97.

SEIU 660. (n.d.). "GR Workfare Project Report by County/Non-County Sponsor: Report Month of 3/94." Unpublished report located in SEIU 660's files.

———. 1997. "Prospects for Workfare in Los Angeles County." Memo. February 21. SEIU 660 files.

———. 1998. "GAIN Participants in Work Experience in LA County." Unpublished report located in SEIU 660 files.

———. 1999. "Organizing Workfare = Protecting Jobs." *660 Voice.* January/February edition.

———. 2001. *SEIU Local 660 30th Anniversary Celebration.* Booklet. Los Angeles: SEIU 660.

Shapiro, Michael J. 1997. "Narrating the Nation, Unwelcoming the Stranger: Anti-Immigration Policy in Contemporary 'America.' " *Alternatives* 22(1): 1–34.

Sharma-Jensen, Geeta. 1997. "Selling W-2 Essential, Conferees Told." *Milwaukee Journal Sentinel.* May 7: Business, 3.

Shaw, Greg M., and Robert Y. Shapiro. 2002. "The Polls—Trends: Poverty and Public Assistance." *Public Opinion Quarterly* 66(1): 105–28.

Shaw, Randy. 1999. *Reclaiming America: Nike, Clean Air, and the New National Activism.* Berkeley: University of California Press.

Shearer, Derek. 1982. "How the Progressives Won in Santa Monica." *Social Policy* 12(3): 7–14.

———. 2000. *The Missing Middle: Working Families and the Future of American Social Policy.* New York: W.W. Norton & Company.

Sheboygan Press. 1997. "Legal Immigrants Need Food Stamps." August 27: Editorial Page. Available at: Lexis Nexis Academic Universe (accessed May 10, 2001).

Sheehan, Tim. 2004. "Child Care Advocates Bemoan Cutbacks." *Fresno Bee.* April 3. Available at: Lexis Nexis Academic Universe (accessed September 2, 2007).

Shogren, Elizabeth. 1994a. "Bill Ties Welfare Reform to Cut in Immigrant Aid." *Los Angeles Times.* May 11: A4, 1. Available at: Proquest-Los Angeles Times (current; accessed June 27, 2011).

———. 1994b. "Plans to Cut Safety Net Leave Legal Immigrants Dangling." *Los Angeles Times.* November 21: A1, 5. Available at: Proquest-Los Angeles Times (current; accessed June 27, 2011).

Silas-Green, Debra. 1997. Testimony to Workers' Rights Board hearing. Milwaukee, Wisconsin (December).

Simmons, Louise. 2002. "Unions and Welfare Reform: Labor's Stake in the Ongoing Struggle Over the Welfare State." *Labor Studies Journal* 27(2): 65–83.

Simms, Patricia. 2005. "Budget Panel OKs Day-Care Cuts." *Wisconsin State Journal.* May 20. Available at: Lexis Nexis Academic Universe (accessed June 29, 2011).

Skocpol, Theda. 1992. *Protecting Soldiers and Wives: The Political Origins of Social Policy in the United States.* Cambridge, Mass.: The Belknap Press of Harvard University Press.

Sloan, Scott. 1998. "Security Guards Pepper Spray W-2 Protesters." *Shepard News.* March 5.

Smith Nightingale, Demetra, and Kelly S. Mikelson. 2000. "An Overview of Research Related to Wisconsin Works (W-2)." Washington, D.C.: Urban Institute. Available at: http://www.urban.org/pdfs/wisc_works.pdf (accessed June 23, 2011).

Soss, Joe, Sanford F. Schram, Thomas P. Vartanian, and Eric O'Brien. 2001. "Setting the Terms of Relief: Explaining State Policy Choices in the Devolution Revolution." *American Journal of Political Science* 45(2): 378–403.

South Central Federation of Labor. 2000. "Symposium Acknowledges Need for Worthy Wages." *Union Labor News.* August. Available at http://www.scfl.org/?ulnid=555 (accessed June 24, 2011)

Sparks, Holloway. 2003. "Queens, Teens, and Model Mothers: Race, Gender, and the Discourse of Welfare Reform." In *Race and the Politics of Welfare Reform,* edited by Sanford F. Schram, Joe Soss, and Richard C. Fording. Ann Arbor: University of Michigan Press.

Staggenborg, Suzanne. 1986. "Coalition Work in the Pro-Choice Movement: Organizational and Environmental Opportunities and Obstacles." *Social Problems* 33(5): 374–90.

State of California Department of Finance. 1999. *Population by Race/Ethnicity Incorporated Cities by County.* July 1990 to July 1999. Sacramento: California State Census Data Center.

———. 2000. "Legal Immigration to California by County: Federal Fiscal Year 1990–1998." Sacramento, Calif. Available at: http://dof.ca.gov/html/Demograp/repndat.htm (accessed January 28, 2001).

Steensland, Brian. 2008. *The Failed Welfare Revolution: America's Struggle over Guaranteed Income Policy.* Princeton, N.J.: Princeton University Press.

Stefancic, Jean, and Richard Delgado. 1996. "The Attack on Welfare." In *No Mercy: How Conservative Think Tanks and Foundations Changed America's Social Agenda.* Philadelphia: Temple University Press.

Stein, Dan. 1995. "Testimony of Dan Stein, Federation for American Immigration Reform." In *Contract with America–Welfare Reform.* Hearing Before the Subcommittee on Human Resources of the Committee on Ways and Means, House of Representatives. 104th Congress, First Session. Part 1.

Stepan-Norris, Judith, and Maurice Zeitlin. 2003. *Left Out: Reds and America's Industrial Unions.* New York: Cambridge University Press.

Stewart, Linda. 1997. "W-2 Allows Mothers Time to Find Child Care." *Milwaukee Journal Sentinel.* September 25. Available at: Lexis Nexis Academic Universe (accessed May 1, 2007).

Strom, Stephanie. 2008. "Funds Misappropriated at 2 Nonprofit Groups." *New York Times.* July 9. Available at: http://www.nytimes.com/2008/07/09/us/09embezzle.html (accessed June 23, 2011).

Suárez-Orozco, Carola and Marcelo Suárez-Orozco. 1995. *Transformations: Migration, Family Life and Achievement: Motivation Among Latino Adolescents.* Stanford, Calif.: Stanford University Press.

Swank, Duane H., and Alexander Hicks. 1984. "Militancy, Need and Relief: The Piven and Cloward AFDC Caseload Thesis Revisited." *Research in Social Movements, Conflict, and Change* 6: 1–29.

Swartz, Rebecca, Jacqueline Kauff, Lucia Nixon, Tom Fraker, Jay Hein, and Susan Mitchell. 1999. "Where Did Families Go When AFDC Ended in Milwaukee?" The Hudson Institute and Mathematica Policy Institute. Available at: http://www.mathematica-mpr.com/PDFs/w2report.pdf (accessed June 23, 2011).

Tait, Vanessa. 1998. "Knocking at Labor's Door: Workfare Workers Organize." *New Labor Forum* 3(fall–winter): 139–50.

———. 2005. *Poor Workers' Unions: Rebuilding Labor From Below.* Cambridge, Mass.: South End Press.

Tarrow, Sidney. 1998. *Power in Movement: Social Movements and Contentious Politics, Second Edition.* Cambridge: Cambridge University Press.

Taylor, Verta A. 1996. *Rock-a-by Baby: Feminism, Self-Help, and Postpartum Depression.* New York: Routledge.

Teles, Steven M. 1996. *Whose Welfare? AFDC and Elite Politics.* Lawrence, Kan.: University of Kansas Press.

Tienda, Marta, and Leif Jensen. 1986. "Immigration and Public Assistance Participation: Dispelling the Myth of Dependency." *Social Science Research* 15(4): 372–400.

Tilly, Chris. 1996. "Workfare's Impact on the New York City Labor Market: Lower Wages and Worker Displacement." Working paper no. 92. New York: Russell Sage Foundation. Available at: https://www.russellsage.org/publications/category/working-papers (accessed June 23, 2011).

———. 2011. "An Opportunity Not Taken . . . Yet: U.S. Labor and Current Economic Crisis." *Working USA: The Journal of Labor and Society* 14(March): 73–85.

United States of ACORN. 1998. "1500 ACORN Convention Delegates Take Downtown Milwaukee By Storm." *United States of ACORN* July/August: 1, 7.

United States Student Association. 2002. *2002 Organizing Guide.* Washington, D.C.: U.S. Student Association.

Unz, Ron. K. 1994. "Immigration or the Welfare State: Which Is Our Real Enemy?" *Policy Review* 79(fall): 33–38.

Urban Institute. 2001. "Welfare Reform Turns Five." Press Release. August 21. Washington, D.C.: Urban Institute. Available at: http://www.urban.org/publications/900346.html (accessed March 12, 2002).

Urevich, Robin. 1998. "A Thin Khaki Line—Between the Poor and Their Representatives." *Random Lengths.* June 26–July 9, p. 3.

U.S. Bureau of Labor Statistics. 1999a. "Local Area Unemployment Statistics." Available at: http://146.142.4.24/cgi=bin/surveymost (accessed TK).

———. 1999b. "Geographic Profile of Employment and Unemployment, 1998, Section III, Table 23." Available at: http://stats.us.gov/opub/gp/gpsec3.htm (accessed TK).

———. 2010a. "Economic News Release: Employment Situation Summary." November 5. Washington: U.S. Department of Labor. Available at: http://www.bls.gov/news.release/empsit.nr0.htm (accessed June 23, 2011).

———. 2010b. "Occupational Employment and Wages, May 2009. 39-9011: Child Care Workers." Washington: U.S. Department of Labor. Available at: http://www.bls.gov/oes/current/oes399011.htm (accessed June 23, 2011).

U.S. Census Bureau. 1991. "1990 U.S. Census Data, Place of Birth by County." Available at: http://www.homer.ssd.census.gov/cdrom/lookup/1000165532 (accessed June 23, 2011).

———. 1997. "Population Estimates for States by Race and Hispanic Origin: July 1, 1996." Washington: Population Estimates Program, Population Division, U.S. Census Bureau. Available at: http://www.census.gov/population/estimates/state/srh/srh96.txt (accessed June 23, 2011).

———. 1999. "State Population Estimates: Annual Time Series, July 1, 1990 to July 1, 1999." Available at: http://www.census.gov/popest/archives/1990s/ST-99-03.txt (accessed June 23, 2011).

———. 2001. "Statistical Abstract of the United States, Table 577." Available at: http://www.census.gov/prod/2002pubs/01statab/labor.pdf (accessed June 30, 2011)

———. 2010a. "Historical Tables, People. Table 3. Poverty Status of People, by Age, Race, and Hispanic Origin, 1959–2009." Available at: http://www.census.gov/hhes/www/poverty/data/historical/people.html (accessed June 23, 2011).

———. 2010b. "Historical Tables, Families. Table 4. Poverty Status of Families, by Type of Family, Presence of Children, Race, and Hispanic Origin, 1959–2008." Available at: http://www.census.gov/hhes/www/poverty/data/historical/families.html (accessed June 23, 2011).

U.S. Conference of Mayors. 2009. "A Status Report on Hunger and Homelessness in America's Cities: A 27-City Survey." Washington: U.S. Conference of Mayors. Available at: http://www.usmayors.org/pressreleases/uploads/USCMHungercompleteWEB2009.pdf (accessed June 23, 2011).

U.S. Congressional Budget Office. 2005. "Changes in Participation in Means-Tested Programs." Economic and Budget Issue Brief. Washington: U.S. Congressional Budget Office. Available at: http://www.cbo.gov/ftpdocs/63xx/doc6302/04-20-Means-Tested.pdf (accessed June 23, 2011).

U.S. Department of Health and Human Services. 1998. "Human Services Policy: Aid to Families with Dependent Children: The Baseline." Washington: Office of the Assistant Secretary for Planning and Evaluation. Available at: http://aspe.os.dhhs.gov/hsp/AFDC/afdcbase98exhib.htm (accessed August 10, 2001).

———. 2009. "Fiscal Year 2010 Budget in Brief. American Recovery and Reinvestment Act." Available at: http://www.hhs.gov/asrt/ob/docbudget/2010budgetinbriefc.html (accessed July 24, 2009).

———. 2010. "News Release: Race and Disability Discrimination Complaints in Wisconsin TANF Program to Be Resolved by Statewide Agreement." April 29. Available at: http://www.hhs.gov/news/press/2010pres/04/20100429b.html (accessed June 28, 2011).

U.S. General Accounting Office. 2000. "Welfare Reform: State Sanction Policies and Number of Families Affected, GAO/HEHS-00-44." Washington: U.S. General Accounting Office. Available at: http://www.gao.gov/new.items/he00044.pdf (accessed June 22, 2011).

U.S. House of Representatives Committee on Ways and Means. 1998. *1998 Green Book.* Washington: Government Printing Office.

USC News. 2011. "USC Dornsife/Los Angeles Times Poll Majority of Californians Want Special Election on Tax Increases." April 23. Available at: http://www.usc.edu/uscnews/newsroom/news_release.php?id=2392 (accessed June 23, 2011).

Valocchi, Steve. 1990. "The Unemployed Workers Movement of the 1930s: A Reexamination of the Piven and Cloward Thesis." *Social Problems* 37(2): 191–205.

Van Dyke, Nella. 2003. "Crossing Movement Boundaries: Factors that Facilitate Coalition Protest by American College Students, 1930–1990." *Social Problems* 50(2): 226–50.

Van Dyke, Nella, and Sarah A. Soule. 2002. "Structural Social Change and the Mobilizing Effect of Threat: Explaining Levels of Patriot and Militia Organizing in the United States." *Social Problems* 49(4): 497–520.

Varga, Jim. 2001. Video recording. Interview for Ernest Savage. "The Price of Poverty." Documentary film raw footage.

Verberg, Steven. 2011. "Unions: Critics Contend Proposals on Dues Collection, Voting 'Pretty Fatal'; State Budget Crisis." *Wisconsin State Journal.* March 4: A1. Available at: Lexis Nexis Academic Universe (accessed June 30, 2011).

Voss, Kim, and Rachel Sherman. 2000. "Breaking the Iron Law of Oligarchy: Union Revitalization in the American Labor Movement." *American Journal of Sociology* 106(2): 303–49.

Wacquant, Loic. 2009. *Punishing the Poor: The Neoliberal Government of Social Insecurity.* Durham, N.C., and London: Duke University Press.

Wahla, Lisa. 2001. "Workers Allege Hostile Milieu." *Valley Press.* October 7. Available at: http://www.avpress.com/n/susty3.hts (accessed October 8, 2001).

Walters, Steven. 1998. "Assembly Supports Food Stamps for Immigrants." *Milwaukee Journal Sentinel.* May 14: 5. Available at: Lexis Nexis Academic Universe (accessed May 23, 2001).

———. 2007. "Severe Cuts Loom for State Child Care." *Milwaukee Journal Sentinel.* January 29. Available at: Lexis Nexis Academic Universe (accessed July 31, 2007).

Watanabe, Teresa. 2010. "Aid Figures Cause Alarm: Antonovich Calls for Change as Payments to Children of Illegal Immigrants Increase." *Los Angeles Times.* September 6: AA3. Available at: Lexis Nexis Academic Universe (accessed October 8, 2010).

Weaver, Kent. 2000. *Ending Welfare As We Know It.* Washington, D.C.: Brookings Institution.

Weaver, R. Kent, Robert Y. Shapiro, and Lawrence R. Jacobs. 1995. "The Polls—Trends: Welfare." *Public Opinion Quarterly* 59(4): 606–27.

Weicher, John C. 2001. "Reforming Welfare: The Next Policy Debates." *Society* 38(Jan.–Feb.): 16–20.

Weier, Anita. 2003. "GOP Legislators Put Doyle Cabinet on Hot Seat." *Capital Times.* March 27: 6A. Available at: Lexis Nexis Academic Universe (accessed June 30, 2011).

Weinberg, Sylvia B. 1998. "Mexican American Mothers and the Welfare Debate: A History of Exclusion." *Journal of Poverty* 2(3): 53–75.

Welfare Mothers' Voice. 2000. "Open Letter to Janet Reno, United States Attorney General." Reproduction of letter. October 26.

———. 2001a. *Welfare Mothers' Voice* (spring).

———. 2001b. "Victory! Goodwill Loses W-2 Contract." *Welfare Mothers' Voice* (summer): 1.

———. 2001c. "Welfare Warriors Celebrate Eviction of Goodwill's Employment Solutions From W-2 Gold Mines." *Welfare Mothers' Voice* (fall): 18.

Welfare Warriors. 2000. "Open Letter to Janet Reno, United States Attorney General." October 26.

———. 2001. "Flyer: Bloated Empire Photo Bus Tour." A distributed flyer.

Wentworth, George. 2011. "How the Great Recession Changed the Politics of Unemployment Insurance." Presentation made at the Reconnecting to Work Conference at the Institute for Research on Labor and Employment, UCLA (April 2).

West, Guida. 1981. *The National Welfare Rights Movement: The Social Protest of Poor Women.* New York: Praeger.

Wheeler, Tim. 2002. "NOW Pickets Bush's Workfare Scam." *People's Weekly World.* June 22. Available at: http://www.pww.org/article/view/1423/1/94/ (accessed August 4, 2006).

Whitebook, Marcy. 2001. *Working for Worthy Wages: The Child Care Compensation Movement, 1970–2001.* Berkeley, Cal.: Institute for Industrial Relations, Center for the Study of Child Care Employment. Available at: http://escholarship.org/uc/item/2050r9pv#page-1 (accessed June 30, 2011).

Whitebook, Marcy, Carollee Howes, and Deborah Phillips. 1990. *Who Cares? Child Care Teachers and the Quality of Care in America. The National Child Care Staffing Study.* Oakland, Cal.: Child Care Employee Project. Available at: http://www.eric.ed.gov/PDFS/ED323031.pdf (accessed June 30, 2011).

Whitebook, Marcy, Laura Sakai, Emily Gerber, and Carollee Howes. 2001. "Then and Now: Changes in Child Care Staffing, 1996–2000." Technical Report. Washington, D.C. and Berkeley, Cal.: Center for the Child Care Workforce Institute of Industrial Relations and University of California, Berkeley. Available at: http://www.irle.berkeley.edu/cscce/wp-content/uploads/2010/07/Then-and-Now.pdf (accessed June 23, 2011).

Whitney, Jean. 2003a. "Dark Skies Cloud County Job Hunt; Assembly Labor and Employment Committee." *San Mateo County Times.* March 6. Available at: Lexis Nexis Academic Universe (accessed September 8, 2007).

———. 2003b. "County Child Care Money on the Block." *San Mateo County Times.* April 1. Available at: Lexis Nexis Academic Universe (accessed September 8, 2007).

Whoriskey, Peter. 2009. "More Employers Fight Unemployment Benefits." *The Washington Post.* February 12. Available at: http://www.washingtonpost.com/wp-dyn/content/article/2009/02/11/AR2009021104311.html (accessed June 28, 2011).

Wichman, Julie. 1997. "W-2 Workers Want Workplace Rights." *Shepard Express.* August 28: 4, 6.

Wilayto, Phil. 1997. *The Feeding Trough.* Milwaukee: A Job is a Right Campaign.

Williams, Claudia, and Ariane Hegewisch. 2011. "Women, Poverty, and Economic Security in Wisconsin and the Milwaukee-Waukesha-West Allis MSA." Washington, D.C.: Institute for Women's Policy Research. Available at: http://www.iwpr.org/publications/pubs/wome-povery-and-economic-insecurity-in-wiconsin-and-the-milwaukee-waukesha-west-allis-msa (accessed June 23, 2011).

Wilson, Yumi. 1998. "Day Care Costs Test Welfare-to-Work Plan Guarantees Sought for Middle-Class and Poor Workers." *San Francisco Chronicle.* January 28. Available at: Lexis Nexis Academic Universe (accessed June 30, 2011).

Winston, Pamela, Andrew Burwick, Sheena McConnell, and Richard Roper. 2002. *Privatization of Welfare: A Review of the Literature.* Washington, D.C.: Mathematica Policy Research, Inc.

Wisconsin Budget Project. 2011. "Comparative Analysis of 2011–13 Biennial Budget." Available at: http://www.wisconsinbudgetproject.org/budget_comparative_analysis_2011-13.pdf (accessed April 7, 2011).

Wisconsin Council on Children and Families. 2011. "Effects of the Biennial Budget and Budget Repair Bills for Working Families." Available at: http://www.wccf.org/pdf/budget_repair_bill_031411.pdf (accessed April 7, 2011).

Wisconsin Department of Children and Families. 2008. "Wisconsin Works (W-2) Background, Philosophy, Goals." June 16. Available at: http://dcf.wi.gov/w2/background.htm (accessed June 23, 2011).

Wisconsin Department of Workforce Development. 1999. "Milwaukee County: Regional Workforce Profile." Division of Workforce Excellence, Bureau of Workforce Information.

———. 2000. "Chronology Since January 2000: Department of Workforce Development Actions Related to the Administration of the Wisconsin Works Program By Maximus, Inc." Madison: Wisconsin Department of Workforce Development.

Wisconsin Immigrant and Refugee Coalition. 1997. "WIRC Calls for State and Federal Action to Help Immigrants and Refugees." Press Release. June 18, Madison, Wisconsin.

Wisconsin Immigrant and Refugee Coalition and Wisconsin Child Nutrition Alliance. 1998. "Hearing on Senate Bill 419, Relating to Food Stamps." Press Release. February 10, Madison, Wisconsin.

Wisconsin Joint Legislative Audit Committee. 1999. "A Review: Wisconsin Works (W-2) Expenditures, Department of Workforce Development." February. Madison, Wisc.: Wisconsin State Legislature.

Wisconsin Legislative Audit Bureau. 2000. "Audit Summary: Food Stamp Program." July. Available at: http://www.legis.state.wi.us/LaB/reports/00-8tear.htm (accessed June 23, 2011).

———. 2001. "Wisconsin Works (W-2) Program, Department of Workforce Development: An Evaluation." Madison: Wisconsin Legislative Audit Bureau.

———. 2005. "An Evaluation: Wisconsin Works (W-2)." Madison: Wisconsin Legislative Audit Bureau.

Wisconsin Legislative Fiscal Bureau. 2009. "Wisconsin Works Time Limit Changes (DCF—Economic Support and Child Care)." Report for Joint Committee on Finance, Paper #225. May 27. http://legis.wisconsin.gov/lfb/2009-11Budget/Budget%20Papers/225.pdf (accessed June 24, 2011).

Wisconsin State Journal. 1997. "Group Asks Legislators to Restore Welfare Cuts to Aid Immigrants." *Wisconsin State Journal.* June 18: 3C. Available at: Lexis Nexis Academic Universe (accessed June 30, 2011).

———. 1998a. "Assembly Backs Food Stamps for Refugees." *Wisconsin State Journal.* May 14: 1B. Available at: Lexis Nexis Academic Universe (accessed May 5, 2007).

———. 1998b. "Poor Teens to Get Free Day Care." *Wisconsin State Journal.* June 9. Available at: Lexis Nexis Academic Universe (accessed May 5, 2007).

———. 1998c. "Teen Moms to Get Break on W-2 Child Care Cost." *Wisconsin State Journal.* August 22: 3B. Available at: Lexis Nexis Academic Universe (accessed May 5, 2007).

———. 2000. "Legislative Changes May Make Child Care Subsidies More Available." *Wisconsin State Journal.* April 25. Available at: Lexis Nexis Academic Universe (accessed May 10, 2007).

———. 2009. "Safety Net Services That Are Being Swamped." *Wisconsin State Journal.* May 5: A7. Available at: Lexis Nexis Academic Universe (accessed June 30. 2011).

W-2 Monitoring Task Force. 2000. [Memo. April 13].

W-2 Workers United. 1997. "W-2 Is Slave Labor! Fight Back with W-2 Workers United." Leaflet.

Wolch, Jennifer, and Heidi Sommer. 1997. "Los Angeles in an Era of Welfare Reform: Implications for Poor People and Community Well-Being." Summary and Full Report. Los Angeles: Southern California Inter-University Consortium for Homelessness & Poverty.

Wood, Tracy. 1988. "Private Approach to Public Welfare: An LA Innovation." *Los Angeles Times.* Available at: Lexis Nexis Academic Universe (accessed July 18, 2002).

Worthen, Helena, Steve Edwards, and Diane Stokes. 2002. "An Activist AFSCME Local Confronts Welfare Reform." *Labor Studies Journal* 27(1): 25–43.

Yoo, Grace. 2001. "Shaping Public Perceptions on Immigrants on Welfare: The Role of Editorial Pages of Major U.S. Newspapers." *International Journal of Sociology and Social Policy* 21(7): 47–62.

Zahniser, David 2002. "County Ignores Recommendation to Privatize Welfare-to-Work Program." Copley News Service. Available at: Lexis Nexis Academic Universe (accessed March 19 2002).

Zald, Mayer N. and John D. McCarthy. 1980. "Social Movement Industries: Competition and Cooperation Among Movement Organizations." *Research in Social Movements, Conflicts and Change* 3: 1–20.

Zedlewski, Sheila, Gina Adams, Lisa Dubay, and Genevieve Kenney. 2008. "Is There a System Supporting Low-Income Working Families?" Low Income Working Families paper no. 4. Washington, D.C.: The Urban Institute. Available at: http://www.urban.org/uploadedPDF/311282_lowincome_families.pdf (accessed June 23, 2011).

Zedlewski, Sheila R., Linda Giannarelli, Joyce Morton, and Laura Wheaton. 2002. "Extreme Poverty Rising, Existing Government Programs Could Do More." Series B, B-45. Washington, D.C.: The Urban Institute. Available at: http://www.urban.org/UploadedPDF/310455.pdf (accessed June 30, 2011).

Zedlewski, Sheila R., and Pamela Loprest. 2003. "Welfare Reform: One Size Does Not Fit All." *Christian Science Monitor.* August 25: 9. Available at: Lexis Nexis Academic Universe (accessed September 21, 2011).

Zeese, Kevin. 2011. "One-Year Anniversary: The Incredible Shrinking Obama Health Care Law." *Truthout.* March 24. Available at: http://www.huffingtonpost.com/kevin-zeese/one-year-anniversary-the-_b_838535.html (accessed June 23, 2011).

Zemlicka, Jack. 2011. "Massive Cuts Proposed for Wisconsin Legal Service Providers." *Wisconsin Law Journal.* March 10. Available at: Lexis Nexis Academic Universe (accessed April 11, 2007).

Zimmerman, Wendy, and Karen C. Tumlin. 1999. "Patchwork Policies: State Assistance Programs for Immigrants Under Welfare Reform." Occasional paper no. 24. Washington, D.C.: The Urban Institute. Available at: http://www.urban.org/UploadedPDF/occ24.pdf (accessed June 30, 2011).

Zullo, Roland. 2000. "In Search of the Silver Lining: The Privatization of Welfare-to-Work Services in San Diego County." Madison, Wisc.: Industrial Relations Research Institute, University of Wisconsin–Madison.

Index

Boldface numbers refer to figures and tables.